# THE ALGORITHMIC PHILOSOPHY

# THE ALGORITHMIC PHILOSOPHY

---

## VOLUME II

## AN INTEGRATED AND SOCIAL PHILOSOPHY

## BIN LI

# CONTENTS

*To my father, Yuqi Li, for his good health and happiness*

Perhaps the first satisfactory thinking theory in history
Strikingly revealed the mystery and true face of human minds
A creative conclusion of hitherto philosophy
and an opening of its new stage
A solution to reinventing and reactivating social sciences
A necessary and correct application of IT
and AI principles in the humanities

~

## ABSTRACT

By combining Kantian philosophy with computer principles, unprecedentedly, this book presents a "software-based" theory of mind, namely, "thinking = (Instruction + information) × speed × time". This means that discrete thoughtful entities interact like chemical reactions under spatiotemporal conditions, while users of this theory can use natural language for research and avoid getting bogged down in technological complexities. Considering the economic factors, surprisingly, it gives rise to a series of inferences and new principles, such as the sedimentation, distortion (the subjective turn), and solidification of thought, combinatorial explosion and infinite development, convergence and divergence, and so on. The psychological system thus becomes attached to the thinking system. After deconstructing the "Being" from multiple angles, the knowledge development model shifts from the traditional "great convergence" to the "Big Bang". As a result, various philosophical branches and schools since ancient Greece are integrated into a critical and creative unity which, encompassing plurality and secured by the "Algorithmic Logic", is termed the "Higher-Order Consistency". On this basis, a unified and general social science is founded, and the coherence among the social sciences, humanities, and natural sciences is achieved, ultimately leading to the concept of "total knowledge system". This is called the "Grand Synthesis". By reinterpreting topics such as freedom, democracy, ethics, institutions, organizations, money, markets, religion, language, culture, science, engineering, and common sense, this book illustratively demonstrates the efficacy of these unique "Algorithmic principles". The author expects that this "Algorithmic Philosophy" will spark a revolution in philosophy, humanities, and social sciences, revitalizing their due vigor and enabling them to keep pace with the revolutions in information technology and artificial intelligence.

**Volume I includes:**

Chapter 1 The Goal of Philosophy is to Discover a Proper Theory of Minds

Chapter 2 The New Principles and New Knowledge this Thinking Theory can Bring

Chapter 3 The Algorithmic Thinking Theory

Chapter 4 The Thoughtful Entities

Chapter 5 The Psychology

Chapter 6 The Fundamentals of Philosophy

Chapter 7 The Ontology

**Volume II includes:**

Chapter 8 The Social Philosophy (I)

Chapter 9 The Social Philosophy (II)

Chapter 10 The Social Philosophy (III)

Chapter 11 The Social Philosophy (IV)

Chapter 12 The Philosophy and Methodology of Science

Chapter 13 Greek Philosophy

# CHAPTER 8
# THE SOCIAL PHILOSOPHY (I)

## §92. Introduction

According to the common division of research objects, the objects of philosophical reflection can be divided into two categories: natural and social. Of course, the object of philosophical reflection also includes the thinker oneself, and the thinker oneself can be divided into two aspects: the natural (or physical) and the social (or thoughtful), which fall into the above two categories. These principles seem simple, but it is not easy to explain them strictly and logically until Algorithmic Theory is used.

Earlier we explained the world as a whole, but the holistic perspective is flawed. What people call "whole" is actually just a face, a part, of the world of objects. When we look at an object as a whole, we have to ignore some details, ignoring the discreteness and relative independence of its parts. The numerous contents of the object world are often only felt and comprehended when the lens is zoomed in and the specific parts or individuals are protruded. This distinction is sometimes referred to as the "macro-micro" distinction. This distinction is not merely akin to "the two sides of one coin", as the conventional wisdom suggests, since the conventional perception implies that they are a unified whole. This perception ignores the plurality of the contents. The "whole" itself contains elements of subjective imagination, which is a simplification made by people due to their limited observational and computing power. "Whole" does not exactly encapsulate the "parts", and the unique contents in the parts cannot be obtained until observers go close to them.

In fact, we have elaborated on each part of the world according to the traditional classification of philosophy. Of course, in the previous discussions, although the emphasis changes from time to time, our universe of discourse is not intentionally confined. We do not assume that people only think about natural objects and not about social objects when they think, nor do we specify which particular types of objects the ontology applies only to. Thus, the preceding statements are in principle applicable to society, although they are not sufficient for the goals of social philosophy. The basic principles of Algorithmic philosophy, which we have repeatedly emphasized, are important throughout the book, as are the specific routes, materials, and methods for deduction in specific fields. The latter is important because readers often do not see the many connections between a particular topic and the Algorithmic principles in advance, until these connections are logically articulated.

In the social realm, the power of Algorithmic principles is enormous. The Algorithmic principles were initially proposed in response to the needs of social research. Many problems in the social field have not been solved for a long time. Some of these questions were repeatedly discussed by early scholars in search of answers. Because they have been permanently in suspense, currently, they have become invisible, disappeared from professional literature, and seem to have ceased to exist. The current social sciences are rather dull. One exception is the impact of information technology and artificial intelligence, which has sparked a few passions. And I narcissistically believe that such dullness and such passions are the precursors of the emergence of Algorithmic Theory. ATT was mainly born for a unified social science. It is itself a result of the information technology revolution and an application of the principles of information technology in philosophy and social sciences. Simplicity of its form, fluency of its logic, comprehensiveness of its coverage, and powerfulness of its arguments are enough to set off another revolution in the fields of philosophy, humanities, and social sciences. Just as the natural sciences eventually emerge and separate from philosophy, a unified or general social science needs first to return to philosophy to generate itself, and it is only after solving a series of related philosophical problems that it can finally become independent, relatively.

Encouraged by the success of the natural sciences, the concept of "social science" has gradually taken shape in modern times. If scholars can succeed in the study of nature, why can't they in the social study? Why can't such success reach the point of establishing a "social science" that goes hand in hand with the natural sciences? Therefore, one of the ideas of the earlier social science researchers was to imitate the natural sciences to discover certain established mechanisms, and then to reason from them, and use mathematics as much as possible. This brings us to the path of determinism. This determinism conflicts with freedom, subjectivity, "irrationality", "self-correlation"[1], uncertainty, plurality, and development. It manifests itself in the opposition between the mainstream and

---

1. It needs to be emphasized that as a dynamic phenomenon, self-correlation, including self-realization and self-falsification, and their prevention or mitigation, must all be conditioned by Algorithmic concepts such as thoughtful discreteness, smallest unit of thinking activity, serial processing method, and so on.

heterodox schools, or the debates between economics and other humanities and social sciences. It also manifests itself in the incompatibility between the theoretical approach and the historical and empirical approaches: is the world presented to us all at once while we know it step by step, or is the world presented historically while we humans can know it once and for all? Or, in the framework of determinism, can and how can plurality and uncertainty arise? What is their significance? Determinism also leads to tension between the social sciences and social engineering: since everything is decisive, so should the course of action, so there should be no essential distinction between social science and social engineering.

Logical breaks like these abound (the macro-micro fracture is also an example). Such breaks are not a trivial matter, but a major and fundamental one. It shows that some basic principles and methods related to social research have yet to be established. This is a view that has existed in the academic community for a long time. Now we know that the answer to these problems is a one-time solution, that is, a highly unified and holistic theory of thinking that can solve all of them at once. Not only that, but some slightly more specific theoretical problems can also be solved herewith, such as the relationship between democracy, freedom and autocracy, the essence of currency, etc. The opposition between democracy and autocracy is still a prominent feature of today's world; a breakthrough solution to this theoretical problem requires the introduction of Algorithmic Theory. What we need shall be a scientific, objective, and comprehensive clarification, not rigid political dogmas. Questions about the nature and theoretical status of money are directly related to the materiality of thought. When these Algorithmic contributions are taken together and compared with what came before, we can see why social science has not been convincing and why we can now confidently claim that we have really discovered the foundational principles and methods of the general social science.

This and the next three chapters focus on the philosophical aspects of Algorithmic social science. This will inevitably restate something that has already been published. Nonetheless, these restatements will take on new angles and approaches as much as possible, and will also include my new gains in this field.

## §93. Run out of the Predicaments of Extreme Rationalism

When it comes to people, behavior, and social phenomena, it seems naturally logical to transplant or apply the methods used for physical and natural objects. These methods presume that an object has certain established characteristics or properties, that there are certain mechanisms or "temperaments" within it, and then making logical deductions from them, from the simple to the complex, thereby explaining certain observed phenomena. This is the theoretical approach. Another way is to directly observe the phenomena and draw certain patterns or laws from them. These laws can be used as the basis for theoretical deduction, which can then be applied to different occasions. Theoretical and empirical methods are often used alternately, or in combination.

However, when the subjects of research were changed from matter to humans, these methods that were considered general were not so easy to use. Indeed, researchers can find certain fragments of human behavior that seem suitable for the natural science methods. Here, the way people behave has been stable, predictable (or has certain fixed "patterns"), and can withstand repeated tests of empirical data. Social scientists, especially economists, often cite such examples as evidence of the "success" of social sciences. However, in the social sphere, evidence to the contrary is numerous. A large number of practical observations show that actors often do not act according to these fixed patterns or laws. Their behaviors are either unpredictable or present significant interpersonal and situational differences. Since those fixed patterns have been predefined as "rational", deviations from them are considered "irrational". Behaviorist psychology and economics are devoted to collating, enumerating, and studying these "irrational" phenomena, and their literature has become very popular in the new century. The complexity, heterogeneity, "self-correlation", uncertainty (or unpredictability), and developmentality of human behavior and society have become so significant that many scholars tend to give up their attempts, no longer insisting on the term of "social science". Ludwig Wittgenstein, for example, said, "we may not advance any kind of theory ... All explanation must disappear, and description alone must take its place."[2] When I sent a manuscript of Algorithmic Theory to a professor for comments, the reply I received was that the idea of establishing a unified theory was currently "unsellable".[3]

The theoretical method is a rationalist approach that is characterized by demonstrating the logic, rationality, or optimality of each aspect of the deductive processes to prove that the conclusions are acceptable. In economics, this approach is expressed as neoclassicism, which is characterized by the representation of the "temperament" of each actor as a function as if it were a physical object, and from which economic phenomena are then derived. The optimal solutions

---

2. Ludwig Wittgenstein, "Philosophical Investigations", translated by Anscombe, Hacker, and Schulte, Wiley-Blackwell, 2009, §109, p. 52. The ellipsis is added by me.

3. However, efforts for synthesis have always been ongoing. For example, in "The Cambridge History Of Philosophy, 1945-2015" (edited by Kelly Becker et al., Cambridge University Press, 2019), one of the four parts of the book is entitled "Bridge Builders, Border Crossers, Synthesizers, and Comparative Philosophy".

of the system of related functions and equations produce the state of "equilibrium". Each phenomenon is interpreted as an "equilibrium" while economic phenomena as a whole are considered the "general equilibrium". Economics formed in this way is not much different from mathematics, logic, or natural science, and if the "actors" are replaced by physical objects, its conclusion will be much the same. One superficial difference is the "respect" for the "preferences" of actors. It is considered sacrosanct. With this reason or "excuse", these subjective aspects of decision-making, which are actually also represented as some functions similarly to those of the objective aspects, are completely separated from the objective aspects. In this way of "highly respecting subjectivity", economists have tried to make their doctrines appear as if they were the "science" about people rather than matter.

Supposedly, it is not too much to whip such doctrines. Neoclassicism is just a variant of extreme rationalism. The soul of extreme rationalism is that people can directly obtain the truth of things, and the process of knowing is secondary or can be ignored. That is, the computing time is zero and the speed is infinite. Even if no thinker is willing to explicitly endorse such a rationalism, it is necessary to assume it as a counter-reference for Algorithmic Theory. I believe that this rationalism actually has many variations in almost all disciplines and contexts. We have exposed and will continue to expose and critique each of these variants in relevant chapters. However, too much criticism is useless and wasteful in terms of the goal of building a new system. Next, we will briefly review and explain our main ideas for solving these problems, and why Algorithmic Theory will decisively lead us to a "basically proper" unified social philosophy and social science. In this unified system, this rationalist approach will be corrected, its merits and characteristics will be restated, but its basic ideas will not change. Basic principles of the scientific method will remain unchanged here, although the specific principles, methods, terms, perspectives, and specific disciplinary forms will change significantly.

It can be said that Algorithmic Theory is simply a "technical" theory about how the activities of the human mind are carried out. The human way of thinking is externally manifested as the activities of a computer. Now, let's borrow the activities of computers to re-explain how the activities of the mind work. Economics and the social sciences, at least initially, will remain the same as before, except that they had to be deduced on this new premise. It's as if the technical characteristics of a factory are not primarily determined by economists, but rather that economists just understand these characteristics and then draw economic conclusions based on them. In this sense, Algorithmic Theory is also known as the "Algorithmic framework", framing any relevant research.

The assumption that multiple Instructions coexist is a pluralism. Therefore, the Algorithmic deduction begins and ends in pluralism. It's an intrinsic and mutual consistency. Meanwhile, it is strongly supported by evidence from adjacent disciplines, as well as important empirical facts. If this hypothesis is (tentatively) acceptable, then the subsequent deductions can be done by philosophers and social scientists themselves. The combined effects of limited computing power and big data will *reasonably* lead to a subjective turn (or "mental distortions") in the thinking of actors. This turn may not happen all the time, but frequently and widely. This conclusion, although somewhat vague, is reliable. The subjective turn causes the actors' behavioral traits of "irrationality", difference, uncertainty, inaccuracy, irregularity, etc. Distortions will cause distortions again, and so forth. In the fields of philosophy, humanities, and social sciences, the distortive manifestations can be extremely colorful. Subjective individuals observe each other's (including researchers') behaviors, thereby feeling, supposedly, that "people as objects are significantly different from physical ones". Heterogeneity is a consequence of Algorithmic bounded rationality, which allows a wide variety of differences to exist in a mixed manner. Thus, convergence and divergence, equilibrium and disequilibrium can coexist in this all-encompassing system. The sedimentation, solidification, accumulation, marginal change of stock, and the combinatorial explosive effect lead to infinite development. "Development" has become a prominent feature of human society that is different from the natural world.

This theory will give its own solutions to philosophical problems such as static and dynamic, absolute and relative, innate and acquired. In particular, in addition to the "first-order laws" that traditional philosophy and social sciences focus on, the Algorithmic theory emphasizes the discovery of higher-order laws, and is committed to building a matrix and a general system or platform for first-order laws and specific research. In principle, the laws revealed by the traditional mainstream doctrine are considered to exist in it only locally. On their sides, there are to be a great deal of things that are different from them, shunned or ignored before. Now, we will say that the existence of these things is a "law", and the mixedness, plurality, conflicts, and development are all "laws". Cannot we say so? I think we can. Even if these statements are inaccurate, they argue or predict that a large number of "non-mainstream" phenomena will occur with a fairly high frequency, and these phenomena are true facts. In other words, they are substantially and empirically meaningful, and hence are not some empty arguments. Therefore, I call them the "higher-order laws". From these high-order laws, a fluent and complete philosophy of science, and methodology of social science, can be derived. Together, they form the Algorithmic system of social philosophy and social science principles.

As a kind of "informal institution", ethics are "endogenous" as an example of the Algorithmic knowledge stock theory, along with formal institutions such as laws and organizations. In other words, they are all products of sedimentation, distortion, and solidification of knowledge. Such ethics can be a major subversion of dominant views since ancient times. Mental distortion is the life and foundation of ethics, without which there would be no ethics at all, and in the same way there would be no law, politics, or all sorts of official or non-governmental organizations. The market economy is actually based on the current computations supported by these knowledge stocks, namely, this two-tier structure of "stock + flow". Capitalism emphasizes that in the face of limited computing power and big data, it is necessary to systematically open up the current computing of individuals, and seek continuous innovations on the basis of a large number of repetitions, waste, failures, and crises. *The combinatorial explosion between Instructions and information strongly tends to support "higher-order rules" such as freedom and democracy, which* allows us to reconnect Hume's severed subjectivity and objectivity within a logically unified framework, putting freedom and order, democracy and power properly in their respective places, and thus comprehensively and innovatively addressing those major issues of social philosophy (This "addressing" certainly involves a large amount of existing literature).

The above are some applicative examples that illustrate some of the concrete results that can be Algorithmically achieved in the field of social philosophy. In the final analysis, these concrete results depend on the philosophical view that thought is a kind of real entity that can be juxtaposed with matter, that they cannot replace each other, that the problems of thought and its solutions are its own affair and have nothing to do with external objects, that the correspondence and inconsistency between it and external objects exist concurrently in principle and hence we do not have to take any particular position in general, that the relations between different ideas are also relations between different entities, and that their interactions constitute the "society". In short, the minds, as the characteristic beings, are the objects to which the word "society" is mainly intended. *When we study society, we mainly study the minds.* Moreover, it is precisely because the minds are such material and substantial existences that they can become the objects of our study.

## §94. "Society" is Primarily a Collection of Specific Mental Entities and Their Relations

Extreme rationalism holds that the human brain can grasp the truth of things, and that the temporal process is relatively secondary, and that those parts of the truth that have not yet been grasped will sooner or later be grasped, and that the errors and imperfections that arise in the cognitive processes are purely procedural, temporary, and insignificant. In short, human's grasp of the truth is the primary and standard doctrine. This philosophical doctrine fundamentally excludes the necessity and possibility of social issues and social sciences.

Imagine if, in the face of nature, all the truth can be easily obtained, and if the best solutions to all problems can be easily found, then what is the need to establish human relationships? In this case, interpersonal relationships would just be a name for something that is naturally established or occurs in acting in accordance with the acquired truth, without actors' any deliberation. For example, this is like a solar or lunar eclipse. These phenomena are simply results of the natural movements of the Sun, the Earth, and the Moon in their respective orbits and spatiotemporal contexts. In order to produce such outcome, the Sun, the Earth, and the Moon do not need to do anything; they do not need to deliberately "goal" it, and "relish" it. Because solar eclipses, lunar eclipses and other phenomena have actually been included in the movements of these planets from the beginning, and they are their "due meanings". In other words, the emphasis on solar and lunar eclipses is nothing more than an "interpretation" of the planets' movements, and this interpretation is not independent of them.

These beliefs persist even when social problems are of obvious importance and their solutions cannot be directly derived from the natural sciences. This is because it is believed that the laws of society and the laws of nature can *eventually* be reconciled (just as two relatively independent fields of the natural sciences are believed to be united). Therefore, the methods of the natural sciences can be simply transplanted to the study of society. This is the ultra-rationalist version of the model of "unification of the natural sciences and the social sciences", and in fact, it is also a way for the natural sciences to cancel the social sciences.

This most classical philosophy still quietly dominates the intellectual world to this day, no matter what resistance it encounters. The way to break down this philosophy is to cut out the arbitrary and unnecessary redundancy of "optimistic eschatology" that exists in it, and to highlight the status of the human minds as one of the many primordial elements in any philosophical, scientific, and intellectual processes. Thereafter, the thoughtful entities will begin to act on other entities, i.e., to develop the mental activities. In principle, any thinking processes should be aware of their own existences, pay attention to and manage their own existences, and integrate this higher-order consciousness into the results of the first-order thinking. The natural sciences also need to realize that they are only a kind of human thoughts themselves, so they should also consciously accept their own limitations, development, and plurality. *In fact, the understanding and interaction between human beings must start concurrently with the understanding and interaction between human and nature, and they are carried out side by side and intertwined,* and there is no question of which is more "basic". Social issues are integrated and unified with natural issues in a pluralistic and interactive way, rather than in the way of extreme rationalism. This is the great turn of philosophy and the re-establishment of social philosophy that we want to achieve.

We must see social existence, social action, and social phenomena as the material and substantial objects that are relatively independent of nature, and of which thoughts are the main components. In most cases, physical objects are only subordinate here, and are of interest to the needs of computations that take place here. In other words, a premise for the relative independence of social philosophy and social science is to regard thoughts as relatively independent realities and entities. There are many types of thoughts, and their contents are rich, and the social contents account for only a part of them. It is not enough for human knowledge as a whole to gain independence from other types of entities, but also to have relative independence between different thoughtful entities within the body of knowledge. In this way, the part of thoughts with social contents inevitably acquires its relative independence.

People's philosophical attitudes on this issue have always been equivocal and ambiguous. When people talk about the term "social phenomenon", they mainly mean that it has a physical form and appearance. It seems that only in this way does a phenomenon finally qualify as a "phenomenon"— because it "manifests". For example, constitutions and laws generally have their visible forms, governmental and religious institutions have their stately buildings, and people's assemblies, speeches, ballots, media, currencies, and commodities have their distinctive physical forms (impressive shapes, colors, sounds, etc.). While observing and feeling these physical forms, people experience the contents of the thoughts inside them. This sense of "fullness" makes people forget to think about who the protagonists of the so-called "social phenomena" or "social objects" are? Ideas or substances? Between the ideological and physical elements of social objects, which one serves which? For example, when someone goes to a courthouse to fight a lawsuit, is he/she going to see the courthouse? Of course not, he/she is to deal with a group of people, including judges and defendants. But is the "dealing" with these people directed at their flesh? Of course not, in fact he/she is to be engaged in ideological activities with them. As a result of the trial, more thoughts and memories will be generated. These memories will form a document, which is then to be transmitted to a wider range of other interested persons (and to be executed as a sentence).

Max Weber gave a subtle but substantive answer to this question a hundred years ago with his "sociology of understanding". He said that social objects are different from natural objects because they are human beings, the same kind of researchers, and they are communicative to researchers, so social research is first and foremost about understanding the meanings of social behaviors.[4] What Weber failed to point to directly is that the so-called "meanings of social behaviors" are actually the ideological contents of social behaviors. The ideological contents are, firstly, the contents of the actions consciously given by the actors themselves (e.g., "I go to court to fight a lawsuit"), and secondly, they are understood by other interested actors (e.g., in an election where the media understand a support for a particular candidate as the support

_______________

4.  Max Weber, "Economy and Society: An Outline of Interpretive Sociology", translated by Ephraim Fischoff et al. 2 Vols. Los Angeles: University of California Press, 1978.

for a political party). Social research is the study of the minds of actors—although the researcher also has his/her own thoughts, and the researcher uses his/her own thoughts as a tool to study the minds of actors. In view of this, we must develop appropriate methods for studying thoughts, including the knack for distinguishing between different thoughts, between different individuals' thoughts, and between different thoughts of the researcher and the actors. This brings us to Algorithmic Theory.

Of course, this distinction between primary and secondary cannot be developed into the point as the traditional monistic "either/or". Thoughtful entities are prioritized just on their coexistence with physical entities. The flip side of this relationship is cooperation. Moreover, it is precisely because mental and physical entities can coexist *at the same level of logic*, rather than *at different levels of logic*, as traditionally believed, that they can *cooperate* with each other. The thoughtful contents are combined with a physical shell to form a complete social object. Ideas and physical entities are not incompatible, not categorically repetitive as Ryle put it, and not inscrutably raveled in any capricious manner. Since they are entities, the ways in which they relate and cooperate are specific, not arbitrary. This point can be used to refute the allegation that the materiality or substantiality of thought shall be denied because it cannot interact with a physical entity in a physical way (e.g., they collide with each other).

Another example of the cooperation between ideological entities and physical entities is that the thoughts sometimes exaggerate their "physical shells" in order to express their substantial existences, and to achieve the effect of impressing somebody. The exaggerated "physical shells" include the national flag, the national anthem, election materials, the imposing and exaggerated shapes of the buildings of certain institutions, commercial advertisements, and so on. A large number of physical materials or physical means are used to transmit information, make computations, express ideas, etc. It is only between entities that such a concrete relationship arises.

## §95. "Society" is Primarily a Collection of Specific Mental Entities and Their Relations (continued)

Since only specific (and not any) thoughtful entities constitute society, what are these particular entities? The answer is that they are those about human relations. For example, when a male doctor receives a female patient, he could have literally treated the patient as a living organism and only used his medical skills on her. At this time there is no human relationship between them. However, the patient is also a human being, and she has legal, ethical, sexual, and economic status, which requires the doctor to integrate those interpersonal relationships into the way he really treats her. "Relationship" is a common term, but it needs to be further questioned: what exactly does it mean? Is it some floating object in the air? And, where does it exist?

As soon as we ask this question, we will realize that it only exists in the minds of the persons concerned, and it is just some thoughts there. As a result of the education the doctor received, he has the idea of how to treat patients as social beings. This idea was accepted by him and he is willing to follow it as a code of conduct. This process of "acceptance" acts as yet another mental activity, leading to the generation of new data in his mind outside of the contents educated. These data form a mechanism to implement the above idea of "how to treat the patient as a social being". It is important to note that "knowing a guideline" is not the same as "committing to the guideline"; the latter involves more data that are qualitatively different from the former. These data also include the doctor's own expectation of the corresponding data in other people's minds.

For example, he may foresee that a doctor's code of conduct is widely known to others (including bystanders and those with direct working relationships), and is also expected by patients. That is, he foresees the relevant thoughts in the minds of others, and how they may react if he violates the professional norms. Therefore, when we usually speak of "interpersonal relations" or "social relations" in general terms, their "specific existence" is actually nothing but these specific thoughts in the minds of the people concerned. These thoughts exist as entities, and their specific natures determine that the persons have specific relationships with each other.

Does the above point of view mean that if the patient is completely unaware of her legal, ethical, sexual, economic, and other rights in the above situation due to the lack of education, can she not enter such "interpersonal relationships"? The answers to this include: first, the patient's ignorance may not be perceived by the doctor, so even if the patient does not request it, the doctor may provide the patient with the same equal treatment as other patients without discrimination; second, even if the doctor perceives the patient's ignorance, exploits it, and does not provided equal treatment for the patient, he will still face the risk of being held accountable by law and professional standards. In other words, even if such relationships do not exist in the eyes of the patient, they still exist in the eyes of many other relevant people. Without the latter, and the extensive substantial presence of relevant thoughts in other people's minds, the existence of these social relationships will not be secured.

As mentioned above, interpersonal relationships can be considered to occur simultaneously with the relationships between human and other entities, and both belong to the most basic phenomena in the object world. However, since extreme rationalism and physicalism have occupied the mainstream of philosophy (they clearly converge on this point) in advance, we are compelled to explain why it is necessary to specifically justify the relatively independent "person-person" relationship in addition to the "thing-thing" and "person-thing" relationships, and social philosophy and social science can therefore have their unique statuses. Our approach is to argue for the relative independence of all things, and eventually to a situation where academic research can start anywhere, for any object, and that different studies only need to compare their efficiency and effectiveness, and there is no longer a need to argue for the "legitimacy" of an object itself.

## §96. Mental Distortions, Constructions, and Reconstructions

The style adopted by Algorithmic Theory deeply links itself to constructivism. This is certainly not a repetition of traditional constructivism, but an important addition and adjustment to it.

"Constructivism", as the name suggests, is the idea that the mind is "constructing" something. But what is the mind? How does it "construct"? What does it use to "construct"? Questions such as these can be answered comprehensively with Algorithmic Theory. That is to say, the term "construction" exists only when the brain is born with something such as Instructions, and the processes and results of "construction" are the processes and results of Instructions processing information and generating "data" or "knowledge", which is in principle different from the original information and the Instructions themselves. There is no "invisible hand" operating the constructive processes, which are the results of the running of Instructions themselves in a roundabout way, that is, with the support of previous operational achievements, hence the constructive processes must be limited by the functions of Instructions, the speed of operation, and other factors.

Constructivism gives an impression of being freewheeling, which is one reason why the term is sometimes avoided.

However, Algorithmic Theory can borrow this term for philosophical expression.

*The act of knowing is a constructive activity.* This long-standing idea would be clearer and more accurate when it is expressed Algorithmically. The reason why this view has been put forward and emphasized is that it is traditionally mistaken that only the field of decision-making and action is arbitrary, and that a cognitive process is only a passive "reflection" of external objects. However, without a proper theoretical framework, it is difficult for actors to effectively process pure raw information, and this theoretical framework is often the result of earlier subjective conception of the knower. A detailed study of examples from the cognitive processes would show that this point of view is very convincing.[5] Of course, from an Algorithmic point of view, the subjective conception process of the theoretical framework can also be compatible with simple inductive processes of some original information, because the theoretical framework was probably obtained, at least partially, through some earlier inductions of this or other knowers' experiences; however, as the simple, rigorous, and econometric-alike inductive method might have been too slow, the knowers turned to the subjective, crooked, fast, and estimative methods instead, to make a theory as a frame. In this way, those various points about the substitution and combination of theory and experience can, in principle, serve as some corollaries to this roundabout production method of thoughts.

A comparison between a cognitive process and a decision-making process shows that the main difference between them is not the difference in the methods used or in the reliability of the results. Cognition can be subjective while in the field of

---

5. Michael Huemer, "There Is No Pure Empirical Reasoning", Philosophy and Phenomenological Research 95 (3):592-613 (2017).

actions, some certainties, such as a certain moral code or a certain action proposal, may be "objectively" and stubbornly made. Therefore, the difference between a cognitive process and a decision-making process lies mainly in the different questions they answer, and actually they are at different stages of an entire thinking chain. Due to the limited computing power, it is difficult for the entire thinking chain to be rigorously and deductively streamlined into a solid whole; hence, the knowledge system is disjointed and modularized. As a result, they are quite different in many specific characteristics.

It can be thought that the constructiveness is mainly due to the bending of the mind. Although we can repeatedly argue that even the knowledge built up by deductive and other reliable methods is, in the final analysis, not related to external objects, but resulted from the "game" of thinking itself, there is a limit to the resonances that this argument can have with readers. Subjective Algorithms, on the other hand, are quite different from the above because they *explicitly* ask a thinker to give his/her own opinions or choices during computing. How the computing route is, and what the result is, depend to a certain extent on the thinker oneself. If the thinker does not subjectively make a choice and give a decision on these questions, the computations cannot proceed again. This causes a different feeling in everyone's mind. Everyone would agree that something is being "constructed", even if the choices in each case are often limited, or even if people do not know (or disagree) that the mental activities are simply processing information with a finite number of Instructions alternately, or that they are just referencing a limited stock of knowledge. Compared to a deterministic fixed route, the free space here is already very large.

The outstanding merit of the word "construction" is that it emphasizes that human knowledge has emerged as an unprecedented new thing in this world, and that mental activity has increased the variety and number of things in the world. The tones of pluralism, heterogeneity, discreteness, and marginal development have been brought out here—even if these meanings remain latent rather than articulated. This is a subtlety of language.

Since subjective thoughts are generated, they are not easy to disappear. They have to exist in some places for some time (even a long time), but people's computations and actions are continuing, and life has to go on minute by minute, continuously. There's no room for waiting all the time. Then, the subjective thoughts will be used as raw materials and put into computations again, which may lead to further subjectivities. A person will process his/her own subjectivities continuously, even deeply, and will also refer to the subjectivities of others for computation, or compute upon the subjectivities of others (e.g., gambling). Since the population is large, the processes of construction and reconstruction caused by it must be very complex, and the resulting personalities and differences will also be very diverse. Then, scholars shift from the before-action world to the after-action world, and to the actions themselves. When we say that social science is the study of thought (as being and behavior) itself, that is, it is primarily the study of thinking and the world after thinking.

Here we must again touch on the issue of convergence. However, there are many reasons to argue that convergence is not easy to achieve, or that the paths to and states of convergence are diverse. For example, when a person does something controversial, he/she may not revoke it and return to the desired "right" practice; instead, he/she may take some remedial actions to further salvage the controversial practice (similar to the often said "adding mistake to mistake"). As long as the energy and resources at his/her disposal are large enough, he/she can stop the convergent process for a long time.

A topic that arises from this can be lengthy, so we'll have to leave it at that.

In dynamically interactive social networks, it doesn't always make sense to distinguish between which objects or factors are fundamental and which are derived (or constructed). For both the actors and the researchers, one cannot expect to be at the very beginning or end of history. All processual objects and factors will have to be faced, and the so-called "beginning" or "end" is just a method that we use to understand a process, or a hypothesis that we use to deal with the problems at hand.

## §97. What on earth is the "Social Structure"?

The "structure" and "function" of society are terms commonly used by sociologists and in the general literature. People use these words with great vigor, but rarely interpret them precisely. Even if experts do explain, they are vague and unconvincing. Now, I believe that under the Algorithmic framework, we can devote ourselves to a substantive and thorough explanation or interpretation of these terms.

Traditional scholarship is "explaining, explaining, and re-explaining", while constructivism is "constructing, constructing, and reconstructing". As soon as it is constructed, the physical objects are marginalized, and the center of the lens is aimed at thoughts themselves. What is "constructed" is nothing else, but the thoughts, and the "shapes", structures, functions, and "scales" of the thoughtful entities, and so on. And where do these mental entities exist? Not elsewhere, of course, but in the human brains.

The stock of knowledge in the human brain is structured. What does the word "structure" mean? As has been discussed[6], "structure" refers first to the existence of objects of different

---

6.  Bin Li, "A Preliminary Exploration of Principles of General Social Science:

natures, and secondly, to the existence of some *close* relationships between these objects of different natures. It is important to note here the word "close", the theoretical meaning of which we have already discussed Algorithmically in the previous sections. Since the word has now become an important and tenable theoretical element, our discourse is actually different from other existing discourses. Where there is this close relationship, the relationships between the entities next to them are not so close. The close relationship is identified by contrast in the middle of relatively loose relationships. Because of this close relationship, words such as "structure" and "structurality" are distinguished from words such as plurality, heterogeneity, and mixedness (although the connections between them are also obvious). Moreover, this close relationship is not primarily quantitative (although it can sometimes be described in quantitative data). *The relationship itself is qualitative, polygonal, or heterogeneous,* so much so that when we try to describe it in terms of data, we use multiple variables and data types, resulting in a fragmented database. However, the word "structure" first brings to mind buildings, specifically the basic framework of an architecture. Actually, this is the best illustration of the word "structure". The individual beams and columns of the building frame are in different positions and have different shapes, but they interconnect and interact to form a tight whole. From the perspective of system theory, a "structure" often has some synergistic effect, the effect of "one plus one is greater than two". If the idealization, perfectionization, or mystification of system theory is avoided, a structure can also be called a "system".

Because of the synergistic effect, a structure cannot be

---

The Algorithmic Approach" (in Chinese), Beijing: China Renmin University Press, 2012, Section 4.1, pp. 97-113.

simply divided into individual parts for analysis, but needs to be viewed and analyzed as a whole. This is one of the basic meanings of the word "structure"—of course, the whole refers to a finite "whole" of elements that are closely related, rather than an all-encompassing whole, and this finite whole is still in the pluralistic, heterogeneous, loose, and mixed "Algorithmic world". However, this is not enough, another meaning of "structure" refers to the opposite of "quantity", thus it is used to resist quantitative relations, and it emphasizes that those heterogeneous elements in the structure and their heterogeneous relationships *cannot be reduced* to quantity only, and hence completely generalized by quantitative data. Then, where the word "structure" is used, it is a reminder to let go of quantity, to leave quantity for a while, to know that quantity is only a local feature of things. Not only is quantitative analysis not a complete substitute for qualitative analysis, but in most cases, it should be seen as an adjunct to qualitative analysis, not the other way around. This is especially applicable to the misuse of quantitative relations in economics. With the help of monetized commodity trading, neoclassicism in economics attempts to reduce all relations to quantitative ones. That is, it is an attempt to destroy all structures. If we don't understand it from this perspective, we often don't know what the word "structure" is talking about, and we may think that what it says seems plausible in some sense, and in other senses it says nothing.

The "structure" is just a foundation, a framework. In its "above", "below", or "inside", the actions take place. A behavior is both supported and limited by it. That is to say, there is also an emphasis on a specific heterogeneity in the word "structure", namely, the differentiation of flow and stock, as well as the particularly close relationship between them (for example, the sociologist Giddens uses the term "structure" in this sense, which he calls "structuration"[7]). This relationship is still similar to that in architectural activities. Within the large frame of a structure, the construction workers fill in the materials and carry out the constructive activities. The structure as a stock exists before the activities, and it quietly waits for the initiation of the activities because it has been prepared for them. Therefore, when people talk about a structure, it means that a behavioral flow is about to happen. And, obviously, the life cycle of a structure as a stock is generally longer than a single action. The roundabout production method lurks here. Now, we're going to make it clear.

Ultimately, however, all of these depend on establishing a proper atomism. Many atoms with different physical or mental properties combine and interact with each other, and recombine and react with each other to produce a variety of structures. Large structures can be built on top of small structures, creating a world of "structural forests".

## §98. What on earth is the "Social Structure" (continued)

The stock of knowledge in the mind is actually structured. This structure is made up of multiple relatively independent databases, and coexists with a large amount of fragmented knowledge. Together, or individually, they have impacts on current computations. Multiple structures can also coexist, thus the number of structures can also be very large. A structure can also have a variety of relationships with one another, such as competition, collaboration, containment, etc., depending in part on how we define a structure, just as we define a system or an object. One of the reasons why the concepts of system and

---

7.   Anthony Giddens, "The Constitution of Society: Outline of the Theory of Structuration", University of California Press, 1984.

structure arise is that the physical and visible existences of the objects that make up the system or structure are loose in comparison with "one object"—despite that they are not "loose" from certain invisible perspectives. In the computational economy, vision is not unimportant, nor are the benefits of the convenience of terminology. Nonetheless, not only are physical objects visible, but data objects are now also "visible" and are treated in the same way as physical objects. This requires us to seek other terms. Then, the existing word "system" or "structure" meets our requirements, i.e., it exists as *an object*, and it is *obvious* (note the Algorithmic meaning of this word) that it contains many different elements that are relatively "visually" independent. We can now use these terms in such a relative, completely disenchanted context.

Where there is an overall structure, there is the word "function". *"Function" refers to the role that a structure plays in an activity it serves.* The role played by a particular structure may be broken down into multiple functions, which are performed separately or jointly by the elements that make up the structure or system. Hence, the word "function" is inherently allied with concepts such as structure, system, stock, whole, etc. When we say that an element or entity has a certain "function", it means that it will have a certain impact we expect on the activities, and thus serve a certain overall goal.

The reason why we spend time interpreting these concepts is to explain how macro and micro issues are connected, and how Algorithmic atomism can be used to construct macro social concepts.

There is a structure between different pieces of knowledge in a person's brain, then, is there also a structure between the knowledge of different individuals? Yes, of course. In the Algorithmic framework, a number of different reasons can be cited to illustrate this structurality. For example, when a large part of an individual's knowledge comes from socialized education, the education will inevitably inculcate some systematic knowledge, and hence the knowledge pieces inside the brains of different individuals will be either identical or similar, or they may *match* each other. Thus, after the individuals invoke these knowledge pieces to make behavioral decisions, their external behaviors will have some certainty, consistency, or compatibility. Different Algorithmic persons can also achieve interpersonal consistency or match through mutual agreement, because it is easy for people with a common or compatible knowledge background to negotiate and reach consensus.

What is an "interpersonal consistency"? It is that people should have multiple choices, but they all make a particular selection. It's like people could have walked freely in any directions in an empty square, but instead of doing so, they line up. The behaviors of different individuals are so closely related to each other that when we look at the social phenomenon in a macroscopic and holistic way, we see a certain orderly "structure". Structures like this exist not only in many concurrent activities, but also overtime. Through these flows, we seem to see the stocks themselves, and also see the structures in the stocks of knowledge. These stocks were originally scattered in everyone's mind, but the feeling was so strong that these intangible things seemed to become tangible. Together with the rendering and promotion of ideas by the physical materials mentioned in §94, the thoughtful elements are finally combined with the physical elements into a whole, and figuratively become something like a solemn building. In other words, they become the "social structures" that hang high over the heads of us ordinary people, like towering roofs that we can see when we look up.

These "roofs" both protect us and restrict and correct our behaviors. They are powerful and seem to oppose the actions of the people and the activities that are alive today. Even, they make us wonder where they came from. They are like the "universal before things" or the "human knowledge thesaurus" that we feel are hanging over our heads or somewhere not far from us. However, this is not true. They are in your, my, his, or her heart as your, my, his, or her ideas. Even if these ideas are produced by our predecessors or others and then instilled in us, our acceptance of them has a conscious and voluntary component (recall the "authorization mechanism" in §56, Vol. I) —at least, we agree with the reality that "these ideas exist in people's minds and are not easily changed". When we sometimes complain about or even criticize them, we are often unaware that another part of our mind has been actually involved in their construction (this internal inconsistency is a common Algorithmic phenomenon), and therefore we ourselves shall be more or less responsible for them.

Now we can see how the "social structure" is closely related to Algorithmic Theory, or how Algorithmic Theory has become the basis of social structure from multiple perspectives. Without the roundabout separation of stock and flow, there would be no social structure; without the sedimentation and solidification of the knowledge stocks, there would be no social structure; and without plurality, heterogeneity, and mixedness, there would be no environment for the social structure to emerge, exist, differentiate, and disintegrate, and thus there would be no social structure.

The nature of social structures can also be understood in terms of its negation. For example, an earthquake happened somewhere and a house collapsed. However, because the long, large, and rigid structure of the house was not completely destroyed, it could support and protect, and hence there might have been some air gaps in the rubble that allowed the victims to survive. Moreover, whether in an emergency or peacetime, existence of such large hard objects can create a large number of "air gaps" that can be used by people. This is what we often call "exploiting loopholes". The effects of "exploiting loopholes" can be negative or positive in ethics. For example, a particular social change aims to replace a particular institution that is an integral part of the social structure. However, the old institution is resilient and cannot be completely destroyed. If the new institution is not beneficial enough, then the remnants of the old institution will have a certain protective effect on social order, making a social change relatively modest. However, as a rigid or "solid" entity, institutions have a certain degree of integrity, leading to the fact that a specific institution is either retained or replaced in its entirety. However, society has to operate continuously in time without interruption, thus this structure is like the "Neurath's ship" that can only be replaced while it is being used, which makes it even more difficult to reform. From this we can understand why reforms, both of the past and at present, when they have been mainly aimed at human minds, have not been easy to succeed.

# CHAPTER 9
# THE SOCIAL PHILOSOPHY (II)

## §99. Individuals and Their Behaviors

Just as everything in the world can be a relatively independent object with an individuality, so is an individual person, or the "individual". The individual is a collection of biological and ideological elements, occupying a relatively independent space and carrying out relatively independent movements or behaviors.

The first element of a behavior is its purposefulness. This purposefulness is a concept that only human beings can understand, and it exists in their consciousness. Just as many other physical phenomena have no causes (or we don't know about them), human purposes can arise, exist, and disappear freely and arbitrarily—of course, "freedom" and "arbitrariness" here may also be the results of an observer's understanding and judgment of the person concerned (or "oneself at another moment") as the observee, and in fact they are all limited. A researcher can explain to some extent how a particular purpose came about, but this does not often affect the relative independence of the purpose and its arbitrariness for the actor. The actor may arbitrarily and free-wheelingly determine his/her own purposes and spiritual values, but this does not mean that one will determine anything as a purpose. One's plot in determining one's own purposes, interests, hobbies, values, etc. is subtle, volatile, and highly personalized, making it not easily understood by outsiders. An original or ultimate purpose can change into many instrumental purposes, and vice versa. As discussed in Chapter 5, Algorithmic Theory can provide the basis for all these phenomena, as well as the absence of purpose and the inseparability of ends and means. The plurality and heterogeneity require us to go to each specific situation to explain the specific phenomena there and to deal with the various irregularities there.

A typical behavior is intentionally initiated by an actor for a certain purpose[1]. However, the limited ability of individual software and hardware determines that the behavior can only be a combination of limited and specific elements in a specific spatio-temporal environment. The individual is like a dot that moves through the social world. Individuals condense their behaviors with the help of various subjective and objective Algorithms, so that the contents or meanings of a behavior have both the locality of a specific situation and the globality of the social world in its own unique way. Therefore, the individual behavior is worth knowing even to a human observer. Researchers need to put aside their own thoughts and opinions, and, preparing for the next step, first understand the specific ideological states and ideological activities of actors. This is the basis of social research.

The finitude of connotations of behaviors also leads to the interweaving of individual successes and failures, as well as the

---

1. No matter how behavior is classified, as Max Weber did (Weber, Max. "Economy and Society: An Outline of Interpretive Sociology", translated by Ephraim Fischoff et al., 2 Vols, Los Angeles: University of California Press, 1978, pp. 24-25), the classification itself needs and can be re-founded within our Algorithmic Framework.

individual's awareness of it. As a result, individuals are constantly moving back and forth between theory and practice through experimentation, evolution, and other methods. Expanding to the social level, this leads to externalities including unexpected successes for society. Environmentalists emphasize negative externalities while Adam Smith emphasized the positive externalities through his concept of "the invisible hand". However, with an Algorithmic perspective, the scenarios we can infer are much more diverse, comprehensive, and realistic. For example, if a person's actions for a specific purpose are secretly observed and evaluated by another person, and then the latter intentionally and furtively encourages or discourages the former, it comes to the Algorithmic concept of *Semi-Internalization*. It can be argued that the "invisible hand" mainly describes this phenomenon of semi-internalization. It is not exactly an externality.

Algorithmic Theory undoubtedly reveals the widest range of interpersonal differences. In this way, the philosophical issue of the "Other" is naturally Algorithmical. The "Other" became a philosophical issue, apparently because philosophers finally discovered how mainstream thought had excluded other people narcissistically, and even instrumentalized others. Under the monism of extreme rationalism, the knowledge in people's minds is first assumed to be the same. At this time, people naturally find no motivation and reason to get to know others—Just reflect on yourself, and you will know everything. Second, from a perspective similar to the concept of "division of labor" in economics, the knowledge in people's heads is assumed to match each other. Such a view of knowledge is a limited understanding of the quantitativeness of knowledge: although it is obviously not so easy for a person to obtain all knowledge, with the help of the "division of labor", it is still possible to obtain all knowledge. Therefore, this view of knowledge more or less implies that one can follow the clues from one's own knowledge and then infer the knowledge of others. Although this idea also logically allows a certain logical status for others, it is still far from enough. It is now only through the introduction of elements such as pluralism, conflict, "individualized versions of knowledge", human dignity, the right to self-determination, etc. that others can enjoy full importance. One shall not just rely on "extrapolating oneself to others" to understand others, but needs to completely put oneself aside, and curiously understand and treat others with respect and even awe. In addition, it is necessary to have a comprehensive and holistic understanding of the similarity, compatibility, independence, communicability, and non-communicability of others relative to oneself. In other words, it has to be under the Algorithmic framework.

Social science was mainly used to discover specific social laws, while social philosophy was mainly used to provide basic ideas, principles, and propositions in a narrow sense. However, these have been just specific rules or orderliness. In my view, an appropriate social philosophy should, in a broad sense, first and foremost explain the plurality and mixedness of society, and how concrete and orderly things coexist with other various things in it. All the theoretical or ideological elements must be present at the outset. This includes, but not limited to, physics-thinking, time-space, stock-flow, dynamics-statics, individual-society, self-other, end-means-consequence, subjectivity-objectivity, monism-pluralism, consistency-conflict, relativity-absoluteness, finitude-infinity, freedom-determinism, convergence-divergence, conservative-radical, etc. Only when the actors have all arrived can the show start off.

However, behind all the actors, there is actually only one actor, and this is the Algorithmic theory. Through this theory, as long as we understand how the human thinking system works, all other social elements can be naturally derived, and the characteristics that the social sciences have, or should have, in relation to the natural sciences, will naturally be acquired. Even if you would have wanted to avoid them, it will be impossible. In light of this, I don't think it's too much to call Algorithmic Theory a "unified theory" (even if it embraces and emphasizes plurality). It can be said that the richness of the theoretical elements brought about by this has reached the level of following everything, supporting everything, and serving everything. Therefore, any discussion that will set out can only be regarded as illustrative (repetitively or freshly), and can never be comprehensive or perfect—not even of a basic soundness. Again, the important thing is the principles and methods, and after mastering such principles and methods, anyone can establish their own Algorithmical analysis and discourse.

## §100. Institution

The significance of ideological and interpersonal differences based on Algorithmic Theory would never be overemphasized. The infinite possibilities for knowledge outcome brought about by the permutations and combinations of Instructions and information would never be overemphasized. These are unprecedented discoveries, and their impacts on the existing body of knowledge must be unpredictable and inexhaustible. For example, these inferences can play a key role in explaining phenomena such as institutions and organizations. Together with other Algorithmical and existing theoretical elements, they can be synthesized into a coherent, comprehensive, and satisfactory theory of institutions and organizations.

For a specific object or goal, the actors can propose multiple computing results for selection. As noted earlier, the ideas or "standards" of right or wrong have been gradually developed through the comparison of the computing results. This is because the quality of the computing results is generally bound to be uneven. The single "standard answer" demonstrated by mathematical economists is usually a further result of deep computations, and hence of elimination of many primary results. If there are multiple indistinguishable choices available at the same time, they should also be understood as products of reprocessing of those primary results, rather than the products at the very beginning of computations.

Thereafter, some knowledge is favored, valued, and respected above others, and the actors are determined to use this higher quality knowledge with a higher degree of intensity in future computations (and, of course, in proper contexts), rather than lower quality knowledge. Keep in mind, however, that this comparison is often not absolute, that higher quality knowledge shall not be absolutely satisfactory, and that lower quality knowledge shall not be thoroughly useless, hence the latter may also be stored for a later purpose. It is an irregularity and mixedness, i.e., states of concrete knowledge are often not so simple as to satisfy us completely.

One piece of knowledge is specific to a single object, while another may be specific to a range of objects. The latter is often more respected than the former for the sake of a computational economy. From here the concepts of law, regularity, and rule can be derived. For example, "There is a river in front of my house" is object-specific knowledge, while "a long travel should be by car rather than on foot" is a rule of conduct for a range of objects. The difference between rule, regularity, and law is that "rule" usually applies to subjective behaviors, while "regularity" and "law" can apply to objective phenomena, although "law" is simultaneously and especially a kind of rule. Therefore, the Algorithmic distinction between the process of knowing and the process of action is a necessary step in developing the concept of "rule". As discussed in Chapter 7, the computational economy is also a necessary basis for the distinction between generality and particularity. If we ignore the economic aspects of computing, we do not need to consider whether one computing result will also be applicable to a range of other situations, and therefore we need to cherish it.

However, these usual concepts of law and rule are still specious and need to be further revised. "A long travel should be by car rather than on foot" is certainly a rule, but "there is a river in front of my house" is not a "rule" at all? Not really. The river in front of my house will not easily disappear; it will continue to exist for a long time. This will inevitably affect *all* computations related to this. For example, it affects all of my travels. If I forget this one day, I risk suffering. That is to say, in the many computations involved, as long as this factor is involved, it must be taken into account, and a fixed value ("there is a river in front of the door") must be taken for the relevant variable (e.g., "the geographical condition of my house"). This value will govern all these computations. Then, is it a "law" or a "rule"? Apparently, it should be. In this respect, it bears a strong resemblance to the rule that "a long travel should be by car rather than on foot". The latter sentence has an abstract concept as its subject, which makes people not hesitate to define it as a "rule". The abstraction of the former is implicit, but its abstraction is higher than "it rained on the day Mike got married" which, also as a piece of knowledge, is difficult to extend to other occasions or places.

With this detailed discussion we intend to show that *a lot of knowledge has the nature of "rule" (or law),* hence our theorists' longstanding curiosity about concepts such as rule and institution is actually superficial. This curiosity stems from the obscuration of extreme rationalism, which theoretically blinds us to the need for rules and institutions—even though this need is easy to recognize in common sense.

The curiosity about rules and institutions also stems from the phenomenon that in a certain decision-making process, some variables follow rules to obtain their values while other variables are open, and their values are to be computed on the spot and then improvised. As a result, the entire scenario is like a moving wheel, which rotates around the axle. The axles don't move, only the wheels move. This binary combination has particularly aroused the curiosity of social scientists. This is the case, for example, of the relationship between freedom and the rule of law. It has aroused scholars' simultaneous admiration for the two and metaphysical reflections on the ultimate relationship between them.

In my opinion, this is a bad habit. For those macroscopic and persistent social beings, people always have to introduce some eschatological scenarios and then seek explanations from them, but a theory of thinking processes has been enough to explain it.

The ubiquitous heterogeneity of both subjective and objective aspects leads to different degrees of grasp of different variables. By the time a particular computing process is unfolded, some variables have been safely valued, while others have not. This does not mean that the latter will never be able to have a fixed value like the former, nor does it mean that the fixed values that the former have already achieved will never change in the future. However, these differentiated scenes themselves have eternal significance. It is unlikely that one would have known so little about the objective world in advance that everything in a computing task would require current computations, or that one would have been so omniscient and omnipotent in advance of a computing task that there would be nothing to do with the current computations for the task. This is in terms of the limitations of the ability to develop knowledge at any given moment. Strategically, the usual computational arrangement is to reduce the number of pending variables in the current computations to a level that the current computations can afford; for this reason, one must consider coarsely valuing variables if one cannot value them exactly. Even if the valuing must be as simple as just "patting one's head", one must do so—until there are acceptably few variables left for current computations. Therefore, the coexistence of closed variables and open variables is not only a necessity, but also a subjective design.

Theoretically, one could discriminately open or close certain variables in one computing process and others in another while still satisfying the requirement of minimizing the number of variables that need to be decided on an ad hoc basis. Indeed, some crude computations that lack discipline (such as in a super-centralized dictatorship) are carried out capriciously at will. However, the economy obtained by changing the variables back and forth in this way is still not sufficient. Since some variables must be closed, it is obviously more reasonable to first close those variables that have obtained high-quality values while opening those variables that have not yet obtained high-quality values.

This is a proactive strategy with a perception of the characteristics of roundabout computing. It should be said that people have understood this early (albeit not completely), so they carefully choose the variables that should be fixedly valued and carefully plan how to value them. The knowledge thus acquired may be epistemic or action-oriented; it is written down in textbooks, passed down from generation to generation, and widely disseminated for people to follow in computations or actions (as codes of conduct). In fact, we are now back to the topics such as "sedimentation of thoughts", convergence, equilibrium, etc.

Because this widely spread knowledge is of high quality, people not only rely on it in computations but are likely to believe it and even worship it. In current computations, actors must rely on existing knowledge and may not have sufficient time to examine it, but this does not mean that the actors will be superstitious in the first place to fully believe in it. The actors usually test the reliability of the knowledge cited to a greater or lesser extent, and even propose amendments to it. Thus, the widely spread knowledge is constantly being adapted and reconstructed. The interaction between of two processes results in that, in most cases, the knowledge that has been deposited and widely spread will finally be trusted and hence will establish its prestige. Over time, words such as "knowledge" and "rules" will be monopolistically and exclusively applied to these pieces of knowledge, so that when people mention these words, they think of the "most correct" knowledge, or the most "sacred" rules of conduct. People mistakenly think that this "established" knowledge is the standard model of knowledge, and that all other knowledge will evolve into this "eternal" knowledge in the future.

## §101. Institution (continued)

However, such imagination is unhelpful and unnecessary. A person in the historical process of computation cannot know whether a certain knowledge is eternal or not. We researchers and observers are also in the midst of historical processes, and although our opinions may often differ from those of the actors involved, we cannot know it in the end. Algorithmically, as long as the lifetime of a certain knowledge is long enough and the computational economy obtained is sufficient, it is okay. Even if it's not perfect, it can gain a foothold when it can outperform other thinking outcomes that compete with it. Taking a step back, even if *some* knowledge is indeed eternal, it cannot completely solve problems of human beings, because from the perspective of discreteness, plurality, and quantitativeness of knowledge, a particular individualized knowledge is only an infinitesimal part of the whole knowledge. Thus, in order to justify this claim of extreme rationalism, it must prove that all or most of the knowledge has this characteristic.

Therefore, let's go back to the general Algorithmic view, that is, *the stocked knowledge is generally imperfect, and it was mainly because of the computational economic considerations that the knowledge was relatively fixed.* This general point of view should be applied here in particular to concepts such as "rules" and "institutions".

A "rule" is a fixed value for a particular variable in a series of different computations. This concept is particularly applied in a context of decision-making on actions. For example, individuals can set rules for their own behaviors and hold themselves accountable for compliance. Correspondingly, "institution" can be used as a rule, especially in a context of interpersonal relationships.

With the abundant Algorithmic elements mentioned above as a preparation, an institution is now easy to understand and explain. For example, it is only from the perspective of "information + Instruction" and the combinatorial explosion of information and Instruction that we can understand that thinking activities are divided into many steps, and that the next step after one step is in principle of infinite choices. Only by understanding this infinity can we understand that "knowledge is about making you abandon your choices and embark on a definite path". Although the differences among rules, institutions, and other types of knowledge are meaningful, they are not very prominent or important. When recognizing the equality or juxtaposition between the entities of people and the entities of things, we can recognize the similarity of rules, regularities, and laws. When recognizing the disconnect between decision-making computing and cognitive computing, we come to realize why it is important to use different terms such as "institution" especially for interpersonal relationships, rather than simply using the extant other words.

Only when we have theoretically portrayed the freedom of human minds in advance can we logically argue that because human has consciousness and free will, the establishment of institutions must go through the steps of consultation, promulgation, and enforcement, and it is impossible to simply "describe" the laws of mechanics as physicists do, to "establish" an institution. This characteristics of institutions (as social beings) are determined by the characteristics of the human mind, just as the characteristics of biology are determined by the natures of living organisms, and therefore biology is different from physics.

*Institutions are only a stopgap measure, just as any other knowledge is a stopgap measure.* This concise view needs to be emphasized, and it needs to be reconciled with other views at all times and everywhere—until we are finally saved from the entrenched extreme rationalism. This is not to devalue the role of institutions and stocked knowledge. On the contrary, it is only from this perspective that we can understand how difficult it is for institutions to be socially established; therefore, institutions must in principle be regarded as important social developmental achievements. The establishment of an institution must begin with the generation of an idea about it, followed by interpersonal consultations, and then spread to an extensive scope. In these processes, there must be countless obstacles such as questioning, protests, rejections, and evasions. Violations of an institution should also be effectively punished in order to set examples for other people. If too many institutions are promulgated densely, it will also cause restrictions and inconvenience to the actors, and will inevitably be resisted. If an institution that established with great difficulty is amended, abolished, or re-enacted, it will impose significant transition costs on society. All these factors lead to the fact that the number of institutions and the frequency of their modifications can only be maintained at a certain level, so that a certain ratio between freedom and order is maintained.

The types of institutions are diverse. According to economists, institutions can be divided into two types: "formal institutions" and "informal institutions". The former includes formal political, legal, corporate, and social organizational systems, while the latter includes ethics, morality, customs, informal organizations, etc.[2] Below we are to enter into the discussion of these topics respectively (continuously or intermittently).

## §102. Morality and Moral Worship

A concrete example of understanding institutions is understanding morality. To understand morality, we need to look at it in a concrete, real social context. There we find examples of morality, observe its characteristics and operations, and then seek theoretical explanations. Why do we adopt this "theory-experience-theory" sequence? This is because we (as Algorithmic People) have a limited ability to make inferences, and we have multiple approaches to inference from reality. At this time, in order to improve efficiency, it is necessary to collect materials in reality and use them to correct the theoretical direction. *Theoretical inferences that are too far from reality will inevitably have a lower applicative value.* The real world can provide a wealth of elements that we may not have noticed yet to support and enrich theoretical inferences, often furtively. In the interval between our object-oriented applications of ATT, we can also apply ATT to methodological discussions to better understand the Algorithmical unity.

If we only make general reasoning regardless of a specific

---

2. This division was made originally by Douglass C. North (1991), "Institutions", Journal of Economic Perspectives. 5 (1): 97–112.

situation, we may come to the conclusion that morality is needed everywhere, or that morality is not needed anywhere. In fact, something as concrete as morality is always associated with *a particular situation*, and it does not exist everywhere and at all times. Therefore, an analysis that does not include contextual factors is probably erroneous or arbitrary—and this contextuality is associated with heterogeneity and plurality, which we need to keep in mind.

Now let's talk about "honesty" and "trustworthiness". First of all, it can be seen that these moral codes are all *requirements* for behavior, so they fall within the scope of "social engineering". They are not the requirements for all aspects of a behavior and all its links, but only for *specific* aspects or links. Honesty deals with the issue of delivering a truthful message, while trustworthiness demands accountability for one's own commitments. Obviously, these pertain to problems that only exist in the Algorithmic world, and this world exists as opposed to the world of extreme rationalism or neoclassicism. In the neoclassical context, the speed of computation is assumed to be infinite, so there is no question of information transfer (as a type of computational activity) and therefore no question of honesty or dishonesty. And because a behavior of the individual is assumed to be "determined" in this context of extreme rationalism, like a machine that runs mechanically, it does not matter whether he/she keeps his word or not. *It is only in an Algorithmic environment where individuals reasonably have a wide range of freedom and choices that the individuals are likely to be "reasonably" trustworthy or untrustworthy.*

By understanding these environmental conditions, the meanings of moral propositions can be understood accordingly. In an environment where information transmission has a cost and distortion of information is prone to occur, if everyone is honest, the cost of information transmission will be significantly reduced. In principle, this benefits society as a whole, and hence for everyone. In the same way, if everyone is trustworthy, others can feel secure when taking their own actions according to promises, which is beneficial to social cooperation. Even if we randomly select some practical examples and examine them, it is easy to find that a function of most moral codes is to achieve social interests by restricting personal actions, so that people in society can ultimately get more rewards.

However, moral codes are rough and often they fail to account for some peculiarities of specific situations. For instance, honesty is sometimes stupid or cruel, and a lie can be well-intentioned. Nor should a false promise be kept, although those misled by the promise are entitled to an apology or compensation. There can also be conflicts between different moral codes. There is no well-developed system of norms in society to reconcile these conflicts, and at best there are only some complementary practices. However, a core meaning of moral codes is not to require actors to *carefully* study and weigh what should be done under each specific situation, but to ask people *generally* not to weigh, not to think too much, not to try to cross the red lines, and just to follow the codes themselves. If it really requires careful and adequate weighing and computing, the moral codes themselves would not have to exist, and it would be tantamount to entering the ideal, "frictionless" neoclassical world in which they can deal precisely with any particular problems with absolutely correct knowledge across time and space. A meaning of the words "norms", "rules", etc. is to *refuse to allow themselves to be sufficiently flexible* while requiring people to act in a *fixed* way *whenever* the corresponding conditions are triggered, without *regard to the specific circumstances*. In practice, even if certain specific circumstances are properly taken into account, the number of cases that are considered must be significantly fewer than those that are not, otherwise the application of a moral code may not be economical or worthwhile.

This is like the example of the structure of the house mentioned earlier. Moral codes are like these hard beams and pillars, ruthless, inflexible, and "unnegotiable". Not only are they arbitrary, and society tolerates and accepts this arbitrariness, but *it is just to use this arbitrariness to regulate other computations*. In most cases, moral codes are enforced rigidly and stubbornly, with few exceptions that attract social attentions and debates. Our statements here are especially for those who prefer mathematical methods, so I invite those who love rigorousness more, to pay more attention to the following discussion. In a system of a large number of variables and functions, how do you find the value of a particular variable? Let's put aside those standard mathematical methods. It is necessary to know that in a specific practice, actors have to, in mathematical terms, solve "giant equations" everywhere and all the time, and the equations in each problem are different, and the actors may have to communicate and/or negotiate with each other. In this way, we will know that the difficulty of real thinking lies not only in its method, but also in its computing power and whether the time and resources are available; if not available, those "perfect" mathematical methods demonstrated by economists shall be useless. In practice, if there are no variables that are fixed in advance as the "constants", chaos may occur, and any relevant variable will not be able to have a valid or reliable value for a while (the "fundamental uncertainty"). Henceforth, let's take a look at the realistic, workable methods.

First of all, the actors know that accurate computations are not possible, and that a feasible way is to fixate the values of some variables before dealing with others. However, a fixed value can only be temporary, and will probably be adjusted again according to the subsequent computations of other variables. Then, as mentioned earlier, a strategy is to *prioritize* the variables that have the easiest or most reliable values to be fixated, so as to minimize the possibility of subsequent readjustments. But how do you find such variables? This is the role of the stock of knowledge. Because of the cost of preserving knowledge, most of the knowledge stored in society is of high quality, especially those that are screened for use in various educational projects, which are usually of higher quality. The makers of this knowledge have usually already considered future changes and other special circumstances to a greater or lesser extent. While this consideration can never be exhaustive, it is generally more comprehensive than other knowledge (which involves a certain equilibrium in economics). Education includes both intellectual and moral teachings. As previously noted, there are similarities between them. Educational engineering implies that, for the sake of Algorithmic economy, the variables fixated by the actors using this educated knowledge usually do not need to be adjusted (even if it is imperfect), or, even if they need to be adjusted to a greater or lesser extent, adjustments required for this knowledge are relatively small, so the risk for the actors adopting it is relatively low. Based on these variables valued fixedly, the actors relatively easily, and riskily, value the rested variables, and then decide on a course of action in this specific situation. This is a real "Algorithm" used in the real world.

Obviously, the above process is a process of "approximation and re-approximation" and "arbitrariness, and more arbitrariness". The "solutions" obtained by this are necessarily different from those obtained by accurate mathematical methods. These are two different systems, just as one is a world without gravity and the other is the world with gravity, in which the objects must be very different in their routes of motion, states of existence, and even their own properties. Even if the "solutions" of these two systems are equal in an individual case, it must be purely an accidental, superficial coincidence. The mechanisms behind them are fundamentally different. Further, it cannot be considered that the neoclassical or extreme rationalist "solutions" are "optimal". As far as the goal of explaining reality is concerned, due to the various real physical properties of computational activities, the Algorithmic descriptions and interpretations must be closer to reality, and therefore more "precise", "rigorous", or "accurate". In the neoclassical or extreme rationalist world, there are no rigid things such as the institutions, norms, principles, models, morals, etc., and the human thinking in it is fully flexible, elastic, or malleable. This is just a hypothetical situation. It can be argued that this is only a preparation for those early thinkers to interpret reality, or a rudimentary simplification of reality. The Algorithmic approach can be a supersession of this rudimentary one.

### §103. Morality and Moral Worship (continued)

The combination of limited sensory, computing, and acting abilities leads to the fact that individuals often behave in a small area while social cooperation in a wider range of areas can lead to greater benefits. These two aspects are mutually causal, and they concurrently occur. This is just as good as the emergence of the gravitational force that makes motion a physical issue. This is also the soil from which selfishness (or the concept of "homo economicus" in economics) arises, and thus morality and altruism.

The moral codes attempt to lead people to a relationship of exchange and collaboration in order to realize a certain far-sight or foresight. This is the basic mechanism by which moralities work. For example, if you help someone today, you can expect to receive help another day. The Algorithmic limitations of individuals put an individual always in a specific, limited situation or state, *and not simultaneously all situations or states*. In such dynamic social conditions, the need for morality is in fact always very urgent. It can be said that even without the teachings of those saints, some morality will also "automatically" arise and exist, indispensable and "inveterate", in every place where there are humans' activities. The role of saints is to articulate the moral needs of society, design or interpret specific moral codes, and thus promote the conscious growth of moral norms on a larger scale, as well as the realization of more social cooperation.

However, the exchange mechanism is imprecise and unreliable. Those most reliable and most important exchange activities constitute formal economic behaviors. Thus, the importance of the exchange relationship in the moral realm has declined. The moral obligations imposed on people are not mandatory, but rely on voluntary self-awareness. Thus, a moral behavior of individual A may not be compensated by its beneficiary B, but by another individual C. Generous moral acts may be rewarded with a stingy or even zero reward. The time, place, and manner of a return, if any, may not match the expectations of its recipient, and so on.

Therefore, in order to increase the attractiveness of morality, people began to reward moral behaviors and virtuous people, and punish immoral behaviors and "immoral people". How can such rewards and punishments be applied? The way to do this is to praise the former and condemn the latter, verbally and publicly. As an Algorithmic effect, personal reputation has real value, then the reputation-driven reward and punishment mechanism will have a practical effect. However, it is important to emphasize that some other things are happening here, rather than just the mechanism of interest in running. What was originally a question of interests has now taken a turn and become the question of good and bad, and a distinction between the noble and the mean. It is detached from the scale of interests and becomes absolute. *It directly becomes a value*. This is a turn, a *bend or distortion of thinking*. I believe it is not enough only to adopt the economically transactional approach to address moral issues. If we cannot speak of this bending and turning, we have not yet touched on the essence of morality.

The reason for this bending is Algorithmical. Because a weak transaction mechanism alone is not enough to motivate actors to fulfill their moral obligations, the trade-offs in the decision-making of the actors must be detached from cost-benefit analysis to a certain extent. Society requires the actors to adhere to moral principles regardless the situation, and not to weigh the costs and benefits. Hence, it's a simplification of computing, bringing a certain amount of computational economy. Nonetheless, it is not entirely sufficient that the actors believe that moral behaviors will be praised by others. It would be better if the actors *truthfully* think that moral behaviors are really noble and worthwhile; only in this way will moral behaviors be carried out resolutely without relying on social supervision. *Such a mechanism is akin to a deception or self-deception, or some kind of brainwashing and mind control*, except that it is usually beneficial to society. This mind control even goes so far as the saints themselves seem to believe that morality is the ultimate end and value, such as Kant's equating "morality in the heart" to "the starry sky overhead", and the Chinese Confucians who believe that morality is the laws of the universe.

In favorable terms, morality belongs to the spiritual values that human beings themselves create, just as human beings can freely create other spiritual values independent of the physical world. *"Creating value" itself is an Algorithm of human beings*. People often refer to things that are initially beneficial as "good", simplifying and exaggerating them. Although this introduces imprecision, it facilitates memory and computation.

For example, since some Chinese audiences love certain Korean products (e.g., the TV dramas), there has been a "Korean fever" (or "Korean wave") in China, and people have started to chase other things from Korea. In fact, this kind of "value-based" Algorithm is frequently used in the social field.

However, the underlying logic will eventually work. When the social conditions that lead to the emergence of a particular moral code change, the code will gradually decline and change. For example, the establishment of the social security system makes a pension no longer dependent on children, then the filial piety gradually declines, the adults are not as expectant of childbearing as before, homosexuality develops, and the tolerance of homosexuality in society also increases. This will seriously impact traditional family ethics.

This is an example of how we Algorithmically see the multiple facets of morality concurrently. This neutral, relative analysis is like a relativistic analysis of institutions. Some social philosophers absolutize and sanctify institutions in the same way that they absolutize and sanctify morality. In this book, I would not like to become a "social engineer" by getting bogged down in the debate over specific moral propositions, as previous philosophers have done. I am still meant to view morality and institutions as the makeshifts in the dynamic and expansive social processes, recognizing their inevitable evolution in the longstanding and persistent "knowledge explosions". This approach does not preclude the possibility that through a specific Algorithmic analysis, some parts of human nature and morality are believed to be "everlasting" (e.g., the concept of natural law, an idea of great practical importance)—even if other parts are mutable. This analysis shall be different from the traditional determinist analysis. The fundamental factors and the social phenomena, the short-term and the long-term, are both connected and independent of each other. For example, the factor of interests (in a narrow sense) can dominate the evolution of morality in a long-term and fundamental way, but this does not mean that morality can be completely dissolved by interests. The movements of these two are carried out at different places, times, and paces. Moral values and moral behaviors can enter the processes of interest game as some wholes under certain circumstances, but their inherent contents are not something that can be filled by the interests themselves; they are independent of interests. Economic relationships are essentially higher-order relationships that are built on non-economic relationships. Relatively, such non-economic relationships and constructs are of the first order or lower orders.

## §104. Organization

Organization and institution are twin brothers. An institution refers primarily to a pre-established rule while an organization refers to a group of people acting according to specific rules, and usually with a subordinate relationship between them, i.e. some people are directed by others. To understand an organization, we first need to recall the relationship between stocks and flows, and thus between the stock of knowledge and behavior and current computations, and we also need to think Algorithmically about the relationship between passivity and initiative. In common parlance, what is "doing things"? The core of an organization is that it needs to, on the basis of stocks, do things initiatively, and unite many people to do things as if they were one person.

Equally salient is the fact that both institutions and organizations are the products of conscious behaviors, i.e., when the actors enter into the institutions and form the organizations, they *know* that they are doing so. "Institutionalization" and "organization" are not merely descriptions of observers, but conscious activities of the actors.

It is clear to individual A which family, which work organization, which association, or even which underworld organization he/she belongs to, and he/she himself/herself actively strives for or passively accepts. The relevant knowledge, language, and conventions are the knowledge, language, and conventions actually used by the actors in actual operations, rather than being secretly referred to by observers. For example, if a regiment is attrition in battle, and the number of soldiers is only equal to that of a company, then it "naturally" and "automatically" becomes a company? No, the higher authorities will still see it as a regiment, and at best they will say that it is "an understaffed regiment", unless the authorities decide to abolish it. However, the abolition of the regiment requires the occurrence of specific acts and procedures of "abolition", rather than "unconsciously" happening without the acts or procedures. This is different from the saying that when it rains, the road becomes slippery. In the latter case, the fact, as well as an observer's proposition about the fact, can be established without the "approval" or "cooperation" of "actors". However, in the former case, "this regiment is a regiment" is an agreement or a construct. This kind of agreement or construct exists in the minds of the actors involved, and constitutes their "mental equipment" to function. The observer can question the legitimacy of such an agreement, however, the "agreement" is the defining feature of this mental equipment. If there is this equipment, this "regiment" will be there; if this equipment is gone, this "regiment" will no longer exist. The observer's challenge will only take effect after persuading the actors to change the agreement.

This method is an application of the "consciousness approach", which refers to the method of treating an actor's consciousness as a real existence or action and an independent variable. This independence is both relative to conscious activities of observers or other people and relative to physical entities. *A large number of social phenomena and their explanations need to rely on direct description or narrative of conscious activities of the actors, as well as their own logic used in their actions.* An organization can display its existence through a variety of physical means such as buildings, clothing, physical signs, rituals, etc., to reinforce the impression of its members and observers, but its core essence is the specific thoughts that exist in the minds of the actors, including conventions, beliefs, understandings, knowledge, and so on.

Another salient feature of organization is that it is a way to coordinate *current computations* between multiple people in *real time*. A rule also coordinates interpersonal behaviors, but it is usually agreed upon and announced *in advance*, and when it comes to the time of current computations, it is usually too late to change the rule. As a result, the institutionalized coordination is either rigid, inappropriate, or inadequate. After each person has acted in accordance with existing rules, their behaviors may still not be harmonious, and hence need a further coordination. This principle is similar to the principle of personal self-coordination. An individual may have built up a stock of knowledge in advance, but it is still insufficient at the end of the day, so there is a need for the current computations. In addition, whether it is a rule for self-coordination or a rule for the regulation of a group, when it was produced or introduced, the person(s) concerned must have generally considered its applicability to current computations, then he/she/they might have consciously narrowed its applicative scope to leave room for current computations. Therefore, current computations are in principle indispensable in group decision-making. This is an extension of the binary working structure of "some variables to be valued by knowledge stock + the remaining variables to be valued at discretion".

Then, how can this kind of coordination be carried out? One of the ways that can be thought of is to deliberate and vote on every organizational affair on the spot of problem-solving. It is true that in some organizations or some organizational activities, people deliberate and vote on a regular or irregular basis, continuously or intermittently. However, such activities are time-consuming and labor-intensive, and are usually only used to make important decisions. According to practical observations, a permanent and more general arrangement is to create administrative posts, implement an individualized-head-responsible system, and then bring all executive or administrative personnel involved under the management and command of the head. That is, to establish a *hierarchical administrative system*.

Why not ask for a book or something, but a person to establish the coordination of the current computations? This is a question that deserves to be answered carefully. We will not repeat the incompleteness of the "dead" stock of knowledge. A human is "alive", and he/she can face the particularity, complexity, concreteness, and novelty of the problems on the spot. Because of the need to make decisions, he/she has to confront and consider all the unavoidable issues that affect the decision-making, regardless of whether there is an adequate knowledge base. He/she must make a "tradeoff" on the current problem on the basis of his/her existing knowledge and computing power, and then arrive at a relatively optimal decision that he/she can draw. That is, his/her decisions, regardless of their quality, are usually of the *factor completeness*. The individual who is the head of the organization also often consciously and "automatically" links current decisions to other knowledge and experiences in his/her head, thus seeking greater consistency. The individual in the present earthly world usually integrates and reintegrates, unifies and reunifies, his/her thoughts and knowledge, to form a stylized system. Since his/her education and experiences are mostly socialized, similar or compatible to those of most adults in many aspects, this system can be seen as a *"miniature version of the human knowledge thesaurus"*(albeit very incomplete). The systems in the brains of different living adults can be different or very different from each other in other aspects, but the systematization and refinement themselves are similar, and it can be thought that they belong to different *styles* that are competitive more or less. There is a significant distinction between such a system and any "functional knowledge" that is written in books, stocked, and used for educational purposes. Now, under the guidance of Algorithmic Theory, we can re-try to study and summarize the characteristics of this personalized knowledge system, so as to put it on paper as much as possible, but its details, timeliness, and novelty form a barrier to protect it from being completely paper-based.

Therefore, when a large number of executives in an organization choose to obey the commands of the head, they must have paid special attention to the characteristics of the thoughtful system in an individual's brain, and its ability to be "refreshed realtime on the spot". The comprehensiveness, unity, and timeliness of the decisions made by the individual leader are considered to exceed those of multi-person consultation and voting in many executive scenarios. Even if the decisions made by the leader at different times are inconsistent with each other, the internal structure of the decisions made at a specific time can be *relatively unitary*, so that the different behaviors of the organizational members will be relatively and concurrently coordinated. Of course, the deficiencies in the knowledge and perspectives of the individual are also significant, but they would rather endure such deficiencies while subscribing to the individual responsibility. Additionally, they can compensate for the weaknesses of this system by staffing advisers and assistants, or selecting and replacing the head of office. They would rather choose a different person as their head than change the system of individual responsibility.

Another characteristic associated with the hierarchical system is the coercive power of the organization. In the Algorithmic world, there is not only cooperation, negotiation, and persuasion, but also deception, intimidation, and coercion. People were born into specific social relations and organizations (e.g., state, family), which were arranged by others and can then be regarded as the results of certain coercion. The more important coercion is reflected in the fact that individuals voluntarily join an organization, but are coerced and punished by the organization. Let's look back and ask: why did the individuals voluntarily join this organization in the beginning? In this regard, the traditional transactional theory holds that it is the result of individuals seeking to join the organization in order to obtain other benefits by giving up certain rights and instead giving the organization certain powers to coerce and punish themselves. This exchange view is undoubtedly reasonable, but on top of this, we would like to add that such calculations of an individual may not always be successful, and he/she may suffer losses and ultimately regret it; this is because joining a particular organization implies signing a framed and "wholesale" contract while other matters are still to be determined on an ad hoc basis, so that the final overall outcome has been difficult to fully foresee. In collective actions, individual disobedience can sometimes lead to significant marginal losses, leading to an organizational incentive to impose severe penalties on those who disobey. In short, it can be argued that all of these are just the Algorithmical or boundedly rational effects.

## §105. Organization (continued)

An Algorithmic person is a person with limited reason or rationality under the definition of Algorithmic Theory. Because the knowledge in their brains is limited, and the way, scope, and means of their existence are limited, Algorithmic people need to communicate, negotiate, make contracts, participate in social activities, and so on. In short, I believe that various individual behaviors in the real world are formed according to such Algorithmic logic. In other words, in principle, I believe that the behaviors of Algorithmic people create phenomena in the real world, or that Algorithmic people are exactly the real people. Therefore, when we describe or state a behavior or phenomenon in the real world, that description or statement now takes on a new meaning, that is, we can be considered to be describing or stating the behavior of an Algorithmic person and the phenomenon he/she causes. This meaning has not always been explained, and sometimes it is necessary for readers to understand in the context.

Through an Algorithmic interpretation of institutions and organizations, we are entering the central part of the social sciences. New elements, real or endogenous, will increasingly be incorporated into the process of theoretical analysis and inference. In the next section, we will be devoted to the issue of communication between people. Through communication and negotiation, people build organizations. Of course, under dynamic and decentralized conditions, this kind of "negotiation" is not necessarily tangible, face-to-face, nor does it have to be done all at once. There may be certain traditions and customs, according to which new members enter an organization passively or actively, and then learn and experience the characteristics of the organization or the contents of the relevant "contract" in the specific daily operations of the organization. Some organizations are free to withdraw, others are not, but the members can express their views within the organization, protest, or file motions to amend or add to the contract. Since the members have already enjoyed the benefits of the organization in advance, and are staying inside the organizational complex network of rights and obligations, this constitutes a reason why these organizations (e.g. a state) are not free for a member to quit.

However, some small, formal organizations can be entered or exited explicitly and freely. These organizations were established either by contract or by "purchase". The method of "purchase" mainly refers to employment. An employer buys the power to make the employees subordinate to him/her, and the employees relinquish control over their physical and mental resources on the condition that they are paid, leaving them to the commands of his superiors. This approach is particularly reflective of the materiality or substantiality of thought, since the employer buys primarily the power to control the employees' minds, thus using their intellectual and physical resources. At this time, an employee is in an interesting state. This state, while familiar to us, is actually quite bizarre. That is, the employee temporarily puts aside his/her own purposes and turns to the purpose specified by the employer, or simply to carry out the employer's instructions, and mobilizes his physical and mental resources (and even some of his/her own external resources) to achieve this purpose. It's as if the employer has taken over control of the employee. Without the Algorithmic decomposition and analysis of the thinking system, we cannot understand this "takeover"—Of course, such a takeover is conditional, and the employee oneself remains "alongside" to concurrently monitor and evaluate this takeover. The employee will regain control of himself or herself at intervals when the employer is temporarily out of managerial control or after the employment terminates. By the word "alongside" here, we actually mean that the relevant monitoring and evaluating procedures are inserted into the computing processes from time to time. This insertion mechanism has been described several times before. It can be used to dispel the confusion that has traditionally surrounded this issue.

Related to this is the concept of "role play", i.e., the individual plays some kind of "social role". What an organization or society requires for actors is sometimes not specific actions, but rather some vague descriptions of specific posts or roles. The person assigned to a role or post then acts actively and creatively based on his or her own understanding of the descriptions. Successful creative performance is not only likely to be rewarded extra, but also may refresh the employer's perception and requirements for the post or role. We now recognize that these effects are all Algorithmical.

Through activities such as employment and role play, a kind of coordination is formed between the actions of many individuals, and these actions jointly serve a specific large-scale "behavior", or serve the production of certain large-scale products or services. The latter is easy to understand. A puzzling part of the former lies in the fact that it seems to produce some kind of "superman" who is above common individual persons in the society[3], and can dominate this society. This is, of course, an imagination, done with the help of a process of abstract thinking. In fact, it is a patchwork of many ordinary people, and hence is nothing more than the result of a simple expansion of the image of an ordinary person, and its consistency, coordination, and unity can also mainly be understood anthropomorphically from the perspective of ordinary people. Without the foundation of the individual,

---

3. Nietzsche, "Thus Spoke Zarathustra", translated by Walter Kaufmann, New York: The Viking Press, 1966.

concepts such as organization and "superman" will be difficult to understand.

Individuals in organizations often act solely on "the logic of the matter itself" (i.e., the "structural factors") and give little consideration to the stakes. This is not to say that the pros and cons analysis method is not applicable here, but that the pros and cons analysis itself requires the temporary abandonment of the pros and cons analysis because the stakes are not obvious, or too obvious to question (e.g., the orders of the boss and the organizational supervision mechanism do not allow any trade-offs or flexibility on certain tasks), or existent only in certain parts, and so on. The logic of an organization is often that only by giving up the local trade-offs or flexibility and focusing on completing a large product or action can a certain large-scale interest be obtained. The possibility of such a large interest, in turn, requires that members must mechanically follow orders. In an environment with widespread interpersonal conflicts and looseness, the possibilities for such large benefits should be present, perhaps even endless.

Then, the larger the organization, the more the benefits? As mentioned earlier, a major function of an organization is to execute, and its typical pattern is that multiple people carry out the wills of one person. This will lead to a relatively large scale of organizational actions, with a relatively small intellectual content in them. Even under guided rather than coercive commands, the wisdom from the guided commanding system is still bound to be limited. Even if the head only assigns a specific goal to guide the subordinates, the subordinates' thinking can be restricted significantly because goal setting is itself part of computations, and therefore part of intelligence. It is true that decision-making of the head is often assisted by some assistants and departments, and in a large organization, the leadership is made up of multiple people. Arrangements such as these improve the quality of organizational decision-making, but they are not necessarily sufficient to hedge against the challenges of expansion of organizational sizes, nor is it possible to fully solve the problems by delegating or outsourcing, since the complicated managerial tasks cannot be fully described and arranged by prior paper agreements, just as they cannot be regulated entirely by pre-established rules.

This means that as an organization grows, its marginal benefits will fall while other additional costs may rise. Some additional costs may be incurred by communication, consultation, oversight, bureaucracy, etc. We don't need to go into the details here, but an analogy may suffice: the chaotic universe has evolved over a long period of time due to mechanical factors, forming planets and galaxies of different sizes. In the same way, when ideological activities are subject to economic factors similar to gravity, human society will also form organizations of different sizes and types, the overlapping and intertwined complex relationships between organizations, and the coexistence of organizations and free individuals. There are more conflicts between free individuals than in an organization, but the richness of ideas, the decisiveness of actions, and the possibility of innovations are greatly increased among the free individuals, and they compete with organizations all the time, and their respective advantages and disadvantages go up and down.

### §106. Communication & Negotiation

Even in those cases where communicative problems are assumed to be non-existent (e.g., the hypothetical "auction market" in economic theory), few theorists assume that the mindful events of one person can be easily known by others. Apparently all scholars are inclined to think that such an assumption is ridiculous. However, from the neoclassical standpoint, there may also be an explanation for this: thoughts are not real entities, and do not belong to actions, so they do not "exist", and information and communication are about the entities that really exist, so people's minds are not the objects of information transmission.

Such a philosophical justification may seem absurd, but it may not be just my own fabrication. Moreover, according to the logic of extreme rationalism, people's minds will correctly reflect the external world, then if you have to understand the thoughts of others, you may instead reflect on your own thoughts only—Obviously, this is consistent both with the tendency of mainstream philosophy to ignore other people and with its Laplacian information determinism that disparately treat thoughts and information.

With this understanding, we can find that scholars seem to tend to particularly respect people's preferences, temperament, spirit, emotions, and other "irrational" things. Clearly, however, the respect does not mean seeing the "irrationalities" as analogues of thought (if so, they will fall in logical trouble), but as something *different from thought*. In this way, three separate things are created: information, thoughts, and the "irrationalities". This separation provides scholars the "freedom" to talk about science and humanities at the same time. Obviously, it is in this sense that economists are determined to explore individual "preferences" (and then incorporate them into their mathematical equations).

The above discussion is intended to illustrate the subtlety of the problem of "communication" in social philosophy. This subtlety is like the subtlety of thought. In essence, it is still concerned with the question of the substantial status of thoughts. Now that the question of the substantial status of thoughts has been resolved, communication, negotiation, and interpersonal exchange can acquire a philosophically substantial status.

This is one reason why language did not become a

philosophical topic until the twentieth century—language is a tool for communication. Philosophers, however, seem to have been driven by a reckless curiosity, or an inscrutable sense of novelty, to enter into this topic. When they rushed in, not only did they not wake up, but they seemed to be stunned. They put forward a lot of equivocal propositions, said a lot of dream words, and ended up in self-denial.[4]

Attempts at the philosophy of language have largely failed, and philosophy has learned little from it. However, it can be considered historically the precursor of the theory of mind. Philosophers started from the perceptible and explicit object of "language" and marched into the realm of thought, which is in line with the common order of research from the simple to the complex. Cognitive science, on the other hand, can be seen as taking over the baton of language and logic and making the transition to the theory of mind. They all asked more questions than they answered.

"Words are the voice of the heart". It is impossible to produce a satisfactory theory of language until the theory of mind has its proper form. Conversely, after the theory of mind is produced, the problem of language is to be solved easily.

Language reflects the contents of the mind. Hence, the structure of thought largely determines the structure of language. According to Algorithmic Theory, such a structure should be non-discriminatory between races, ethnicities, and eras. This can be seen as the basis for Chomsky's "transformational-generative grammar", and thus as the reason why different linguistic systems can be translated and understood by each other.

According to the principle of computers, a communication system is attached to a computing system, which is used to

---

4. Richard Rorty, "Consequences of Pragmatism: Essays, 1972-1980", Minneapolis: University of Minnesota Press, 1982, pp. 217, 75, 216.

perform a functional branch of computing, that is, to exchange data for a computer with other computers. The same goes for natural language. As mentioned earlier, it is not surprising that high-level language systems developed for this purpose have different characteristics than the Instruction system (e.g., there must be a subject in a sentence in natural language, but not in Instructional sentences). Since there is no neural connection between the bodies of different individuals, thoughts must be transformed into other physical means of expression, and this requirement determines the characteristics of language: it has the contents of thoughts, but it must put on the cloak of physics.

Thoughts must first be translated into language before they can be delivered to others, and after they are delivered to others, the recipients must read (or hear) the language and transform it into thoughts again in order to understand and hence achieve the purpose of communication, and vice versa. This process of "thought-language-thought" is similar to the process of encoding and decoding in a computer. The classical telegraphic process can be used to visually understand the mechanism of language: human language becomes telegraph codes, the telegraph codes are sent by radio waves, and the person who receives the radio waves and the telegraph code can then decode them reversely according to the same way of encoding before they can be read. The two ends of this process belong to linguistics while the middle belongs to telecommunications. Telecommunication engineering has not been easy to develop. The above process shows that both the encoder and the decoder need to use *the same encoding system* in order to communicate successfully. In other words, two people communicating must have learned the same language *beforehand* for the communication to be complete. Either they (as depicted in spy movies) get together to share the same encoding system, and then carry it with them so that they can communicate in different locations, or they can get it locally in their respective locations. This further requires that coding systems should be public knowledge (if not confidential) that is accessible to all people and can be taught or learned anytime, anywhere. Moreover, it is best to have only one encoding system, without having to transcode (translate) each other again, which is the most economical method.

From this we can understand what a vast and costly engineering program the human language systems are. Linguistics has traditionally been subsumed under the category of "humanities". Now, after the formal creation of the category of "social engineering", linguistics should be re-subsumed under "social engineering" and become a well-deserved member of it. A "single language system" is just an ideal. In fact, because of the long geographical distances and the barriers of mountains and rivers, the communality between languages is only realized to a certain extent and within a certain range. There are so many different linguistic systems on Earth that they have to translate into each other, and the relationship between them is inevitably complex.

## §107. Communication and Negotiation (continued)

Spoken language is a permutation of sounds, and written language is a permutation of words, letters, symbols, and ultimately graphics. Alphabetic writing is actually a kind of graphics, a physical means. A finite number of sounds or graphics can be combined alternately and repeatedly to express different meanings. There is a similarity between language and thought. The words are arranged chronologically, one by one, moving forward. It's as if thoughts are being generated one by one along a time series. The two ways are similar. Sometimes they can also be synchronized: ideas are being generated, and simultaneously (in fact alternately) being expressed with language. As the saying goes, "talking while thinking". This scenario can be used to visualize the way ideas and language work together.

The mathematics of permutations and combinations is useful here. Not only can simple vocal or graphic elements form words, which are arranged chronologically, but they can also be re-formed into sentences, paragraphs, articles, books, and libraries, so that an extremely rich content of ideas can be recorded and expressed. If ideas can all be expressed with language, then all the permutations and combinations of all words constitute again the "human knowledge thesaurus", namely, all thoughts or knowledge (although there must also be a lot of thoughtful garbage). This idea is related to "large language models"—Of course, this is just an assumption. Since this collection is practically infinite (e.g. such an "article" can go on without ending), it is impossible to discover all the knowledge in this way.

The seriality of thought leads to the seriality of language. The barriers to communication caused by this seriality may be more serious than people think. No matter how rich the stocks of knowledge in a person's mind are, when he/she communicates with other people, he/she can only say or write word by word, and sentence by sentence. And when you speak, others can only listen, and when others speak, you can only listen. Even when there are many people gathered, it is usually only one person who can speak, and the others can only listen. This seriality severely limits the efficiency of interpersonal communication. The walkie-talkie machine, which was popular in the past, vividly illustrates this feature: after a person has finished speaking, he/she must add an agreed term to indicate the end of the speech; then, the communication channel is transferred to the control of the other party, and the former person can only listen but cannot speak, and the latter person can only speak but cannot listen.

Then, is it possible to "listen while talking" (or "reading and writing") in everyday life? Literally, yes, but in these cases, since the human brain has only one thinking process, it has to switch frequently between the operational control of speaking and listening (or of reading and writing). Not only does this increase the total amount of computations in the brain (since this "switching" is itself another additional computational operation), but it is also bound to be error-prone. This principle can be used to explain why "one mind cannot be used for two purposes".

"Seriality" and "finite communication per unit of time" go hand in hand, and together leading to significant time-consuming and other costs associated with interpersonal communications. Therefore, the number of people a person knows and the number of friends he/she makes are all limited. It is only recently that the academic community has recognized the theoretical significance of the distinction between "strangers" and "acquaintances". Acquaintances not only have a certain understanding of each other, but also know that the other party understands themselves and recognizes their status as acquaintances, and that the other party also knows that they "know that the other party understands themselves and recognizes their status as acquaintances". The existence of this *high-order* effect is a necessary condition for their smooth communications.

However, there are still significant limitations to these interactions. Even between two close friends or loved ones, there are actually a lot of things that the other person does not understand. Moreover, people's knowledge, opinions, experiences, habits, and personalities are constantly generated, and it is more necessary to communicate with acquaintances continuously or intermittently. Expanding the scope to an organization, a region, and a society makes communication even more of an onerous task. As a result, the skills, techniques, patterns, arrangements, customs, and so on of communication are of great social significance.

If you look at the mode of a meeting, you can appreciate the challenge of communication even more. If a meeting is attended by a large number of people, it often becomes either a "one vs. many" mode or a free party. In the former way, most people can only hear the speech of one person, and the indispensable discipline in the room limits the freedom of the attendees. In the latter case, people can't share important public information and ensure they have met the people who matter to the meeting. This party shows a lively scene, but in fact, it just means communicating with a few people for oneself. In an organization of a certain size, most members are unknown to each other, and in order for them to know each other well, they must get along for a long time. This is the cause for a deep affection between classmates or colleagues who have been getting along for many years in a stable environment— since there are actually not many opportunities to make good friends in the "passerby" society, which makes the relationship between classmates or colleagues much more valuable.

This restriction is reflected in the field of mass communication, and its effect is even more prominent. What exactly is the "public opinion" in a country of hundreds of millions of people? Should we ask everyone to shout to the sky to give the answer? This method may be useful in small meetings, but it is useless in large communicative scenarios, because it is an extremely heavy computational work to quickly receive, synthesize, and refine the voices of hundreds of millions of people. In this sense, the role of media and leaders can be highlighted. A good leader is able to feel, synthesize, and refine public opinions efficiently. When it comes to state affairs, everyone generally has certain opinions and demands, but they may not express them well; however, when a leader gives a speech, many people may praise in unison: "You have spoken our minds!" This situation is one of the lucky few, and in most cases, public opinions are ambiguous.

Therefore, mass media gained a market. The media make representative or leading statements in relatively short lengths. *They not only reflect public opinions but also lead and shape public opinions.* Everyone's focus (i.e., attention) is usually different, but when they focus on an issue together, a common attention is formed. The media tries to draw public attention to themselves. However, the carrying capacity of public attention is limited, which determines that the *number* of public agendas in a society is also limited at a given point in time (e.g., there can only be one headline in a newspaper). If there are many public affairs to be discussed, they can only be carried out one by one and in sequence. In fact, the "communication" between the media and the public is mainly in the *one-way* mode. Audience feedback is usually limited to a fairly low level. This has given the media the title of "fourth power". This power can be manifested in such Algorithmic effects: news about national leaders has long dominated the media, while news about the lives and preferences of ordinary people has mostly taken a back seat.

Can the Internet be used to alleviate this elitism? To some extent, of course. For example, at least as a means of public opinion polling, can large language models such as ChatGPT be used to actively and continuously summarize and refine public opinion without waiting for the people to consciously express their opinions? Nonetheless, on the other hand, in the era of the Internet and self-media, a new problem has occurred, that is, when a large amount of good and bad information is presented to readers simultaneously, it brings a huge challenge to the reader's discernment. Some misleading and fraudulent information is almost impossible to identify in the first place, and can only be held accountable ex post facto. In some cases, however, it is useless to pursue accountability after the fact, because it is already too late.

Does the drastic increase in the means of information dissemination "solve" the problem of communication? Not necessarily. Since computing power has increased, the resultant data become richer, and hence there is much more information that needs to be transmitted and re-processed. The center of social attention is not departing from computing, but is more concentrated on the problem of computing. This is because, in the context of the combinatorial explosion, the increase in computing power brings richer returns. This is the effect of "a rising tide lifts all boats". Readers may ask: Is this effect "Algorithmical" again? Of course, all of the discussions and narratives here can be Algorithmical.

## §108. State

One of the main steps towards the unification of the social sciences is the integration of economics and politics. One of the main challenges in integrating economics and politics is to address the relationship between commodity transactions and political activities. On this topic, traditional economics has provided a basic theory, namely, the doctrine of public goods. The public goods theory holds that the scale of public goods is too large and their nature is relatively special, beyond the scope of private production and exchange, thus they have entered the social field and are jointly financed, built, and used by the whole society. This is where the state comes from. However, according to the mainstream economic theory, since human rationality is deemed perfect, how can there be the problem that the scale of public goods is too large to be borne by the private economy? Why can't private individuals form larger and more complex enterprises to produce public goods? Why can't the use and charging of public goods adopt the ordinary private model but require the inaccurate method of public finance? It can be seen from this that the core of the problem of public goods is finance, accounting, communication, and so on, and the limitations of computing power have led to the creation of public goods. In other words, *the public-goods theory needs to be based on the Algorithmic theory of bounded rationality.* ATT depicts how "small and simple" people's computing power, and thus their collective behavioral capacity, can be, which then highlights how "large and complex" a certain product (or service) can be, beyond the scope of private commitment, and hence becomes one of the public goods.

The large size and complexity of public goods relative to individuals (e.g., public roads are frequently used by many individuals, making it difficult to monitor and toll), combined with their other concrete and particular properties (e.g., natural monopoly), lead them to be built collectively and operated free of charge or at low fees. *Transactional relations exist here only partially, or to a lesser extent* (e.g. linking tax payments to political rights), *which are intertwined with those various structuralities inside and outside public goods.* With the development of commodity transaction technology, the transactional methods are likely to be expansively used in the public goods sector (e.g., commoditization of carbon emission credits). The introduction of these economic methods is undoubtedly a step forward due to the traditional neglect of the economic aspects of government activities. But, in the final analysis, as long as a public good remains a public good, its key feature is that it is generated and operated in a non-private economy including the compulsory financing and expenditure within society, the ambiguity of its user and funder identities, and the *overt* asymmetry between users and funders, etc. Public services are run in an organized manner. The organizations are often structured hierarchically, and the relationships between people are often one-way rather than strictly reciprocal.

Another way to understand this organizational character is to recognize that the "transactional relations everywhere and all the time" described by mainstream economics are a simplistic idealized model designed to facilitate the theoretical analysis, of interest to researchers themselves. This is not to say that the true face of social activity is like this, nor is it to say that it will be like this in the future. If people had not understood economics in that neoclassical way from the outset, or rejected this neoclassical method, it may be easier for them to come to this pluralistic scenario of politics and economy. Of course, after this roundabout process from neoclassicism to Algorithmic Theory, our understanding of this social plurality has deepened.

Public goods, as a concrete example, can help us understand the sources of the state's coercive power. Public goods as a whole are provided to all members of society without discrimination, and in general, no one can be exempted. If a person refuses to pay taxes on the grounds that he/she is to give up access to a specific public service, the state also has reason to impose a tax on him/her. This is because he/she may have access to public services in other circumstances, or at other ages. Some public services, such as national defense, are implicit; even if one does not intuitively feel them, one actually benefits from them. In extreme cases, even if one does not receive any public services, or has access to very few services, one will be forced to pay taxes and be "served" by the state mandatorily. This is because such individuals are difficult to identify and exclude from the specific operations of the state. Moreover, the wills of such individuals may change at any time. If the state allows such a freedom, it would be beyond the capabilities of existing technical means, or the managerial operations may be extremely costly.

That is to say, freedom actually has a price, and this price is a typical feature of the computing economy, and the coercive power of the state is a kind of "bending" that occurs under the pressure of this price, and it responds to this price with the Algorithmic crudeness and arbitrariness. Hence, *without an Algorithmic economy, there would be no state, no political affairs.* Even in places where decentralization and human rights are most important, we find the existence of the coercive power of the state. It is implausible that the "pre-state" society was imagined as some kind of perfect society without violence. In a clan or tribe, it is believed that some form of coercive force must exist. The importance and urgency of certain public matters do not allow decisions to be made on the basis of unanimous consent among members. Algorithmically, "anarchism" can only be a utopia. Further, if the people completely reject some forms of public administration, they will be subjected to "free" violence and criminal activities in the "completely free" society, just as the beasts in primeval jungles can invade human settlements.

On the other hand, in civilized societies, the coercive power of the state is a key reason for negative consequences of the state. Coercive force is characterized by the fact that, once it has been decided to be used, it does not take into account the revolt of the objects on which it is exerted, because its aim is just to suppress or destroy it. Therefore, it is not flexible enough and not precise enough when it comes to regulating social relations. Wise people have long recognized the dangers of the coercive power of the state, and therefore, they advocate the most cautious and restrained use of coercive power, replacing the use of coercive force with other gentle means as much as possible. Coercion is mainly used as a last resort, or as a deterrent.

Algorithmic Theory can help us establish a framework for comparing coercive and voluntary. From a social point of view, the advantage of voluntariness is that it makes use of the information in the specific spatio-temporal environment in which the person concerned is located, as well as the computing power of the person. Coercion excludes the use of these resources and instead suppresses the wills of the person with the will of the collective or the society. Although in a single case the suppressive elements are individual and limited, in the day-to-day and large-scale use of the coercive power, the individualities suppressed can be very rich and the overall social cost is likely to be enormous. However, those who wield power are constrained by the limitations of their own attentions and may lose insight into this. It is unrealistic for a traditional society to expect those in power to "wake up" to this. Limiting power cannot rely solely on the diffusion of the notion that "power requires one's own restraint" (although it is also helpful), but on a *concrete* establishment of institutions that employ personnel other than the persons in power. The effectiveness of supervision is enhanced when the persons with significantly different knowledge backgrounds supervise the governors.

Of course, the above perspective can also enlighten us to recognize the weaknesses of voluntariness, decentralization, and democracy at the same time (e.g., short-sightedness, chaos, slowness, etc. in some cases). In fact, *a comprehensive and correct view shall be in the comparison and combination between coercion and voluntariness, centralization and decentralization, arbitrariness and democracy.* It can be considered that *Algorithmic Theory is the inseparable foundation of political science* that, as a social science, is mostly based on the premise of bounded rationality. The existing political science is not precise and coherent enough, and has not yet been integrated with other social sciences. Introducing the neoclassicism of extreme rationalism in economics, using it as a frame of reference, and then introducing Algorithmic Theory, and then basing political science on the comparative discussions between them, is a method proposed by me to improve political science.

## §109. Law

Law is the most typical form of institution. People write laws on paper as evidence, spread them widely, comply with them when acting, and supervise each other lest one break them in current operations. Other laws are believed to exist in specific cases or in people's minds, difficult to put into words, which reflects the Algorithmical views of theory and language. I believe that the Algorithmic legal philosophy is a radical reformation of the traditional existing jurisprudence, and this reformation has already begun implicitly from the first page of this book, then the discussions here are just an extension of the previous sections.

One of the essentials of the Algorithmic legal viewpoints is to *look at law from the two-layer computing architecture of "flow + stock"*, and then realize that a necessary condition for a law to be law is that the thinking should have to be distortive and arbitrary. Since humankind is in the process of history, and history has no end, how can it be categorically affirmed that something can be determined and compulsorily implemented? How can it still be claimed to be "sacred"? Therefore, an inevitable consequence of Algorithmic philosophy of law is to let law go down the altar (while letting morality go down the altar) and become a kind of *social engineering knowledge* that exists in relation to other types of knowledge.

However, if certain knowledge is to be implemented by the coercive power of the state, why isn't it the highest quality and most reliable knowledge? The answer to this question can serve as a source of the conservativeness of the law and its good social reputation. Absolute perfect knowledge envisioned by extreme rationalism is unattainable, and among the knowledge that is Algorithmically available, there is often a distinction between high and low quality. High-quality knowledge is generally the result of thousands of years of cumulative computations by human beings, and is generally not something that can be recreated by any short-term current computations. However, reference to this knowledge can significantly improve current computations, making them significantly more relevant than the results without such knowledge. Thus, such knowledge (and of course it has other characteristics suitable to be law) is established as law. The implementation of such knowledge as laws has had good social effects (reinforced again by becoming laws), which in turn further enhances the reputation of the law. This is an example of the "smart rule of law".

The rule of law can also be less intelligent. For example, in the framework of roundabout computing, since something must be determined in advance, this is determined as law today, and that as law tomorrow, capriciously. This kind of drastic change is especially prevalent in authoritarian countries, where the ruler, driven by the inevitable Algorithmic short-sightedness, opportunistically uses the law to bind people than himself. Practical observations show that such speculation has only succeeded in a few cases while at other times the reputation of law itself has been tarnished, and the people have gradually ceased to believe in law and act in accordance with law. When opportunities to use good laws to improve current behaviors are lost, the competitiveness and governance of the state will imaginably decline. This is not to say that high-quality knowledge has completely disappeared from this society. Due to the limitations of current computing power, the amount of knowledge that people can change is always limited, and the amount of knowledge that can be destroyed is also limited. However, in the above case, the knowledge has to be idle, discarded, and not put into use. The difference between idleness of knowledge and its "operation" is the difference between idleness of a computer program and its operation. This difference should be considered "Algorithmical".

In practice, another rather unsuccessful rule of law is to expand the scope of legal jurisdiction to an extreme, so as to reduce the freedom of actors in current computations to a very low level. As the scope of legal jurisdiction expands, the quality of the law will inevitably decline, and its effects or productivity will also decline. The arbitrariness and rigidity of the law will become prominent. Those overly draconian laws are certainly not liked by the general public, and are usually only the instruments of authoritarian governance. The ruler excludes himself from legal obligations, but demands that the people obey the strict laws. China's Qin Dynasty is an example of this failure of the rule of law. It perished in the violent revolt of the people. The other form of monarchy was the conservative governance that reduced the scope and intensity of legal jurisdiction to a particularly low level, leaving a large space to morality, customs, religion, and rulers' discretion. A typical example is the Confucian system in China. However, the Confucian system is degenerative, periodically descending into disorder, chaos, and war, resulting in another type of failure.

These "multiple difficult choices" reveal the fact that "law has both advantages and disadvantages". The dilemmas can also be inferred Algorithmically. Thus, which system would be comparatively preferable? The answer to this question may be found through the "theoretical-empirical shift", because a pure theoretical answer to this question may involve too many computations, and social practice can take our place in these numerous computations, so that we can infer conclusions by directly observing the historical facts of different countries at their different historic periods. In comparison with the two Chinese examples mentioned above, the rule of law society in the West is clearly characterized by continuous progress, which indicates that the laws there shall be relatively appropriate in terms of both quality and quantity.

*Modern Western society is actually a combination of the two Algorithms of "rule of law" and "laissez-faire".* The scope, scale, and strength of the rule of law stop where its marginal gains are rapidly declining, giving way to laissez-faire. Law appears either where it has to unavoidably play a role, or where it is best suited to play its role and therefore is most welcomed. The Western law is delicate and strict. In the other realm of freedom, the protection of human rights is also sharp and rigorous. As a result, a good combination between current computing and knowledge stock is realized. Meanwhile, in view of the distortion and rigidity of law, the state has set up legislative entities to adjust law with due procedures. There are also numerous arrangements in the judicial system and certain legal provisions so that the laws actually implemented have a certain degree of flexibility and can adapt to special cases and to changes of circumstances.

## §110. Law (continued)

Understanding the true nature of human reason and how it operates is the key to understanding law and correctly answering many questions of jurisprudence and philosophy of law.

First of all, it needs to be recognized that the dynamic and networked society demands norms for human interactions almost everywhere and at all times, and these norms are first and foremost produced, used, and developed spontaneously and freely in this private and secular society. Algorithmic people frequently need to make mutual agreements, commitments, supervision, and punishments. Even in the absence of formal laws, law-like mechanisms operate in every family, community, clan, and tribe. Only a few norms need to be raised to the national level to become law. Therefore, from the quantitative point of view, statutory laws will not be numerous, let alone comprehensive. Even if the person who writes the law tries to make it "all-encompassing", he/she will not be able to do so. The laws enacted in any era are, first of all, needed by that era, and can be used to play an effective role in the regulation of social relations. This is a requirement for the economy of computation. Because laws are often of great importance, they rarely include empty, useless, or impractical clauses. Once a law has been passed, its existence will be of inertia; it will be continuously and unchangingly in effect unless it is necessary to revise it. These are all boundedly rational or Algorithmical effects.

Bounded rationality also leads to the fact that the internal logic of a law cannot be completely consistent. Compared with other types of knowledge, law focuses more on logical consistency. Even so, this is still relative. When logical inconsistencies occur, there are often multiple technical means of coordination within the legal system. For example, delimiting the applicable population, period, or region of a particular provision is one such "technique". From this perspective, the formulation of many legal provisions can be interpreted. Another way is to formulate procedures: since it is not appropriate to make one-size-fits-all provisions on specific matters, then it is necessary to stipulate some procedures for decision-making, that is, who needs to participate in the decision-making, what kind of processes and links must be undertaken, and what decisions and information need to be released or notified, and so on. This is called "due process". Obviously, this is a *"higher-order"* approach: regularity that was not established at the first-order level is found at the higher-order level.

Legal reasoning is reasoning among different legal terms and/or cases. A country's entire legal system resembles a hodgepodge, always barely maintaining some kind of unity. It is a daily job of legal persons to prove that their claims (whether legislative or judicial) can be supported by certain legal provisions, or at least do not conflict with existing law. This process is similar to any day-to-day epistemic, logical argument. What the Chinese call "Jiangli" (讲理, reasoning) is to infer one's own claims based on existing inferences that are considered to be generally accepted. This is an activity that will inevitably occur under dynamic conditions and in the presence of stocks. However, its effectiveness is still limited, and it would be naïve to expect that by reinforcing the rigor of reasoning, it will necessarily be approved by other parties concerned. Any logical system is not rigorous enough, and loopholes in a law often exist. In particular, from the perspective of the "combinatorial explosion", we can infer that it is impossible for legislators to take full account of the specific circumstances that their enacted laws will be applied, and that a new reasoning is to just tentatively apply old rules to new problems, in response to new social conditions. All these "Algorithmic" elements point to the fact that the so-called "judiciary" is in fact a difficult and empirical work, and that the work of judges is potentially creative.

This brings us to the realm of the common law. Theoretically, this judicial system, which has not been very long, can be called a miracle of human civilization! It expresses powerfully a deep suspicion of written law and a clear distrust of legal professionals. It apparently believes that law is difficult to express accurately through words, and that fairness and justice exist in the hearts of ordinary people. For professionals, the primary task is not to make laws and enact them in society, but to understand and appreciate the specific contents of "naturally existing laws" from ordinary people. Judges should first and foremost be neutral and even stay out of the matter, primarily in charge of procedural rules, rather than actively or even personally investigating cases. Substantive arguments should be conducted by the prosecution and defense in a confrontational manner with the help of lawyers, and so on. What "Algorithmic" points of view these are!

Of course, the Algorithmic point of view does not mean a mere one-sided emphasis on this "tacit knowledge". The Algorithmic view not only acknowledges the importance of the elements such as tacit knowledge, common sense, automatic computation, subconscious, and unintended consequences, but also emphasizes the importance (and finiteness) of conscious activity and thus language and text. It brings the two together and puts them in their right places, thus achieving a total unity. In this sense, statutory and written laws are, of course, also important. One cannot give up self-expression just because one is not able to perfectly monitor, describe, and express oneself. Self-expression can be combined with "passive or indirect expression" (or what others understand from the person's words and actions) to complement each other. Statutory law cannot be understood as perfect, nor can the thoughts in the minds of ordinary actors. We shall not go to the other extreme like some rigid natural jurists who have worshipped the ideas of ordinary actors as something absolute. As soon as we come to the Algorithmic orbit and realize that any human thought or system of thought is necessarily an imperfect mixture, then all theoretical confusion tends to dissolve, or take a back seat.

Law, morality, religion, science, and so on are all different forms of human knowledge, and therefore all obey the universal characteristics and evolutionary laws of human knowledge. In principle, no knowledge would be eternal, and in order to construct a theory, it is not necessary to assume which knowledge must be eternal, although there may be certain laws or knowledge that have not changed much since the dawn of time. The latter phenomenon, if it exists, is linked to the permanence of the subjective and objective conditions that determine it; as these conditions change, these laws or knowledge will also change. We shall assume that the requirement that the law remain as unchanged as possible does not come from some other mysterious reason, but from the Algorithmic economy itself. For the time being, it is particularly important to recognize that law is also a stopgap measure that needs to be weighed for its benefits and harms from time to time, and should be changed, increased, reduced, or reconstructed from time to time. The thinking of ordinary actors contains elements of conservatism and innovation simultaneously, so the jury system is also a system that takes into account both old-fashioned and innovative. And as far as the old-fashioned part goes, it's not entirely mysterious. For example, through computer simulation, we can decompose and infer step by step what "common sense" the minds of ordinary people contain. This inference is of course hardly complete, but it can be progressive. As long as the evolution of common sense is much slower than the progress of computer simulative engineering, then it can be inferred that the common sense of ordinary people will be cracked and formalized in whole or mostly one day, just as artificial organs were not good enough at the beginning, but now they can replace natural organs in some places of the body.

This brings us to the AI-style questions: can the human legal system be digitized? Can a trial be aided or replaced by machines?—especially in the age of large language models, where AI agents have become quite good at sorting out coherent results from fragmented data. If the simplicity of written law is a strong requirement in the era of manual operation, then in the digital age, can law become more complex, precise, and lengthy? Can the entire legal system be integrated with the help of artificial intelligence engineering to be more orderly and intelligent, or even more flexible? Can the systematic social analysis supported by artificial intelligence also give legislative suggestions? Can the digital legal system provide guidance or advice for individuals in realtime actions? In this direction, the imagination, speculation, and discussion that can be carried out seem endless, and realistic, to a certain degree. Those ancient and time-honored legal principles now seem to be facing severe tests and challenges, and I believe that the many Algorithmic principles will be able to play an important role here.

## §111. Politics

As said earlier, one of the major challenges facing political theory is elucidating the relationship between political and economic activities. The current mainstream neoclassical economics is absurd, and it prevents the integration of economics and political science. In neoclassical economic theory, commodities can be infinitely subdivided, and then priced and traded by individuals with perfect rationality, so that the market "solves" all the problems at once. It leaves no room for political activities. To clarify their relationship, firstly, economics needs to be transformed into the Algorithmic economics. Algorithmic bounded rationality can be compatible with any real, irregular form of a concrete commodity, and thus gives rise to public goods, as well as the organizations used to produce them—governments, or the state. The state uses coercive power to a certain extent to ensure the production and supply of public goods, as well as public services. This is where political activity comes from. Of course, this logic has put economics prior to politics, which, reflecting the idea of "economic imperialism", is not fully appropriate. Then, in an alternative word, the above logic pertains to a "convergence" of political science and economics.

When the state exists as an organization, it has to carry out activities such as ideological research and development, personnel selection, communication, negotiation, debate, legislation, justice, and administration, which are broadly called "political activities". The state is not created for producing a single public good, but for the supply of most or all of the public goods. Even if certain public goods are not needed for a while, the state will continue to exist in order to await the emergence of, or actively develop, new public goods demand. This is the independence of an organization from its products. This is one of the manifestations of the "procedural" character of roundabout production.

An "organization" is a virtual individual, not a real individual. Since it must act in unison (in order to produce large public goods), but its individual members are scattered, each with relatively small or weak abilities, and in kind of conflict with each other, the formation of an organization means that these individuals actively imagine a large "superman" in which they play the various parts of the superman and act in harmony with each other (while temporarily setting aside their own unrelated personalities). One consequence of this is that the superman has to have his own independent "mind", or some basic "personalities" or "Algorithms", in order to govern his various actions. This is a requirement of bounded rationality. The existence of such fundamental Algorithms that distinguish themselves from the work of everyday thinking, makes it seem as if each virtual individual has his own philosophy. Ideology, as a part of social engineering, provides such fundamental Algorithms. It was created for the superman by some scholars and modified by others. It is also put to a formal vote when necessary, and then passed down from generation to generation.

Another consequence is political discourse. The underlying assumption of mainstream economics is that people communicate with each other silently, i.e., that people know what they do by observing each other's behavior, and then, at best, they have a little bit of talk about "price" and so on, and then "everything becomes fine". In a business, people are only assumed to act according to some technological requirements (i.e., the "production function"), and therefore there is no significant "discourse". A salient feature of "discourse" is that it is conscious and highly subjective. Discourse conveys not only information, but also opinions, and hence arouses the interactive debates. This subjectivity is a prominent feature of political activity. Not all aspects of the production of public goods need to be debated. Some aspects are determined by technology while others are socially agreed. Usually the so-called "political activities" only focus on aspects of people's differences, such as distribution of interests, choice of values, and conception of administrative actions. This requires expression, dissemination, mobilization, negotiation, debate, and so on. These activities form a central part of political behavior. In fact, similar activities exist in firms and any other organizations, but the logic of narrow mainstream economics cannot extend to these activities, cannot connect with them, and thus economists simply pretend that they do not exist.

Another characteristic of organized activity is its unidirectional nature, rather than the reciprocity that prevails in the market. Traders in the market are often assumed to be anonymous and do not know each other's specific identity. A transaction is usually a one-time action. After the end of the transaction, the traders no longer have regular contacts with each other. As a result, they have to settle their relationship with each other on the spot and in real time, and no one owes anyone anything thereafter. Even if one owes the other, the debt between them is usually explicit, precise, and even documented. However, a prominent feature of organized political activity is the unidirectionality of behavior, that is, in a certain activity, only the beneficiary or the victim appears, and the other party is missing. This is the case, for example, with the exercise of power. Those in power demand that the other parties obey their commands, without on-the-spot considerations. Civil rights are also exercised in this way: a right holder only makes a one-way claim, not knowing who the giver is, so it is even less likely to ask the giver to appear. When an obligation is fulfilled, it is simply the fulfillment that happens, and the identity of its specific beneficiary is also ambiguous.

Of course, under the thinking of economic imperialism, these one-way behaviors can also be explained by the "objective" existence of transactional relations; however, this transactional relationship is vague, loose, imprecise, subconscious, and also of large-span and long-term. This is significantly distinctive from commodity transactions that take place under clear and strict protection of law. To ignore this distinction would be to ignore the distinction between political and economic activities and to deny the importance of the issues we have raised.

Moreover, in the logic of political science, there has always been a tendency to be wary of and oppose monetary transactions. Why is this? Since Algorithmic Theory has demonstrated the theoretical "legitimacy" of common sense, we can now combine common sense with theory to answer this question with ease. This can be explained for reasons such as the difficulty of monetarily pricing for a "political good", the negative and sensitive stimulus of mispriced monetary transactions that would distort interpersonal relationships, the large number of people involved that brings the difficulty of universal and fair charging. On the other hand, money has not been completely withdrawn from the political sphere (e.g., campaign contributions), but is strictly restricted and directed.

It is also necessary to look at political activities from the dual structure of stock and flow. Law is a stock of knowledge, while politics can be understood primarily from the perspective of current computations. Politics controls the current computations in public affairs in order to deal with those affairs that the judicial system cannot handle. "Executive (or administrative) power" can be defined in this light. Administrative staff are usually in their offices permanently. Even if they have nothing to do, they must be in a waiting state in order to launch actions at any time when needed. Urgent public affairs require recourse to certain entities and staff with sufficient resources and mandates to initiate urgent and realtime actions, rather than allowing it to be left to the last minute to launch a public forum and then discuss from scratch how to organize institutions and mobilize personnel. This is the scenario where a truly proper theory of dynamics is bound to come. In this direction, it is possible to argue for the necessity of power for society, and what exactly this necessity is, rather than being caught up in the political rhetoric of worship or attack on power.

With power comes the need for oversight of power. In this way, we enter the key political issue, the struggle between autocracy and democracy.


## §112. Politics (continued)

If an individual leader can integrate conflicting ideas and perfectly supervise himself, why does he/she need again the supervision of others? Why do other people adopt the mechanism of "authorization + supervision" to the leader instead of a complete and pure democratic system? Why and under what circumstances is the collective decision-making of many people superior to the decision-making of an individual? Conversely, why and under what circumstances does the system of individual responsibility prevail over the democratic system? Historically, why is the democratic system becoming increasingly prevalent in the world?

Questions such as these plague philosophers. They are an

integral part of the core of social philosophical questions. It can be argued that the basic answers to all these questions are hidden in the Algorithmic analysis, especially in the Algorithmical comparison of individuals, others, and groups. How is an individual person different from others? In the final analysis, it is actually the biological or "technical" factors that determine everything: the lack of neural connections between people decisively leads to the emergence of "individual" as an independent computational subject, his/her various characteristics, and interpersonal thoughtful differences. This lack of neural connection makes people unable to feel each other's pain and happiness, so they mainly and intensively use their own pain and happiness as a guide for actions (selfishness). This inevitably leads to an inadequate and untimely understanding of the sufferings and joys of others, and the decisions one makes on behalf of the organization may be biased. Such biases are unlikely to be corrected by strengthening the leader's own knowledge system. Although autocracies attach great importance to the (moral, political, intellectual) education of a monarch, it is clear that the role of education is very limited (and marginally diminishing) in terms of practical effects. On the contrary, one of the advantages of assigning supervisory power to others is that, first of all, it creates a strong check on the leader in terms of administrative *purposes*.

Secondly, there is the heterogeneity of knowledge and the asynchrony of behaviors. The physiological independence of an individual's body leads to the fact that one's computations and actions are relatively independent and often asynchronous, rather than synchronous, with others'. When the leader is happy, others may not be happy; when he is angry, others may not be angry, and when he is excited, others may not be excited. This asynchrony creates a containment that can prevent impulsive and ill-conceived decision-making. This kind of consideration is central to the design of modern polities, as political scientists generally recognize that any decision is in fact a "current decision" that cannot fully take into account the "whole", "globality", or "generality" beyond the situational limitations. It can be said that law, as a "representative" of predecessors, can inject many historical elements into the current decision-making to make it global to a certain extent, while the supervision of others further contributes to it especially by injecting those contemporary elements that scatter widely in space, far beyond the place where the head is located.

Inferred from the principles of neoclassical and extreme rationalism, it shall be undoubtedly ideal that any public decision be made with the full participation of all actors involved. This ideal is not easy to achieve, especially among large groups of people. But it can serve as a frame of reference to help us evaluate the variety of public decision-making systems that actually exist. The Greek city-state's pure direct democracy was closer to this ideal because of its small size that made it easy for citizens to gather and deliberate. Even so, however, the dilemma in the city-state was still prominent. As mentioned earlier, in the serial mode, the length of statements in a meeting is actually a matter of combinatorial explosion. If a specific decision is made that would affect the whole state, exactly the "full discussion" must be impossible. Any discussion processes shall be concise and efficient, and optionally, can be followed by a vote. The voting procedure can subsume those "unspeakable rationales" or "unspoken truths" into the decision-making, so that a meeting is not easy to be manipulated by those eloquent people. Voters do not have to clearly state their reasons for voting.

From an Algorithmic perspective, the voting system must be a public decision-making system that needs to be used often or regularly. The rationale here is very obvious and convincing.

Extreme rationalists, based on their belief that "everything can be clarified", marginalize the vote system; however, they have neglected the fact that the criteria and methods of judging knowledge are kind of subjective themselves, and also neglected the core significance of the time process of thinking activities. Among numerous individuals holding different versions of knowledge, the vote can be used both to forcibly end computations and debates to arrive at a decision, and to ensure peace throughout the public decision-making process. However, the voting system is also an averaging system, which gives the (weighted or unweighted) average opinion of everyone. It avoids the lowest quality opinions, but may also miss the highest quality opinions. Nevertheless, high-quality opinions can be highly persuasive, and, given enough time and a relatively sufficient debate, it would be increasingly possible to become the mainstream opinion.

Representative systems make communication relatively easy by reducing the number of participants in a meeting, thus making democracy more applicable to a wider range of governance. The establishment of special committees within the parliament has further improved the efficiency of interpersonal communication. However, although the systems designed around interpersonal differences are important, their effectiveness is limited. Interpersonal communication and interaction are costly and in many aspects repetitive and homogeneous. It can be daunting that new representatives have to make the mistakes their predecessors have already made and reset the knowledge their predecessors already have. It is also difficult for a chaotic deliberative body to make a series of consistent decisions over a long period of time and govern the country in an orderly and systematic manner. The pace of interaction between multiple persons is also often slow. Factors such as these point to some of the benefits of expert governance, or a centralized system.

The centralized system greatly saves time for communication and negotiation, and the centralized decision-making process can be simple and efficient. Meanwhile, the head of the group can gather experts in various fields to systematically develop a decision support system to help the leadership improve the quality of decision-making and expand the scope of decision-making. From this point of view, decision-making under a centralized system, although not as broadly representative as a democracy, is expected to be better than a purely individual decision-making. In particular, decision-making under individual responsibility is not only rapid, but also expected to be more continuous. The disadvantage is that, in addition to the above points, the limited computing power of the individual leader will ultimately limit the number of tasks that the leadership can handle. If the individual head of state does not understand his/her own limitations, it may lead to a serious backlog of state affairs (a negative phenomenon that is quite prominent in Chinese historical records), thereby delaying the operations of the system. Another conspicuous disadvantage is that over time, the knowledge system of the head of state becomes obsolete, but perhaps he/she is unwilling to update it; if there is no mechanism for replacing the head, affairs of the state are bound to fall into great danger.

Therefore, a relatively good system in the present world is a certain fusion of democratic factors and centralized factors. The constitutional system of separation of powers in the United States can be regarded as a typical example of this. The United States has set up a strong presidency in order to take advantage of the benefits of centralization. At the same time, specific arrangements have been set up for the presidency, such as an electoral system, a term of office, and the mechanism of impeachment, so as to limit and correct the presidency. At the same time, the Congress, which shares power with the president, is in a tense state of almost year-round meetings.

Interestingly, in terms of political style, today's Democrats are more clearly using what we call "mainstream Algorithms" while Republicans are more likely to adopt "alternative Algorithms". In short, everything in politics is almost Algorithmical. Political phenomena can be a stark illustration of the core meanings of the word "Algorithm": a forced and stopgap trade-off in an environment full of "subjectivity"; there is no best, only better.

Algorithmic knowledge accumulation mechanisms have a natural tendency to improve interpersonal communication. This is because improvement of knowledge also includes improvement of the knowledge about knowing and dealing with others. Thus, in general, future generations are always able to understand each other better than their predecessors. In addition, the development of information technology has historically facilitated person-to-person exchanges, which is also conducive to the development of democracy. It can be said that the political system of contemporary America is better than ever in concurrently achieving the following governance goals: broad representation, strong and sophisticated management, flexible and rapid response, and so on.

The discussion here is only exemplary. The comparative analysis of democracy versus autocracy will continue after the discussion of economic issues.

# CHAPTER 10
# THE SOCIAL PHILOSOPHY
# (III)

## §113. Money as Thoughtful Entities

Algorithmic pluralism can be seen as a "scientific", "rational" pluralism that coexists with the Algorithmic unified logic (monism), and the Algorithmic pluralities can be divided into the preset or primitive one and the endogenous one. The former refers to the plurality that exists before human computation, which is the reason for computations to be initiated, i.e., the computational activities set out to target, eliminate, or mitigate the plurality, while the latter refers to the plurality that arises from the computational processes as a result of the subjective turn, or mental distortions. These pluralities, combined with the coherences revealed before the emergence of Algorithmic Theory and the coherences established by the other Algorithmic principles, serve the goal of the "grand synthesis".

Pluralism is important. Obviously, only after our Algorithmical elucidation can pluralism truly enter the core analytical process of philosophy as a novel theoretical element. It allows us, after elucidating the general and rough principles, to enter directly into the discussion of some specific topics without having to undergo those tedious transitive deductions. What is being done here is just the transition based on the principle of *"the real world as both the theoretical prototype and the prototypical theory"*, or the logical sequence of "Algorithmic principles—the real world—specific issues": Algorithmic principles endogenize *in principle* the "real world" as the unified matrix or "platform"; we find problems in the real world while we are no longer surprised by the existence of any problem (as a plurality); nonetheless, specific research work (in itself as another plurality) is still necessary, and these research efforts proceed with or without the application of Algorithmic principles.

That's how economic issues are raised. There are activities and phenomena called "economy" in the real world, and now we will face them, describe them, and explain them. These efforts will be carried out within the framework of a unified social science, alternated and intertwined with other social discussions from time to time. However, these efforts cannot be exhaustive, and any research work is only fragmentary. Between these fragmentary workings, we have to fill in intermittently with plurality. At this point, "plurality" may seem like a fig leaf, a cover-up, but there is no way around it, we have to let it exist. Its presence reminds us that we are always in an imperfect thinking process, and that our concepts and ideas are mostly expedient. Then, what is the "truth" behind these expedient measures? For this, we need to know that, in principle, it is always possible to continuously delve into the matter, which may to a certain extent negate the "illusion of plurality"; however, in principle, there is no end to the delving, and we still have to stop somewhere before we "label" certain parts of it as "plurality" again.

These are the basic attitudes and methods we adopt when introducing economic issues.

These attitudes and methods allow us to start with *a direct description of economic activities*, followed by partial deductions and explanations, thus forming a style of writing that blends narratives with analyses—Of course, this style is not uncommon, but we are only now theoretically "justifying" it.

Among the many types of social activities, economic activities mainly refer to those that use money, or are *closely* related to the use of money. The use of money is a distinctive *sign* that distinguishes economic activity from other activities. The reason for saying it is a "sign" is that economic activity, by its very nature, does not require using money as an essential or necessary characteristic. For example, in less commoditized economies, money is rarely used, but these activities (such as production activities) are still economic activities. It is only in the modern market economy that the use of money is closely (still not entirely) linked to economic activity. This sign (or definition) is not perfect, but it is more convenient and worth adopting than other criteria. For example, to say that economic activity is "related to the production and exchange of material goods" would seem to imply that other activities do not involve it. To say that economics is the study of "saving" seems to imply that other activities do not need to save. To say that economics is the study of "rational behavior" seems to imply that other activities are not as rational as economic ones, and so on.

The use of money as a sign or definition of economic activity reflects how real actors in the real world understand and define economic activity (e.g., people often say that economic activity is about "money"). At this point, our researchers can reach an agreement with real actors. Money is not only an "inherent" existence in the real world, but also can exist as an Algorithmic inference. ATT can be used to comprehensively explain all aspects of the birth of money, so as to theoretically endogenize money. This is an important application of Algorithm Theory.

The endogeny of money in the Algorithmic theory is, first

of all, to connect with the existing monetary theory, and to provide a basis for it. In the exchange of goods, in order to reduce the *number* of price conversions and thus reduce the *cost of calculations*, it is necessary to introduce a general equivalent. That's money. Secondly, money is not only a price unit, but the "thing" actors also want to *hold in their hands and be under their control*. That's to say, it must firstly be a kind of *physical entity*. This is because there has been a spatial distance between money and its owner, and this spatial distance creates a sense of insecurity, for it can possibly lead to the loss of possession of the money by the money owner. Holding money in one's hand, or storing it in close proximity, increases his/her control over it. Furthermore, it is only in the *continuum of time* that actors are willing to accept the money, because the money accepted by the actors can be used for *future* purchases. In other words, money can be *stored*. This, in turn, requires that money itself be non-perishable, in addition to the characteristics that it is small in size, easy to divide and carry. After an appropriate commodity has been selected and widely used as money, money can then be used as a means of payment, legally recognized to pay off debts.

These processes show that the creation of money must be premised on the existence of time and space, which is a concrete Algorithmic arrangement that has grown up in the real world. In this way, we unravel the mystery that money is not compatible with mainstream neoclassical economics, where the spatio-temporal factor is abstracted from the beginning.

However, this is not enough. In particular, it should be emphasized that behind many specific Algorithmic elements, money typically reflects the physical, material, or substantial characteristics of ideas. *The rejection of money in mainstream economics is consistent with the philosophical rejection of thoughtful entities (or substances) since ancient times.* Now that the *question of the substantial status of ideas has been clarified, the question of the nature of money can be answered accordingly.*

## §114. Money as Thoughtful Entities (continued)

Money is one kind of mental entity that people deliberately stipulate with each other. In the neoclassical conditions that deny the status of a real entity of thought, money cannot be defined, and people do not know what it is, where it comes from, and why it moves in society. Now it's different. All thoughts are entities or "real entities" or "substances", and none of them arise noncausal, nor do they move effortlessly, or gratuitously. Their creations and movements have real impacts on the real world. At these points, money, as a kind of thoughtful entity, is indifferent.

Money was first a kind of concrete commodity, and now it has become credit money. As long as the central bank of any country wants to create money, it writes a number directly on its accounts, and money is thus created. This historic change clearly manifests the essence of money, which is that it actually has nothing to do with the physical means used to represent it (gold, silver, banknotes, bills, electronic symbols, etc.), but is itself an agreement between people, an ideological kind of entity deliberately created by people. However, since this ideological entity reflects an agreement *between people*, there is the question of credibility, and all physical means have actually been used to solve this credibility problem (while meeting the other requirements mentioned above).

However, the problem of trustworthiness is not unique to money, and there are many types of information related to this problem. The message "there is a river in front of my house" can be questionable. There is also the problem of credibility in the orders given by a commander to his subordinates. Some of these problems do not have ready-made solutions (e.g., online rumors), or they can only be solved by the actors themselves (e.g., how to verify the authenticity of military orders). The peculiarity of money is that it is used frequently, dispersively, and independently by a large number of individuals. In the early days when instant verification was lacking, a piece of money had to be verified by both actors at the spot of a transaction in the absence of its maker (and thus the authoritative verifier), and hence it is worth using public, institutional means. These technical means could sometimes obscure the true nature of money, misleading observers into believing it is not ideological at its core.

The nature of money is somewhat similar to that of items such as tickets. They are all thoughts, but they must all be dressed in a "physical garment" so that they can be seen and/or "touched" by others. Even today's electronic forms of money, such as those that operate on a mobile phone or computer, unnecessarily cryptocurrencies such as Bitcoin, are of their *physical forms.* For example, if you're sending money to someone else, you'll have to do something about your bank account on your phone or computer. Even if the consequence of this operation is only some change in the magnetic records in the bank's computers, you must act to achieve it. This change in the magnetic records is not just a physical change, but represents the change of a certain social attitude, and potentially reflects the collective recognition of the event by countless anonymous individuals in society. The physical elements and the ideological elements go hand in hand here, mixed and intertwined. This is a process of collaboration and interaction between the two kinds of entities.

Just because it is an entity of thought, just as the quantities of other thoughtful entities have real influences, the quantity of money has a real influence. One might think that the quantity problem of money is special, different from the quantity problem of other ideas. Not at all! When theorists are puzzled by the question of the quantity of money, they have been actually ignoring the fact that the quantity of any thought or information has a real effect. Even if we were to reproduce only words here, it would have a real effect, because it would have to be done with the help of some kind of *actual operations*. The replication activities must consume time and resources, and the replicated words must take up space, and will work and cause real effects. The question of the quantity of money is more complicated than the reproduction of such information, because it is different from the manufacture of counterfeit banknotes, but it means that the central bank issues a greater number of genuine certificates. Each document is identified as a separate document of the same nature but with a different identity, which exists in its own specific independent space, is possessed by the same or different persons, and moves along the same or different lines and rhythms in the economy—At this point, we can even add that even counterfeit banknotes are quantitative, and that the real effects of counterfeit banknotes are similar in some respects to genuine banknotes, although in other respects they are different.

What exactly is the quantity of money? This question seems to have become unclear now after the abolition of the gold standard. We only know that it refers to the quantity of a certain "economic value". This economic value is abstract, but in fact, it is controlled sequentially, or serially, by reference to the historical value of the currency. It can be said that this abstraction is very prominent and distinctively reflects the existence of abstract concepts as entities.

Although the quantity of money is theoretically determined by both the size of the economy and the velocity of money, in practice, it is difficult to determine that a particular money supply is sufficient and appropriate. If the theoretical "optimal amount of money" is a specific and fluctuating value, then the boundedly rational perspective leads us to conclude that, given the limited computing and operational capacity of central banks, the actual money supply is usually either excessive or insufficient. Moreover, the widespread heterogeneity in economies necessarily makes it impossible for the money supply to be fully structured. These can all be understood as *manifestations* of a bent mind—since thinking bends everywhere. The fact that the economy has to use money is itself a consequence of the bent mindset.

However, after the creation of money, the bending intensified further. Another manifestation is that because a monetary regulation is often *more convenient than other means of regulation*, and is becoming increasingly convenient thanks to the innovation of monetary forms, both government and the private sector are becoming more enthusiastic about using money. The scope of entities that manifest their value by money is expanding, and the scope and size of the market, and thus the fields of use of money, are expanding. This is tearing the whole society in the direction of embracing more money. Then, the pursuit and worship of money gradually appeared. Money as a form of value is simple, straightforward, and powerful, which stimulates people's enthusiasm for the pursuit of monetary wealth, and prompts people to become more diligent than in the era of underdeveloped money. On the other hand, it may also mislead people into ignoring important values that cannot be monetized.

## §115. Limitations and Singularity of the Price System (1)

Another consequence of the use of money is that the entire economy has established a comprehensive quantitative accounting system expressed in monetary units, thus making quantitative analysis a prominent feature of economics. Even in everyday life, when people think of "economy", they think of mathematical calculations such as which is bigger or smaller, addition or subtraction, and so on.

However, through the idealization of neoclassical economics, the price system has been absolutized and perfectionized. The actors were assumed to have unlimited access to communications and to be able to precisely and perfectly process economic data, resulting in a general equilibrium price system. What the average reader doesn't know is that in a purely neoclassical model, commodity trading can only happen once, and then there is no reason to happen again, because all the factors that affect costs and benefits (both distant and future) have assumptively been taken into account and all the economic values have been assumptively "extracted" from them, accurately and entirely. This absurd state of affairs actually reflects the enduring tradition of thought, the notion of extreme rationalism. It's like Plato's Idea of the "table", once it's established, there's no reason to change it.

This is contrary to common sense and inconsistent with the original intention of economists. The basic idea of economists was that ordinary people can build an effective economic system even if they only act in their own self-interest and consider only a few easily accessible variables, including price. This Smithian idea is actually very Algorithmical. The concepts of "selfishness" and "homo economicus" should first and foremost refer to the fact that each person should primarily think about one's own circumstances, the things that are *near* or *close* to oneself. Why? Obviously, because there is a cost to the transmission of information, you are often the only one who knows you and your circumstance best. Therefore, "taking care of oneself" has basic rationality from the perspectives of both an individual and the society. Combined with the Algorithmical principles and perspectives, we can further realize that economists assume that people are selfish, mainly for the convenience of subsequent mathematical analysis, which should not be misunderstood as that if a person cares about others, it is not conducive to the optimal allocation of resources within the social scope. One takes the happiness of others as one's own, which is the freedom one has in determining one's own purposes. Second, compliance with social norms such as ethics and morality shall be an inevitable result of Algorithmic people making selfish computations in a dynamic and boundedly-rational Algorithmical world. Now, these no longer need to be presented as stand-alone hypotheses.

In short, Algorithmic methods can help economics theoretically return to its original purpose, which is to re-evaluate the effectiveness of market systems in the Algorithmic context, or the real behavioral environments.

The finitude of computing power is a key. Whatever factors could have been included in an actor's own current computations for pricing, and whatever Algorithms could have been adopted if one has wanted to, however, the decisions must be made within a limited time and a limited number of computations. The stock of knowledge, including the memory of historic trading prices, sustains and limits the actor. A transaction means that the computation is forcibly closed once, that is, one's knowledge and attitude towards the world is "concluded" once. The resulting price is not only the manifestation of limited information, but also the manifestation of the finite Algorithms that contain subjectivity. Therefore, the price will reasonably change in the future.

Prices are not only temporary, but also partial and individual. The actors are not often collectively traded as is assumed by mainstream economics. Such an assumption is only intended to obscure and eliminate the spatial, and thus communicative, factors. Since everyone is in a specific spatial position, and this position has a certain exclusivity for others, the "unified market" is also an illusory imagination. It is true that a "market" is where traders are gathered, but any market is always in a specific position and its size is always limited. Even an electronic market on the Internet today is limited in size. Although the Internet has greatly broken through the constraints of geography on individual behaviors, it is still not enough to completely eliminate the geographical factors and change the physical natures of ideological activities. For example, while it is easy to enter and access any web address as long as we know it, we are often unaware of its existence due to our attention limitations, so much so that the website itself has to attract us through advertising. The means of communication contribute to the dissemination and convergence of price information, which, together with the simplicity, loudness, and hence accessibility of the price information itself, makes it easier than other information to disseminate and respond (thus inducing arbitrage activities), so that the prices generated in different places will move much closer to each other. However, this convergent effect is always relative and to a certain degree, and prices remain dispersed, individual, temporary, and continuously generative. These basic characteristics will not change.

This is what economic theory shall go to re-describe and represent. Nor should such a price be regarded as a perfect measure of the value of a commodity or any property or action. It must *coexist* with other complex and diverse information and serve collectively as a basis for actors' computations of evaluation and judgment. It just stands out a little more than other information in some cases. Such economics shall also be consistent with its role as a part of the pluralistic social science.

Theorists could be satisfied with this new price theory. This is because, first, only such an explanation is factually conforming, and the factually conforming explanation shall be a really successful explanation. Second, economists no longer need to scrape together a general equilibrium system. The general equilibrium theory shall be abandoned; its rational elements shall be replaced by the new doctrines.

## §116. The True Meanings of "General Equilibrium"

The limited capacity to act, both physically and mentally, leads to the fact that people can only divide labor and then produce goods, and thereafter exchange and use goods. The limitation of an individual's immediate production capacity means that even if one has the productive capability of a particular commodity, in a special space-time scenario one may not be able to produce it by oneself (and thus be at a temporary disadvantage), so one can only buy that commodity. While the roundabout method of production requires that actors must possess a certain amount and variety of capital to produce, the limited immediate productive capacity also leads to the tendency of the actors to possess limited capital and to transfer the excess to others (in place of the holding of financial assets). These are very Algorithmic truths. The general equilibrium theory roughly correctly proposes that it is necessary to pay attention to the equilibrium of aggregate supply and demand in the whole society, which is the key to economic stability. The word "roughly" is used here for the same reason as mentioned above, namely, because "aggregate" itself is a less accurate term, and it only makes sense in the context of "mental distortions" —that is, it is in the simplification and approximation approach. The reality is that the forces of supply and demand are always encountered separately in each specific trading situation, and they are equilibrated at some places, but may not at other places. There is no *actual process* of "matching the supply and demand at the aggregate level first, and then allocating it to all specific locations". This process is a superfluous hypothesis.

In the real scenario, the so-called "supply-demand balance"

simply means "the price remains unchanged", that is, the current price is the same as the price made earlier in time. This is to say, those related concepts and discourses must be understood in a dynamic context, otherwise they are meaningless. Keeping the price unchanged means that the price is stable over time. Logically, the reason for stability may be that neither supply nor demand forces have changed, or that supply and demand forces are increasing or decreasing synchronously. However, considering that the probability of the latter scenario is very low, and it is very difficult to achieve the "synchrony" practically, it can be seen that changes in supply and demand forces usually lead to changes in prices, and prices either rise or fall most of the time. Here we interpret the price change entirely as a change in the forces of supply and demand, which is also a simplification and distortion. In fact, actors can set prices in any way they are willing to use, not necessarily simply taking into account the changes in the quantities of supply and demand (e.g., pharmaceutical manufacturers insist on supplying at a fixed price during an epidemic for ethical reasons, refusing to increase prices, while consumers queue up to order). Any real Algorithm can be included in the Algorithmic framework.

When supply and demand are out of balance, it is not meaning that the sky is going to fall—just take it easy and go to adjust the price. The flexible price system is designed for such adjustments. Price changes are one of the most legitimate ways to use the market system. By adjusting prices, supply and demand are rebalanced. However, this equilibrium, like any other equilibrium (or balance), is limited in scope. In a market, supply and demand are generated almost continuously due to the large number of people, and prices are also generated and fluctuated almost continuously. When it comes to each individual, one usually neither trades every minute or every second nor stops trading until one day he/she makes an "overarching, lump-sum" trade. An individual's transactions are usually intermittent in order to intersperse with their own other actions (this intermittence can certainly be argued Algorithmically). Price movements are intertwined with the stillness or movements of other aspects of economic activity to constitute the general state of an economy at a given time.

There are many, almost innumerable, ways to adjust economic disequilibria or imbalances. For example, companies can speed up or slow down production to adjust their inventory levels. It is particularly important to understand disequilibria in the context of failures and catastrophes, which is what the word "disequilibrium" means. This means that particular economic consequences do not satisfy the expectations of the actors. Of course, some unintended consequences are good and helpful in many cases, but this has usually not been focused on in economics. Bad consequences happen when, for example, a company produces so much that it has to sell at a loss, or an economic crisis occurs, a company closes down, certain employees lose their jobs, and so on.

The original meaning of general equilibrium should be that the overall economy is stable in the *time channel*. Since partial or individual failures in an economy are inevitable, this "stability" really means that the failures have been offset with successes, leading to a *rough stability* at the macro level, so much so that the government does not need to intervene. That is all. However, according to the Algorithmic principles and actual situations, the economy usually grows continuously and "automatically". With this in mind, "general equilibrium" can be understood further as a sustained and stable growth of an economy, and it further implies that the various parts of the economy either increase at an equal velocity, or although their increases are not isokinetic but cancel each other out, and thus the aggregate increase is still at the same velocity. According to the principle of heterogeneity, we know that such a situation of "exactly canceling each other out" is very difficult, and hence, we can deduce that a stable isokinetic growth will be difficult to achieve in the presence of important structural changes.

The general equilibrium, only when it is reinterpreted in light of the above pluralistic, structural, and dynamic approach, is clearly of practical significance. By contrast, the neoclassical, static general equilibrium shall be a mere pavilion in the sky, or rather, a precursor to meaningful research. Also by contrast, we can understand why economies are often not balanced. However, the study in the neoclassical approach has been seriously overdone. It should not become the mainstay, the core of economic research. The main, central research should fall from heaven to earth. The Algorithmic theoretical models on the earth can grow and move closer and closer to the real world. Among them, "equilibrium" is clearly an important issue for actors. Meanwhile, this issue shall be largely considered in the time frame. For example, whether the actors want to expand the scale of an enterprise or accelerate an innovative process, the key consideration shall be on the ability of the market to withstand or absorb it over time. An equilibrium for it is not unimportant, but only becomes important dynamically. Otherwise, the company concerned can grow big at will, or ramp up R&D at will, and then wait longtime for the structure of the other economic parts to grow to match it. The time frame also requires that these radical decisions shall be made taking into account the natures of the supporting structure of other enterprises and customers, otherwise the qualities of the additional products produced may be deviated. In short, structural issues and process issues are now juxtaposed with quantitative issues, rather than being "represented" and then eliminated by quantitative issues or price issues.

These are extensions of the micro price theory, on which the subsequent discussion continues.

## §117. Limitations and Singularity of the Price System (2)

Algorithmically, the function of the price system is not only limited, but also specific; it is a unique and stylized signaling system. Although its role in the economy is not perfect, it is relatively effective, quite interesting, and even singular. As long as we are free from those static, absolute philosophical concepts, these understandings will enter our theoretical horizon. The recognition of the finitude of price information is the basis for understanding its effectiveness and singularity, and these two aspects are mutually reinforcing.

There used to be theories (e.g. Marxist economics) alleging that the value of commodities has already been "determined" at the stage of production. Thereafter, in circulation, the actual price is only a "reflection" of this value; at best, it fluctuates around the value. The value of a commodity is like that the commodity has been added with another screw in the production stage, and afterwards, no matter wherever the commodity travels to, this screw will always be there, maintaining its position and characteristics. In fact, such a price theory is quite in the style of Plato's determinism. Although it emphasizes the importance of production costs, after all, it completely physicalizes the price problem, divorces it from human beings, and even makes human beings become the servants or tools for physical objects to "realize themselves". Neoclassical price theory attempts to correct this error by pointing out that the utility of goods is subjectively evaluated by consumers, and that consumers' situations and opinions are not easily predicted in advance at the production stage, and they are subject to changes. However, the neoclassical price theory, which looks at consumer preferences absolutely, and looks at the computations of the actors concerned monistically, is not fundamentally different from the previous approaches that mechanically and deterministically dealt with all economic problems. It's still a pot of rice parboiled.

We need theories that include both subjectivity and objectivity at all levels and links. From an Algorithmic point of view, are production costs completely objective? No! What resources are consumed by this act? How are these resources valued? And furthermore, how much does a commodity cost? Views on all these issues are kind of subjective. This subjectivity is usually prominently reflected in how inventories are valued, how depreciation is calculated, how revenues are recognized, and so on. Readers who are familiar with accounting shall be quite familiar with the subjectivity in accounting. The presence of externalities, such as environmental effects, suggests that impacts of production activities are actually beyond the scope of accounting. Although the purpose of cost-benefit accounting is to try to identify all the effects of production and other business activities, then value them, and then subtract costs from revenues, it can be said that none of these steps can be done perfectly or undoubtedly.

Some people may ask rhetorically: Although the calculations cannot be perfect, the amount of money spent can be a standard for the calculations, concise and definite, then why bother finding fault with it? That's right! In this dilemma of economic accounting, the emergence of money is like a savior, and it solves this problem simply, directly, and roughly. Accounting is actually based on monetary revenues and expenditures. Calculations based on monetary flows and balances, even if substantively imprecise, are objective and easy to agree on. Even if you need to fine-tune it, it's also much easy at this point. I am by no means nitpicking, but I am using this to explain that the accounting method is exactly an example of what we *Algorithmically* call the "*patterning*", "modularization", or "solidification". With the help of this pattern established by the use of money, conclusions about costs of goods are drawn directly *without taking into account other miscellaneous factors*. Rather than determining the costs with consideration of all big or small factors, it first uses this simple, direct, and *partial* method to figure out the costs, and *then*, based on the easy results, gropes for solutions to other problems accordingly. Even if people know this is imperfect, they would have to tolerate it.

At the stage of selling goods, a salesperson tries to sell the goods *while knowing the costs of producing them*. Moreover, the basic goal of the seller is to recover the costs recorded under *the goods*—and preferably make a profit, of course, through the sale of *the goods*. In the same way, a buyer calculates to buy. Thus, they start the negotiation and pricing process.

Supposedly, the seller can hide his "hole card" about the cost of a good, just look at the maximum price that the buyer can afford, and then try to sell at this maximum price (as long as it is greater than the cost). However, the buyer can also do the same, treating the other party as the buyer is treated. This leads to a complex game process. Other players can also join in between, further complicating the situation. These assumptions can be generally more or less true. The resulting analysis forms an important part of the economics literature.

This kind of game can sometimes lead to a long-time process and other high costs. This highlights the value of honesty. "Big players" who own large quantities of goods and face many counterparts may turn to use some simple pricing strategies, such as the cost-plus method. As long as the selling price is higher than the cost by a certain amount or percentage, the seller will decide to sell the commodity at this price. This is very common, whereas a difficult situation is: what to do when the selling price is lower than the cost?

The practical experience is that the seller at this time is usually going through a painful ordeal, and he/she will resist it fiercely. The memory about the cost of the product is *strong,* and its dominance is *prominent.* The severity of the situation will be significantly higher than in the case of a normal profit obtained. Supposedly, if a seller produces and operates multiple commodities at the same time, he/she can pursue the balance between the total revenue and the total cost of all these goods, and does not necessarily care about the balance between the income and cost of a single commodity. That is, he/she can subsidize some product lines with others. However, if subsidies are carried out in an unruly manner, where does the responsibility system work again? How are the employees judged to be rewarded or punished? Logics like this require the company to *prioritize* accountability based on the *correspondence* between the cash flows, and hence the cost-benefit analysis of any *particular* product. It is not that the subsidy system will be completely avoided, but that the responsibility system should take great precedence over the subsidy system. This shall be true within an enterprise, and be true to the entire economic system: *there is a serious bias towards the cash-flow-based accounting system; the economy is dominated by it, and by the memory of it.* This is like an impulse to retaliate: whoever causes the damage will pay the price. It's an *Algorithm.*

Of course, this Algorithm is a manifestation of a bent mind.


## §118. Limitations and Singularity of the Price System (3)

A flow of money is followed by a flow of behavior. A proper flow of behaviors requires people to hold money sometimes and commodities some other times. The flow of behaviors is a consequence of the actor forcibly closing computations and independently settling the current action. To a certain extent, it is the result of ignoring the past, ignoring the future, and ignoring other matters. Although current computation involves the past and the future, it is ultimately free and independent on its own. The resulting current price is the price that really "exists". Past and future prices don't really exist, they exist in the brain, either as memories or as predictions.

However, mainstream economics doesn't see it that way. Mainstream economics has a vague, strange character. It seems to connect the past and the present, and the present is a continuous extension of this connected "whole". The original marginalist economics seemed to describe the actual dynamic economic process while defining the word "margin" as the latest event in time. Unfortunately, however, this dynamic definition was quickly rejected by subsequent neoclassical economists, who redefined the margin as a certain differential property of a function, thus conforming it to the needs of the static theory. They then demonstrated that the overall profit or utility maximizes when the marginal benefit is zero (i.e., the marginal benefit is equal to the marginal cost). In this way, it seems that the dynamic theory is "perfectly" integrated with the static theory. However, instead of moving further towards the development of dynamic theory, this has made dynamic theory redundant, secondary, or unnecessary (meanwhile, the vaguely dynamic temperament of the word "marginal" casts a flattering but mysterious aura over mainstream economics). It is in this sense that the marginal determination of prices becomes the golden rule of mainstream economics, demonstrating the consistency between the complex mathematical calculations of economists and the simple decision-making models of ordinary people.

What a clever piece of wisdom!

Now, let's re-observe and understand the characteristics of prices in an Algorithmic, and therefore real, environment.

The price is characterized by its outstanding flexibility. It is often a *restless, radical* force compared to other kinds of information. While seeking and predicting price trends from other information, people take price changes as a fresh and strong stimulus to alert themselves. They start from sharp price changes, follow the clues to find out the reasons behind them, and then understand the changes in economic conditions. A price is like a puppy that you are holding on to for a walk, running around you, jumping back and forth, thereby "regulating" your walk. The reason for this is that the current behavior is relatively independent, and in the final analysis, it is not subject to the history, the future, or the stock. It only relates to them, and is not determined by them. People's preference for historical prices and memories is a kind of bias towards traffic, and people break away from these historic fetters and stubbornly decide on the current novel price, which is also a bias towards traffic. On the point of "bias towards traffic", they are consistent. Practical observations show that when there is an imbalance between supply and demand in the current period, prices often deviate from the historical trajectory and move violently. It's a brutal process. It brings windfall profits to one side and unexpected pain to the other.

When readers agree with the "principle of marginal determination of prices" in a textbook, perhaps they have empirically provided the following footnote to such a theory: the market price is the guide of the economy, and the historical prices and stock assets are often helpless against the market price. Marginal decision-making is actually for the binary framework of "stock-flow". This is true even according to its own discourse. However, the neoclassical "stock-flow" framework mainly refers to the "capital-product" framework, and nothing else. What is real interesting in the marginal approach, however, lies not in the fact that a particular product is relative to the capital goods in which it was produced, but in the inventory of that product throughout the economy, including the goods in use and the second-hand goods stored in the hands of users and consumers. These commodities, traded at varying historical prices, are the most vulnerable to spot price shocks. Especially for a durable, bulky, and high-value inventory, when the price fluctuates violently, the owner will be under psychological pressure every day, and even have to face the choice of "sell or buy" all the time. A rise in the market price will motivate the inventory holder to sell for profits, or may push speculators to accelerate their purchases. After these two forces cancel each other out, the balance will be used to affect the price movement. This leads to the familiar wave in other asset bubbles, as well as business cycles.

A price theory is a qualified price theory only if it logically includes all of this simultaneously. However, even in this case, the implication of the principle of marginal decision-making remains specious. If the current transaction that exists relative to the entire inventory market is understood as the "margin", it is tantamount to saying that "the price is determined by the current price, and the current price is determined by the current transaction", and in the end it is equivalent to saying that "the margin determines the margin". It's a tautology. Then, where exactly is the rationale of the marginal decision-making principle as understood by average readers?

Obviously, this means that *inventory can be valued at market value*. Changes in market prices change perceptions of the value of any inventory of the same kind that exists in the economy, resulting in a continuous or intermittent revaluation of these inventories. It is ultimately unreasonable to reject a reaction to price changes, and it is also naïve to assume that all inventories can be cashed out at market prices, whereas only the market-price-based revaluation and adjustment is a relatively realistic and feasible approach to accounting. This is a compromise and a real way for the price system to work. Here, the price mechanism is both useful and limited, and it is quite specific. This specificity is also manifested in the fact that price is linked to the volume, and a particular price is only valid relative to the actual volume of the commodity transaction from which the price was generated, and does not necessarily mean that it will be valid for any new offer. In this sense, price information is not actually isolated, it is followed by a combination of a series of structural information. The fact that price information is singled out to separately aggregate and disseminate can only be understood as a simple and approximate use of price information.

Henceforth, market price is used to value existing assets and is of great economic significance. It allows people to get rich without earning an income, and allows a country's economic power to rise above (or below) the level indicated by its gross national product. It has broadened the range of commodities and allowed the credit and financial sectors to grow. The resulting economic pattern is quite different from what is described in traditional textbooks. It could even be said that this opens a window through which it would be enough to change our perception of the natures of the economic system, and enough to change the general tone of economics.

## §119. Economy as a Subjective Valuation System

By understanding the finiteness and specificity of micro-pricing, we can understand a large number of important economic phenomena, as well as the way the economic system operates and moves as a whole.

First of all, it should be emphasized that economic analysis does not need to avoid the real economy and society. Mainstream economics starts with abstract analytical models, and the models, parts, or branches are shown off one by one; however, at the end of a textbook, the overall face of the economy still does not appear. Now, our order is reversed, and the real world is presented to us from the beginning as a whole, as a theoretical matrix and platform. The real world is endogenized from Algorithmic Theory in principle, and presented to us as an inference, a prototype theory, and a philosophical principle. But this presentation is only a rough line, and we still need to refine it, and to drill into it for detailed explanations. The next step is the specific work to be done in "economics" as a sub-discipline of general social science. Note that this "concrete work" is only to enter the matrix and do detailed work, not to change the matrix, not to propose new basic assumptions. The limitations of the Algorithmic person's field of vision require and allow us (also as Algorithmic persons) to work in such a step-by-step, one-by-one, or serial way, and communicate and coordinate with the parent or platform at all times. Such applied work, even if it is superficially similar to the existing compartmentalized work, is fundamentally different.

The Algorithmic micro-pricing mechanism suggests that prices are influenced by subjective opinions in a number of ways. This subjectivity is usually not manifested significantly in trading ordinary, small, and consumable commodities. This is because these commodities are not easy to hoard and therefore not easy to profit from the movement of time. Coupled with the fact that mainstream economics is accustomed to ignoring dynamic processes, speculative behaviors such as hoarding for profit are not present in its basic theory, and at best are only concerned as extensions and exceptions. However, if you look at real life, you will know that speculation is almost universal in any commodity trading activity but varies in size and intensity. For example, in the past year, there has been a relatively high level of inflation in the United States, and shoppers often buy a little more food than usual as long as it is non-perishable. It's almost become a habit. This habit leads to supermarket shelves running out of stock from time to time. The shortage has further exacerbated the rise in prices.

As mentioned earlier, the prices formed by transactional flows will lead to the revaluation of stocked goods. This effect is prominently reflected in the durable goods sector, which further causes far-reaching wealth effects. For example, over the past two decades, the Chinese mainland has experienced a great bull market of real estate. The economic and social behaviors of people who "feel rich" have undergone extensive and profound changes, which in turn have led to dramatic changes in many industries related to real estate, both near and far. Because of the large population, the amount of this new "virtual wealth" is also huge, which it in turn significantly affects the whole world. As a result, for example, the global luxury industry has seen an unprecedented expansion.

It is only natural that Algorithmic people are more accurate at valuing goods with a short lifespan and less accurate at goods with a long life hence requiring a larger range of computations. People often rarely consider those medium- and long-term events while merely assuming that the medium- and long-term prices move in the same direction as recent prices (valuation models such as these can be developed empirically). This Algorithm exacerbates the volatility of a spot price, as in luxury goods. The practical value of a luxury good is not large, and its usefulness is often psychological, which leads people to value it inaccurately, and thus its price fluctuates greatly.

When the durable market grows, it will be more suitable for financial investment. This means that a trader does not participate in trading for the purpose of supplying or using the goods, but only to earn the difference between prices to make a profit. There are not many commodities that can accommodate large-scale investments. Special markets (e.g. primary product market) are opened for these commodities, and standardized contracts are drawn up for the trading. The virtual trading volume is sometimes higher than that of a spot market. When the trading activities become frenzied, they can in turn distort the prices in the spot markets.

However, this is only the beginning of the discussion of

financial investment. Generally speaking, financial investment is not negative, but a major development of the commodity market. This means that people who have funds beyond their personal consumption needs, according to certain conditions, transfer the excessive funds to those who need them, so as to hold various forms of financial assets such as notes, bonds, contracts, and stocks. The development of financial markets is heavily dependent on legal documents, and thus on the level of a country's legal system. In order not to affect the actual use of funds, holders of financial assets can often transfer financial assets to a third party again instead of recovering the original investment when they need funds again. It is usually much easier to hold, preserve, transfer, and deliver financial assets than physical assets, thus the possession and transfer of them replaces the possession and transfer of physical assets to a certain extent (note the Algorithmic implications of this comparative perspective), which leads to significant savings. A person who possesses and uses a physical asset does not have to worry about an unexpected redemption of funds that would otherwise forcibly disrupt his/her business activities, and a person who relinquishes his funds to hold financial assets usually does not have to worry about his investment not being redeemed. Re-transfer activities create a secondary market for financial assets, which can be used to re-price financial assets in a continuous manner. When the price of a financial asset involves a wide range of factors and a long period, the subjectivity of its pricing is strengthened again, and it can produce a "virtual wealth" effect similar to that of the real estate market.

*Stocks are those stocks, and elements are often those elements, but their different permutations and combinations, and thus the productivity of different "postures" of the assets, are varied.* It can be argued that the pricing of an asset, which is significantly subjective, reflects the evaluation of such a "posture" by the people receiving the service of the asset. *Meanwhile, this "posture" shall play a concrete role and intermittently form a concrete service to people in order to strengthen its value.* People evaluate an asset directly, or indirectly and intermittently through receiving its services. This "virtual economy" has become an important part of advanced economies. The popularity of the word "virtual" is obviously due to the rejection of the substantiality or materiality of thought in traditional mainstream philosophy. This rejection developed into a branch of physicalism in economics, which valued things over people, and the tangible over the intangible. People who like to use the word correctly recognize the fact that the price of an asset depends to a large extent on the opinions of the person who actually uses it, but incorrectly describe any deviation from it as "illusory". Asset prices are not illusory because assets can be sold and exchanged for currency. In this respect, it is as "real" as any other commodity prices. Even at the point that "a particular price implies a condition of a certain trading volume", it is the same as other commodity prices. However, the volatility of asset markets is sometimes particularly high, surpassing that of ordinary commodity markets. However, all relevant differences are just at certain degrees, technical, or detailed. There is no essential difference between them.

The development of the market will also lead to an expansion of the range of goods. Art, collectibles, odd stones, cryptocurrencies, and much more can all be traded. At this time, in addition to the various physical elements of the market, traders will pay special attention to ideas of others and study them as *factual objects*. Some actors also deliberately try to influence and steer other actors' opinions in order to profit from them. Sometimes wealth is so easy to acquire that it seems to come out of thin air. However, Algorithmically, this is not true. Although actors' behaviors are often absurd from a third-person point of view, this does not mean that they are what the third person whimsically wants them to be. There have been its own evolutionary laws. Their behavioral patterns are personalized, complex, and not easy to observe, and observers sometimes do not think that any of them is worth studying in detail, but this cannot be used to prove that the traders' behaviors are just arbitrary, lucky, or "walking randomly". It is the computational economy and big data that prevent researchers from understanding them precisely, and these obstacles are likely to be mitigated with the development of research techniques. Afterwards, researchers may learn more about the rationale inside them. Secondly, the perspective of computational economics tells us that resources are finite, and when people benefit from investing resources to develop a bubble economy, other aspects of the economy may be affected by insufficient input, or the future of the economy may be jeopardized. A more subjective part of the economy will rise and fall significantly, and it is more unstable than the rest of the economy. Empirical observations show that the resulting crises are also more frequent. This characterizes the Anglo-American economic system. In contrast to this, the German-style economic system does not rely so much on asset prices like the Anglo-American system. Each type of economic model has its own advantages and disadvantages, and all reflect certain styles to a certain extent. Of course, this does not mean that one style is not superior or inferior to another, but that it is not easy for anybody to compare, judge, and choose.

### §120. To Survive Motions

The Algorithmic perspective allows us to realize the importance of the truth that "a person can only do one thing at a time", so people's social roles (including economic roles, of course) are constantly changing, and the assets and objects with which people deal are constantly changing. The resulting effects of economies of scale and scope[1] lead to the endogenous and directional development of people's comparative advantages, which in turn leads to the social division of labor. The social division of labor, in turn, creates the need for collaboration and transaction, increasing the frequency of social interactions. Economies of scale and scope will also lead to the intensive and partial advancement of certain behaviors that often manifest the deepening of thought, one-sidedly, then break the existing equilibria, and enable the economy and society to develop in the midst of "creative destructions"[2].

This principle that "a person can only do one thing at a time" first makes "social interaction" feasible and independently meaningful. Some observers wonder why people "interact" with each other, and buy and sell commodities frequently; since they "interact" to sell and buy, the two opposite processes can cancel each other out, so don't they need to interact or buy and sell? Honest thinkers would ask questions like this. Self-righteous people who think they know everything often laugh at such questions. In fact, this is a typical extreme rationalist or neoclassical question, and its answer lies in the Algorithmic principles, which require a wide range of in-depth elaboration. On this basis, we need to understand the concept of "behavior" and its finitude. Finally, it comes to the proposition that behaviors of limited contents lead to the fact that the contents of human interactions, including those spatiotemporal elements, are always limited, specific, and unique, and often cannot cancel each other out.

---

1. According to the terminology of economics, the economy of scale refers to the effect caused by pure quantitative change(s) in a given structure, while the economy of scope refers to the effect caused by change(s) in the structure itself, namely, qualitative change(s).

2. Hugo Reinert and Erik S. Reinert, "Creative Destruction in Economics: Nietzsche, Sombart, Schumpeter", in Jürgen G. Backhaus et al. (ed.), "Friedrich Nietzsche (1844–1900): Economy and Society", Springer, 2006, pp. 55-85.

Therefore, the election of a president generally does not lead to a blackmailing of the president by the electorate so that the blackmailers could exploit the president's administration. Similarly, individual stocks can affect the stock market index, but they are not enough to cause the index to lose its independent significance. A chef still often needs to go to a restaurant for dinner because he/she cannot always serve himself.

The resulting dynamic topics are wide-ranging. The demands for commodity trading proliferate because of money. Money is like a fast lane (another metaphor is the "blood vessels in the body") in the economic system, and once you enter it, you will usually get the best of both worlds. This means buying commodities with money when you need them, and when you want to "avoid" them, you can simply and conveniently hold money, or sell them for money, or sell them for less liquid financial assets. Individuals with limited physical and mental abilities in a spatiotemporal environment do not always enjoy being surrounded by physical assets. In a given circumstance, people only need to use a specific asset, and prefer to stay away from the drag of other assets. That is, people like to expand at times and "*slim down*" at other times. Accordingly, commodities are occasionally chased or abandoned. The Algorithmical "particle economics" (or "chemical economics") leads us to recognize this characteristic of the economic system.

Commodity trading can happen only if people's behaviors are *asynchronous*, i.e., people often do different things at the same time. Otherwise, if people always do the same things, both buyers and sellers will not be able to find a counterparty. Asynchronicity is first and foremost a natural state, because the synchronicity of behaviors of individuals who grow and move in different locations, if any, must be accidental unless there is some specific coordinative mechanism between them;

therefore, asynchronicity can be a normality. Second, people endogenously cultivate asynchronicity with each other in order to alternately occupy resources in terms of time, thus conserving resources.

Asynchronous behaviors can be coordinated with each other or not. When it's better coordinated, fewer resources can serve more people, or, the same resource can quickly go from person to person. This is the rationale of the so-called "seven lids match eight bowls". This is a basic principle of the market economy. This is also how money works. Money itself as a commodity can be turned over and over again by the banking system to create more money that is several times its original amount.

The realization of such savings requires that the combination of people and resources be reconfigurable or replaceable: either resources (e.g., money) can be moved between different people, or fixed resources (e.g., roads) can change the users frequently. Otherwise, not only will the savings not be realized, but the effect could be reversed. For example, it can be taboo for people to exchange old clothes with each other, so that a person will have many sets of clothes for one's own use. One person can only wear a small amount of clothes at the same time, and the other clothes are left in the wardrobe as stock, waiting to be invoked. Another example is housing. Some people own more than one house, which they take turns living in on different days.

Assets with different attributes bring different dynamic effects. In the latter case above, the dynamic performance is more stable, with the disadvantage of greater waste, while in the former example, a consequence of increased asset utilization is the increased risks in the dynamic process. An asset needs to have a relatively high utilization rate, and the relevant economic conditions and people's expectations for the future must be relatively stable. As soon as some shock causes expectations to change, turmoil will occur, and even intensify. For example, natural disasters such as earthquakes and floods often cause shopping mall shelves to be emptied by consumers, not only because of temporary supply reductions, but also because people suddenly and unusually increase their stocks of supplies. These vicious circles, and in the opposite case, virtuous circles, characterize the market economy. Such a market economy is like a "cage ride" in an acrobatic show: the faster the bike in the cage rides, the higher the bike rises, and on the contrary, its height decreases. Asset prices are constantly *stimulated* or *suppressed* by traffic activity. This is how the business cycle is formed.

Economic activity is rarely characterized by linear movements, often accelerating or decelerating. It is in this sense that classical marginal economics takes on an important significance. We don't need to dwell on that again. However, a special example of the marginal effect needs to be mentioned here, which is the so-called "bottleneck effect": heterogeneity leads to some "bottlenecks" in the operation of the economy from time to time, and then blockages occur. If bottlenecks can be eliminated with smaller inputs, it is possible to achieve much greater economic benefits than such inputs. Modern Monetary Theory has many negative implications, but one positive is that it identifies more "monetary bottlenecks" in the economy, so that by injecting money, it is possible to achieve a certain amount of economic growth—and then reclaim the injected money. The use of "helicopter money" to heal the traffic stagnation caused by the coronavirus pandemic is a media joke tinged with "Modern Monetary Theory", and the logic is the same as J. M. Keynes's claim that "digging holes in the ground"[3] can create GDP.

---

3. John Maynard Keynes, "The General Theory of Employment, Interest And Money", Cambridge University Press, 2013, pp. 129, 130, 220.

Some readers may have thought that discussing these everyday examples does not make much theoretical sense. On the contrary, it is only in the Algorithmic realm that it is possible to systematically sort out these bits and pieces of material to illustrate the anti-neoclassical truth that economies "survive in motion". Moreover, the most important task of economics is not to establish those "general theoretical models" that go beyond these individual cases, but rather to go into these specific descriptions and analyses by comparing them with more general models. Only the latter can be connected to the ultimate goal of research—economic policy, while the former cannot. The former is just preparatory work.

## §121. The Statics in Motions

Statics is not to be discussed until in a dynamic context, at least in a context where dynamic and static are combined and mixed. Now, I think it's worth sorting out a little bit about this.

The physical world is inherently a combination of dynamic and static. Static, of course, first refers to the invariance and constancy in intuitive feelings. However, many parts of a motive object remain constant, as do some laws. The latter, in particular, can be seen as an extension of statics. All kinds of statics bring convenience for us humans to recognize and treat them. At this time, the human mind with limited abilities can calmly study them and deal with them. This is a condition for the sustainable development of knowledge. By extension, as long as the rate of development or change in the objective world is lower than that of the human mind, the human mind should still be able to handle it. The introduction of velocity helps us establish a flexible and "soft" worldview and achieve a gradual transition from static to dynamic.

However, after the introduction of the human mind, some wonderful changes took place. A wonder of this lies in the fact that the human mind is a system of continuous development. This continued development is spectacular compared to the natural world. Although there are changes in nature, even continuous changes like the Big Bang, they cannot be considered "developed" and "improved". Words such as "development" and "improvement" are mainly used in human society. Although this developmentality is based on the immutability of the Instruction system and the relative stillness between the physical world and the mental system mentioned above, it is ultimately bizarre. Although development needs to be conditioned by value judgments, which are only a matter of human beings, at least the amount of knowledge is growing objectively (and its content is actually constantly changing or improving). This adds a relatively independent, explosive system outside of the physical world. At this time, the physical world is often only assumed as an external object, a background, despite its specific changes. Even if it changes, its name does not change. This contextualization and fuzzification is actually a kind of staticization—changes of the external objects do not significantly affect the internality, and therefore, they are assumed to be "just there", regardless of whether they change or not. This is effectively the equivalent of assuming that they, as a whole, do not change.

Now we know that this staticization comes from the serial computing of the human mind. Serial computing leads to the roundaboutness, and the roundaboutness requires that the stock of knowledge be placed "alongside" of the mind, in a state of waiting. During this period, it shall not be changed. Unless it changes due to memory decay, damage, etc., it must remain unchanged so that when current computations invoke it, they can still recognize its natures as before and thus take advantage of the natures. Thinkers cannot allow unexpected changes in the stock of knowledge, otherwise the computations will be out of control. Of course, a knowledge stock is powerless to change itself without the intervention of current computations. In the thinking system, this coexistence of dynamics and statics is a manifestation of plurality. Such coexistence shall be inadmissible by monism. *In this way, monism can be further interpreted to mean that any partial independence can be instantaneously extinguished, implying that the computational speed is infinite.*

As a kind of statics, an equilibrium now has to retreat to a corner as a locality or partiality. The Algorithmic framework creates the conditions so that it can "comfortably" return to its right place, its origin or "home".

After returning to the partial, what we can discuss first is the neoclassical "stable equilibrium": imagine that a certain system, even after experiencing multiple "shocks", will still return to equilibrium in the wake of a short period of turbulence—like a cockroach or the "Alien" in movies who can't be killed. What we are saying is that even if such a system exists, it is not a universal, typical case, but a special one. More importantly, in order to illustrate the natures and advantages of the economic system, we do not have to "generalize" or "beautify" it in this way. While economic systems have a tendency to self-heal, they also tend to self-sabotage (e.g., innovation), and they concurrently have tendencies to move towards equilibrium and tendencies to deviate from equilibrium. There is actually an equivalence between these two types of opposite statements.

Only by moving beyond this misuse can we recognize the real, vivid, interesting, and useful examples of the concept of "equilibrium".

Equilibrium usually refers to a relative statics achieved through a certain behavioral process (physical or mental). Once here, the actors can no longer move forward. This inability to move forward refers to the inability to continuously and effectively carry out this series of tasks that are closely related in accordance with the existing pattern of behaviors. Then, the actors either go to rest, or change their places, change their topics, and devote themselves to other matters. In terms of mental state, the persons are either satisfied, helpless (e.g., under a Nash-style stalemate), desperate (e.g., as a consequence of experiencing a failure), and so on. Economically, in particular, it can be understood as a *vulnerable* state of "exhaustion" (rather than a "state of stability"): all opportunities have been exploited, and one step further is a precipice or a catastrophe. The psychological background of this state is that if people are particularly satisfied with the status quo, they will not stop, but will continue to move forward (the so-called "insatiable" or "much will have more") until they are not satisfied with the status quo. In other words, the equilibrated state at this time is a state of life that is psychologically boring. People have to accept the status quo or repeat the old way of life. People are trapped in it, unable to move about. Or, from a macro perspective, the economy at this time actually contains a lot of small crises that are left to fend for themselves. Some people are complacent, some are trembling, and some are hesitant and confused. At this time, the macro "equilibrium" can be understood as the balance between the specific proportions of various social mentalities. Conversely, "disequilibrium" means that their proportions have changed. In general, these proportions can be interpreted oppositely for economic upswings and for recessions or crises.

Another meaning of equilibrium is that *in most cases*, the level of intelligence contained in the status quo of society is *basically* optimal for a challenger. This is not because this intelligence is objectively and absolutely superior, but because the arrangements for real life have been mostly the result of *a great deal of* conception and testing by *countless predecessors*, and therefore, they are less likely to be improved. It should also be taken into account that the challenger oneself is not an alien, but from this same society, inheriting the knowledge of this same society, thus the intelligence gap between him/her and the object society is usually not very large. This leads to what Soren Kierkegaard called an attitude of "anxiety"[4]. In real life, sometimes the status quo may not be good-looking, and it is especially easy to be despised by young people. Challenges of young people are often not successful, but rather raise their own awareness of society and respect for traditions. This is one aspect. Another aspect of this argument is that, *from the point of view of the contemporary people*, the real society is always *slightly* disequilibrated[5] (this slight disequilibrium is linked to the impossibility of completely changing the social stock in the short term that we have already mentioned [§23, Vol. I]), and thus can be improved by the contemporaries in a few respects, or to a lesser extent. This improvement is only marginal. Moreover, the task of challenging reality can be daunting, because the intelligent difference between the challenged and the challenger is often small, and it is not easy to determine which new idea will succeed; and, once it is determined, there would be a "winner-takes-all" effect, and the income distribution would be heavily skewed in favor of the winners, at least in the perception of the contemporaries.

The above view of real life further derives its *mystery* in our eyes. Its mystery and "anxiety" are the basis of all empirical research, and the psychological basis for attaching importance to practical activities. Therefore, in social research, as in natural science research, researchers have attached importance to empirical testing and practical effects. Reflected in political

---

4. Soren Kierkegaard, "The Concept of Anxiety", Princeton University Press, 1980.

5. Traditionally and habitually economists refer to "slight disequilibrium" or the "degree" of disequilibrium baselessly in theory. Now, in the Algorithmic framework, equilibrium or disequilibrium can always, or in principle, be a matter of degree, scope, or other technical issues.

activity, people attach importance to the results of opinion polls and public votes. People usually do not blame public opinions, but investigate public opinions, especially to *feel* the new trends of social change. An amazing thing is that in the midst of collective, highly-intensive political interactions, we sometimes find those superior opinions quickly turning into public opinion. Thus, democracy is a tool not only for the pursuit of stability, but also for powerful development and innovation. In this way, an Algorithmic equilibrium is not completely static and stable, and the traditional concept of "equilibrium" can be further transformed into a certain form of development based on slight imbalances, such as "consensus-driven development", "sustainable development", and so on.

## §122. Economic Growth

The most striking Algorithmic dynamics is the phenomenon of continuous development. Looking at the economic data year by year, you will find a very regular growth. However, this extremely prominent and important phenomenon cannot be explained by the existing mainstream neoclassical economics. This is because growth has been identified by economic research as being primarily caused by innovation that is not compatible with neoclassical economics.

In the Algorithmic framework, while critically embracing the neoclassical concept of equilibrium, innovation can be readily explained. The secret lies not elsewhere, but in the weak, simple, yet transparent functions of meta-computing. Computations, and thus the process of human thinking, begin here, and naturally, they develop and innovate. Firstly innovation is not because the future of knowledge development is broad, but because our history and accumulation are very limited. If we look back and understand this finiteness, *then* our future can be opened up and the infinite nature of knowledge development can be understood. Henceforth, the growth comes not only from the accumulation of physical wealth, but also from the development and innovation of knowledge; from the expansion of the quantity of knowledge, and from the improvement of knowledge quality; and, from the information-driven innovation, and from the innovation of Algorithm improvement. In short, these various ways of development, whether simple or complex, can now be easily understand in principle. The sum of developments at the individual level constitutes the phenomenon of a sustainable development at the macro level.

This is a mechanism that is unique to human society. This mechanism should be attributed mainly to how knowledge is developed as revealed by Algorithmic Theory. There is no phenomenon of development in the physical world. Since no long-term memory effect in the animal kingdom has been observed, there shall be no significant developmental phenomenon in it. Humans are particularly fortunate in this regard. The standard of living today is in principle better than in the past—people sometimes mistakenly think that the life they are living is the best life they can get. The word "best" here reminds us that development is also the result of a subjective evaluation of dynamic consequences, and that the purposes of human actions have a certain stability, commonality, and irreversibility, which leads to the fact that the ordinary measures of developmental results can be basically acceptable (and also inevitably controversial in some aspects) for most people. It's like a horse-drawn cart always running in *one* direction, so the distances it travels can be accumulated, rather than canceling each other out.

By comparing this continuous development with the following situations, we can better understand where our human luck lies. One is a degraded life. How frustrating and frightening will such a life be?! I believe that those who have been in it have experienced it. The other is a static or cyclical life. In traditional philosophy, an ideal state is often conjectured in this way: stillness, fulfillment, happiness, desirelessness, and so on. It is the end point of development. Now, however, with the Algorithmical purpose theory, the *static ideal has been eclipsed*, and we know that purposes also can be endogenous, so when people are in a certain state of happiness, it will not be long before the happiness would disappear; monotony, boredom, insipidness, and dissatisfaction will recur, and people will inevitably move towards other higher goals. This "insatiable desire" is actually a commonsense truth, so it is surprising that people would believe in some static society while knowing this truth! It can also be reflected in the division within philosophy. Now, the static, ultimate ideal is Algorithmically eliminated, which will facilitate the establishment of a dynamic, integrated view of happiness, that is, happiness lies not only in the realization of a certain state, but also in the process of perpetual improvement or development itself.

However, real historical records show that growth was not always achieved, and sometimes failed. This requires us to further examine the causes of growth, especially its social mechanisms.

The first is the "pluralistic growth model". This refers to people who are in different places and relatively independent, mainly using their own local resources for development. They do not exchange information and knowledge individually, or do not communicate adequately. At this time, the levels of knowledge they possess are uneven. However, they are still evolving relative to one's own past. Coupled with the accumulation of material wealth, each will achieve relatively independent growth. A simple arithmetic addition of these individual growths yields the macroeconomic growth statistics. Because of the independence of individuals, the plurality of knowledge, and the barriers to communication, we can believe that this *"pluralistic growth" constitutes an important part of the total growth*, even for today when the means of communication are highly developed, and a large amount of personal knowledge converges on the highest level of knowledge available in society (as shown in Diagram 8, §123). Although results of development are not fully measurable by monetized statistics, the statistics on economic growth will remain one of the most concise and effective ways to measure development relative to other indicators.

The second is the hedging mechanism. The sum of the individual development outcomes mentioned above is only a simplification. In fact, due to individual differences, fates of individuals at the micro level vary greatly and fluctuate. Reflected in statistics, some people's growths are hedged by others' failures or declining outputs, and macro data are then the results of this hedging, or offsetting. However, it is in this sense that we can recognize the wonder of the phenomenon of a continuous growth. This kind of wonder seems unfelt when analyzing human beings as a whole, but now it can be strongly felt. This needs to be explained. One explanation is that because innovation is risky and disruptive, there is a distinction between aggressive and conservative strategies. An aggressive strategy may yield higher returns, but it can also lead to larger losses; in short, it can exacerbate the instability of life. On the other hand, if you are too conservative, growth will slow down and life will become monotonous. Consequently, people have learned the skill or knowledge of maintaining a certain balance between radical and conservative until innovation occurs in a less drastic way that can be sustained over time. This strategic innovation management (both knowledge development and knowledge utilization) must have permeated the way of life since ancient times, both at the individual level and at the social level. Sometimes innovation must be suppressed or controlled.

Finally, there are control mechanisms at the national level. Algorithmically, it can be said that the truth of the market economy is not complicated at all. *The reason why "laissez-faire" is the golden rule of the market economy should be understood mainly from a negative perspective, that is, it is not that individual behaviors should not be coordinated at the macro level, but that a government is often unable to do so. And, since individuals' knowledge is developing, this governmental "inability" can be endogenous and distinctly permanent.* If strict coordination is imposed (as is the case with a planned economy), the output will not grow but fall. Therefore, we have to adopt a laissez-faire approach, allowing the actors to coordinate and fend for themselves. There is by no means no negative behavior in the market; reversely, negative behaviors must be abundant, but they are statistically masked by positive phenomena. Moreover, it is not the case that the state is incapable of coordinating all aspects of individual conduct. Certain social functions can only be undertaken by the state, and some other social functions can be competitively undertaken by the state, thus being used to suppress negative phenomena. As mentioned earlier, specific functions of the state depend on the natures of the matter that the government coordinates. The principle of heterogeneity can vaguely guarantee that this possibility exists.

In terms of growth specifically, it can be argued that the emergence of a "state" in the ordinary sense from scratch is usually conducive to it. A society without a state is jungle-like, and everyone can offend others by force. The emergence of the state has monopolized the use of force, which has led directly to savings in security expenditures. When an individual cannot rob others of their wealth, he/she can only turn to seek cooperation interpersonally. In order to attract others to cooperate, it is necessary to look for win-win projects that can increase the total output (as pointed out in game theory). In particular, when the state is democratic, governmental actions can be understood as the result of social consultation, and voluntary social consultation, if it leads to the requirement of governmental intervention in some respects, can be understood as *conducive to growth, at least from the point of view of the actors consulted.* Thus, voluntary negotiation actually means a screening mechanism in heterogeneous societies: only projects that are conducive to growth are selected and implemented.

Government as an organization, according to the organizational theory that we have proposed, can be used to reduce social conflicts, establish certain order among people, and thus increase total output. This principle is similar to that in the establishment of innovation management by individuals at the micro level. Further, we can argue that a certain combination of government and market is the most conducive to growth (this optimality also varies with the specific conditions of each case). When the governmental intervention decreases, other things being equal, society will lose its growth because it is too chaotic, and when the governmental intervention increases, it will lose growth because it lacks innovations. The "socio-chemical" Algorithmic perspective can also tell us that when the number of free individuals is large, the growth will be relatively stable because of the strong hedging of each other, and when the scale and intensity of collective behaviors are too large, the growth will be less stable because the hedging is weakened.

# CHAPTER 11
# THE SOCIAL PHILOSOPHY
# (IV)

## §123. The Knowledge Spindle

Since computing power is limited, people have to make trade-offs between topics, and they can't indiscriminately compute on everything. In terms of tense, people usually tend to prioritize the present, the real world in front of them. The second is to pay attention to history, which can be understood to be motivated primarily by the focus on the current real world. In order to solve real-world problems, it is often necessary to care about the history that produced the present world. For example, a strategy for a city tour is to visit its historical sites, to read about its historical materials, get a sense of past events, and then look back at the present, and you will know and feel about it quite differently. Why? This is because historical events have not only left visible traces in reality, but also left invisible traces in history books and materials, and in the thoughts and behaviors of local people. The invisible relics are not in the light, but in the dark, and we have to find the doorway to reach them; otherwise, our understanding of reality will not only be incomplete but even miss its essentials. This is where the unique value of "humanistic tourism" or "cultural tourism" lies. After reading the historical materials, talking to the locals, and experiencing their way of life in depth, the tangible materials under the sun will become alive, and become the one integrated with ideologies and cultures. The impact of historical events on tangible and intangible stock is often a natural, undesigned, and unstoppable process, and involves a huge number of people, thus its size and intensity are generally very high. Even if someone (e.g., an authoritarian ruler) tries to erase or tamper with the historical relics, the amount of the physical or computing resources he/she can devote is generally comparatively small. It is relatively easy to destroy buildings and tamper with official history books, but it is extremely difficult to change the memories, thoughts, remnants, private documents, and behavioral characteristics.

However, people seem to have placed too much emphasis on history compared to their concern about the future. Historical events are always turned over and over again by generations of people trying to obtain new findings in them. The reason for this, of course, is first of all because historical events are the "existences", the facts, and these facts have been completed and established, definite and unique, so understanding them will not waste energy, while the future is the "nothingness", a possibility, undecided, and therefore theoretically infinite; if we study these possible situations one by one, it is not allowed in computing power or in the economy. Diagram 8 illustrates the comparison, where the present part attracts the most attentions, followed by history and then by the future. The amount of attention that people have invested in each period decays with the distance from the present, and eventually tends to zero. This indicates the finite scope of each person's concern, as well as the finite quantity and quality of knowledge all people possess.

However, our interpretation of the status quo does not mean that we agree with the perfection of the status quo.

This allocation of computing power is more or less formed under the domination of a static, false worldview. As a result of the dominance of the convergent rather than divergent philosophy of knowledge, the idea of infinite development has not yet been able to gain philosophical dominance. This inevitably leads to the fact that the real society under the influence of philosophy ignores the future, and is even more reluctant to study and speculate on the future in detail. Although projections of the future can be impossible to be completely reliable, according to the principle of heterogeneity, there must be a certain percentage of them that can be quite reliable. In particular, *speculation about the future can in turn influence our present behaviors, so the benefits shall be enormous, generally greatly outweighing those of the study of history.* Moreover, the forward-looking research method can include historical research as its precursor and an integral part, which can help historical research to adjust its direction and posture to be more meaningful and practical.

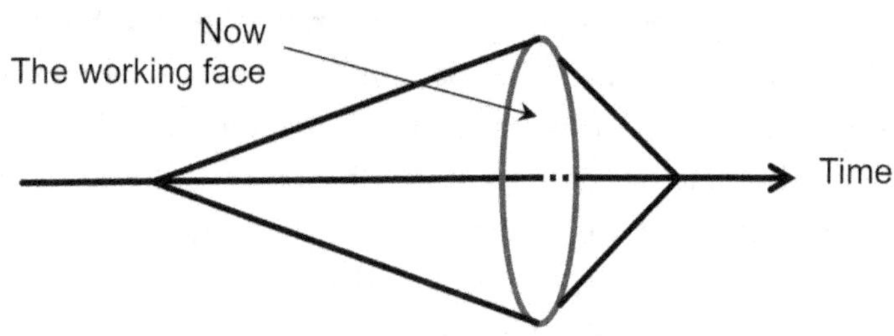


**Diagram 8: The Knowledge Spindle**
The knowledge spindle can be used to illustrate the time structure in the knowledge systems of an individual or society, or the distribution of different pieces of knowledge in high or low qualities.

The above is the first usage of the "knowledge spindle". The knowledge spindle can also be used in a different way, which is to divide it according to the levels of knowledge development. The concept of "equilibrium" means that we always put into practice what we consider to be the most reliable, or "best" knowledge. Since such knowledge is heterogeneous and pluralistic in general, it is also relatively large in quantity. In Diagram 8, it is represented by a circle (which in engineering terms can be called the "working face"). The knowledge below this optimal level (on the left) is the not-so-good knowledge that has been stored in human memory and has not yet been discarded. The lower the quality of the knowledge pieces, the fewer of them are retained. At the same time, because knowledge is always in development, there are still a lot of immature knowledge and ideas in research above the optimal level. Although these ideas are new, they have not been decided to be put into practice as optimal knowledge. The process of knowledge development is that the current knowledge system, the circle as the working face, constantly absorbs the knowledge on its right side, and "excretes" the old knowledge to the left side. The working face is advanced from left to right along the time axis, to develop.

Both of the above uses of the knowledge spindle can all be personal or social. In the social sense, especially in the second use, most people can be understood to stay inside the circle most times, which is a collection of the existing best and mature knowledge including consensuses and pluralities, while a smaller amount of people stay left or right as laggards or pioneers respectively, and in occasional cases—Of course, it may be debatable where each individual piece of knowledge is located. The total volume of the spindle is limited, which means that the quantity, quality or contents of human knowledge are actually limited. The "set of existing knowledge" is a subset of the "human knowledge thesaurus", and the difference between the two includes the lost knowledge and all the knowledge that is possible but not yet in possession.

## §124. Multiple Dynamics

The above is mainly a rough look at economic issues. Now we need to return to general, comprehensive social issues including a number of non-economic ones. Some of the previous statements can be regarded as fundamental, and now we will deepen and expand them a little. The first is an extended discussion about the dynamics in the Algorithmic world.

Sustainable development is undoubtedly beautiful. It is one of the freshest and brightest discoveries in the Algorithmic world. In addition, there are a variety of non-neoclassical dynamics that deserve to be mentioned and listed here.

One is cyclicity. As mentioned above, cyclicity can be understood as a kind of statics. However, in terms of individual microscopic experience, it is dynamic, because a cycle is often defined at the macro level, but it is new to certain individuals, such as young people. A generation often has to face the same problems as their predecessors and construct the same knowledge to deal with these problems, and the way to deal with the problems has been almost the same for thousands of years, lacking development. Given the existence of heterogeneity and discreteness, development is not pervasive everywhere in the Algorithmic world. For example, the business cycle contains elements of repetition, although other elements in it are fresh and changing. Such statics and cyclicity shall not be understood as ubiquitous or universal in the economy and society, nor can they be, conversely, denied or devalued because of the existence of other dynamics.

The second type of dynamism can be called "evolution". This means that certain economic and social elements will inevitably change, and this change is not necessarily positive. It just goes where it has to go, as if an object is hit to fall onto the ground, unstoppably. It's impossible to leave it as it used to be. Main reasons for this include that there are many factors that change people's psychological and mental activities, such as the learning effect that leads to changes in personal strategies, and the tendency to dislike monotony and repetition in psychology that leads to changes in personal preferences, and the computing power saved in repetitive life that needs to find its new targets. At the macro level, for example, a stable institutional framework will continue to enact new laws. Although the governance of the state will become more and more refined, individual freedom may also become less and less, and the vitality of society will continuously decrease, to the point known as "social rigidity".[1]

The third type of dynamics is "attenuation". This effect, which has already been mentioned, mainly refers to the fact that a process of mutual objectification or self-objectification usually continuously decays or attenuates until it ends at a point. The reason for this is that since this re-objectification process is arranged serially, the energy and resources are consumed repeatedly, and the accuracy of actors' predictions continues to decline, then, after several rounds of speculation or games, the actors are no longer interested in the re-objectified activities, and thus becomes inactive. In the final analysis, this diminishing (or discursive) effect is similar to other diminishing marginal return effects in the Algorithmic world, which is to say that intensive activities focused on a specific object will not continue indefinitely, but will generally converge, so that it would be necessary to move elsewhere.

---

1. Mancur Olson, "The Rise and Decline of Nations: Economic Growth, Stagflation, and Social Rigidities", New Haven and London: Yale University Press, 1982.

The fourth dynamic can be called "developmental dependence". This refers to the fact that when the economy and society suddenly come to a standstill for some reason, society would be unable to maintain its static cycles and would fall into crisis due to over-optimistic expectations of the development. In other words, certain economic and social problems are to be solved depending on development and growth, even if the development does not improve something but only barely keeps it afloat. Employment issues are just like that. Technological progress has led to a reduction in the number of workers, and full employment will not be achieved until the workers saved are absorbed with new investment, and thus by greater economic scale.

Another manifestation of development dependence is the fact that a significant proportion of the new population is unable to find jobs without adequate education and training, as a higher level of economy requires a higher-quality labor force. This exacerbates society's responsibility in education. A higher level of economy may also be based on a more refined division of labor, so that the internal linkages and interdependence of the economic system will be strengthened, which will require a higher level and stronger institutional arrangements and macroeconomic management to protect against systemic risks. Because, this kind of economy with a higher level of structure is more likely to collapse as a whole. As soon as one part of it is attacked and destroyed, the effects will quickly be transferred to hurt the other parts. People may only be able to serve a high-level division of labor system, but lack the ability to survive in isolation (limited computing power and memory capacity require that workers can only be trained to a limited extent), then, when a holistic disaster occurs, it may be more destructive than in a low-level economic system.[2] Higher-level

---

2. Bin Li, "Foundations of Algorithmic Economics: The Cognitive Revolution

economies are also more based on people's subjective perceptions and expectations, especially asset prices, which rely heavily on the mindsets of actors. Because of the subjective and unstable nature of the minds, prices in asset markets periodically collapse to the detriment of the entire economic system.

The fifth dynamics can be called "limited collapse". The long-term sustainable development of a country will create a kind of fear from its prosperity, fearing that overdevelopment will eventually lead to a systemic collapse and a return to its primitive state (as the saying goes, "climb high, fall hard"). This concern is justified because development is a constructive process that involves subjectivity. Since there is subjectivity, there is mental bending, and hence, there may be a process of correcting this bending. However, "correcting" does not require a complete collapse of the structure, because it must be only partial (and hence involving a small number of events). Second, people don't have the ability to completely return to the primitive state, this is because due to the limitations of knowledge storage capabilities, knowledge will be partially discarded during its sedimentation. Even if some knowledge is deliberately preserved as historical heritage in some places, it may have been abandoned by the general public and hence is unable to be generally reactivated immediately. This does pose a danger to the safety of human survival, but in the final analysis, this kind of risk is unavoidable, since people have to give up certain knowledge, and they have to choose on their own what knowledge to give up. The knowledge that people possess and actively use is always a finite subset of all existing knowledge. On the other hand, this finitude leads to any social, systemic collapse that can only be limited. Because of the

---

and the Grand Synthesis of Economics" (in Chinese), Beijing: Economic Daily Press, 2019, Section 7.1.7, pp. 576-578.

limited options available after the collapse, after subsisting and waiting for a period of time in a low-output crisis state, society can only choose to roughly return to its pre-crisis mode. Even if certain adjustments and corrections have occurred simultaneously, and will probably continue to occur, they must be based on maintaining most of the previous structural elements. This factor confirms the validity of the status quo to a large extent, and forces development to be one-way and incremental, to a certain extent.

The sixth type of dynamics is the change of human psychology in the dynamic world and specific situations. For example, when the objective situation changes positively, people may become overly optimistic, and vice versa, they may become overly pessimistic. People become stubborn when they are convinced of something, and when their beliefs collapse, they become inferior, hopeless, and so on. Such psychological ups and downs are often only processual. The psychological activities of actors in specific circumstances are like the above because the actors may not understand the big picture beyond the circumstances (hence the so-called "perspective" problem). Then, after the "truth" is revealed, the person concerned may be annoyed, or laugh at oneself, and everything might become dull. Nonetheless, in fact, we will never be able to escape the fog of time and space, and the "truth" revealed is not necessarily the "real truth". Even if it is true, there will continue to be an endless fog, and the psyche will continue to undergo all kinds of tortures. Many of the "significant" social phenomena to be explained are, in fact, related to the various states of mind in the dynamic and structured social world, which require us to have a high-order awareness and management of them.

## §125. Multiple Dynamics (continued)

The seventh dynamics can be called "alternating ups and downs". That is to say, it is difficult for a specific, one-way movement to be maintained continuously; instead, it might experience relative slowdown or decline, and eventually be replaced by an opposite process. From a macro perspective, development is also stepwise and alternate, and even waxing and waning. Progress in aggregates is merely the result of hedging these micro or macro processes.

At the micro level, the basic reason for this alternation is the tentative nature of human behaviors. Bounded rational individuals are always trying to act. If the effect of an action is good, it is possible for an actor to continue and even intensify it until the marginal effect is reversed. After the reversal, it is probably best to go on in the opposite direction, supplementing the aspects that were neglected or hurt in the previous stage. This results in a *constant swing* in behaviors as an inconsistency that happens to one person. This inconsistency can also manifest itself in different individuals, and even occur in a group or society on a larger scale. The effects of inconsistent behaviors may reinforce or diminish each other again. Or, even if they don't interact directly, after a simple statistical summarization, the macro data becomes relatively flat, not as violent as the data of the individuals. However, since rationality is always limited, the hedging effects generally cannot be completely precise; therefore, it can be speculated that although the aggregate statistics fluctuate slightly, they will never be of no fluctuations at all. Even, in some years, they break down. They are exactly what has happened. This kind of fluctuation differs from microscopic fluctuations in degree only, and they are essentially the same. Only a perfectly rational route would assume that the positive and negative effects are exactly canceled out.

This situation can be explained even from the point of view of knowledge development. While it can be argued that knowledge development is stubbornly continuous and monotonous, the pace of innovation can be variable. There may also be an asymmetry between the disruption of existing assets caused by innovation and the building effect of innovation. There may be processual inconsistencies between fundamental innovation and application of innovations. There can also be a temporal dissonance between the speed of innovation and its spread. Large-scale disasters can destroy physical wealth, or they can destroy the stock of knowledge by destroying populations, thereby altering the social distribution of knowledge. It is impossible to fully explain the phenomenon of fluctuations without independently examining the existence and movement of such knowledge.

The above theories can obviously be used to explain the rotation of political actors and the change of social trends. However, it is important to focus on the phenomenon of long-term fluctuations in civilization. Historically, the rise of a civilization has usually been the result of a continuous play of certain factors, resulting in an increase in the return to scale. Civilization has grown continuously on the basis of these factors, leading to prosperity and achievement. But, in principle, the power of any factor is limited, which brings a limit to the heights that can be attained by the civilization on which it is based, as well as a limited period of history of the civilization. In the human world, there are some special ideological factors that will hinder the continuous growth of civilization. For example, in today's United States, economic growth has led to a sustained increase in wages, which weakens the competitiveness of American products relative to other countries, thereby expelling capital out of the United States. After development, people tend to spend more and work less— after all, that's what development is all about. Wouldn't development be counterproductive if it didn't lead to higher incomes and living standards?

If those specific factors that support the rise of a civilization are time-limited, then their disappearance will also lead to the decline of that civilization. Competition from other peoples and regions also has a continuing equalizing effect, since all people have the same basic abilities in thought. However, these specific factors are sometimes soft, which need to be examined again. For example, the rise of the Mongols in the thirteenth century apparently stemmed from a right combination of their leading cavalry technology and military management. Genghis Khan imparted this holistic military ability to his retinue and descendants, thus maintaining a military peak for several decades. However, after that, with the end of the conquest, the military ability was rendered useless, and the Mongol rule was found not only mediocre but crude, which led to an inevitable decline of the Mongols. On the contrary, American civilization is built not only on the superior geographical conditions of the North American continent, but also on its institutional framework marked by the Constitution. This system not only ensures freedom to stimulate active innovation, to include and absorb other civilizations, and to spread knowledge and cultivate talents, but also ensures the overall social order in which new knowledge can be transformed into concrete products for the benefit of the masses of the people. This system is widely and deeply rooted in society as a kind of widespread knowledge, and is strengthened and revised by continuously demonstrating its practical effects. As a result, the American civilization is very tenacious, and even in the face of all the resistance brought about by wealth and affluence, it still shows no signs of decay two hundred years after its founding.

The eighth dynamics builds on the seventh one, called "eternal turbulence" or "the impossibility of absolute stability".

Algorithmic Theory can be used to illustrate from

numerous perspectives that microscopically stable is often not only impossible, but also that social turbulence is frequently quite intense. The subjectivity of people's thinking and behavior is one of the key causes of instability. Such subjectivity is difficult to completely cancel each other out, and thus the structure and state of society exist as a subjective and limited construction as a whole. No one can completely guarantee that this "Neurath's ship" is safe and reliable. Alternating between left and right, expansion and recession, is inevitable. At the micro level, continuous innovations cause turmoil, interpersonal games cause turmoil, knowledge dissemination causes turmoil, and the withdrawal of experienced people, the entry of unskilled novices, all cause turmoil, coupled with turmoil from the physical world, and so on. What can make us believe that stability, harmony, and peace can be everlastingly achieved? What power can remove all these factors that lead to turmoil? In fact, the "peace and prosperity" described by writers was often an illusion, and its taste can only be told by those who have really experienced it. For example, what a hard and uneven trajectory China's sustained high-speed growth over the past decades has actually been on! It cannot be denied that "happiness and stability" exist in a certain range, period, or people, but excessive stability will bring paralysis, pride, and excessive optimism. These subjective factors accumulate over time and can eventually cause a disaster and major change. If we recognize that "behavior" is nothing more than just a flicker of activity in the middle of a multitude of stocks, then the end of one behavior can only be deemed a precursor to the beginning of another. This perpetuity can be predicted theoretically.

In particular, the perpetuity of instability should be understood in terms of the limitations of governmental action. Actions of the government are generally aimed at maintaining the stability of society at the macro level. However, this does not mean that the government can provide whatever hedge force that is needed by society to maintain its stability. The government's ability to serve is constrained by its productive capacity. From the perspective of thoughtful materiality, the limitations of the government's productive capacity are even more prominent, because a fairly high proportion of government services are thoughtful, involving the production of various thoughtful products. In particular, this large-scale productive activity is not something that can be done by mere personal intuition, but is inevitably guided by certain abstract theories that are largely indivisible as public goods. There are not many opportunities for these theories to be tested in practice, therefore, the governmental policies supported by these theories are often risk-taking and cannot always be expected to be successful. For example, "Modern Monetary Theory", as a new policy doctrine, is currently in a situation where it is being used at risk. This brings us to what I advocate: in the face of the sustainability of turbulence, the goal of macroeconomic policies should be lowered, the tolerance for economic fluctuations should be increased, policy operations should not be done frequently, and the operations should be carried out in a decentralized rather than centralized manner, and so on.[3] The effects of policies must be relative, and policy makers shall in principle accept this relativity as long as the effectiveness reaches a certain degree.

## §126. Centralization and Decentralization

The main conflicts in the world today are between autocracy and democracy, or, to put it more neutrally, between

---

3. Bin Li, "Foundations of Algorithmic Economics: The Cognitive Revolution and the Grand Synthesis of Economics" (in Chinese), Beijing: Economic Daily Press, 2019, Section 8.3.2, pp. 745-747.

centralization and decentralization. The theme has been around the globe for at least three centuries, and it remains stark today. This seems surprising. One of the major reasons for this is that the scientific mechanism between them has not yet been clarified. I believe that *before the Algorithmic theory, the social sciences have not yet opened even the most basic chapters of this topic.* The social sciences do not yet know essentially what autocracy is and what democracy is. In the final analysis, this is because of the lack of a proper theory of mind. Since even fundamental problems of the theory of mind have not been resolved, it is not really surprising that neither democracy nor autocracy can be defined—because they are both questions about the basic way of computing among many people.

With our theory of thinking, in fact, readers can answer the question of democracy and autocracy on their own even without our elaborating on it. The basic architecture of the human brain's thinking can be understood as a certain memory capacity, paired with a "central processing unit" with specific functions. Inter-multi-person computations, i.e., social affairs, imply multiple independent memory capacities, each with a separate "central processing unit", in which social computations are carried out in conjunction with each other. "Democracy" means that these independent units of computation, i.e., individuals are equal to each other, and they each answer the same social problems and then vote on the outcome. A typical "autocracy" means that one of the "central processing units" acts as the dominant unit of computing, and the other units of computing feed information to it, and then separately carry out the decisions it makes.

In this way, it is easier to analyze the advantages and disadvantages between democracy and autocracy, or between decentralization and centralization—we can also assume other scenarios for comparative analysis, such as "all computing units are directly controlled by a center + data is stored separately", "all computing units are directly controlled by a center + data is stored in a unified manner", "a single super high-speed computing unit + data stored in a unified manner", and so on. Centralized decision-making, because it uses global information from each individual, is likely to result in better outcome than an ordinary individual. However, according to the Algorithmic principles, decision-making of the leader is still done by a finite number of computations, and the "central processing unit" in the head of the leader that undertakes the computational task works the same way as that of any other individual; therefore, the contents of the decisions made are generally still limited, subjective, and imperfect, and they lack, and hence are subject to the tests and corrections of other people.

This problem can be understood in particular from the perspective of computational workloads. The information in the possession of n individuals is now gathered and allowed to be computed by one person, whereas this information could have been processed by n computing units concurrently. It stands to reason that either the processing speed of the computing unit of this leader shall be n times that of ordinary people, or the computing time shall be n times that of ordinary people; otherwise, there is no guarantee that the computational results will reach the level of n parallel computations of n people. This is a basic inference.

However, the leader can also be defended. Since the independent computations of these n individuals are necessarily parallel, when the data of n people is aggregated, some parts of them may appear repetitive, and the leader can distinguish their importances and sift through the data, and thus does only the necessary computations that amount to less than n times that of the average individual. In addition, the quality of decision-making can be improved by providing the leader with assistants, specialists, and specialized equipment that the average individual is unlikely to afford.

The opposing argument is that the motives of the leader's decisions cannot be guaranteed to be good enough. Even if others fully communicate their motives to the leader, the leader can ignore them. There is no way to prevent the leader from making decisions in favor of himself/herself and those close to him/her. The hired assistants and experts must be the result of the selection of the leader according to his/her own judgment and preferences (this dependence is an Algorithmical inevitability), which may not be objectively professional enough, and there is no guarantee that they will work sincerely for the benefits of these n individuals.

The internal systematization of the system of the thoughts of a leader and his/her subordinates may be higher than that of a simple collection of the thoughts of the n independent individuals. However, the flip side of this systematization is that it can also systematically and stubbornly deviate from the correct answer, even far away. In this absence of a hedging mechanism, the subjectivity (or even a "systemic subjectivity") of an individualized version of knowledge can be particularly worrisome. The correct answer can no longer be given by a specific third party, but is left to the judgment of the leader himself/herself. He/she has to generate his/her own schemes for decision-making on the one hand, and judge these schemes on the other, and the knowledge, methods, and skills for making such a judgment are inevitably subjective in themselves (just as the leader is inevitably subjective when selecting his/her assistants). If he/she believes a certain scheme is correct, he/she may stand on the side of this scheme and actively stifle other schemes. At this point, while the "specialized computing" is delving deeply, it is only going further down the wrong path.

Let's look again at the computations made by the n

independent individuals. Due to the large differences in their personalities and thoughtful systems, their respective computations may be much different from the beginning. Although the good and the bad are mixed, the richness of the ideas will be significantly higher than that of the computations dominated by the leader alone. There may be conflicts between these ideas, so it is inevitable to argue endlessly (this democratic phenomenon is often gloated over by authoritarians). The resources of a single person are limited, so the depth of his/her computations is also limited. However, due to the social heterogeneity, some of the individuals may voluntarily increase their input to deepen the computations, and others may also join them, or even raise funds from society to build a strong research institution. In particular, given that a voluntary joint effort requires the consent of each collaborator, a successful project can be an indication that the research project has withstood the scrutiny of multiple people, and therefore, its quality is likely to be high. Under dictatorial conditions, questions such as what to study, how to study, how much to invest, and so on are all constrained by the dictator's vision. If the dictator believes that there is no need for more R&D, the scale of R&D will not expand.

In this way, a democratic society is rich in thought, stable, and may be powerful. This "distributed" computing method of "each part of the data is equipped with a separate independent computing unit" has great advantages. Moreover, this independence and parallelism are ensured by the independent, decentralized brains and bodies, which constitute a natural mechanism for diversifying risks.

The next question: if this democratic mechanism is seen as superior, then the dictator can also imitate it and try to have this superiority, cannot he/she? The answer to this question involves one of the core problems revealed by Algorithmic Theory, namely, the stock of knowledge. The stock of knowledge, including hard software, is a prerequisite for an individual to generate personalized ideas and decisions. It is constantly growing and changing. If a dictator wants to succeed in imitating a democratic society, he/she must first have this stock of knowledge, not all at once, but continuously. However, the stock of knowledge in an individual's mind is not only huge, but, as mentioned earlier, subconscious in its many components. Individuals may not be aware of their existence, let alone describe them exactly. Then, how can it be completely "reported" and collected to the leader of the group? Moreover, even if it can, the operational workload required would be strikingly enormous.

In this regard, the defender of the dictatorship may say that the leader can use supercomputers to process the information and knowledge of the whole society, and thus break through the limit of computing power. However, this perception is only static. The possession and use of these machines may have an advantage in the short term, but in the long term, the technology that the leader can use can also be used by other organizations and individuals. Unless the dictator has taken a complete control of the society and deliberately prevents the spread of new technologies, it is impossible to stop ordinary people from using the supercomputers. As a result, the level and complexity of individual behaviors are bound to rise, which will finally nullify the leader's use of the supercomputers.

## §127. Centralization and Decentralization (continued)

However, the challenges facing democracy are also enormous. The weakness of democracy lies first and foremost in its high dependence on means of communication. In principle, social affairs require interpersonal communication in extremely large amounts. Nor should the benefits of plurality and diversity be exaggerated. A lot of what is communicated is repetitive or overlapping. Even in terms of interpersonal differences, the communicative activities will eventually fall into diminishing marginal returns, and then lead to either public decisions or deadlocks. The red tape and slowness that democracy brings are not always tolerable. Therefore, there are reasons to speed up the democratic processes. To this end, one of the ideas is to draw on some of the advantages of centralization. It is only when centralization develops into an authoritarian dictatorship that it turns negative in value. Ordinary centralization is just a means of social organization and is widely used in democratic societies; it does not necessarily contain ideological significance in itself.

One way to simplify the democratic processes is to introduce a proposal system for public deliberations. A deliberative body does not make proposals by itself, but only votes on a wide variety of proposals. Individuals or organizations with certain qualifications may submit the proposals. The contents of a bill are compiled by the proponents as *an independent unit of computation*, and then the deliberative body simply says "yes" or "no" to it as a whole. Obviously, this arrangement can significantly reduce the overall workload of the deliberative body, and at the same time provide an opportunity for experts to use their expertise to internally rationalize the bill. It can be argued that when the bill is submitted for deliberation, there is usually less selectivity and flexibility inside the bill, and it is not worthwhile to vote on each part separately. A voting action is actually only for those parts of an entire social process that involves major decisions.

Another way to simplify is to distinguish between decision-making and execution, and leave the latter to the executive department that runs the hierarchical head-responsible system. In principle, both decision-making and execution are categories of computing activities, despite the fact that the decision-making process also involves executive work (so congressmen must have assistants), and that there are also decision-making problems in the executive process. However, there are still differences in degree between them. The Algorithmic economy makes it unnecessary to distinguish them completely; instead, it requires only this distinction, no matter how accurate the distinction would be.

We can call the "market + government" or "congress + president" system some kind of "mixed system", but this statement is inaccurate. The Algorithmical rationale shows that such a structure should be regarded as a unified whole, with a high degree of interdependence between its internal parts, which cannot be summarized only by the word "mixed", neutrally and eclectically.

Around the world, democracy has a clear advantage and is still on an upward trajectory. Democracy not only has the correct foundation in terms of the purpose of governance, but also has a strong ability to deal with practical problems after strengthening the legal and administrative systems. Today's markets and democracies are attractive to developing countries because they can be effectively innovative and stable.

Authoritarian system is a system formed by forcibly shutting down computations in the face of time pressure and the problem of factor completeness, hence its inherent characteristic is to emphasize the immediate or short-term decisiveness. No present, no future; this is its basic idea. Therefore, it tries to prioritize the best knowledge available *currently* and put it into *practice*. In a quasi-static, slow-moving society, the conservativeness of the system in knowledge development does not seem to pose a significant disadvantage; however, in the long-term national competitions, this system is bound to eventually lag behind democracy. This can be a logical conclusion.

There is a natural connection between the statics of

authoritarian systems and extreme rationalism. Because extreme rationalism emphasizes the existence and uniqueness of the ultimate truth, this ultimate truth will eventually be distorted as the best knowledge that exists currently in any era, as people at that time could not imagine why this optimal knowledge could be wrong and to be replaced in the future. In the final analysis, the fallibility of knowledge can only be proved with the help of Algorithmic principles. Thus, through an alliance with the intellectual leadership, the ruler could then claim to have possessed the "truth of the universe". The rulers would monopolize the rights of intellectual research in their own hands, and then ostentatiously show off their "erudition" and "greatness" to the whole society. In the absence of such a basic theory of thinking and knowledge development like ATT, rulers will consciously or unconsciously become hostile to diversity and freedom in order to simplify their computations. Rulers will despise not only the minds of ordinary people, but also their emotions, desires, and wills. Rulers, in particular, despise the history, traditions, and social stocks, and exaggeratedly understand the regime's ability to act in the present. The governing logic will attempt to show that any decision will be "sound and reliable" only when it comes from the top. They will only relinquish power when they are forced to do so. Regimes may concentrate a large amount of power that they actually find difficult to wield, and then simply and brutally exercise those powers. Even, regimes will not hesitate to declare war on any established system or custom, trying to change the world overnight. This has the potential to be devastating. In fact, these speculations are largely the facts of yesterday and today. What we are now emphasizing is that the occurrence of these facts could have been theoretically foreseen. In the absence of voting pressure in a democratic system, an authoritarian system can sometimes manifest certain long-term vision in its operations, however, because the change of its leadership is generally not institutionalized, and because the individual leader has a prominent moral hazard, this long-term nature is very limited (for example, it may benefit from a long-term vision supported by a specific piece of knowledge, but it may not obtain the long-term benefits generated by renewal of knowledge), and its performance may be otherwise more unstable in the medium and long run.

By absorbing the advantages of democracy, autocratic systems also evolve. However, whether ultimate control of society is given to the people or to the autocrat, and whether to divide power among multiple entities or to concentrate power in a single body seem to be some unavoidable and *Algorithmical* questions. It seems that the boundary between the two cannot be finally erased through quantitative evolution—the existence of the topic of "ultimate control" is really an Algorithmical effect. China's miraculous development in the past decades seems to provide new supporting evidence for authoritarianism. However, as long as we recognize that China's development is ultimately an *intellectual imitation*, and that centralization can be conducive to the imitation, then it can be concluded that this evidence is not sufficient to falsify any existing general views. Instead, the "imitation" perspective can be used to dissolve other successful developments under authoritarian regimes in general terms (e.g., Germany, Japan, and Russia before World War II, and thereafter, Taiwan, South Korea, Singapore, etc.). A further corollary of the "imitation" theory is that when a developmental process of catching up with developed countries tends to come to an end, it is likely that this will also be the time when the energy of this particular strategy is exhausted. China's story is not over yet. Next, it is likely to pay the price for its overdraft.

A tragedy of history lies in the fact that, at a critical juncture in history, some important people may have deliberately understood, evaluated, and chosen between various systems for the sake of the development of their own country and nation, but they made the wrong choice because they could not get effective help in theoretical analysis. The evidence of practice is pluralistic and not easy to interpret. As the social sciences are not developed enough, the dominant regime is unable to concisely explain its own strengths and thus win more support. Dictators may be ambitious, but they don't know why they have failed. "Limited power" is just an empirical and common-sense slogan, and it is not as persuasive to many thinkers as imagined. Some well-wishers try to persuade autocrats to consciously push for the transition to a democratic society, but they may not be as eloquent as the dictator and his/her advisers. In the face of the failure of democracy and the pressing practical problems, the embrace of centralization, and the danger of centralization, have risen from time to time.

Ideas are valuable. An appropriate social philosophy might be able to clarify all the important social issues at hand from the ground up. To this end, Algorithm Theory is willing to sit in this very seat and be tested.


## §128. Artificial Intelligence and the Future of Humankind

The success of large language models shows that the economics of computation is still a key factor in determining the success or failure of program development. Because a large language model only computes based on the linguistic form of knowledge and not on semantics, it gets rid of the huge workload of semantic computation. It uses computers' usual strengths (e.g., speed) and strategies to only seize a few or individual links in human thinking that a computer is good at and make full use of them, while ignoring other links of human thinking activities. This shows that even with today's most powerful computing power, an AI developer has to be concerned about the combinatorial explosion that will lead to a spike in computing tasks. Under this pressure, large language models are actually adopting an opportunistic approach.

However, in any case, it is clear that AI has ushered in its unprecedented golden age. The prevailing opinion in the media seems to be that computers are not only becoming more and more "thoughtful" like humans, but that they seem to be going to surpass human thinking and thus have to be managed and limited. Perceptions within the professional community are less optimistic than those of the media and the public. However, because the speed of machine computing is so fast, as long as it has mastered certain techniques and the "secrets" of human computing, it can use them to the extreme (e.g., computer chess players practice millions of times at night between chess game days). From this point of view, its knowledge accumulation will proceed very fast, and the computational results will be able to understandably surpass those of humans in some aspects. Especially in professional fields, experts will control it and use it to develop new knowledge (including compiling computer programs) in place of human researchers. For existing social, even common-sense knowledge, computers should also be able to simulate and reset, or surpass on the basis of replications. Because, no matter how complex this knowledge is, it is always limited in quality and quantity. I do not intend to give any further alarmist warnings as a result of this. The machines must be managed properly, and I believe they will be.

What needs to be discussed now is humanity itself. Since the dawn of computers, technologists have been at the forefront. Perhaps the technological upheaval was too swift to be reflected on its philosophical and social implications. Worst of all, however, a significant proportion of humanities and social science scholars are still in a state of contempt and hostility (even jealousy) towards new technologies, and have not seen a logical connection between the two. Humanities scholars have always refused to "scientize" their thinking. Now, science and technology themselves exude a distinctly humanistic atmosphere and temperament, how will humanistic scholars feel about this?

It would not be surprising if humanity were to one day accept the management and services of e-doctors, e-judges, and even e-officials. A machine may not be better than a human everywhere playing these roles, but it also has outstanding advantages that humans do not possess (e.g., efficiency, precision, stability, neutrality, etc.). This is not a debasement of human beings, but a manifestation of human intellect, and therefore it will mean the enhancement of human beings' own worth. Although we are now borrowing computer principles to elucidate the structure of human thinking, the computer itself is a model and mirror image of human thinking; in its early years, it imitated people, not being imitated by people. It's like borrowing a mirror to see what we look like. A car will run faster than a person, in fact, we can also say that the car is "intelligent", and it can even be said that any appliance around us contains intelligent elements. The purpose of building a stock of knowledge is to let it *automatically* provide answers to our questions. A tool is a tool, and its nature and status have not changed at all on the computer. Only people who don't really understand the principles of computers, or writers who like to sensationalize, will consciously or unconsciously confuse this, and then lead to all kinds of exaggerated psychology such as fear, inferiority, and jealousy about computers.

While emphasizing the narrowness of traditional scientific thinking and its necessity to extend to the fields of common sense and humanities, we must also emphasize that the latter is equal to the former, and that the latter is not "nobler" than the former. Moreover, there is a need for competition, collaboration, and complementarity between the two. Unfortunately, the current situation is that before the basic principles and methods of the humanities and social sciences are to be clarified, artificial intelligence has hit. In other words, the status quo is two levels behind what it should be. Therefore, what humanities and social sciences need is to catch up. My opinion is that the first step is to understand the basic principles of the humanities and social sciences by using the Algorithmic principles, and hence to know how we can use technology. The second step is to reuse technology for a better society. Machines will become a stimulus, a challenge, and a catalyst for us to exert our own efforts. In collaboration with machines, humans need to explore further and develop their comparative advantages. As long as the right combination between human and machine is achieved at a higher level, another door to high human development is likely to be opened.

Following in the footsteps of information technology, the development of biotechnology seems to have the power to subversively change human life. However, if humanity has not yet grasped the basic principles of ethics and morality, it would be doubtful whether humanity will be able to formulate new ethical norms to adapt to technological changes at the present time, then the human ability to embrace such subversive will also be questionable. However, technological innovations shall be unstoppable. If the innovations cannot be actively coordinated, they will happen in a chaotic and even destructive way. When we take a comprehensive and prospective look at all these, we will find that human society seems to be on the eve of great changes.

An established trend of change is the wave of democratization and globalization. Although there may be some twists and turns in this process in the future, its end is already in sight. In the future, the world will most likely enjoy a unified global government. In this unified territory, although autonomy may vary from place to place, it is bound to share some unified institutional infrastructure. These systems will do their best to protect freedom and innovation, but they will also lead to equalization, homogeneity, and uniformity in some respects. These two sides are not fully compatible. An Algorithmic perspective will allow us to predict that some form of rigidity and a slowdown in development will occur. After we get out of the confusion of the static view of happiness, we will in turn realize this hidden concern about the future of humanity.

To some extent, information technology seems to be able to alleviate such concerns by using information technology to assist in institutional innovation and management improvement. Since institutions, like other knowledge, act only as an expedient measure, sooner or later, they are bound to be updated. In principle, this is the case. This principle is present throughout the book. The process of creation is also the process of restructuring, and there is no essential difference between the two. However, real institutional experimentation can be costly and even brutal, and one of the alternatives is to experiment in a simulated environment (e.g., the "metaverse", a buzzword), and then continuously adjust and refine the schemes of institutions and policies. The latter includes not only a programme of new regimes and policies to be enacted, but also a detailed transition plan. Such a transition plan could cover those closely related, if not all, groups of people, with detailed (at least more detailed than at present) measures to redistribute benefits. According to the Algorithmic principles, we know that it is impossible for this kind of plan to be perfect and complete, but it may be possible to achieve much more perfection and accuracy than the current coarse institutional reforms, and can take more care of personality and particularity. Whereas real-world experiments need to be done with caution, simulated experiments can be carried out boldly and actively.

I think that both humanities and social science scholars might have wasted too much time in the past. Algorithmic Theory now presents us with a clear path that will allow us to carry out a large amount of new research work quickly and efficiently. The general public will finally see that this large cluster of disciplines will have great practical value, and will no longer be just a trivial "talk" in an ivory tower. It is only through this practicality that we can show the public that the work of the past has finally not been in vain but become a kind of preparation for the practicality that can be shown today.

## §129. Matching and Marriage

In addition to economics, law, and politics, the application of Algorithmic Theory in the social field can be very broad. Here is just one example of how Algorithmic Theory can be used to construct philosophies about love and marriage.

It starts with the personality of a person. As a kind of knowledge system, the innate hard software of individuals, together with the acquired knowledge stock, jointly form a person's personality. According to some findings from genetic studies, most of the hard software parts are universal and do not vary from person to person, and the differences exist only as a small fraction. However, for the birth of love and the goal of choosing a mate, this small part is the key.

Secondly, what has not been mentioned above is that in the development of knowledge and the development of personality, the knowledge that was generated ahead in time has an advantage, because it can govern the direction of the subsequent knowledge development to a certain extent, thus influencing people to choose or avoid the later knowledge. This is the *path-dependent effect of knowledge development*. According to this reasoning, hard software has priority over general knowledge development. Individuals can choose knowledge that suits their innate nature, systematically developing their own Algorithmical style of behaviors.

It can be considered that hard software, together with some knowledge developed early in life, constitute the *basic character* of an individual. This basic personality is used frequently in life, has a large range of influences, and thus is relatively less easy to change. Traditional fortune tellers and astrologers have divided the basic personalities into a number of categories. Aside from the mysterious metaphysics in such work, it can be argued that there shall also be some truth in it—and in the relevant work of psychologists.

Since basic personalities can be divided into various types, there is a question of whether or how they match each other. A prerequisite of mutual affection between a man and a woman is that the gap between them is neither too big nor too small. Sometimes one wants the other to be the same or similar to oneself, and sometimes one wants the other to be different from and hence complementary to oneself. But this is just a rough interpretation. Specifically, what exactly "matched", "tacit understanding", "harmony", or "getting along well" is must be psychologically very complex and subtle. Even if the two persons are in love, they may not be able to clearly explain the reasons themselves. This complexity is consistent with Algorithmic Theory. However, just like the method of making judgments about right and wrong, good or bad, the matching of personalities can be defined relatively and subjectively, if not completely objectively. It is in the process of dealing with different individuals that a person knows what is "in love" and what is not. When people with matched personalities deal with each other, they understand each other well, highly efficiently, and have fewer conflicts, thus both of them are relaxed and happy, and on the contrary, they will have more misunderstandings and conflicts and produce much more mental pains. Therefore, one needs to pay special attention to the basic character of oneself and others. This is undoubtedly ideal if your partner is compatible with you in terms of basic personality and temperament. In fact, this compatibility is important not only in gender relations, but also in partnerships of any nature.

The above perspective will predict the occurrence of an interesting phenomenon: love at first sight. Although a personality has many sides, it cannot be ruled out that there is such a harmonious and tacit understanding between the appearances, temperaments (as personal default, usual, and basic attitudes, psychological states, etc. to life), and personalities of two people that they enter the rhythm of love as soon as they know each other. Of course, it can also be speculated that the probability of such an event must be very low. According to most people's experiences, the "others" they have encountered were not satisfactory enough, i.e., desirable in some aspects and not in others. We live in a state of widespread irregularity and variability. Some people fall into bitter love in a dilemma and embark on a tortuous life. Some people choose to be tolerant and live a normal life. However, there are also those who started out in a bland relationship but developed into a passionate one, while others started out in a passionate relationship and ended up breaking up. There are those who choose celibacy in disappointment, and there are those who never give up their pursuit and hope in celibacy. Some people have been divorced many times and have gone through ups and downs, but in the end they are happy in some unassuming relationships.

The reason for this is that human personality is not only influenced by innate factors and factors early in life, but also is formed and changed throughout life (for conceivable reasons, the pace and mode of change must vary from person to person and from time to time). "Character" is actually a rather simplistic concept. As an individual grows, he/she is influenced by more and more others, but also to be educated. Although foreign knowledge can also be independently selected to a certain extent, individuals mainly adopt the method of "introduce it first, and then revise it". If the evaluation and revision of imported knowledge are not sufficient (in fact, they will generally never be "sufficient"), then this knowledge will conflict with one's own nature as a relatively rigid element. Such people are often confused, tormented, and struggling mentally. But, on the other hand, certain knowledge can also lead individuals to point their fingers at their own natures and to try to limit or change their existing personalities (e.g., someone who recognizes that his/her nature is an obstacle to success and thus tries to restrain it). If one's spouse's nature is not quite suitable for oneself, one can still find a way to gradually improve their relationship with each other. Observations show that this is not an unusual fact. Nonetheless, since hard software cannot be deleted, he/she need to pay this additional price for it for the rest of their marriage. These factors further contribute to the complexity, diversity, and variability of human personalities and interpersonal relationships.

However, the management of hard software and affective life by the mind itself can also be relatively unsuccessful. For example, the occasional "first-sight love" affairs can be exaggerated and developed into the long and well-known stories of a prince and princess that passed down intergenerationally to the world. In times of ancient hardship, people were prone to fantasies, which always alternated with brutal realities. People didn't know yet how to unify them within a single framework. Then, with this misunderstanding, the "first-sight love" was regarded as a "deserved" and "standard" love style. This is just as Plato enshrined the heavenly "Ideas" as the "truth" of all things on earth. In fact, this way of thinking should rightly (and Algorithmically) be called "idealism", an extreme notion about ideals. Idealism leads the person to believe that "every Jack has his Gill", that is, everyone has a spouse somewhere who is absolutely suitable for him or her, and therefore his or her mission in this life is to find the spouse.

This kind of thinking occupies and controls the minds of people from the very beginning, so that men and women are always focused on the small probability of this distant scenario, ignoring the reality in front of them, and simultaneously giving up the opportunity to use quite simple logical thinking to arrive at important insights. The occlusion of reason makes people psychologically overly sensitive; as soon as one discovers the "merits" of the other party, he/she exaggerates it imaginatively, and on the contrary, when one discovers the "shortcomings" of the other party, he/she immediately falls into pessimism and disappointment, and then gives up. After cohabitation or marriage, the attitudes are reversed: all the "merits" of the other party are taken for granted, and all the "shortcomings" are demanded to be "corrected" as soon as possible.

The joys and sorrows, ups and downs that people experience in their affective life, just like the hardships, twists and turns experienced in social life. Based on my observations and speculations, I suspect that the general state of human sexual life may be much worse than it appears to be. Because the "prince-princess" monism dominates the field, it has brought too much conflict and pain, and this monism also forces people to endure the conflict and pain hiddenly while busy covering up the truth.

A true and comprehensive doctrine can be used not only to promote harmony and success in society, but also to bring more harmony and success to private lives. In my own life experience, "tolerance" is a word I heard relatively late. Now, I know that it has great value, and this value also needs to be theoretically justified. This justification must at least start from theorizing the significance of others. Sexual characteristics and differences are special cases of interpersonal differences and thus interpersonal relationships. On the basis of Algorithmic pluralism and dynamics, it should be possible to develop a relatively comprehensive and sound philosophy of ethics and life, which will be both a synthesis and a development of existing philosophies.

## §130. Society, Culture, and Religion

After developing a theoretical system about the generation, existence, growth, interaction, conflict, and infinite development of ideas, we would have little more to say, not only about social philosophy, but about philosophy as a whole. Because almost all the issues that can be seen have already been covered, what is needed now is only annotations, extensions, and local applications. Of course, this should in no way be understood as the end of philosophy or social philosophy, but only as a conclusion of its previous stage. Since the development of knowledge never stops, so will philosophy and the social sciences.

We imagine that society as a whole is presented to us. Now, we think of this society as the result of the human brain functioning and acting in an Algorithmic way. Of course, this does not prevent elements outside of consciousness from being mixed with the result. Since heterogeneity, plurality, complexity, etc. are the goals of Algorithmic theoretical argumentation, we will not be surprised that no matter how unexpected or bizarre things we find in this real society, whether or not we have noticed these things beforehand, they would in principle be deemed proof of the predictability of Algorithmic Theory to a certain extent.

That is to say, Algorithmic Theory will give a foundation of heterogeneity, diversity (plurality), and complexity to the unity of all discourses on society to date. On this basis, Algorithmic Theory elaborates on the further unity of them. As a theory of thinking, ATT is first used to explain the thinking and psychological mechanism of individuals, so as to form the distinction between static and dynamic, stock and flow, and institution and behavior. Politics, law, and morality together form the formal or informal institutional framework of society, in which economic or non-economic behaviors unfold and marginally change the institutional or non-institutional stock, extending towards an infinite future. Historiography records the trajectory of history. All kinds of academic activities first describe and explain, and then influence real society, so that they also become part of the society sequentially and cyclically.

After each specific topic has been divided from "society", the rest of the territory reserved for "social philosophy", "social science", or "sociology" often seems to be less important or even somewhat empty. This is also like the concept of "natural science". As soon as it is talked about, the listeners can't help but ask: what part of the natural world are you talking about? Yes, at the end of this chapter, I don't intend to add any more details, but rather devote the rest of the space to cultural and religious issues.

The concept of "culture" is commonly used, especially to refer to specialized spiritual activities, such as education, art, entertainment, religion, etc., a considerable proportion of which are closely related to serious issues such as economics and politics. For example, there is no better way to understand the life of an era in detail than to read the literary or artistic works about that era, such as novels, films, and television dramas. However, due to space constraints, it is impossible for a literary work to record real life mechanically and lengthily like a monitor. It can be seen from this that literary creation and fiction are actually driven by the computing economy, thereby using typical and dramatic techniques to condense and reproduce life. One of their goals is to deal with big data. The reality and efficiency achieved in this fiction may be unsurmountable by other works of the social sciences. This is how literature can acquire a role in social science.

However, despite this, cultural activities are at least formally relatively independent of political and economic activities. They have a definite, symbolic presence in society. In the terminology tradition, there is also a clear border between them and political & economic activities. Even if there is a connection between the two, the connection is generally implicit, loose, or indirect. The rationale for this independence, as mentioned above, is easy to understand when we recognize the mind (or spirit) as a relatively independent entity. At this time, spiritual activities do not necessarily arise in response to the needs of worldly activities or practical interests, and can have their own independent pursuits. It can be confusing, it can be curious, it can be loved, it can be entertained, it can be narrated, it can be meditated, it can be fantasized, and so on. However, these activities can all be incorporated into the framework of concepts such as Instructions, data, computations, Algorithms, etc. In the context of subjectivity and psychology that have already existed as an important part of the Algorithmic framework, culture as one of the contents of the Algorithmic framework is natural.

Here it is necessary to say a few more words about religion. In ancient times, religion was the product of psychological counseling, comprehensively in areas such as explanations of the world, attitudes towards failure and suffering, problems in sex and marriage, social and entertaining needs, and so on. Today, its metaphysical content is becoming less and less convincing, while its social and moral functions are tenaciously maintained. People need to shape their own *basic attitudes* about society, life, and others. This is an Algorithmic effect. Laws often only provide injunctions on *what not to do*. However, this is not enough. The variables faced by people are infinite, and thus it is not enough to know where they cannot go; they also need to be *positively guided*. This distinction between negative and positive *should be seen as an Algorithmic effect*. Furthermore, positive guidance is often blunt and harmful, if it is mandatory. Therefore, the flexible religious or ethical persuasions (such as Confucianism in China) will be welcomed by society. Meanwhile, the ethical persuasions are not only about kindness, but also about intimidation (as well as obedience, praise, and worship), just as modern society relies not only on education, but also on the coercive power of the state. From this we can see some of the basic elements that social engineering in general should have. This has been and is to be the case today, and I think it will also be so in the future.

This book focuses on theories and principles that should be avoided from falling into trivial and exhaustive accounts. Therefore, I would rather stop here for the time being. In the discourse of the Algorithmic philosophy, we still lack the last piece of the puzzle, which is the philosophy and methodology of science. Of course, there is nothing special about this part, because they are already included in the previous discussion, either explicitly or implicitly. What follows is only a slight reorganization and expansion.

CHAPTER 12

# THE PHILOSOPHY AND METHODOLOGY OF SCIENCE

## §131. Types of Knowledge

Since the Algorithmic theory puts diversity and difference before all specific analysis, it creates conditions for us to comprehensively view, organize, and study the entire knowledge system of human beings. Much of what has been done in this area can be critically incorporated. In turn, we can establish a fluent, comprehensive philosophy and methodology of science consistent with other philosophies.

Computing is serial, so some knowledge, as the computing results, must be tried and given before it can be evaluated and selected, and if the evaluation and selection are insufficient, a lot of half-baked knowledge will continuously exist, or even exist for a very long time. However, because human beings with finite computing speeds do not know exactly what kind of evaluations and selections are really and truly "sufficient", it is possible that various types of knowledge at different levels of development can coexist for a long time. Moreover, the subjective turn of thinking, that is, mental distortions, will actively and endogenously add a lot of diversity and difference to the knowledge system. This is the basic principle that diversity, plurality, and difference prevail over all specific analyses.

It is believed that knowledge was first developed by ordinary people. Since the number of ordinary people is extremely large, and they compute in parallel in their respective positions, they must have produced an extremely rich and complex knowledge. This richness must be beyond our imagination today. This is because a large number of thoughts must have gone unrecorded, or have lost their records so that we still don't know they have ever existed. Even today, the loss of knowledge must be occurring commonly.

The specialization of knowledge development must be slightly later than the generation of knowledge, but it would not have been delayed for too long, because specialization is not difficult, it can exist in the forms of witchcraft and others, it can be large or small, and it did not have to wait for the establishment of the institutions for modern knowledge development. Professionals make a living from the development, management, and application of *certain types* of expertise. This is because their brainwork, like manual labor, is also a physical and substantial work, hence, the value of their work can be recognized by ordinary people, and in turn, they can form a relationship with ordinary people in terms of division of labor and trade. The emphasis on the phrase "certain types" here is due to the heterogeneity of knowledge. Not all knowledge is suitable for specialization. Some knowledge, even if it would be specialized later, was not necessarily at the time. Specialization is conditional. Even if it is not convenient for us to enumerate these conditions at this moment, we can still deduce one or two of them. For example, specialized knowledge must be uneasy to learn, otherwise, it would spread to common people before its specialization. The application of specialized knowledge shall also entail a considerable amount of work, otherwise, these specialists would not be able to work full-time, but part-time, etc. In conclusion, this problem is very much an economic one.

Over time, there will be more and more areas of specialization. The increase in the productivity of society would accommodate more and more financial support of intellectuals, whose work will further promote the increase of the productivity. This creates a virtuous circle. Nonetheless, there is generally no complete separation between intellectuals and ordinary people. It is common for each person to engage in both mental activity and physical activity, but the natures and proportions of their work vary from person to person. Moreover, activities of ordinary people specialize to varying degrees and in different ways, and both their mental and physical activities can be specialized. Some also develop specialized skills that combine the two (typical examples include journeymen and athletes). These truths seem to be commonplace. Now, however, they are only theoretical in the Algorithmic framework, and hence can be articulated clearly and thoroughly. In particular, we would like to emphasize how diversity and heterogeneity have logically and naturally shaped the society before us, and the actual states of the knowledge system before us, or, in other words, the various "irregularities" in front of our eyes. Once these irregularities are clearly and Algorithmically sorted out, they are actually to become "regular" and orderly again. Furthermore, after the discovery of these regularities of real society and real objects, we can also realize that the original idealized and rationalist "models" are in turn "irregular", irrational, and kind of distortive.

Regarding the types of knowledge, first of all, all human knowledge in the Algorithmic sense is regarded as "knowledge", and then knowledge is to be classified. All the results of thinking are called "knowledge", not only because of the convenience of wording, but also because they must have had certain reasons or usages to be produced. Even if some thinking results cannot be clarified as to where to be used for the time being, the person concerned may still cherish it and retain it for some reason. This can be a normal occurrence in dynamic computations. In particular, many computing results have been stored and even passed down from generation to generation; no matter what we as posterity would say about them today, they must have been justified and valued in the eyes of their real users. This method of treating the choices or decisions of real actors generally as the results of optimization, and then as an argument, can now be called the *"equilibrium argument"* (similar to what Leibniz called "preestablished harmony"[1]). In traditional mainstream scholarship, equilibrium argumentation is a necessity, even the only one. This approach to the equilibrium argument has actually eliminated its value. Now, its value as a *relatively useful argumentation strategy* with *limited significance* will only be properly highlighted in an environment that acknowledges the existence of the mixture of equilibria and disequilibria.

According to the above ideas, knowledge can first be divided into two categories: book knowledge and practical knowledge. The former is collated and summarized by specialized personnel, written in books, and then stored and disseminated. The latter is not written in the book, but only in the brains of actors, and a part of it is used only for their own lives and destroyed with their deaths, while another part is only used for word of mouth. Practical knowledge can inevitably be lost, but there are parts of it that would persist tenaciously. The examples include the ways of life of some families, the characters of the people in some regions, the cooking methods of private dishes, and so on. The tenacious existence of this

---

1. See Section 4.4 in Look, Brandon C., "Gottfried Wilhelm Leibniz", The Stanford Encyclopedia of Philosophy (Spring 2020 Edition), Edward N. Zalta (ed.), URL = <https://plato.stanford.edu/archives/spr2020/entries/leibniz/>.

knowledge is a testament to their importance. Sometimes, we refer to this knowledge as "common sense" in general, but it is not accurate enough. Only the relatively general part of this knowledge is suitable to be called "common sense", and the rest of the knowledge may be more unique and complex than some of the book knowledge.

The importance of book knowledge is, of course, to intellectuals. However, the overemphasis on it can lead to a disdain for practical knowledge, which in turn may lead to social discontent against intellectuals. To use a common saying: only when it is put in its proper place is it truly cherished.

The outstanding feature of book knowledge is that it is suitable for specialization and is suitable for printing on books. That said, it doesn't have to always be the most important knowledge. Intellectuals are generally dissatisfied that their actual status in society has not reached the "deserved" height, but in fact it is because they have not yet understood this truth. Some important knowledge is not booked because it is too fragmented in form to be collated and hence is not in line with the requirements of systematization and scale of book knowledge. The next example is that some knowledge (e.g., deception, pornography, etc.) has moral or customary taboos, and it is not appropriate to be booked. The third example is that some knowledge is time-sensitive or special and does not have time to be booked, or has little value for dissemination, although it may be very important to the people concerned.

Another characteristic of book knowledge is that it is a part of all existing knowledge, which leads to the fact that the mere combination of all book knowledge, even if this can be done, is not enough to form a *comprehensive* guide for actors. That is, it lacks what we call "factor completeness". The average level of this aggregate in depth of thought may exceed that of practical knowledge, but it is flawed in the breadth of coverage. Therefore, it may not provide a complete answer to any practical question. If some parts of it have a tendency to exaggerate themselves, they might hide their weaknesses and mislead their readers. This is one of the reasons why practitioners are often somewhat dissatisfied with book knowledge.

However, book knowledge is also diversified and characteristic, including science, technology, literature, art, mythology, religion, and many more. It is not appropriate to list its specific classifications here because they are too common (for example, see the catalog of a library). However, according to the above logic, another inevitable conclusion is that different pieces of book knowledge are not necessarily compatible with each other, and each must have some independence to a greater or lesser extent.

## §132. The Birth of Science (1)

We live in an era when most people have been educated in science and humanities, so they take it for granted. Therefore, one of the themes and pursuits of modern philosophy was to start from science and go back to its roots, that is, the question of the nature and status of other knowledge (including the so-called "irrationalities"). This is obviously because scholars who had been over-trained by science were somewhat unfamiliar with other types of knowledge bases that are broader in scope. This root-seeking process is the opposite of the process that produced science back then.

As mentioned above, we can argue that in the pre-scientific era, various kinds and various levels of knowledge were mixed, and this mixture then produced differences and comparisons, prompting people to *sift* through knowledge. It can be assured that the sifting of knowledge is by no means a phased or temporary phenomenon, but exists at any time from the first moment of computation. People select and preserve knowledge of higher quality or value, and eliminate knowledge of lower quality or value. Over time, the persons concerned would ask: how can knowledge of higher quality or value be discovered, identified, or developed? This is a Socratic question. Socrates is famous for advocating and exhorting people to discern knowledge and pursue high-quality knowledge. This can be seen as the beginning of rationalism. Nonetheless, there can be no doubt that this question and such a proposition must have existed before Socrates, but in Greece in the time of Socrates and after, it became a large-scale and remarkable social current, attracting attentions of common people.

Rationalists rightly believed that *there were differences in quality or value between different pieces of knowledge, and therefore they needed to be carefully identified and discriminately treated. This can be seen as the rudimentary form of scientific thought.* This is what I want to emphasize. The core feature of science (or something similar; in the time of Socrates, the name was "knowledge") lies not so much in its methodology or other aspects, but in its *relative position* in the whole body of human knowledge. "Science" is the name given to the most reliable or valuable knowledge people have. With the uneven quality of the knowledge system, there is a need to distinguish in between, and thus there is a need to define certain high-quality knowledge, and then there is the emergence of the *knowledge subsystems* such as "science".

This characteristic of science determines that the scope and scale of scientific knowledge are necessarily limited. This limitation refers not only to the limited knowledge available in any era relative to the infinite potential for knowledge development, but also to the fact that scientific knowledge must only account for a small proportion of the total amount of knowledge available in its time, and by no means the whole of it. In terms of domain of discourse, it is only one type of discourse among the many discourses involved in human knowledge, that is, the cognitive (rather than practical or action-oriented) knowledge. In terms of level of development, it refers to high-value knowledge and generally excludes common sense knowledge. This is not to say that the relatively reliable knowledge in common sense cannot be used as the content of science in principle, but that since science is a product developed by scientists and used to improve society and hence bring exchange benefits to scientists, only when it is different from common sense can it be recognized by ordinary people or other groups of people, so that scientists can obtain the exchange benefits. This requirement further narrows the scope of science. Scientists define common sense as science, which doesn't make much sense. The concept of "science" can only be meaningful when scientists popularize the unique knowledge they have deliberately developed as "scientific knowledge".

The "exchange" mentioned above is a general term. Scientists exchange scientific knowledge as a product for society, gaining benefits such as money, reputation, and social status. But this exchange usually does not take place like an ordinary commodity exchange, but rather in a tortuous way, such as in return for research resources, faculty positions, awards, etc. To do this, the research results must be novel and not repetitive. This possibility is guaranteed by the limitless potential for knowledge development. Therefore, without an Algorithmic framework, the generation of science will not make sense, and science will become "a tree without its root". Second, the results of relevant research must be received, understood, and ultimately accepted by society, otherwise, the exchange cannot be realized, and science cannot be disseminated to the world for the benefit of the people.

The interesting thing here is that the research results are made by people who understand them, but they have to be tested by people who don't know them. What should be done next? There are at least two ways; one is to make the research results a *marginal development* of existing knowledge. To do this, the person submitting the results must explain how the results develop existing knowledge. Readers try to make sense of new knowledge based on what they already know. This process is actually kind of similar to the common learning process. Nonetheless, if the gap between new knowledge and old knowledge is *too large*, it will be more difficult to understand and accept new knowledge. There is also another process in between, which is logic testing. The readers can review the author's reasoning steps in the publication. If they don't find a mistake, they tend to accept the new one. However, as mentioned earlier, no logical operations can be considered perfect, so the absence of an error in reasoning temporarily does not lead to 100% acceptance of the new results. Another way is empirical testing, that is, to test whether the new results are consistent with the facts. Since the purpose of a research result is often to explain facts, empirical testing is an inevitable and logically natural testing method, rather than a new method that is fundamentally different from logical testing. The results of well-designed experiments, such as Galileo's two-ball experiment on the Leaning Tower of Pisa, are often enough to silence critics. However, there are often multiple interpretations for the results of most experiments. This is because many different factors and their different combinations can all cause an equal outcome. The infiniteness of factors leads to the fact that even if readers tentatively agree to accept or reject a new discovery, this consensus may be overturned at some point in the future. From an objective point of view, the examination and evaluation of any research results is, in principle, endless.

This means that the process of evaluating scientific knowledge is, to a certain extent, a compelling or subjective process. The inability of evaluators to dismiss a particular research result often leads them to accept it (at least temporarily), just like students have to accept the contents in a textbook temporarily. The degree to which the research results match the subjective experiences of the reviewers may significantly affect their evaluation. As a counter-example, it is also possible that a reviewer may, for some reason, become very supportive of the research he/she reads, or even more than the author. This is because the author may have been tentative in making the hypotheses and results since he/she could not deny them. In extreme cases, a researcher may have abandoned his or her original conclusion, but that conclusion is accepted and persisted by other readers until it is commonly accepted one day. This possibility is logically present.

In order to be compelling, methods and arguments are key. Relatively rigorous reasoning, rigorous methodology, and strong evidence are all useful for convincing a group or sub-group of scientists. A sub-group sometimes contains not numerous scholars, so it is not very difficult to convince them. Even results with obvious flaws are sometimes accepted. Even if the main conclusion is later proved to be wrong, it is possible to obtain a certain positive evaluation because of the contributions of its other elements. The advantages and disadvantages of specific knowledge are innumerable, and how can they be judged together?! A mediocre paper may be accepted by a scientific journal for one reason, and it may be that it deals with a topic that the reviewers are concerned about, and this paper just develops *on the basis of existing results*. The author only did an ordinary job like an ordinary person— Of course, ordinary work itself does require logic and evidence as well. In any respect, the scientific work may not be entirely unique, and therefore, *scientific standards, if any, are likely to be pluralistic, technical, or flexible.*[2] Everyone has a sky of their own

---

2. This is what Feyerabend called "anything goes" to the extreme. See Paul Feyerabend, "Against Method", London: Verso, 1984, pp. 23-28.

above their heads. It is only in this sense that science is unique. It's just as common sense is unique.

## §133. The Birth of Science (2)

Since there are only technical, detailed differences between science and other knowledge, which of the differences should be discussed here? In particular, it is necessary to discuss the conservative strategy of scientific research, and why this strategy produces radical and revolutionary results.

This topic is closely linked to the factor completeness and the forced closure of computations. As has been repeatedly stated above, in view of the urgency of decision-making, ordinary actors must forcibly close computations from time to time to reach a decision. For this reason, even those questions involved in computations that are difficult to satisfactorily answer must be answered riskily, even shoddily. Scientists, by contrast, belong to the "leisure class" or are interested in working on less pressing issues in addition to their daily tasks. There is no clear time limit for the study of these questions, and it is not important whether the answers can be reached at the moment. Or, they deliberately pick out less pressing questions to study. These issues are often considered "foundational" and of universal significance. Of course, it is also possible that these problems come from big, urgent, and practical problems that cannot be solved for a while, and the scientists have made long-term research plans and determined to overcome them while tolerating current expedient measures.

Since there is no explicit or urgent time requirement for scientific research, it is, of course, necessary to pursue knowledge that is *as reliable as possible*. Conversely, if scientific research has been intended from the outset to pursue reliable knowledge, there should be no explicit or urgent time frame. Otherwise, if a clear or urgent time frame has been set, it is unlikely that reliable knowledge would be obtained under the conditions of limited computing power. You can only choose one or the other.

Then, among the many achievements of knowledge, how to pursue or identify reliable knowledge? To this difficult and divergent question that many philosophers have asked, the Algorithmic answer can be very simple, that is, before people become scientists, in the process of evaluating and selecting the results of daily thinking, they have already acquired some methods to pursue or identify reliable knowledge. The training in scientific research has enabled them to acquire more skills. For example, deductive reasoning is used more than other unreliable reasoning, reliance is placed on facts as much as possible, universality is prioritized (with relative neglect of particularity), certainty is prioritized and then used to expand the results, and so on. They apply a combination of these methods and techniques to select *relatively reliable* knowledge. In other words, this task is actually simpler than commonly considered. They just pursue to discover or conceive knowledge that is *more* reliable or of *higher* quality than the knowledge of ordinary people, which shall be enough for their work to be accepted as "science". As for what "absolutely correct" knowledge is, they don't have to care. Moreover, the standards for ideal knowledge are not completely and objectively given in advance; instead, that relatively correct knowledge will endogenously cultivate the standards for judging knowledge. These standards, as knowledge as well, are also subjective, relativistic, and developmental. This leads to the possibility that the actors involved in the historical process would be very satisfied with certain scientific achievements, without knowing that those achievements are actually only relative and historical.

This is not to say that scientists' motivations and attitudes are necessarily unserious. In fact, scientists usually adhere to the highest standards of their work, adopt the most prudent attitude, and gather the most sufficient evidence to conceive, discover, evaluate, and select scientific knowledge. If they are not satisfied with the results of research, they will not draw a conclusion, and they might rather continue to explore for many years and fail again and again. Even if they don't get valuable results for a long time, they won't lower their standards and perfunctorily do things. This is the *research strategy of conservatism*.

But there is also a radical side to this strategy. Not to draw conclusions means not to have a satisfactory conclusion, but to be dissatisfied with the current findings, and to continue to explore while recognizing and believing the potential for knowledge development. Therefore, this method minimizes the time spent on shoddy work, and allows a scientist to get closer to the most valuable clues and answers as quickly as possible (although it does not help practitioners make practical decisions at the moment). The less bending happens, the more energy can be used to "straighten it out" in those "undug fields". Henceforth, scientific research has, from time to time, produced major and radical discoveries that have shaken human society. It can be said that scientific research has now become the main way for the development of new knowledge in the evolutionary human society. Knowledge in the field of practice is also summarized to a certain extent and is reflected in textbooks and in the activities of higher education institutions. Therefore, intellectuals have become the main force to develop knowledge and push society forward.

We can compare the radicality of scientific research with the radicality of common sense. The radicality of common sense lies in the bold use of alternative Algorithms and the swiftness of conclusions, while the radicality of scientific research lies in sticking to the mainstream Algorithms, regardless of how far away the conclusions are or how many roads to take. The conclusions drawn by ordinary people, while precisely in line with the needs of action, are often the manifestation of nearsightedness. Such conclusions are often not worth preserving, and the methods used are of little value. From a long-term and macro perspective, they are highly repetitive and circular, and less progressive. However, the conclusions of scientific research, even if flawed, are often well documented and hence valuable in their own right, given that they can be used as future references. Since scientific discoveries are not primarily driven by pressing real-world problems, they often do not *immediately* bring practical benefits to real society. However, over time, its practical value would become apparent. Of course, there is also a significant proportion of research results that, although scientifically or academically recognized, have so far failed to produce obvious practical value.

This perspective is only relative. The long-term horizons of scientists are not unlimited. Sooner or later, more or less, scientists will also have to close and summarize their computations. Scientific questions can go unanswered, but scientists have their limited careers and lifespans, and they cannot always remain silent. Even if there are no important findings, there are usually minor findings, or there are lessons to be learned, and improvements in data and methods. The length of a paper is always limited, and the author must say something before he/she stops writing. Moreover, scientists can also make associations and hypotheses. In the absence of a conclusion, a number of hypotheses can be put forward tentatively or prospectively. The scientists can explicitly state that they are just radical hypotheses, only intended to be the objects of further investigation and selection. This approach is particularly similar to that of ordinary actors. That is to say, scientists are sometimes eager, too, although their concentration and patience are often higher than those of ordinary people. This is likened to the relationship between one hundred steps and fifty steps.

## §134. The Birth of Science (3)

Starting with original materials or problems, scientists use relatively conservative or prudent methods, plus the distortive processing that is necessary but deviously longer than that to common sense, to form the systematic knowledge system that is named "science". Such a system (or its subsystems) is large enough for learners to break away from their daily lives and study for a long time before they can master it. There are materials, theories, and hypotheses within it, and there are relatively reliable parts, as well as problems and controversies. Therefore, science is not monolithic; it is also a mixture. However, as a system, the various elements that compose it are *more closely* related to each other, and their closeness often exceeds their connection with external elements. Such a system has developed from history, thus, it has relatively fixed documentary traditions and even relatively fixed personal connections. Such people, things, and events form a community with relatively clear boundaries with the outside world and other groups of people. Such boundaries are either topical, qualitative, methodological, or merely traditionally documentary, and so on—as long as they are identifiable. For these reasons, scientific knowledge is also constantly evolving and updated. What usually happens are small updates within a larger framework (or "paradigm"). When small updates accumulate to a certain extent, the basic framework or paradigm itself will also be updated; namely, the "scientific revolution" will happen.[3]

After the discourse on science is over, we need to turn to

--------

3. Thomas. S. Kuhn, "The Structure of Scientific Revolutions", Chicago:

other types of knowledge again. This is because, since science is so worthy of discussion, and science is only one type of knowledge, there is no reason to just talk about science.

The difference between technology and science lies mainly in the different questions they answer. Science is about answering questions like "what" and "why", while technology focuses on "how". Bounded rationality, or finite computing power, leads to the relative independences of the two. The tentacles of science are not stretched long enough to reach the practical problems to be solved; this is one way we understand their independences. Therefore, although scientific knowledge needs to be used in technology and engineering, it cannot be relied on alone. Common sense must have played an important role in them. In addition, the irregularity of the knowledge system makes it impossible for technologists and engineers to selectively use the stocked knowledge to solve their practical problems. Often, technical experts are forced to conduct some specialized research on specific practical problems. The results of these studies are attached to the technical field, but there may also be some links to science. This effect exacerbates the fragmentation of scientific knowledge and enhances its interpenetration with technical knowledge.

The kinship between technology and science is less obvious when it comes to morality. However, morality is similar to technology in that they are all about "how". It's just that morality answers the question of how interpersonal relationships are handled, while technology often focuses on relationships between people and things. Moreover, a distinguishing feature of morality is that it is fragmented, functional, and regular. This means that it only relates to some links or aspects of an action, regardless of how this whole

---

University of Chicago Press, 1996, and Imre Lakatos, "The Methodology of Scientific Research Programmes", Cambridge University Press, 1989.

action unfolds. For example, it emphasizes only that "people should be honest" to constrain specific actions, regardless of how a specific action can be done from beginning to end. Technology, especially an engineering project, must guide the action *throughout the process*. Nevertheless, moral knowledge, as the knowledge that guides the society to run healthily, is the result of summarizing and refining human knowledge from generation to generation, and it is quite reliable and precious. It is valued like science. As relatively high-quality or high-value knowledge, they are all collected and compiled into books, taught and passed on historically. From this perspective, we can see the connection between them, although there seems to be a lack of direct logical connection between the scientific "truth" and the ethical "goodness". Therefore, in Chinese culture, intellectuals have always been required not only to be the inheritors of knowledge, but also to be moral models.

These discussions lead us to the establishment of a *total knowledge system*. This task, at least with Aristotle, had become an explicit and concrete endeavor, but it was clearly impossible to accomplish in ancient Greece until plurality was effectively introduced into the core of philosophy. It could not be done without the help of a set of principles articulated from Algorithmic Theory. Now, the basic idea is quite clear. The faces and personalities of each basic discipline have come to life in the Algorithmic vision. Even writers and novelists have their clear roles to play here. The division of knowledge, based on the Algorithmic principles, can now, first of all, allow each discipline to define its own role according to its own definitions. As for the division itself, intellectuals of the past and today have their own understandings, and the correct or valuable understandings have been soaked in the existing literature, and now they only need to be Algorithmically sorted out and marginally revamped.

Such a "total knowledge system" can be used to explain why

there is such a wide variety of departmental disciplines in universities that are still actively being adjusted and expanded. The more knowledge develops, will the division of developmental work become more and more detailed? Will there be more and more departments? Questions like these are important and worth exploring. The "total knowledge system" can also be used to coordinate the relations between scholars in different fields, to avoid those wasteful mutual attacks, and to promote the intellectual development of individuals. Once a person understands the principle of knowledge division and has certain insight into the genealogy of the human knowledge system, one can deliberately, transdisciplinarily, and interactionally develop one's knowledge system to better adapt to one's career and life goals. To a certain extent, this can cure the current ills of intellectual fragmentation and narrowness. The exchange and integration between disciplines may lead to the adjustment and reconstruction of the disciplinary category system, and improve the operational efficiency of the whole chain of development, teaching, dissemination, and application of knowledge. In my opinion, this kind of knowledge system is especially suitable for guiding new students who have just entered colleges, so that they can start to design their own long-term study and research plans early.


## §135. Some Methodological Issues (1)

The Algorithmic ontology has provided a great deal of discussion about methods, but these discussions are mostly about ordinary people and practitioners. As mentioned earlier, scientists do not necessarily have to adopt any unique approach to building scientific knowledge that is distinct from common sense and other knowledge. But, conversely, the adoption of *relatively special* and distinctive methods, or the relatively intensive use of some methods while avoiding others, is also one of the pathways to building scientific knowledge. This pathway is not only for scientists to choose, but also for scholars or intellectuals "other than scientists". Because, with the Algorithmic system of knowledge, we are faced with a new task not only to establish a scientific methodology, but also to establish a methodology for all kinds of intellectuals—a general or special methodology. The overall goal of such a methodology is to explore how to help intellectuals build a kind of knowledge that is different from other kinds of knowledge. Such a methodology would be a combination of existing methodologies and Algorithmic methodologies. Because of this comprehensive or unifying effect, our discourse will be synthetic, outlined, concise, and illustrative. The Algorithmic principles are transparent enough to discourage us from repetitive discourse, and the subject matter of this book does not allow us to dwell too much on specific problems.

Readers may have sensed sort of weirdness that the words "other than scientists" above are in quotation marks. For example, according to the tradition or convention, historiography is not a "science" or a "social science", but does this mean that historiography is "unscientific"? Can a historical researcher talk nonsense like a romance novelist? Doesn't historical research require precise material evidence like scientific research? In particular, under the Algorithmic framework, since the theoreticality of historiography is bound to be enhanced, and its scientificity will also be enhanced, can historiography be correspondingly called "historical science"? Or, what will be the differences between the terms "historical science" and "historiography"? In fact, there is clearly a uniform academic method and standard among the various disciplines included in a comprehensive university, and scholars in various fields usually agree and comply with this without hesitation. However, if we agree to this uniformity, it becomes increasingly unclear what "science" means as a subcategory (the traditional narrower definition of "science" is clearly inapplicable). This difficulty is now exacerbated by Algorithmic Theory. Of course, this is a pleasant annoyance, as it means that Algorithmic Theory brings more uniformity.

As pointed out earlier, intellectuals need to strategically select topics to develop book-based knowledge. "Methodology" does not refer only to the "methods" in a narrow sense, and of course includes such topic selection strategies. For example, to choose a topic that is persistent, general, or certain for research. This seems to be the traditional "scientific" pursuit. In the case of the poverty of scientific knowledge, that is, in the initial stage of science, this pursuit should be justified, because the knowledge of the highest economy, namely, the highest value, should be among the priority pursuits. Those universal laws revealed by the natural sciences must have exerted a magical attraction among intellectuals: if such miraculous knowledge is not worth pursuing, what is there to pursue again? If such knowledge is not to be explored by scientists, then by whom? Obviously, even if such knowledge is not the ultimate truth in the final analysis, it should be a priority, at least. The pursuit of the most certain knowledge that can be pursued must be a preferred strategy of scientists, and even one of their missions.

However, the above strategy, understood from the perspective of Algorithmic economics, also leads to its relativity. That is, when the desired permanence, generality, or certainty cannot be obtained (at least temporarily), then comes the matter of second best. In other words, we have to include and tolerate temporality, particularity, and uncertainty. Second, such inclusion and expansion should be done according to the rankings in terms of the cost-benefit profiles of relevant research activities. That is, the one with the highest "net benefit" shall be studied first, and then the second, and so on. It can be found that the real research activities in many disciplines do indeed fit this assumption.

However, this is only the case for some disciplines. There are other disciplines that do the opposite. For example, apart from the example of historiography, biology began with the detailed recording and collation of animal and plant data, and gradually developed into a certain degree of theoreticality. The establishment of this order of study can be understood that a general extraction had been difficult from the outset in areas like this, and that some objects of study are rare (e.g., rare species) or fleeting (e.g., historical figures and events) and are therefore of great value for the documentation of the source materials. Second, generality, even if it exists, is considered local, whereas research work is aimed at the whole object that should be explained not only in terms of generality, but also in terms of particularity; hence, the explanation of the whole object is the ultimate goal of research work. Another consideration is that exceptional or extreme cases may be significant, and this significance does not contradict the pursuit of generality or universality. On the contrary, researchers recognize that certain hidden regularities manifest themselves in the exceptional or extreme circumstances, which have been usually difficult to observe, and only then can they be caught, and hence be identified as the generality or universality.

This discussion of research priorities is highly Algorithmical, because it is only from an Algorithmical perspective that there are questions of how to use and allocate limited resources, and what to seize and what to ignore. Obviously, our questions and answers are much more comprehensive and rational than Mach's discussions under the mere concept of "economy of thought". Of course, these brief expositions are not enough to satisfactorily answer any specific question, and the main objective is just to present some basic ideas and points. The philosophy of science to date has been fragmented. In my opinion, this is because the basic nature of science has not been explained convincingly before. Now,

Algorithmic Theory answers these fundamental questions in an outline. After these fundamental questions have been clarified, there is reason to try to establish a more systematic philosophy of science. Although this book cannot directly undertake this work, it is going to put forward some clues in this regard.

## §136. Some Methodological Issues (2)

One of the fundamental problems before scientists is the question of the relationship between theory and empirical materials. With the basic framework of "Instructions + information", the answer to this question is actually a matter of course. However, theory is not the result of the Instructional system *operating alone*. The latter can refer to things like logic, mathematics, etc. They use extremely *rare* (not zero) empirical materials (e.g., abstract symbols) and operate as if a new machine self-checks, drills, or rehearses before it goes into real productions. The so-called "scientific theories" actually contain rich empirical factors, while certain theories are the results of the theorists' use of the Instructional system and other knowledge to process the corresponding empirical materials. For example, the basic concepts (e.g., "force") and problems in Newton's theory of mechanics cannot be understood until one has experienced living in the physical world for a long time, let alone the theory itself.

Traditionally, we often understand theory as something close to perfection, and understand the diversity of the real world and the particularity of concrete objects as an interference or destruction of the theoretical perfection. However, something perfect should provide answers in a comprehensive and exhaustive way without requiring people to do anything else. Therefore, this method of combining universal theories with concrete materials is itself a manifestation of the limitations of reason. Now, Algorithmic Theory can help us to establish a new understanding, that is, a theory often embodies an understanding of some aspects of an object. In particular, when the theory adopts the method of "formula + parameters (or independent variables)", it shows that the theory only expresses the local regularity in the properties or changes of the object thing, and the theory has little to do with the remaining parts. That is, the theory is incomplete. It is precisely because of this defect that the application of the theory needs to collect some raw information (e.g., parameters). Audiences who have mastered such a theory have to live in this mixed state of "half-understanding".

From this point of view, it is easy to understand the proposition "people are always applying some theories when they observe the world": this is because people, in the course of time, are *using some semi-finished products to process other materials or other semi-finished products*. When people consciously or unconsciously use a theoretical framework to look at some emerging source materials, it is often the case that either the theory is implicit or the empirical elements of the theory are implicit. The reason for the implicitness of theory is that it is a foundational framework, stuck in short-term memory, and applied repeatedly and frequently to a series of operations. It is often only through a deliberate process of self-objectification that the person concerned discovers it. The empirical elements underlying a theory generally derive from its abstraction, i.e., the concepts contained in it refer to a large number of objects, rather than a single object, and are formed by the person concerned at an early stage of his or her life, or received through an earlier educational process. In the face of new source materials, one has to use certain theories or conceptual frameworks, and the reason for this must be understood: without them, the understanding and grasp of the object will not become easier, but will become more difficult. If the knower rejects theories altogether, he/she will have only the Instructional system to rely on; and, in principle, he/she will have to go back to the first day of human history, begin to re-understand the world, and then progressively concretize the knowledge of the present object within an interrelated framework. Such a path does not necessarily completely replicate the existing theories and knowledge, and may generate new knowledge, but in any case, the time and resources required for the re-computations would not be affordable.

In passing, we can discuss the empiricist view that science is strictly produced from actual materials. This view, despite its well-known flaws, is still prevalent in real contexts, thus, its advantages and disadvantages still need to be clarified. The difficulty of extracting theories from empirical materials to discover is that it is often a combinatorial explosion problem. Hypotheses need to be generated and tested one by one. Leaving aside the creation of hypotheses, even in order to test a hypothesis, it is necessary to assume that other conditions remain unchanged, or it is inevitable that some other hypotheses must be additionally made at the same time. After the previous test is completed, the parameters are changed for the next test, or the other assumptions are to be tested one by one. The latter work will in turn trigger more hypotheses and tests. Such a rapid expansion would make it impossible for the entire task to be rigorously completed to a desired standard. So, what to do? One way to conceive of this is to invoke axioms and common sense to get the audience to agree that some (indeed, massive) tests can be waived, and that the tests should be focused only on a few so-called "core" issues of concern. Once these core tests have passed, the corresponding findings can be declared "tested". In this way, it supports again the idea that people always apply theories when they observe the world. Second, because such empirical research emphasizes empirical testing, it reveals the following meaning: if it is not empirically valid, it refuses to accept the research results. It considers empirical testing (or specific empirical testing) as a necessary condition for scientific results, otherwise, it is considered to be unfounded. Therefore, in fact, this is the conservatism discussed above: Avoid actively proposing hypotheses as much as possible, preferring to *be passively driven by experience.*

In between, it can be called "positivism". Positivism is a tailor-made tool for *impatient* intellectuals who believe that reliable knowledge can be confirmed either by logical or empirical tests, and that logic is consistent with experience. It reassures scientists that they only need to stay within these two areas. Then, a dissertation can be divided into the analytical part and the evidentiary part, and the two seem to patch together a "complete" research work. However, the question from factor completeness is: Aren't there other questions related to this dissertation? For example, does the researcher need to have a certain attitude towards metaphysical or life problems? If a scientist does not have a healthy attitude towards life, will he/she actively and steadily engage in scientific research? These psychological, philosophical, and religious questions that were excluded by positivists may not be directly related to usual natural science problems, but are indirectly connected with them through the scientists themselves in person. In order to improve the efficiency of their research, it is a wise strategy for scholars to narrow down the scope to pursue the most reliable knowledge, but it is wrong in principle to deny the significance of other types of knowledge and methods. Moreover, empirical testing does not tell everything, and the scope, intensity, and meaning of empirical testing are limited, thus, its results cannot be superstitious. Being excessively confined to empirical tests can easily make research work superficial, mechanized, and trivial, and even become short-sighted and formalistic. It hinders the development of people's critical thinking and imagination.

Scientific research, as well as any mental activity, requires ingenious theoretical ideas. Theoretical conception entails the abstraction of a finite number of elements, and then the various arrangements, computations, and deductions are repeatedly carried out in the mind of the thinker. This often involves a simulative process. Since the human brain is often easier and cheaper to manipulate data than the real object itself, theorists are often diligent in thinking, and their clever ideas can replace and surpass a lot of inefficient empirical research. When the scope of thinking expands, deepens, and complexes, the thinker often resorts to tools such as computers. However, any consciously constructed analytical system is limited in the elements it can include. In contrast, only the richness of real objects is unlimited. Thus, there is a threshold between theoretical analysis and experiment or experiences, beyond which theoretical analysis is no longer economical or effective, and at this point, it gives way to empiricism. Through practical activities, a number of controllable parameters in the real object are set to the required initial values, and then the real object is allowed to "operate" on its own, allowing the infinite abundance of factors to interact with each other, and then the results of the actual operations can be observed.

The above process is the reverse of the previous process from experience to theory, and they are collectively called *"theory-experience shift"*. Algorithmic Theory can be used to explain and account for this shift, and often the "shuttle shifts". After the shift(s), the authenticity of the object guarantees in principle the practicality of the verified theory. However, since the factors contained in the object are infinite, and the operational results may be caused by other factors unknown to the researcher, this arouses new risks. Therefore, there is no perfect thing in the world, and the dilemma faced by the actors of bounded rationality cannot be fundamentally avoided by the researchers of bounded rationality, either.

## §137. Some Methodological Issues (3)

Theory and raw information are the two extreme forms of knowledge. In between, there are bound to be a large number of different types of knowledge, which may contain both a certain amount of information and certain parts of theories, and a large number of immature contents as well as a large number of problems. These can all be broadly regarded as some types of "knowledge". This hybridity is a basic inference that can be made by Algorithmic "thinking chemistry". In fact, this is also the case. As a result, the textbooks we see are usually thick and large, containing not only theories and raw data, but also rich contents in between. For this mixture, there are many positive words in literature such as "mellow", "fleshy", "full-fledged" to describe it. On the contrary, if a discourse only includes simple propositions, claims, and the like, the readers or audience may say that it is "dry", "insipid", "stuffless", etc., to express their discontent. This hybridity may come from the computational processuality or not, and hence may serve a transitional process or not. Not necessarily all knowledge will eventually transition to some kind of minimalist forms, and a state of equilibrium that exists locally is not necessarily a minimalist state. Moreover, the infiniteness of knowledge development implies that the total amount of knowledge may increase even for a given static object without the input of new raw information—because the amount of knowledge can be increased by increasing the depth of computations, i.e., by repeatedly objectifying computational results.

Again, there is a need to directly discuss the methodology. A general point of view is that, in principle, it is impossible for researchers not to use the methods used by ordinary actors, and there is no need to deliberately circumvent certain methods. Because, even if all the methods are used, it is impossible to solve problems perfectly and completely. Any method can be seen as "biased" and characteristic in a certain sense. Formalization, for example, is a method that makes computations clear and precise, so that they are easy to manipulate, easy to record, and easy to compare interpersonally or intertemporally. In modern times, this method has been mainly promoted and used by intellectuals, but it must not be said that it was invented by intellectuals, because the ancient methods such as knotted-rope counting or written language can also be regarded as "formalized" methods. But that doesn't mean that intellectuals don't have the power or ability to invent new methods. Since intellectuals and ordinary actors are equal, it is impossible for all methods to come only from ordinary people, not from intellectuals. An electronic computer, for example, is an intellectual invention— if we consider that computer simulation can now exist as a relatively independent "method".

Below, we continue with two traditional methodological issues and then move on to the discussion of computer simulative methods.

One of the issues is the falsification method. One might think that falsification is an invention of intellectuals, but this is not the case. For example, we sometimes ask others, "You say that this person is a good person, and that person is a good person, but who on earth is a bad person? Is there a bad person in your eyes?" This is the falsification method, namely, emphasizing that a proposition should objectively have the possibility of being denied, otherwise, it may not be meaningful. Such cases include the fact that a referred object is concrete or partial, and not everything, or that a nature or action of the object is specific and partially existent, thereby allowing others to exist beside it, and so on. In short, it can be argued that falsifiability is related to finiteness, and therefore, it is compatible with the atomic and chemical Algorithmic theory. However, the reality is that sometimes we can prove a proposition easily that, however, is not easily falsified, and sometimes on the contrary, it is easy to falsify but not easy to affirm. Why? This is obviously because our knowledge is limited, and we don't see the whole picture of the world and the whole picture of knowledge, so we can't simply use the method of elimination. If we know the totality, we can subtract one part from the total to get another part, or subtract another part to get this part. This "either/or" relationship requires knowing the totality. Related to falsifiability is symmetry, which also requires knowing the totality. People who like symmetry always take it for granted that the general state of the world is logically symmetrical. This understanding is a manifestation of perfect rationality—the states of the world always correspond to logical relations; then, if we know a situation on one side of the logic, we can infer its other side. However, in the framework of bounded rationality, there is still a fog ahead of what you grasp, and you do not know whether there is another pole in front of you, nor how many other irregularities exist between the two poles. It's no wonder that some logicians reject the law of the exclusion middle[4]—because you don't know if or not the base your proposition is on is itself appropriate, so you can't simply and directly infer its opposite.

Another issue is the so-called "neutrality". Hume emphasized the distinction between factual and moral judgments, or between objectivity and subjectivity.[5] This distinction was re-interpreted (or misunderstood) by later scholars as "Hume's lever knife", and further believed that for

---

4. Łukasiewicz, Jan (1970). "Selected Works". Amsterdam: North-Holland; Warszawa: Polish Scientific Publishers, pp. 35, 114-126, 331-332.
5. David Hume, "A Treatise of Human Nature", Oxford: Oxford University Press, 1960, p. 469-470.

scientists, it is enough to work in the former field. This view is dominant in academic circles and has far-reaching implications. Nowadays, it has developed into a rigid dogma. Algorithmic Theory is undoubtedly fundamentally destructive to this dogma. The Algorithmical principles help us to believe that subjectivity and objectivity go hand in hand and are difficult to completely separate. At each link in the long chain of computations, it is difficult to believe that only objectivity will occur and not subjectivity. For example, as mentioned earlier, the two propositions that make up a syllogism are connected by the activity of searching, and search is subjective, and it is almost impossible to become purely objective, so it can be said that in any part of the computations, in fact, we can only discuss questions like how much subjectivity there is, or what kind of subjectivity it is, rather than whether or not there is any subjectivity. Accordingly, neutrality can only be relative, derivative, soft, and changing, and is just an alternative technical strategy with limited effectiveness.

The basic conditions for all of these to be integrated into a computer simulative system now seem to be in place. Computers can accommodate both theory (programs as its typical embodiment) and information, and because they are fast and precise, they can be considered an ideal tool for analysis. Programmers have recognized that virtual individuals in computers have both ethical and political issues.[6] Now that the relevant mechanism has been elucidated by Algorithm Theory, the barriers to a basic theory of it could have been removed. Computers are especially useful for deducing dynamic scenes. The popularity of "models" of all kinds can be deemed echoing the general trend of computer simulation.

---

6. For a survey of this issue, see Ken Kollman and Scott E. Page, "Computational Methods and Models of Politics" in Leigh Tesfatsion et al. (ed.), "Handbook of Computational Economics", Vol. 2, North Holland, 2006, pp. 1434-1463.

What they all have in common is that they contain both finite elements and dynamics. The rich contents of a computer simulative system are often by no means something that a paper or book can accommodate. It is important to note that the teaching of many courses today has moved away from traditional textbooks and revolves around some specific pieces of software. This trend shall continue to strengthen. Social scientists shall set the goal of building giant simulative systems about human society in the near future. These systems, or a set of the systems, can range from simple to complex, and can be carried out by a global group of scientists working collaboratively and dividing labor. A completely realistic system may be unrealistic. However, a moderately simplified version of the system may be possible. Some key steps, including knowledge expression and knowledge accumulation, have been taken in advance. Digital technology can be used to automatically collect information on a voluntary basis, or collect information in controlled human-computer interactive games, and so on. As long as the raw materials are accumulated sufficiently, the virtual actors, or "human agents", can compute like running a large language model, and the computations would be close to the real computations performed by real actors. Their differences, if any, would be only technical, not substantial. Another approach is to look forward to the establishment of artificial general intelligence (AGI) and then based on this, to carry out developments specialized in social areas.

## §138. Particularities of Social Science Methodology

As we have repeatedly stated, when Algorithmic Theory is introduced into theoretical models as an ontology of the human mind, society and social sciences are naturally and logically deduced without the need for us to deliberately emphasize their particularities, and the connections and distinctions between society and nature, and between social sciences and natural sciences, are explained appropriately at the same time, so that even if we do not deliberately emphasize the boundaries between them, we do not confuse them. Therefore, with regard to the particularities of the social science methods, only a general and supplementary discussion will be made here.

When we study society, the thoughts of actors are at the heart of the objects of study. The existence of the actors' thoughts as entities and objective reality in the precise way described by ATT may be so rich in meaning that it is far beyond what we can understand at the first sight of this proposition. This perspective undoubtedly requires us to investigate, describe, and understand the thoughts of real people as objective facts. Therefore, it is legitimate not only to describe the thoughtful reality, but also to describe the thoughtful history. In history, not only the usual so-called "thought history" is important, but also the thoughtful status of ordinary actors. For example, the selection and narration of historical events inevitably require the application of a historian's own criteria, but it is not enough; historians also need to respect the views of the actors involved in that particular historical period, and to include in their writings the events that were considered important by the actors (rather than by historians themselves). Applying this principle to the question of scientific standards entails taking opinions of the "scientific community" (Kuhn's words[7]) as a criterion for judging what is science and what is not. Such a scientific concept is historical, and it is consistent with other scientific standards, because other scientific standards may be the views

---

7. Thomas. S. Kuhn, "The Structure of Scientific Revolutions", Chicago: University of Chicago Press, 1996, p. 10.

of present scholars, and the views of present scholars will also become a part of history, on an equal footing with other historical views, although these views of different periods have also developed over time and, in some respects, have been superior or inferior to each other.

That said, scholars may often need to make a clear distinction between their own views and those of the actors, and be flexible in their relationship between the two. When a scholar makes an inference about the activities of an actor, he/she inevitably needs to take his/her own inferences as the inferences of the actor, since any inference is first and foremost one's own. Scholars can assume their own inferences as the thinking processes of the actors, and they can also develop their own thinking processes and the actors' thinking processes separately in a certain sense. In ordinary ontological discourse, scholars can be "self-forgetful" and not mention this distinction. However, a paper or book is often used to express new insights that have not been available in the world before, and for such new insights, the author should not have assumed that the person he/she is writing about already has been holding them, so that the paper or book is not necessary any longer. The author can clearly reveal any implicit meanings of real behaviors, making them explicit. As mentioned earlier, this revelation resolves the asymmetry between the conscious and the subconscious, and should be seen as an epistemic development and therefore of new significance.

Distinguishing the views of actors from our own means that we regard them not only as objects of study, but also as competitors in our theories, and that we develop our own theories with reference to the actors' "theories" as the basis and models that exist before our research activities. The real world, which is composed of physical elements and mental elements, is not only the "prototype" for which we build theories, but also the "theories" that exist before our theories, namely, the "prototype theories". Our goal is to revise and improve such "theories". Such "theories" are like a pot of "thousand-year-old soup", which is mixed with a wealth of practical factors, and has complex interdependences and a large number of "inside stories" that we do not yet understand, so we must treat them with great respect and with great caution. We are generally powerless to reconstruct the world in front of us, nor can we rebuild a "parallel world" that is different from it. Even if we are able to build large models in the future using the computer simulative methods mentioned above, sooner or later such models will be transformed into the courses of actions of real actors, and consequently, even if such large models have ever successfully stayed ahead of reality for a while, they will eventually become the tools for the actors to further complicate the real world. Therefore, in the long run, the complexity of the real world will always be worthy of our awe, and the various Algorithmic regularities will remain unchanged in principle.

The real world, with its rich prototype theories, is a platform for social scientists, from which scholars search for problems, study them, and then return to it with their advising solutions. The work of scholars is marginal, even individual. That is to say, it is impossible for scholars to completely abandon the real world to do something else, and they cannot leave aside the ideas of actors and construct *a whole set* of ideologies that they think are more intelligent, and then form an ideal virtual world with the ideologies, and revel in a game (such as the purely neoclassical system of general equilibrium) that is completely invented by themselves. Such a game is of little significance because of its lack of applicative value.

The distinction between actors and researchers also means that it is difficult for social science to avoid giving advice to actors, and therefore, the social science always has more or less "normative" components. These normative components have already been manifested in ordinary engineering. Engineering, which is primarily based on the natural sciences, actually means that natural scientists discover opportunities for action that exist in the natural world. However, such a suggestion cannot be provided for a physical object, but only for people. Therefore, engineering already had social components at its beginning. There is no such a thing as "natural engineering" that is completely distinct from social engineering. Engineers cannot completely avoid social issues, and always have to intervene more or less in the field of social research. Now, hence, on the basis of Algorithmic Theory, social engineering can go its big way, and the "natural engineering" can be the discipline of persuading people to change existing practices and act in accordance with the proposed new solutions. The main objects of the latter are physical. Their difference is that social engineering not only instructs people to act in new ways, but also instills new knowledge and new ideas in people, thus further making them the basis of new social engineering. That is, it will tend to change the natures of their objects. Any social science discourse, as long as it is published, no matter what posture it takes and what purpose it serves, will objectively have an impact on the minds of the readers. These effects may not have been pursued or foreseen by the authors, or expressly known to the actors. These reciprocating cycles between subjectivity and objectivity will converge in some ways, but some others will have no end, and we can only identify them in terms of time, speed, and characteristic details. The natural sciences will also re-examine man-made objects as their objects, but such research is clearly less important than that in the social sciences.

A research approach that accepts disequilibria as a partial reality is bound to be brilliant and hectic. The general equilibrium system of extreme rationalism actually rejects all problems and all changes, looking arrogant and narcissistic. Now, there are almost countless fields and problems that can be studied, screened, questioned, conceived, and acted upon, and the brains, hands, and feet of researchers have been greatly liberated. Those methodological taboos that pretend to be sophisticated and in fact are full of errors can no longer oppress us, and the various active groups of researchers may be about to thrive. Taboos on topics to be broken also include moral and political ones, such as lies, tactics, mind control, centralization, violence, fascism, and so on. I assume that one of the reasons why the discussion of these topics could not be allowed in the past is that the relevant theoretical principles have not yet been clarified, so the consequences of completely opening up discussions on them are something that the real society cannot confidently bear. However, with the Algorithmical help, the rationality of many universal values has become easy to understand, and thus there shall be no longer fear of public doubts and objections to an open discussion of these taboos. It can even be said that some of the universal values do not necessarily continue to exist as universal values, but may become scientific principles and private knowledge or strategies. People's words and deeds are no longer subject to the strong external constraints of norms such as "universal values". Given that the Algorithmic principles are so simple and convincing, "Algorithmical people" can be consciously self-disciplined. Human society will not forever be entangled in the relevant social disputes, and perhaps will eventually turn this page and find and open up new issues.

# CHAPTER 13
# GREEK PHILOSOPHY

## §139. Introduction: the grand synthesis of philosophy

In Volume I and the previous chapters of this volume, I first introduced Algorithmic Theory as a theory of mind, and then explained how Algorithmic Theory can be used to revamp each philosophical branch and integrate them together. To put it simply, through the introduction of spatio-temporal elements and the thinking economy, Algorithmic logic is generated, which can be used to connect various logical systems into one logical system that, further, can be regarded as equivalent to the Instruction system operating according to the principles of economics, and then can be regarded as the logical mechanism for generating psychological systems. Such a "human mind" coexists as a reality or entity and "interacts" with physical objects, and the interactions between different human minds and between different entities create the phenomenal world that we "see" in front of us. In particular, the knowledge system, and thus the social world, is constantly and infinitely evolving. Since a human mind can objectify itself and other minds in a discrete, serial way, higher-order thinking activities, lower-order thinking activities, and other activities coexist and intertwine with each other as the ontological contents. Algorithmic Theory acknowledges the necessity of metaphysical propositions as hypotheses, but suggests that the metaphysical contents should be condensed, minimized, and versioned, that is, metaphysics should accommodate its finitude of argumentation and the consciousness of its own fitful renewals. In the Algorithmic framework, a method is firstly part of the ontology as an Algorithm of actors, and secondly, methodology is used to explore how the work of intellectuals is technically different from that of ordinary actors, so as to produce the advantageous knowledge that is temporarily unique and helpful to actors. Social issues can reasonably originate from the "Algorithmic natures" of human thinking, and then various social existences and social phenomena, including ethics and morality, can be generated and developed, logically and "naturally". They are interconnected, distinct, and combined with natural issues.

In the following 4 chapters, the grand synthesis will be applied to various philosophical schools, as well as to the philosophies of various periods in history. The following discussion contains several missions at once. First, we are to examine the Algorithmic elements embedded in various philosophies until they converge historically into the Algorithmic theory. This examination has not been presented at the beginning of the book, as is customary for an academic paper, because, given the subject matter of the book, it is more appropriate to include it in the later chapters of this book. Second, it evaluates the merits and demerits of various existing philosophies from the Algorithmic perspective, and shows how they can be critically incorporated into the unified Algorithmic system. Thirdly, the Algorithmic principles and philosophy are further explained in combination with specific topics.

The "philosophy" mentioned here is actually mainly the continuation and development of Greek philosophy. The ancient Greek philosophy basically unfolded all the issues of this discipline called "Western philosophy", but at its core was rationalism. Parmenides' few words laid down its basic style, the separation of "Being" from the rest of the world. Later philosophers interpreted it from different angles. Plato and Aristotle focused on the deductive and inductive methods, as well as the theoretical and empirical approaches, respectively. In the Middle Ages, God took the place of "Being". In modern times, with the rise of epistemology, this place was reoccupied by science. Epistemological philosophy means that what was thought to exist somewhere in the external world is actually an idea in the human brain, so that the question of "what is Being" is transformed into the question of whether subjectivity and objectivity are compatible. *Kant was a big turning point.* Kant's philosophy made the structure of "innate thinking tools + sensory materials" come out, which preluded the basic style of Algorithmic Thinking Theory and Algorithmic philosophy. A group of scholars, including Hegel, tried to dissolve it and pull it back into the orbit of traditional philosophy, but it irreversibly flourished. It can be argued that *the history of philosophy after Hegel has been a comprehensive preparation for the Algorithmic Theory, either by developing logic and analytic philosophy to directly serve the generation of computers and their applications, or by emphasizing the philosophical arguments that will become the inferences of Algorithmic Theory.* The latter refers in particular to the work of schools of irrationalism, pragmatism, hermeneutics, phenomenology, existentialism, structuralism, etc. However, all of these can only logically happen when the "innate thinking tools" are identified as discrete "Instructions" and the behavioral and economic elements are added on. Metacomputations operate serially and roundaboutly in a spatio-temporal environment, and hence subjective turns occur inevitably, that is, the sedimentation, distortion, and solidification of computations, coupled with the sustainable development caused by the combinatorial explosion, can not only integrate many traditionally divided or opposing theories, but also form a relatively novel and satisfactory new system. In it, all types of knowledge have their places, and they exist relative to each other. This is an extension of rationalism, or a unity of the rational and the irrational—there is an equivalence between the two statements. In ontological terms, the Algorithmic philosophy is intended to provide a set of theories about the coexistence and interaction of ideas as relatively independent, discrete entities with other entities.

*Algorithmic Theory tightly sticks to the theme of philosophy, and is closely tied to almost every page of the philosophical textbook.* It is so relevant that a review of the entire history of philosophy is necessary. Meanwhile, at least from my point of view, the logical connections are so overwhelming and so persuasive that we can determine their applicability without having to carefully review every detail of each philosopher's arguments. This is by no means to say that Algorithmic Theory can replace everything, but rather that it is the catalyst and the glue that provide philosophy with some of the elements that have been lacking all along but are extremely basic and necessary to put the pieces together. The basicity and necessity of these elements should be expected to be generally agreed upon by the readers after fully understanding ATT. In this way, I dare to point out that we have made a comprehensive encapsulation and conclusion of the philosophy for more than 2,000 years. Of course, this is not the end of philosophy—Algorithmic Theory has already demonstrated the sustainability and irreplaceability of philosophy itself. After establishing a proper theory of mind, philosophy is bound to begin a new phase.

In view of the fact that this is only a small, outlined book, and the scope of my study is by all means limited, the discussion here cannot be thorough and full, and it mainly shows some basic ideas as the results of my hurried and cursory skimming of philosophical literature. I prefer to discuss the most fundamental things, even those topics that are textbook-level, common-sense, and often less noticed by others, namely, those that are commonly taken for granted and unnecessary to articulate, to find out magnificence. I believe that after clarifying these fundamental questions, philosophy will be greatly improved, and its significance to other disciplines and to the real world will be regained, which would also satiate me for the time being. Therefore, those discussions of cutting-edge, advanced, or specialized topics will not be included in this book if they do not serve these purposes.

## §140. From Ancient Philosophy to Greek Philosophy

Although the contents of philosophy are limited, looking at ancient philosophies around the world, there is no lack of commonality and generality in their enormous differences. For example, in Egyptian philosophy and Indian philosophy, mind-object dualism, dynamics, and circularism can be found. In the vast Indian philosophy, one can even clearly find the idea that some basic elements are permutated and combined to form everything.[1] Chinese Taoists believe that everything is unified in a single "Tao". Unlike Western philosophies, the Chinese Tao is much like a rope that connects everything and thus runs through diversity and dynamics, while Western concepts of the same kind (such as the "Being", "Ideas", and Substance) are relatively concrete.[2]

There was no shortage of a phenomenon in Chinese and foreign history, i.e., there was a certain era of intellectual

---

1.  "Companion Encyclopedia of Asian Philosophy", Edited by Brian Carr and Indira Mahalingampp. New York & London: Routledge, 1997, Section II-8, pp. 140-149.
2.  Ibid, Section II-27, pp. 497-514.

prosperity that everyone yearns for, during which there were many masters, talents, and classic works emerging one after another. In China, this was the Spring and Autumn Period and the Warring States Period, while in the West, it was the Ancient Greek Period. The heterogeneity and structurality of intellectual activity have led to the fact that, although computations were carried out from moment to moment, the output is not evenly distributed in geography and history. Some areas or periods were poor in thought, while others were at the height of their ideas and fame. However, in addition to heterogeneity and structurality, there was another reason that could not be ignored, and that was the advancement of the technologies of thought recording and communication. Before there was written history, there might have been other eras of intellectual flourishing, or of important thinkers and their outstanding works. Considering how long the prehistory was and how vast the world was, you will know that this speculation is by no means untrue. Either most of the ideological achievements of the predecessors might have been not recorded or most of them were lost later, but it cannot be ruled out that their ideas had been passed on from generation to generation through words and deeds, and in the end, they influenced the ideological consciousness of both ordinary people and the thinkers of the era of ideological prosperity. In this sense, completely innovative ideas might be truly rare, and the "masters" might often be people who were good at gathering and organizing the existing materials and revising them, and they were often good at and diligent in writing.

It is surmised that advances in the recording and writing of ideas would sooner or later come to a tipping point where most of the works of thought before this period were lost (e.g., the Kingdom of Greece was devastated by foreign invasions in the twelfth century BC[3]), and from that period onwards, ideas were stored in relative completeness and in detail. This preservation created the conditions for later generations of scholars to "*stand on the shoulders of giants*"; therefore, the repetition of brainwork had been reduced, the development of ideas had accelerated, and its historical context had manifested its richness. Since these "original" works were cited by subsequent generations of scholars, the authors became the giants of history as well.

We seem to be talking about Algorithmic economics rather than revisiting the history of philosophy. Yes, we do. It can be noted that since the Greek language at that time was written mainly with inexpensive tools such as papyrus and reed pens, the written literature was roughly in the colloquial style. For this reason, the written language of the West, although also sort of different from the spoken language, has clearly not been refined, reinvented, and condensed in order to save paper (papyrus). The slight differences between written and spoken language in the West have not changed much from ancient times to the present day. In striking distinction, the ancient Chinese language was written with expensive tools such as animal bones, tiles, bamboo slips, or cloth (the economical form of paper was not invented until the first century AD), forcing the ancient Chinese to develop an extremely concise system of written language. In fact, there is a huge difference between it and Chinese spoken language. This must have seriously affected the expression, exchange, and reproduction of ideas. The colloquial movement of the Chinese written language did not take place until the beginning of the last century, which must have further led the written language used

---

3. Zhiwei Zhang (ed.), "A History of Western Philosophy" (in Chinese, 2nd), China Renmin University Press, 2010, pp. 17-18, and Jean-Pierre Vernant, "The Origins of Greek Thought", Cornell University Press, 1982, p. 10, 36, 37.

by Chinese intellectuals today to be in a state of inadequacy and immaturity.

The economy of ideological activities seriously affects the contents of ideological activities, which is a basic inference of Algorithm Theory. This is a perspective that can help us understand why Greek philosophy is characterized by precision, rigor, and even formality. This characteristic has been developed and has finally led to the emergence of science, which has made a significant contribution to world civilization that no other region has been able to make. This process is consistent with what was discussed in the previous chapter. Science was the result of people's blind, one-sided, resolute, and continuous pursuit of high-quality knowledge regardless of its practicality and timeliness. It tore apart the knowledge system and disregarded the integrity of the knowledge system. In other words, it was the product of a structural development of the knowledge system, which was closely linked to discreteness and plurality, and was also consistent with the tradition of Western philosophy that values individuals and concrete objects.

Of course, there is no doubt that the above characteristics of Greek philosophy were also closely related to the democratic politics in which debates prevailed. Some of the basic meanings of democratic politics included peaceful discussion and hence rational exchange of ideas. When a person could not force another person to obey him, he could either buy him or persuade him. Algorithmically speaking, this led to the relative independence of *public speech*. Although the theoretical status of language was not clarified until after the advent of Algorithmic Theory, its practical use was well understood in the ancient Greek era, so that this particular "rhetoric" has always enjoyed its important position in the West, distinctively from other societies. Beautified, skillful discourse was used to serve the goal of "articulating ideas". Due to the lack of neural connections between people, communicative problems arose as an Algorithmic problem. The arguments and principles involved in the debates should not be "understood but not spoken", as in Oriental literature, but should be presented to ordinary people in an understandable way, and try to influence their positions or attitudes (so as to influence the outcome of the vote). This was how the formalized and sophisticated style had developed. Philosophy and science were great products of democracy and freedom, and this truth had been strongly proved in ancient Greece. [4]

Greek philosophy dealt with a wide range of philosophical questions as well as specific ones. Now, let us in turn comment on some of them, briefly.


## §141. Thales, Pythagoras

The Greek word for "philosophy" is "philosophia", which means "love of wisdom". [5] Obviously, the word might first and foremost reflect the humility of philosophers, meaning that they did not claim to be "wise", but only to "love" wisdom. Secondly, the word also had an advertising component, namely, a call to people for wisdom. This meaning is consistent with the rationalist spirit of Greek philosophy. However, the main reason for the establishment of a specialized discipline is not elsewhere but that the researchers continue to study a specific field or a specific type of problems, so that they have produced

---

4. Although it seems to be common knowledge that democracy contributed to the emergence of Greek philosophy, historians of philosophy rarely explain it in this way. The root cause obviously lies in the inherent hostility of Greek philosophy to democracy (it is manifested in the rejection of sophists). The integration of philosophy and democracy is an important aspect of our "Grand Synthesis".

5. Zhiwei Zhang (ed.), "A History of Western Philosophy" (in Chinese, 2nd), China Renmin University Press, 2010, p. 4, and C. C. W. Taylor (ed.), "Routledge History of Philosophy", Vol. I, ebook, Routledge, 2005, p. 8.

results of a specific scale. Therefore, the division of knowledge based on the Algorithmic economy could be a fundamental reason for the formation of philosophy, and it could also be where the meaning of "philosophy" as a discipline lies. For example, according to investigations, the word "school" derives from the Greek word "skhole"[6] (leisure), and many important Greek philosophers belonged to the "leisure class".

Let's start with the first important philosopher, Thales of Miletus. Thales studied both the origin of the world and its movement. He reduced the origin of the world to a single element, "water". He believed that everything had a "soul".[7] As with other Greeks, the concept of "soul" was primarily used to explain the occurrence of changes or movements. However, the ancient Greeks could not have said slyly, as Newton did, that "a moving object will continue to move as long as there is a force to stop it" (this idea was derived from Galileo and Descartes). The ancient Greeks could only first compare objects to people. Because people start to move by the action of their minds, the ancient Greeks also concocted the same method, believing that the movements of all things also originated from things like minds. That is, the dynamic mechanism of thinking was expanded to the whole world. However, Thales was not able to combine dynamics with statics. He first said that the world was made of water, and that the world was driven by the soul, which was tantamount to assuming a second kind of entity outside of water, and that the two kinds of entities were disconnected. The "soul" is clearly an example of what later writers criticized as "superfluous metaphysics". The advantage of Newton's method is that it avoids the assumption of a second

---

6. Zhiwei Zhang (ed.), "A History of Western Philosophy" (in Chinese, 2nd), China Renmin University Press, 2010, p. 18.

7. Zhiwei Zhang (ed.), "A History of Western Philosophy" (in Chinese, 2nd), China Renmin University Press, 2010, p. 23, and Bertrand Russell: "A History of Western Philosophy", London: Unwin Paperbacks, 1984, p. 45.

entity, simply acknowledging the existence of a pre-theoretical world, and then the theorist emerges with an acknowledgment of the previous state and (pursuant to this acknowledgement) an explanation for the phenomena that follow. In other words, the theorist admits that he is limited in his ability and has only done a little work on a particular part or link of the world. This is exactly the Algorithmical attitude. Furthermore, by describing the Instruction system as a working mechanism, Algorithm theory combines dynamics and statics.

The second was Pythagoras. Pythagoras is a symbolic figure that marks the importance that Western civilization attaches to quantitative relations. In China, there is no such a person who has achieved an important philosophical position by studying mathematics. According to historian Ray Huang, this neglect of quantitative relations was an important reason for the eventual decline of Eastern civilization.[8] However, Pythagoras' view that "number is the origin of all things" is here to be an object of criticism. Although Algorithmic Theory attaches great importance to computations, what we mean by "computation" is not limited to quantitative computations. We think of "computation" as a logical operation, and quantitative operations are only one kind of it. Moreover, as far as quantitative operations are concerned, the binary structure of "Instruction + information" shall be adopted, rather than just information—"number" is merely one type of information. Coincidentally, this approach of placing information at the center of narratives in the one-sided manner is exactly the route adopted by the current information science and information philosophy. Moreover, scholars who take information as the center of their discourse in the one-sided way now go one step further, implying that information could

---

8. See Ray Huang: China: A Macro History. New York: M.E. Sharpe, 1988, p. 48, 129, 168, etc.

be deemed the origin (or essence) of the world, a core viewpoint of the so-called "philosophy of information".[9] I will never agree to this. In my opinion, they have completely failed to grasp the essence of the information technology revolution. This argument is just a simple imitation of Pythagoras's proposition. This consistency, which spans more than two thousand years, is by no means accidental.

Quantity is a certain property of an object, and when it is discussed, there must first be some kind of object. This is a commonsense understanding. For example, we can reduce the origin of the world to a single substance or element, such as water, as Thales did, and then talk about how everything is made up according to a certain amount (or structure) of water. This way of arguing is in line with general logic. However, when we have made this argument, the origin of the world is water, not quantity itself. Pythagoras might have seen this danger, and perhaps at the same time, motivated by exaggerating his own mathematical calculations, went so far as to claim that it was not the object described by quantity, but quantity itself, that was the source of all things. This seems quite puzzling.

However, if you think deeply, you will find that this is actually consistent with a form of extreme rationalism that we have already criticized, that is, it is trying to replace qualitative analysis with quantitative analysis, and then cancel all qualitative analysis, and ultimately reduce the world to something homogeneous, that is, it is only "made up" of a single material without structure. Obviously, this is neoclassical

---

9. This "infocentrism" is currently much equivalent to "pancomputationalism", which is introductorily summarized in the following entry: Gualtiero Piccinini and Corey Maley, "Computation in Physical Systems", The Stanford Encyclopedia of Philosophy (Summer 2021 Edition), Edward N. Zalta (ed.), URL = <https://plato.stanford.edu/archives/sum2021/entries/computation-physicalsystems/>.

economics that only pays attention to quantitative analysis while attempting to eliminate structural analysis. At this point, we don't need to repeat our criticism.

This argument also faces another difficulty. We know that quantitative features or quantitative relations are "constructed" with the participation of the human brain's mental activity, and that the object itself does not tell us about such characteristics or relations. This is like what Locke called color or sound, which is constructed with the participation of the human sensory organs. In this case, to say that "number is the origin of all things" is tantamount to saying that "I", as the person who is studying and thinking about the origin of the world, am the origin (or part of the "origin") of the world, which is to inadvertently and secretly make the logical error of "self-containment". Moreover, according to the above view, "number is the origin of all things" must still be further reduced to the proposition that "I am the origin of the world" (or part of the "origin") before the latter proposition is to be explored again. Although this direction points to the Algorithmic mind-matter dualism, it is not suitable for exploring the origin of the world. When we talk about informational entities, we only mean that information can be regarded as relatively independent objects that can coexist with other various entities, but it does not contain the meaning of "information is the origin of the world".

### §142. Heraclitus, Parmenides

The third important figure was Heraclitus. For posterity, Heraclitus was a questioner. Heraclitus' assertion of the universality and eternity of change or motion must have upset static theorists. The separation between dynamics and statics has lasted for thousands of years, and it continues to this day. This regrettable phenomenon is also surprising. Extreme statics is monotonous and unreal, while extreme dynamics is superficial and hollow. When the speed of change or motion drops to zero, the dynamics become statics, hence, it can be said that dynamics actually contains static. A particular speed of motion, whether fast or slow, must be described in terms of the interaction of at least two aspects: the factors that cause motion and the factors that cause rest. To illustrate the statics, or constancy in motion, Heraclitus introduced the famous concept of "logos". *With this concept, a stream of philosophy was gradually developed that is characterized by the combination of constancy or regularity and differences to explain changes or motions and the whole picture of the real world.* This is like on a trip; sometimes you can take a car, sometimes you need to walk, and you cannot just rely only on a single means of transportation.[10] This approach has become one of the main approaches used in current scientific theories (Laplacian determinism can be a derivative of it); however, it is not actually mainstream in philosophy. The major direction of mainstream philosophy is to try to engulf differences and dynamics with statics and constancy (Heraclitus himself also had this tendency), rather than letting the two sides take their respective places and cooperate with each other. This kind of hybridity requires finding another philosophical foundation. In this regard, Algorithm Theory not only inherits the method of logos, but also solves many problems caused by it. Therefore, it can be considered that it has comprehensively achieved Heraclitus' multiple goals.

It is no accident that most scholars who emphasize change emphasize *dialectics*, as was the case with Heraclitus. For change means a deviation from the status quo, and sooner or later this deviation might develop into its opposite. Thus, at

---

10. This point needs to be emphasized here that the concept of logos is quite similar to the "Tao" mentioned by Chinese Laozi (see He Xin: (See He Xin, "Philosophical Contemplation" [in Chinese], Beijing: Modern Press, 2019, p. 133, 148). Also, Heraclitus' dialectics is similar to Laozi's philosophy.

least phenomenally, the changes seem to be some shuttle motions between those two opposites. This further leads to *circularism*. The proposition that follows seems to be natural: an interaction between the opposites, that is, the "struggle", "leads" to the cycle of changes or motions. However, why is there a "struggle" between them? As soon as this question is asked, the question is exposed: Is this a "trick" of "explaining phenomena with phenomena"? It is said to be a "trick" because even the theorists themselves could be aware of the superficiality of this argumentation, then they have to try to find further explanations. In Heraclitus, this "further explanation" coincidentally resembles Hegel's style of "cunning of reason". In an anthropomorphic tone, he said, "Nature loves to hide"[11]. This sentence structure is similar to Thales's "animism", imagining nature as having a mind and a personality. It sounds like that "nature is very naughty, it wants to play with us a game of 'hide-and-seek', and deliberately does not tell us the truth bluntly, but goes around in circles, testing our wisdom to see if we can dig out the hidden truth".

The Algorithmical process of revising the dynamics and dialectics can be divided into the following steps: 1. Move from the objective world to the subjective world, to identify the constancy hidden in changes as the Instructional system. 2. The Instructional system acts on external information, leading to our pluralistic and mixed understanding of the objective world. Consistency and contradiction are only special cases of the pluralistic ideas, and they do not exist everywhere (dialectic experts actually admit this irregularity). In the Algorithmic framework, it can be argued that objective logos corresponds to the recognized regularity in the subjective system of thought. When a logical or mental system grasps the (local) regularity of

---

11. A. C. Grayling, "The History of Philosophy", New York: Penguin Press, 2019, p. 28.

the objective world, it can be considered that there is a corresponding "logos" in the objective object (this is similar to the generation of the "universal in things" described in §79, Vol. I). 3. The one-way, infinite development of the knowledge system, and thus the social world, can save dynamic philosophy from circularity and meaninglessness. Looking at the dynamics and statics of the physical world from the perspectives of the developing knowledge system will gain a changing vision. Even if an object does not change, our own perception of the object changes, which constitutes another kind of "relative motion". This is an "Algorithmic" way for us humans to get rid of the monotony and meaninglessness that the physical world brings to us.

The fourth is Parmenides. Parmenides' search for eternal and unchanging existence in a changing world can be seen as a response to the problem of dynamics. I still believe that the assertion of "Being", like other Greek philosophical concepts, has a tendency to anthropomorphize. That is, if certain phenomena are seen as the consequences of the actions of a person (or an actor who is functionally similar to a person), then there must be that person (or agent) behind these phenomena—although "Being" was considered immovable. Then, having found this "person" (or agent), the truth was revealed. This is a method of synthesizing and dissolving phenomena. This method differs from the method of attributing specific types of phenomena to specific concepts or principles (e.g., attributing a large number of physical phenomena to the existence of "force"). Since there are many types of phenomena to be explained, a single concept or principle is not sufficient. Even if these numerous concepts or principles need to be assumed to be "existent", they need a unified carrier that can simultaneously have many natures or functions that need to be assumed to exist. Of course,

Parmenides's "Being" is not a person, but an object of human cognition. He just borrowed the working mechanism of human. Obviously, this is because philosophers, as human beings, are first and foremost familiar with themselves. This brings us to an Algorithmic view linked to the approach to consciousness: if we are not even familiar with ourselves, or if we don't even know ourselves, how can we know the world?!

This method of reducing "many" to "one" has a hidden motive, i.e., the computing economy. After "many" boils down to "one", we only need to grasp this "one" and supplement it with secondary means, then we can go back and grasp the "many" again. This approach has multifaceted economics. For example, it saves memory space and computing power. One might say that not only does this lead to savings, but it can also be used for forecasting, which can increase the output of computing activities. That's right. The economy is not limited to cost savings, but also an increase in *output*; these two aspects are logically connected. Although the principle of computing economy is hidden here, we can assume that the people of that time (and anyone of any era) had not fail to grasp this uncomplicated logic. Perhaps, they had not thought it was that important. Or, they might have thought that publicly expounding the truth undermines the persuasiveness of their arguments. Although the rationale for the computing economy means admitting explicitly that the distortions had been deliberately made, for philosophers who had preached their doctrines as truth, this recognition would be self-destructive.

The assumption of "Being" is similar to the assumption of the Instructional system that we have made today, but the difference is that Parmenides lacks the consciousness that "my doctrine is a hypothesis". Because of this distinction, the "Being" as something already known or knowable (Parmenides said, "The thing that can be thought and that for the sake of which the thought exists are the same".[12]), which was originally used to explain "phenomena" (a concept that did not exist at the time), becomes that *the "Being" as true and phenomena as false, and the two sides are opposed, negating each other.* Parmenides must have observed many examples of successful refinement of phenomena. He extrapolated this, and then categorically, "bravely", or "crudely", argued that *all phenomena must be able to be refined again and again, and finally all come under a single "Being". This single "Being" had already been firmly believed to be existent before it was clarified what it exactly was.* Parmenides's own and his followers' descriptions or inferences about the specific natures of "Being" prove the arbitrariness of his proposition. As a result, phenomena were dwarfed or discarded, and what left for us was merely to worship the "Being". This separation was reflected in the distinction between the "path of truth" and the "path of opinion". Obviously, *this distinction was the beginning of the "great split" in Western philosophy.* Although this distinction has encouraged generations of scholars to pursue the truth, and finally set Western scholarship on a unique scientific path, the confusions and conflicts it has created have persisted to this day. Bridging this split, and revising and reconstructing the philosophical principles, have become a primary task of Algorithmic Theory.

## §143. Parmenides (continued)

The "Being" hypothesis also raises an important issue, namely the natures of the object of "Being". No one, including Parmenides, has ever witnessed what Being looks like, nor has he even asserted whether Being can be seen or touched.

---

12. Bertrand Russell, "A History of Western Philosophy", London: Unwin Paperbacks, 1984, p. 67. The facts about Parmenides in this section are based on pages No. 66-67 of the book.

Algorithmically, Being is clearly a fictitious object, a concept generated by the human brain. This concept takes the *form* of a thought, a computational result, a piece of knowledge, or a "datum", and its *content* is some "thing" in the minds of the people (including the readers and me) who talk about the concept. We imagine how this "thing" relates to other objects. We can even simulate these interactions in our minds. This simulative process is like a computer performing some kind of animations, and its dynamics and states can be vividly reflected on the screen. However, this in no way means that the concepts in our minds can act *directly* on real objects. In such performances, not only are the hypothetical objects (e.g., Parmenides's "Being") virtual, but the objects associated with them (e.g., everything related to Being and imagined by Parmenides) are all virtual. What happens are the interactions between these things that are of the same, similar, or compatible natures. They correspond to the interactions between "real objects". "Real objects" are not directly accessible to people, but they can exist as *another* hypothesis in the mind. A "simulated animation" is used as a relatively independent computational process to compare with a hypothetical "real object". At the same time, it is not contradictive between "I recognize that the 'simulated animation' is fictions" and "I strive for the 'simulated animation' to be as realistic as possible", because there is a difference in the authenticity of these different "simulated animations". In terms of common sense, among ordinary people, this distinction is actually very clear and there is no confusion. This is because we are all human beings and all have the thoughts in the same formats, and can objectify ourselves. The above distinctions and truths are easy when people speak to people, and only when "people are not told by the logic of people, but by the logic of things", or under the strange way of thinking of some philosophers, confusions and chaos would occur.

When Chinese philosophers talked about "Tao", or when Heraclitus talked about logos, it could be assumed that they were also talking about some kind of "Being", "Substance", or "essence"; however, these philosophers apparently did not consider these to be identical with the phenomena they were trying to explain. In this regard, Parmenides was different. He spoke of Being as if it were something identical with concrete physical beings—and it was for this reason that questions such as "whether Being should have volume" became problematic. Along this line, philosophy (and later science) has the function of predicting the existence of certain physical entities that have yet to be discovered. For example, Democritus, who was influenced by Parmenides, predicted the existence of atoms. Another example is the prediction of the existence of black holes in contemporary physics, which has been confirmed by empirical evidence.

The verification of these physical entities predicted, which moved from backstage to the foreground, from hidden to explicit, indicates a success of philosophy and science. But what would happen next to the success? Taking a step further, we will realize that these "great discoveries" mean merely the addition of some objects to the world we are knowing about, and nothing else has changed. Thereafter, we still need to continue to understand the world. Far from being alleviated, this task now becomes: what is the other hidden power that dominates this expanded new world? What is the other "Being" that governs these newly discovered physical entities? And, what will happen again if the "Being" predicted by Parmenides is finally confirmed by experience?

Obviously, in a certain sense, *something that is real or substantial must be something invisible, and it must be outside the realm of phenomena.* If it enters the phenomenal realm, we have to retreat *again*, so as to place it *outside* the phenomenal realm again. This grotesque and intriguing process seems to imply that we can never truly discover Being, truth, or Substance. Why, then, do we have to "ask for trouble" in this way? The answer lies clearly in the Algorithmic world, which is that this is nothing more than a reflection of the infiniteness of knowledge development. Knowledge does not reach an end just because it develops, nor does it not develop because there is no end. This endless pursuit is an impulse generated by the limitations of our vision and thinking as a whole. *The "hypothetical entity" is actually resulted from a method under the condition of computational serial processing.* This hypothetical entity can neither be too close nor too far from phenomena. If it is too close, it will be weakened by being too superficial, and if it is too faraway, it will be weakened by being too complex or difficult. Marginal conditions dictate that the retreat must be gradual. However, the pressure of time and space has led to the fact that computational activities must be forcibly terminated from time to time, resulting in a certain historical version of metaphysics. Since then, through continuous revisions, a new version of metaphysics would be formed. Such a metaphysics would be both more useful and more economical.

The specific natures of the above-mentioned Being, Substance, or essence are different or pending in different philosophical systems. What they all have in common is that they can all be used as *objects* of our mental activity. Even thoughtful entities can become our objects through the process of re-objectification. In the Algorithmical context, "object" and "entity" can be synonymous. All objects or entities can be common only in the sense that "they are simultaneously the objects of mental activities", but not necessarily in their concrete natures, nor must they interact directly. However, a chaos in this was about to occur soon in Greek philosophy. Objects or entities of different natures were to be juxtaposed and compared indiscriminately, and their specific natures were forcibly required to be uniform, otherwise, a "philosophical problem" would arise. In some later philosophies, mental activities were thought to act directly on physical objects without the mediation of information, and so on and so forth.

## §144. Socrates, the Sophists

The change of the attitude of the philosophical history towards the Sophists reflects a progress of philosophy itself. The earlier history of philosophy was dominated by the opponents of the Sophists, the rationalists, thus, it is not surprising that the Sophists were judged negatively. However, philosophy is recognizing the meanings of their work, and this process of re-understanding and re-evaluation can only be "completed" at the Algorithmic stage.

The Sophists were professional intellectuals. This required that the contents of their teaching must be able to help students gain a foothold in the society of the time and obtain *practical* benefits, so that they themselves could be rewarded in a *timely* manner. This reflects the inherent Algorithmical contradiction of educational activities: to teach students what they do not understand, while receiving students' selections and evaluations. One way to resolve this contradiction was to select teaching contents with the goal and criterion of practicality. Socrates, on the contrary, taught his students the contents they might not like, and tried to proactively guide the society; instead of receiving tuitions, he was sentenced to death.

The principle of professionalism and practicality is tantamount to the principle of the computational forced closure and factor completeness: if you develop knowledge without practicality, you could, of course, be quite "sound and clear"; but in order for knowledge to be useful in the present, it must be compromised and must accept imperfection. Thus, the Sophists emphasized human's presence in nature and the meanings of an individual, and emphasized actions, languages, skills, and strategies, seeking to prevail in the debates in the democratic Athenian politics. They were clearly the source of social philosophy, social sciences, and the humanities (although ethics is thought to have originated with Socrates). They even discussed the rights and wrongs of law in a more comprehensive manner, with special emphasis on the shortcomings of law.[13] However, judging by the critical attitude of Socrates and his followers, the Sophists of the time may have gone too far in subjectivity, strategy, and opportunism. In this context, rationalism arose as a corrective force.

The confrontation between the Sophists and rationalists is a wonderful page in the history of philosophy. Algorithmically, it touches on, in particular, some of the major and fundamental issues that will shape the development of philosophy for thousands of years to come. These are also the questions that Algorithmic Theory is now focused on answering.

The first question to be asked is: Why did the Sophists, if so important, collapse after the Greeks? The first reason is, of course, the decline of democracy. However, from an Algorithmic point of view, it is clear that some of the contents emphasized by the Sophists, that is, contents that are often referred to as common sense or practical factors, were not easy to systematically generalize, and not convenient for classroom teaching. Moreover, there must be plenty of opportunities for students to engage with these contents outside of the classroom. Second, there were parts of these contents that should not be discussed openly, especially morally. One of the examples was some of the strategies. Children were born to lie. Later, children were taught to be honest at home and at school. This kind of education must have a very positive significance for the construction of society. However, after graduation,

---

13. C. C. W. Taylor (ed.), "Routledge History of Philosophy", Vol. I, ebook, Routledge, 2005, pp. 258-266.

practitioners who went out into society would sooner or later recognize that strategic activities (e.g., lying) were necessary or useful in some cases. Nonetheless, did this mean that educators could talk about strategic activities as freely as they did about other intellectual topics?—especially when there was insufficient preparation with relevant book knowledge.

This involves a common saying: it is easy for people to learn bad, but it is difficult to learn good. It is better to avoid talking about certain negative topics. A truth doesn't have to be told as it is. Because language is not just used to "reflect" external objects, it is itself an act. For example, it is better not to touch on erotic topics, otherwise, there will be certain practical consequences. This is Algorithmical. Doctrines such as this divide the contents of education into at least two parts, one for truth and the other for profit (or "usefulness"). The first part is scientific, the second part is engineering. Therefore, Socrates, who was regarded as the "founder of ethics" by later generations, began to expand his ethics with an engineering proposition: virtue is knowledge. Knowledge was undoubtedly worth pursuing for Socrates, and virtue was also worth pursuing. What is very "Algorithmical" is that he actually interpreted virtue as a kind of "skill".[14] This interpretation was counterintuitive and might have been a bit unconventional at the time, but it should have deepened the audience's impression and prompted people to think. Moreover, ethical propositions, as propositions that explicitly or implicitly direct how people should behave, are indeed Algorithmically engineered or technological. This engineering nature of ethics in particular should be revealed and emphasized.

Then, what is virtue? Socrates went around on this question, explaining it in multiple canny ways. This was

------

14. C. C. W. Taylor (ed.), "Routledge History of Philosophy", Vol. I, ebook, Routledge, 2005, p. 336.

apparently conducive to perfecting his arguments and putting himself in a relatively advantageous position in arguments so as not to be seized by his opponents (and thus there is some truth in the perception of Socrates as a Sophist). However, virtue must include ordinary ethical and moral principles. We can understand virtue in terms of today's game theory perspective. For example, the benefits of being honest can be understood as follows (although Socrates himself did not argue this way): while lying is beneficial temporarily in certain circumstances, lying may be detected by others, and those lies in repetitive games may be inconsistent with each other, leading other people again to easily identify the liar and then to stop believing him/her and not to cooperate with him/her in the future; therefore, in the long run, it is not only noble to be honest, but also wise and advantageous. In the language of game theory, honesty is a "long-term dominant strategy" of the individual in a society of acquaintances, or a "solution" of a long-term equilibrium. Wisdom, knowledge, and goodness can be consistent in such senses. I believe that this may be the implicit meaning of Socrates' argument. This reflects that in the earlier stages of knowledge development, people's views are generally more comprehensive. On this basis, many philosophers, including Socrates, advocated the intellectual and spiritual life, and persuaded people to adopt those visionary ways of life that were essentially conducive to the long-term development of society. This kind of persuasion would literally also be in the interests of the far-sighted intellectuals themselves; however, if ethical norms were not promoted by intellectuals, by whom?

However, there is general agreement that knowledge and virtue are not entirely identical. A wise person is not necessarily good, and a good person is not necessarily wise. Experience tells us that excellent people with both are actually few in life, and the separation of the good and the wise is a real normalcy. After the introduction of various Algorithmic elements, the principle of endogenous comparative advantage in economics can be used to demonstrate this truth. That is, the body of knowledge is pluralistic rather than completely internally consistent. The criteria for judging people and things are not uniform, but pluralistic. This pluralism is not now a dogma that we are forced to accept, but is justified precisely with the logic of monism, and by using the method of reductio ad absurdum: According to monism, even if true knowledge (as epistemic knowledge) and good knowledge (as engineered knowledge) can one day converge into a unity, we are now still in the process of computations, and this processuality guarantees that there must be some disagreements between these two streams of knowledge coming from their different origins.

## §145. Plato (1)

In the intellectual history of the West, Plato created the image of a typical professional intellectual. He was well educated, was familiar with historical documents, respected the work of others, wrote prolifically, argued rigorously and thoroughly and carefully, cited extensively, and founded and presided over a teaching and research institution, all of which set an example for later generations of scholars. His widely circulated writings have made him a master, an authority, and a symbol of mainstream academia. To a large extent, his ideas shaped the way of thinking of the entire Western world. With the process of modernization and globalization, this way of thinking has now spread all over the world. At the same time, the philosophical problems he participated in creating have also persisted into the twenty-first century. This can only be solved with the help of Algorithmic Theory.

Strictly speaking, Plato was not the original maker of the

philosophical questions. Parmenides was. However, Plato, in his professional way, expanded and disseminated the issues, making them permeate the whole world. Given that these problems are so serious in nature and have such widespread impact that they have become a source of split in the academic world, our critique of Plato cannot be taken lightly—even though Plato has actually lowered the tone of Parmenides' absolutism and made ontological philosophy appear closer to common sense and experiences.

This is first manifested in his use of the scattered "Ideas" (eidos, Form, etc.) in place of Parmenides' singular "Being". The Idea of a table is always more intuitive and therefore easier to understand than the "Being" of the whole world. Moreover, with regard to the concrete thing to which an Idea corresponds, Plato did not think that it did not exist as Parmenides did, but that it "both exists and does not exist".[15] This suggests that he was trying to make some kind of compromise and reconciliation. A typical example of Idea is not a natural object, but a human-made object which, together with the concept of "good" extended from Socrates, enriches the contents of engineering. This adds to the variety of contents in the "right knowledge base". The use of verbs such as "participate" and "imitate" for Ideas also shows that Plato understood the formation of the world in the first place from the perspective of a human behavior.

However, these corrections are superficial in nature. On the core philosophical issues, it can even be said that Plato did not show much creativity. Although the Ideas are numerous and scattered, they are in no way intended to lead to pluralism. This

---

15. The materials about the facts of Plato in these three sections, except where explicitly stated, mainly come from Zhiwei Zhang (ed.), "A History of Western Philosophy" (in Chinese, 2nd), China Renmin University Press, 2010, pp. 63-80, and Frank Thilly, "A History of Philosophy", New Delhi: SBW Publishers, 1993, pp. 58-73.

was true even when Plato believed that certain Ideas, such as motion and stillness, could not be combined with each other. He preferred to establish hierarchical affiliations between different Ideas. On the question of the nature of Ideas, Plato obviously magnified the errors hidden in Parmenides' doctrine. That is, an Idea that exists as a kind of *knowledge* in our view is regarded as having the same or similar properties as the concrete thing that gave rise to the Idea, and can therefore be reversed and re-exist with that concrete thing, and *interact* with it. A typical example is that the Idea of a table, an actual table, and a table in the picture, are juxtaposed, equated, and summed up into the result of "three tables".[16] In this sense, Plato followed and strengthened the philosophical tradition of *category confusion* that was initiated by Parmenides, which is to simply compare, equate, analogize, and relate mental objects with physical objects. The concept of Idea was further transformed by Aristotle into the concept of "form" that was first regarded as a component of an object, then, after being separated from the material of the object, could directly enter the human mind. The relevant narrative, almost as a standard, has been pervasive in philosophical literature so much so that even today some authors still believe that the objects of human thinking are not information but directly the physical objects themselves.[17] It has even become a Western-style everyday discourse.[18] This tradition of "rhetorical humor" in the eyes of common readers can hardly hide its philosophical dilemma.

---

16. Plato, "The Republic", translated by B. Jowett, Quality Paperback Book Club, 1992, pp. 361-365.

17. For examples, see Thomas Reid, "An Inquiry into the Human Mind", Pennsylvania State University Press, 1997; J.L. Austin, "Sense and Sensibilia", Oxford University Press, 1964.

18. A common sentence such as "Melancholy almost fell from his body" seems to express the notion of the materiality of thought, but in fact it does so overly, because it hints or requires that the thoughtful entity (melancholy) have specific natures (e.g., weight) identical to those of a physical substance.

Gilbert Ryle's concept of "category mistake" is inherently deficient, but it is quite appropriate to use it here. As readers know, this mistake was to be corrected through conceptualism. In my opinion, its complete correction can only be realized in the Algorithmic era.

The appeal of Ideas obviously lies in that they have their concise forms as the abstractions, simplifications, and generalizations of many concrete things. By understanding the single model of an "idea", one can grasp many specific objects. That is, it is computationally economical. This economy is undoubtedly valuable and worth pursuing. As long as the circumstantial conditions permit, it should even be a priority for actors to pursue. However, this shall not be a reason to elevate it. Ideas should not be exalted because of this, and become something that dominates us as knowers, or even prostrates us to worship them. It's like saying that because someone is kind to me, I call that person a "good person". Whether or not he/she is a good person needs to be examined objectively and broadly, not just by his/her attitude towards me. This is a *reversal of the subjective and objective relationship*—although Plato and his followers might not have been aware of their own motives for this hidden economy. Therefore, when we worship Ideas, we worship ourselves, and we put our own needs above external objects.

Second, there has been insufficient logical basis for an Idea to be elevated as a *universality* and defined as the "essence" of a concrete object. Ideas were clearly generated through the observation of concrete objects. Specific objects generally have a multitude of properties. In the midst of these different properties, since a certain property was also found in many other objects, then, like a "black chicken" becomes a "phoenix", this property leaped to the top of the others, and was upgraded to something that had a dominant power over the whole specific object. It's as if when children play games, some children bully others because they have more friends, or a tyranny of the majority is created under the voting rule of "the minority obeys the majority". A reason why the majority is greater than the minority is precisely the fact that the voting statistics are based on the principle of individual equality, so it is unfair that after the statistics are completed, the majority becomes so "majority" that the minority loses its original equality. Universal properties are actually only a part of the properties of concrete things, and are therefore a kind of locality. Since this locality has risen above the whole concrete things, it is *a reversal of the relationship between the part and the whole*. Even if a universality were to be exalted, it would obviously not be enough simply because other things also have this universal property; new reasons shall be needed here to explain why such universality is so "overwhelming". However, such explanations did not actually exist; or, there are no truly effective or convincing explanations, and the universality is apparently regarded as "overwhelming" only because of its dominance (i.e., computationally economical) in statistics on individuals. Since Plato was unable to further explain where this universality came from, he had developed an excessive imagination and admiration for it, and mistakenly thought that there was behind it something more mysterious, more regular, and more compatible with our human needs—it is speculated that occasional intellectual innovations would fitfully stimulate this spiritual excitement in the direction of Parmenides' monism. Correspondingly, particularities were "blamed" and discriminated against because they are not easy to deal with.

Finally, as a kind of "perfect" thing, an Idea became a concrete thing with the help of "participation" and "imitation", and the purpose of the existence of concrete things was understood to pursue the perfect Idea. Such a logical cycle exists not only in Plato's philosophy, but also in many other similar philosophies, such as Hegel's. Then, why do we have this meaningless cycle? This is a question that readers may often ask. The answer to this question obviously requires the addition of our own human purpose, rather than hiding it and pretending to assume that external objects have their own purposes. However, in order to achieve our own ends, we need the thinking processes and the roundabout assumption of virtual entities that conduct the thinking processes. Specifically, when we live in the phenomenal world, we either need to understand the phenomena or control them in order to meet our own needs; for this reason, we construct models, discover the properties of universality, necessity, etc., and then add particularity, contingency, and other factors to them, so as to realize the explanation or control of the phenomenal world. Therefore, this cycle is not a simple, meaningless logical error but a "productive process" of thinking. It starts with the phenomenon, expands computations, and finally returns to the phenomenon for "delivery". Plato turned the process upside down, starting with Idea and ending with Idea. This is *an inversion of the end and the means.*

## §146. Plato (2)

Corresponding to the above ontology is Plato's epistemology. Since an Idea was eternal and absolute, it could not be a product of human. However, the human soul was "knowing" the Idea, just as it knew a good friend of the past. The immortal soul once knew the Idea in life, and later, the soul lived inside the body and forgot about it. Then, by recalling, one could regain a grasp of Ideas, and observation and learning could help one to do so. In this way, Plato barely combined his ontology with epistemology. His doctrine even dealt with the concepts of "conjecture" (eikasia), "belief" (pistis), "calculate" (dianoia), "reason" (noesis), and so on, which he regarded as the "functions" of the soul.

The doctrine of "re-gaining" Ideas through recalling has become a typical example of the theory of innate knowledge in the history of philosophy. That is, there is indeed something innate in the human brain, but what is innate is not the tool of thinking, but the results of thinking—knowledge. It is a pity that Plato failed to distinguish between the tools of thinking and their results. But, considering that the innate tools of the mind have not been discovered until now, we certainly have no right to blame Plato captiously. The reason why the theory of innate knowledge shall be inferior to the theory of innate tools of thinking is that the former cannot explain a flaw, change, and development of knowledge. It can be said that the absence of this distinction makes the theory of Idea very clumsy and vulnerable. The incorrigibility of the theory of Idea is also reflected in the invalidity of many of Plato's own later corrections. Yet, despite this, the diligent thinker seemed to have approached the heart of the matter. The above-mentioned doctrine of the functions of the soul flashes the shadow of Algorithmic Theory. The four functions of the soul can be approximated as four Instructions or Commands that represent different kinds of computational jobs. In particular, Plato recognized that it is not enough for a thinking process to proceed merely from concrete materials and objects and to carry out empiricist work only. At a certain point, the soul shall turn and move in reverse from the highest Idea, the good, or the "first principle". In fact, this was emphasizing the importance of the theoretical method, pointing out that it can be used (at least) as an initiative, fundamental method.

Believing in the objective existence of Ideas can also be deemed emphasizing the objectivity of knowledge. Algorithmically, this kind of objectivity has at least two meanings: 1. The thinking activities of people to understand the objective world will always lead to some results, and they will not get nothing. Thinking tools process information, and there will always be something to be gained, and nothing will not be obtained. This refers to the concreteness of thinking: the thinking tools, the thinking activities, and the thinking results are all concrete, neither everything nor nothing—regardless of their varied quality and effectiveness. 2. A computing result can be definite, eternal, and interpersonally universal. If the result is A, it is not B; it will not be A today and B tomorrow; it will not be A for Mike and B for Tom. In other words, *we can understand or reinterpret the belief in the existence and objectivity of truth that has prevailed in philosophy since Parmenides and Plato as the definiteness, eternity, and interpersonal universality of the results of the processing of specific information by specific Instructions.* Although this belief has been skewed due to the absence of Algorithmic Theory, which has led to the confusion of this objectivity with that of the ultimate truth of all epistemic processes, the belief, or relevant beliefs, has always been firm. The ambiguity in it can now be clarified by Algorithmic Theory.

Plato's doctrine of "soul first, matter second" is another consequence of the development of the above skewness. The logical flaws are obvious, and they were bound to be criticized and corrected by later scholars, including Aristotle. I'd like not to detail this for now. Another doctrine that has had widespread influence is his tripartite division of the soul, which stated that the soul could be divided into three parts: reason, passion, and desire. This has been the standard doctrine for separating the rational from the "irrational". Even though this doctrine has had different versions in later generations, its basic idea has not changed to this day. In my opinion, this can be clear proof of the originality and creativity of the Algorithmic theory of knowledge, that is, the theory of sedimentation, distortion, and solidification of thinking. The mainstream intellectual community has never recognized that rational thinking will inevitably lead to the generation of knowledge stock under the limitation of computing speed, and simultaneously, the knowledge stock must have the characteristics of "irrationality" from multiple perspectives. In this sense, passions, desires, and knowledge are all similar in character, and they are all inextricably linked to rational activity.


## §147. Plato (3)

Let's now turn to a commentary on Plato's political doctrine.

For Western societies that lead the world with their democratic and liberal systems, Plato's political theory is nothing short of an embarrassment, because it is really and definitely a founding doctrine of communism while it was developed and strongly advocated by leaders in the Western intelligentsia. From Socrates to Plato, who witnessed the decline and failure of Greek democracy, they proposed a doctrine akin to technocracy, which meant that people should not indulge in the war of words in democratic debates, but should perfect knowledge (virtue and truth). Once sound knowledge was established, society could be organized pursuant to the guidance of that knowledge, without the need for democratic procedures. If the ruler could be the ruler of this knowledge, namely, the "philosopher-king", then an ideal state could become a reality.

On the positive side, Plato raised an excellent philosophical question. In a typical scenario, using clear logic and expression, the idea was conceived and proposed. Whatever the idea is, the way it was presented was not arbitrary. This is conducive to a rational analysis and discussion. The attitude of the Western world towards the ideal state in The Republic has also been quite mild and restrained: it was neither blindly condemned nor simply complied with, but studied soberly and reasonably by successive generations of scholars. However, it is clear that no breakthrough has been made in this study until Algorithmic Theory. Academicians have been either speechless on those crucial issues involved or they have been content with some of Plato's pluralistic and comprehensive discourses that made compromises on them. To a certain extent, the concept of the "philosopher-king" is in the interests of intellectuals. Moreover, in the real world, just as "virtue", which represents the overall and long-term social good, is always lacking, high-quality knowledge is often despised or ignored. Thus, the emphasis on knowledge and reason seems harmless. However, the fact that autocracy and democracy are currently still in sharp opposition on a global scale shows that the classical philosophical problem is remaining, and that its solution is in fact demanded urgently!

There is a clear correspondence between the dominance of the philosopher-king over the ideal state and the dominance of the world of Ideas over the real world (no wonder Plato was regarded by Karl Popper as the inventor of communism[19]). Therefore, as long as the basic philosophical problems are solved, Plato's political science will be self-defeating. Algorithmically, when we think of the world of Ideas as the world of human thoughts, this question can be easy to answer.

While we can think of high-quality knowledge (and any other knowledge) as an "objective existence" that is relatively independent of any specific person, it is not independent of all human beings. If there were no human beings, there would be no knowledge, and therefore there would be no such "world of Ideas". At the same time, the world of Ideas is obviously a collection of high-quality knowledge accumulated by human beings up to a certain point in time, which is inherited and mastered by intellectuals at this point in time, and

---

19. Karl Popper, "The Open Society and its Enemies", Vol. I, London: Routledge & Kenan Paul Ltd., 1962.

disseminated to society. Since it was resulted from longtime selection, it is not easy for people nowadays to perceive its slow updating, so that it may be mistaken as the static, absolute, and complete knowledge. However, it is only one part of the knowledge required for successful practice, and the other parts (as "particularity", "contingency", etc.) have been in the hands of ordinary people. Therefore, ordinary people are of indispensable importance in computing. Knowledge, on the other hand, does not function on its own; it always needs to be applied by people. As a person, the "philosopher king" is also limited by computing power and memory, and the knowledge he can master is limited in quality and quantity. There is *endogenously* no person who can fully grasp and apply all knowledge (general, special, high-quality, low-quality, centralized, fragmented, etc.) in a timely manner. The idea that affairs of society as a whole can be controlled and managed by a small amount of high-quality knowledge in a concise form by a few individuals is also *endogenously* unfeasible. These can be the iron Algorithmic laws. These iron laws lead to the absolute unviability of communism, and that power and democracy can only exist relatively, cooperating and competing concretely in the context of time and space. Meanwhile, it should be emphasized that the quantity and subjectivity of knowledge, and the infinite development caused by the combinatorial explosion are indispensable in this rebuttal argument.

Why was universality, as a local element contained in concrete things, mistakenly and reversely regarded as dominating over a whole concrete thing? How did this illusion come about? I think this question needs to be further explained, and Algorithmic Theory can also provide an explanation for this. Parmenides's Being, and Plato's Idea, clearly represented the knowledge that people had *already* achieved about things, but the rest of things had not yet been known. Then, when people acted, of course, they should give priority to the knowledge they had already acquired and acted on the parts of things that they could control. As for the parts of things that were not yet controllable, the measures that one could take (i.e., the management of ignorance itself), if any, were relatively few, and their strength and effectiveness were necessarily weak. Therefore, the objective world formed by people's actions could be regarded mainly as the embodiment of the dominance of knowledge, and the history of humankind could also be regarded mainly as the result of the dominance of knowledge. This is for society (as a result of actions). It is similar in the case of the natural world: an observer always relies mainly on his/her own knowledge to explain natural phenomena, which makes it seem as if the observer's *own* knowledge has *active* dominance over the natural world. This dominance, combined with the obvious, somewhat acknowledged developmentality of knowledge, has led thinkers to believe that the dominance of knowledge would be even greater in the future.

Nonetheless, Socrates and Plato's criticisms of the Athenian system of direct democracy were not entirely unfounded. The citizens' assembly had a large number of people, and its frequent meetings would inevitably cause a major waste of computing power. The limitation of computing power led to the division of knowledge, so it was reasonable to leave specific affairs to specific people to make their decisions and handle them. This is the rationale of the theory of technocracy. The discussions in which citizens came together were a kind of current computations. Regardless of how the citizens' assembly was organized, the nature, scope, and number of matters that it could effectively consider must be quite limited, and the knowledge that was scattered in the depths of people's minds and in the corners of society needed to grow up to be used in the decision-making processes of all kinds of public or private matters in an appropriate way; and, new knowledge needed to be developed in a decentralized, continuous, and routine manner outside of the meetings. This was not completely foreseeable at the site of the citizens' assembly. The close proximity of citizens, while conducive to their communication, could also (Algorithmically and distortively) lead to emotional problems, personal or group grievances, and strife. When the citizens' assembly *gathered* enormous powers, its members might become bold and arrogant, contemptuous of traditions, experiences, and conventions, to the point of abusing their power and making decisions only at will.

It can be found that the improvement of Athenian democracy in later history was carried out in multiple directions. This improvement was undoubtedly driven in part by the Greek philosophy of rationalism. One of the directions was to strengthen and improve the judicial and administrative systems so that they could assume additional functions. The second direction was to implement the representative system. Ordinary citizens did not directly participate in the discussion of politics, but elected their representatives and entrusted them to participate in politics. The political computations were thus divided into the above two sections. Elected representatives were often not only intellectually superior to average people, but also had the time and enthusiasm to engage in politics (which has since finally developed to the point of their professionalization). But that was still not enough. A constitution was also needed to govern all who were alive. As a "dead" text written on paper, the constitution reflects the wisdom and wills of our ancestors, and participates in the management of the affairs of the current world. The powers of all public institutions, including the citizens' assembly, were limited in order to ensure social freedom and to allow it to freely develop new knowledge and avoid using existing knowledge alone to decide *everything*.

The last thing to mention is the philosophy of art. Just one thing to say: as an extreme rationalist, it is not surprising that Plato was hostile to art, just as he despised passions and desires. This position could be renamed the "*anti-Algorithmic position*".

## §148. Aristotle

From the point of view of philosophical history, profound Aristotle can be seen as a complementary figure to his teacher, Plato. Even in terms of the "profoundness", he was trying to make up for what the outspoken Plato had overlooked. However, Aristotle was not able to replace Plato. He was not able to fundamentally overturn Plato's system, nor was he able to correct some of Plato's key mistakes. Most of the time he tried to offer his readers what Plato did not, but at other times he simply echoed and followed his teacher. Although his additions to Plato were important enough to stand up to the teacher, the two failed to merge into a single whole, so much so that the split continues to this day. He had some misfortune because the top spot was already occupied by his teacher, and he was forced to take the secondary seat. Thus, while Aristotle's writings are enormous, our comments here are relatively brief.

Aristotle was a problem-oriented philosopher. Correspondingly, the comments here also deal with a number of relatively separate topics.

The first topic is on the empirical and inductive approaches. Aristotle explicitly rejected Plato's Idea that was separated from concrete things, and instead asserted the reality of the concrete and its substantive status. His vast knowledge and extensive exploration are matched by the title of "encyclopedic thinker". The processing of a large amount of empirical material necessarily requires the use of inductive methods, so it is unsurprising that he is the founder of inductive methods and the whole logical system. Nowadays, induction based on empirical materials has become a daily and major scientific research work, and has even become a sign of the "scientificity" of research work, so that people sometimes even forget theoretical work. With regard to the status of induction and its relation to other methods, Aristotle rightly pointed out that "Clearly then it must be by induction that we acquire knowledge of the primary premises"[20], stressing that induction plays a crucial role in the initial stage of understanding. Furthermore, the economic Algorithmic factor also leads to the fact that inductive methods can be applied to any thinking process, interspersing with deductive methods and other methods, at the expense of some accuracy in order to achieve conciseness and speediness.

The second topic is about logic. The rigorous research methods from Socrates and Plato finally bore fruit in Aristotle, which was the great logic, initiated by Aristotle. Although this original discipline cannot be impeccable to today's logicians, the fact that it has dominated the academic world for 2,000 years is enough to prove its tenability. This tenability must have reached a point where it could satisfy the curiosity of the world and the applicative needs in the meantime. Aristotle's dismantling of the human mind into parts and fragments, such as the subject, the predicate, the deduction, the syllogism, and so on, shows quite clearly how the thinking activity itself is constituted. This is extremely important for later scholars to study the microscopic processes of mental activity. For example, the division between subject and predicate can be seen as the prototype of the "Instruction + information" structure, especially the use of abstract symbols[21], which points to the "constancy of thinking tools" and "variability of

---

20. Aristotle, "Posterior Analytics", translated by Hugh Tredennick. London: William Heinemann Ltd. Cambridge, Massachusetts: Harvard University Press, 1960, p. 261.
21. Jonathan Barnes (ed.), "The Complete Works of Aristotle", the Revised Oxford Translation, Princeton University Press, 1984, p. 40 and afterwards.

information". Again, according to Aristotle, inductive reasoning and deductive reasoning work in tandem with each other. The inductive process provides propositions or "premises", and the deductive process builds on this for further in-depth work. This simple and clear partnership results in a "pipeline" style of serial computing. This is fundamental to understanding computer principles and Algorithmic Theory. Logic and mathematics originally developed relatively independently, but by the nineteenth century they combined to produce Boolean algebra and formal logic, which formed the direct basis for the birth of modern computers. This clear line of development illustrates the continuity between computer science and logic. The birth of computers further promoted the development of logic, making it prosperous like never before. Now, by proposing the concept of "Algorithmic logic", it is finally able to unify different forms of logic into an organic whole. This is also the unification of logic and the theory of thinking. Algorithmic Thinking Theory can be viewed as an extended version of logic, while "pre-Algorithmic" various logics can be viewed as some particulars of ATT (when assuming that the computing time is zero, ignoring the materiality of thoughts, and so on).

Now let's comment on Aristotle's metaphysics (or ontology). Compared to Plato's simple and absolute theory of Idea, Aristotle's "First Philosophy" appears chaotic and fickle. He said that concrete things were "substances" and that their "species" and "genera" were also substances ("secondary substances"). Sometimes he said that essence was substance, sometimes a form was a substance, and he named God "the highest substance", and so on.[22] This confusion shows the self-conflicting dilemma that empiricists often fall into, which is

---

22. Unless otherwise specified, the historic facts about Aristotle in this section mainly come from Zhiwei Zhang (ed.), "A History of Western Philosophy" (in Chinese, 2nd), China Renmin University Press, 2010, pp. 80-101, and Frank Thilly, "A History of Philosophy", New Delhi: SBW Publishers, 1993, pp. 75-94.

different from the Platonic dilemma, but was clearly subject to Plato. For this dilemma, it is certainly easy to criticize. However, it is better in this case to find a way out for it. I believe that this way out is the Algorithmic approach. What Aristotle called a "substance", as mentioned earlier, is a relatively independent object. With the help of such objects, the phenomenal world can be divided into individual substances, the natures of substances, the relationships between substances, and the changes of substances. Natures, relationships, and changes are all attached to a substance or substances. In this way, the number of independent objects would be greatly reduced, and the economy of computation and representation would be greatly improved. This approach is still used today. The computational economy is clearly the decisive reason for this. Because of this, Aristotle defined very different substances in different contexts. He apparently didn't care about their inconsistency. Rather, this becomes evidence that as long as a substance (or entity) can achieve the purpose of computing economy, there would be no need for other "criteria" to define it again. This direction actually leads to pluralism.

However, Aristotle still lacked the consciousness of "bounded rationality", thus, he tried to draw conclusions about the truth of the whole world, and he apparently believed that the objective world was suitable for him and allowed him to do so. This was the kind of metaphysics that was going to entail those excessive, uneconomical, and cost-ineffective computing activities. "Essential being", "being as being", "the what it was to be", "that which is neither predicable of a subject nor present in a subject", "primary substance", "self-sufficiency", "fulfillment", etc., in fact, all indicate the attempts of "lazy thinking", i.e., that since computations had arrived at this point as the "destination" (or "source"), there was a reason not to proceed any more. However, in this interconnected world, this ultimate destination is actually very difficult to find. Even if it does, it doesn't mean anything fundamental enough to make us really see the "end of the world". Like Plato, Aristotle was still anxious to see the "end of the world", so he pursued the "unmoved first mover", regarding God as the highest substance.

Another case of the "superfluous metaphysics" is the assumption that conditions of the world correspond one-to-one to elements of the human mind. Thus, in the tradition of Platonian division, Aristotle liked to first make an all-encompassing outlined wholeness, and then to argue one by one by elimination under this whole, and finally to arrive at a conclusion that logically seemed to make sense, whereas the readers might be confused more. The typical sentence structure is: "There are several situations of something—discuss these situations, affirming or denying them respectively —hence the conclusion can only be..."

Thinking (reason), although present in the discourse, is deemed the same as the object ("in the case of objects which involve no matter, what thinks and what is thought are identical; for speculative knowledge and its object are identical"[23]) and does not exist independently. For a logician with an empiricist tendency, this view seems bizarre. The system of thought was clearly regarded as a tightly cohesive mass within itself, and thus did not distinguish between the flow of thought (although the division between the "active" and the "passive" implies that thinking activity might sometimes have been vaguely regarded as a behavioral flow) and its stock, and, in particular, did not recognize that the stocks of knowledge could exist as finite, individualized "entities" with their specific rhythms of changes. In the discourse of logic, Aristotle arbitrarily interspersed between logical and ontological contents, in which the existence of human concrete

---

23. Jonathan Barnes ed., "The Complete Works of Aristotle", Vol. I, Princeton University Press, 1995, p.683.

thoughts failed to serve as an intermediary of them. I believe that the discussion of logic and language should only be carried out in correspondence with the specific contents of human minds, and should not be rashly jumped into any substantive topics, otherwise, it will cause confusion. According to Aristotle's style, there would have been no obstacle to his identification of the substances or entities of thought, but unfortunately, he was not able to identify thought distinctively, and did not explicitly enter into the approach of pluralism and bounded rationality, which led to his inability to deny and surpass Plato. On the contrary, this deficiency continued into the philosophy of language in the twentieth century, where it caused further confusion and ineffectiveness.

## §149. Pluralism, Skepticism

Some parts of Greek philosophy from the early to the late period are worth mentioning here because they are much more closely related to the Algorithmic theory. The first is the atomism of Democritus (as well as Epicurus, Lucretius, etc.), and the theory of the "seed" of Anaxagoras[24] (as in the later Stoic narratives). Atoms and seeds, as the smallest units, either through permutations or through their combination with environmental factors, evolved and developed into the phenomenal world. From the perspective of the broad effectiveness of Algorithm Theory, this reductive method of "explaining the macro with the micro" has great potential. Algorithmic Theory only expands the application of this reductive method of natural philosophy to the object of

---

24. Unless otherwise specified, the historic facts on Empedocles, Alaxagoras, and Democritus in this section mainly come from Zhiwei Zhang (ed.), "A History of Western Philosophy" (in Chinese, 2nd), China Renmin University Press, 2010, pp. 39-47, and A. C. Grayling, "The History of Philosophy", New York: Penguin Press, 2019, pp. 39-49.

"human thinking". Moreover, such a microscopic approach was naturally linked to the theory of dynamics, so all the above authors have put forward their own unique dynamic discourses. Lucretius, in particular, even developed a panoramic theory of dynamic evolution from nature to society.

Such micro theories can also be readily associated with pluralism. In this regard, Empedocles' theory of the "four roots" (fire, earth, air, and water) shall be mentioned first. As for the basic elements of the world, it is unnecessary for just one; why not assume that there were multiple basic elements?!

Such micro theories can also be readily related to epistemology. Thus, there were Empedocles' theory about the subject-object similarity and the object-sense streaming[25], Anaxagoras's theory about the subject-object opposition[26], and Democritus's "image" theory[27]. The journey from epistemology can also be very close to skepticism or bounded rationality. Thus, Democritus uttered the following very forward-looking, even Kantian statement: "Now that in reality we do not grasp what each thing is or is not in character, has been made clear in many ways...A man must know by this yardstick that he is separated from reality...This argument too shows that in reality we know nothing about anything, but for each of us there is a reshaping—belief."[28]

Skepticism is undoubtedly a philosophical school of great value. In the case of rationalism as the mainstream, it has to carry the other heterodox half of the world on its own, which is really a "heavy responsibility". We say "half of the world"

---


25. A. C. Grayling, "The History of Philosophy", New York: Penguin Press, 2019, p. 41.
26. Ibid, p. 46.
27. Frank Thilly, "A History of Philosophy", New Delhi: SBW Publishers, 1993, p. 39.
28. GS. Kirk; J.E. Raven; M. Schofield. "The Presocratic Philosophers", Cambridge University Press, 1988, p. 410.

because an appropriate concept of "rationality", or "bounded rationality", necessarily requires at least the mutual penetration of positive and negative factors in order to be formed. Factors on the one hand affirm the role of rationality, while factors on the other deny or limit the role of rationality (or propose another kind of rationality, such as the Algorithmical rationality). Unfortunately, skepticism was still significantly weaker in Greece. Assertions as brilliant as those of Democritus were rare, and most other skepticisms took the line of directly doubting or denying the truth or effectiveness of knowledge. For example, Pyrrho argued that arguers could not say what a phenomenon was, only what it appeared or looked to be; therefore, the best thing to do was to remain silent and unswervingly insist on not expressing any opinions.[29] Aenesidemus's ten arguments for doubting knowledge mainly emphasized the difference and relativity of individuals, that is, universal and objective knowledge was not easy to obtain.[30] Agrippa's five arguments emphasized the divergence of opinions, infinite regression, relativity, hypothetical arbitrariness, and circular arguments, and thus advocated doubting all knowledge.[31]

However, it is not enough to destroy through suspicion, and it is also necessary to build, that is, to specify what the "face" of "reason" (or rationality) really looks like, how limited it is, how it develops, and so on. It is not enough for a pluralistic philosophy to merely make ontological statements or assumptions that are distinct from monism. Such pluralism is not much different from monism in terms of methodology. It is just a simple dogma for people to choose from. Accepting such

---

29. A. C. Grayling, "The History of Philosophy", New York: Penguin Press, 2019, p. 120.
30. Frederick Copleston, "A History of Philosophy", Vol. 1, New York: Image Books (Doubleday), 1993, p. 443.
31. Ibid, pp. 443-444.

a pluralism and thus rejecting monism is equally rigid, arbitrary, and divisive. As mentioned earlier, in order for skepticism or agnosticism to enter into the core of philosophy, just like pluralism to enter into the core of philosophy, both of them need to be bridged by an appropriate epistemology. We need to properly characterize the process of cognition, so that it embraces both absoluteness and relativity, and, in principle, shows the prospect of infinite development. Such an epistemology is *technically* pluralistic in the first place, because there is simple and unmistakable logic (including a finite computational speed) that shows that plurality can occur firstly in large numbers. Neither science nor philosophy should refuse to give *priority* to conclusions based on reliable premises such as these. However, such an epistemology does not exclude a prospect of monism; instead, any opponent can present his own monistic argument within this framework. It also does not reject Parmenides's and Platonic metaphysics, because any metaphysician can try to prove his/her claims within this framework. That is, Algorithmic Theory is an all-encompassing "framework" that is methodologically prudent and safe, whereas Parmenides's and Plato's methods have the opposite drawback, that is, they did not start from the most reliable premises, but from the very beginning of the extremely unreliable propositions, and then deduced from the distance to the near. This approach was necessarily inefficient and extremely risky, as it could easily lead to the total collapse of the entire system. This is a wrong approach that reverses the order relative to the correct approach.

Finally, Epicurus should be mentioned again.[32] Epicurus is known for his philosophy of pleasure. In reality, however, Epicurus emphasized the importance of desire in a relative,

---

32. Frank Thilly, "A History of Philosophy", New Delhi: SBW Publishers, 1993, pp. 101-103.

rather appropriate framework. He valued the positive meanings of desire, but also emphasized that the role of desire should not be exaggerated. This attitude is quite "Algorithmical". This is our general attitude toward any stock of knowledge. In the face of the fickle and dangerous spiritual life, desire can be a stable guide of people's behaviors. It is like a loyal and honest assistant, guarding the bottom line of our physical and mental health. It's not remarkable, but practically reliable.

Epicurus' theory of the social contract emphasized freedom of will, as well as the engineering nature of institutions. In this way, the various Algorithmical elements gradually developed from all corners of ancient Greece.

# CHAPTER 14
# MEDIEVAL PHILOSOPHY

## §150. The Algorithmic Meanings of Belief or Faith

Belief or faith can be grouped into the category of Algorithm of "Assumption". The assumptive method is characterized by the fact that the value of a variable has not been easy to determine reasonably, but it needs to be determined now, so it is valued assumptively without a sufficient base. The valuation can be done randomly or discretionarily on any clues. The person concerned may have known that this valuation was subjective, unreliable, and tentative (a famous saying of Tertullian [c. 160-240 AD], Father of Latin Christianity, is: "Because it's ridiculous, I believe it"[1]), or may not know it but mistakenly believe in its reliability.

In the latter case, it can be called a belief or faith. Beliefs or faiths are rarely invented by the believers themselves, but are usually developed by certain people with specific motives (such as trying to survive and avoid punishment after premarital

---

1. Despite this saying not being found in his extant works, Tertullian is generally deemed a fideist. See Amesbury, Richard, "Fideism", The Stanford Encyclopedia of Philosophy (Summer 2022 Edition), Edward N. Zalta (ed.), URL = <https://plato.stanford.edu/archives/sum2022/entries/fideism/>

pregnancy), and because they meet certain social needs, they are adopted, reinforced, and disseminated, and even with mechanisms of emotion, interest, or coercion to instill them in the audience, and finally making them popular. Individuals generally accept a certain doctrine in a half-pushed, half-agreed ambivalent mood. Religions became popular not so much because of the veracity of their teachings as because of their usefulness. Believe because it is useful, and the beliefs cover up the interests behind, weaken the disputes over interests, and thus make beliefs more useful. These effects are all Algorithmical.

Rationalists "understandably" cannot understand the popularity of religions, whereas they don't give answers to all questions of people, but to a part of them only. This leaves a wide space for the fabrication of myths and religious teachings. It can be speculated that in the relatively small and closed living environment of ancient times, this kind of fabrication must have been very abundant and frequent. The poverty of real life opens the door to imagination and fantasy. It is hard to believe that the first person to fabricate a religious doctrine did not know that it was apocryphal and thus would have been "convinced" of his own works. Nowadays, even as a scholar who recognizes the importance of belief systems, I cannot accept religious teachings, not because I know that theism is 100% wrong, but because I am sure that authors of these works, like me, must have no reliable means of knowing the existence of God, and therefore I can assume that the motives for writing these works must contain an element of dishonesty. That is, even if God exists, these authors themselves cannot possibly know about it. Even if some "miracles" have "happened" to them (or those involved) in a misinterpreted way to convince their minds, the vast amount of other "evidence" is clearly unreliable and even bears the marks of manipulation.

The religious doctrines that prevail today are not

necessarily the most brilliant and enigmatic ones, but just among the doctrines that are most fortunate to have their persistent written records. In the relatively closed and lonely conditions of ancient life, religions told people what the world they lived in was "really" like, where it came from, where it was going, what rules they needed to abide by, what otherwise the consequences of a violation would be (no matter how true they were), how to deal with the confusions and pains of their hearts, and so on. Religious stories are also intertwined with useful, beneficial, or entertaining activities in order to make the most of the time occupied by religious activities. In particular, I believe that the flourishing of religions in the Western world has something to do with the free and democratic traditions of Western politics that originated in ancient Greece and Rome (even in the Roman Empire, autocracy was obviously not as strong, strict, and pervasive as in China), because in a relatively relaxed and liberal environment, governmental activities were relatively weak, whereas people's minds, Algorithmically, needed to be guided *positively* and *actively*, not only passively by rules. As a result, religions developed as "informal institutions" outside the government. In China, the government was relatively strong, and the ideology supported by the government was directly involved in the management of people's minds and everyday life, which crowded out to some extent the space for religions to expand, making religions not as prosperous as in the West.

Religions have their origin in ignorance. In other words, religions originated from people's desire to generalize and summarize the world despite a lack of knowledge. This Algorithmical truth was not only recognized and publicly acknowledged by theologians themselves, but also *repeatedly emphasized by many theologians.* Theologians' explanations of religions generally began with rational explanations, but at a certain stage, they resorted to faith, and even openly stated that some parts of the doctrines could not be explained by reason, but only by faith. For example, St. Anselm (1033-1109) talked about the interaction between understanding and faith[2], while Thomas Aquinas attempted to illustrate the cooperation between theology and philosophy and their mutual transformation. He said that the differences between philosophy and theology lay first and foremost in their goals and objects; outside of theology, there was a lot of room for rational thinking about the real world; reason was not omnipotent, not knowing all truths; on top of the real natural world, there was a surreal, supernatural world.[3] "Although those things that are higher than man's knowledge may not be sought for by man through his reason, nevertheless, once they are revealed by God, they must be accepted by faith."[4] Such discussions are quite pertinent to the substitutive relationship between mainstream Algorithms and alternative Algorithms.

In connection with the above point, there are two more figures that need to be mentioned here. One is Roger Bacon (1214-1294). Bacon held a rare synthetic, relative view of mental activity and knowledge systems. He argued that knowledge had three sources: authority, reason, and experience. In fact, this proposition tends to distinguish the accumulated stock of knowledge from the current productive flows. And, on another distinction between theory and experience, he also identified the "external experience" and "internal experience", the latter referring to the results of thinking on various issues. Even if these results were virtues, beliefs, etc., he regarded them as

---

2. Frederick Copleston, "A History of Philosophy", Vol. 2, New York: Image Books (Doubleday), 1993, p. 156.

3. John Marenbon (ed.), "Routledge History of Philosophy", Vol. III, ebook, Routledge, 2004, pp. 268-269 and pp. 291-292; And Zhiwei Zhang (ed.), "A History of Western Philosophy" (in Chinese, 2nd), China Renmin University Press, 2010, pp. 182-184.

4. Thomas Aquinas, "The Summa Theologica", revised by Daniel J. Sullivan, Chicago: William Benton, 1952, pp. 3-4.

some "experiences".[5] These synthetic views are close to the Algorithmical views of knowledge, therefore, I cannot agree with the allegation of the philosophical historian that "Bacon confused science, ethics with religious beliefs, which exhibits the chaos in his mind."[6]

The other was Nicholas of Cusa (1401-1464). According to Nicholas, the human spirit was a unified whole, which was manifested in the four faculties of sensibility, imagination, intellect, and reason. The different stages of cognition were not isolated, but constituted a system of commonality, interdependence, and mutuality. Cusa emphasized the finitude of human cognitive ability, thereby allowing our "alternative Algorithms" to function significantly. For example, he argued that the grasp of God was not achieved directly through deductive reasoning, "but by analogy and the transcendence of reason. In this sense, it is a non-incomprehensible way, an ignorance in terms of precise cognition; however, ... it is also a kind of approximate cognition, knowingly somehow. Moreover, the recognition that God is infinite and cannot be known exactly is in itself a kind of knowledge of God, and a kind of knowledge of our own ability to know. The concept of 'learned ignorance' is used in this sense. ... Cusa denied that we could know the truth precisely, but believed that we could approach the truth infinitely through constant speculation, ... and that the true meaning of cognition lies just in this dialectical unity of 'unreachable' and 'nearer'".[7] Obviously, this kind of rare but

---

5. Roger Bacon, "The Opus Majus", Vol. 1 & 2, translated by Robert B. Burke, University Of Pennsylvania Press, 1928, pp. 3-5 and pp. 583-586.

6. Zhiwei Zhang (ed.), "A History of Western Philosophy" (in Chinese, 2nd), China Renmin University Press, 2010, p. 199, translated by me.

7. Zhiwei Zhang (ed.), "A History of Western Philosophy" (in Chinese, 2nd), China Renmin University Press, 2010, p. 238. The ellipses are added by me. The historic facts here about Nicholas come mainly from this book, pp. 234-238, and Frederick Copleston, "A History of Philosophy", Vol. 3, New York: Image Books (Doubleday), 1993, pp. 231-247.

still incomplete thought would not be completed until the Algorithmic age.

## §151. Realism vs. Nominalism

For the ontologists of the Greek day, medieval Christian philosophy must have been a big surprise to them. An arbitrary and obscure philosophical hypothesis had been developed to such an extent that philosophy itself was about to become its "handmaiden"! The reason for this unbelievable phenomenon cannot be found solely within philosophy, and it is clear that the establishment of the Roman Empire was an important reason for the flourishing of Christianity, theology, and thus the religious philosophy. The empire needed a unified rule, which shall be why they needed a unified religion and philosophy. How could an empire tolerate pluralism? The causality that social forces and interests have an influence on the direction, degree, and content of mental activity should be established as an Algorithmic principle. Because, like any other activity, computing activities are physical or material activities that compete for resources. If computations were effortlessly carried out from beginning to end at once, they would be difficult for other materialized factors to affect.

The Being of Parmenides, and the Idea of Plato, now were replaced by the concept of "God". Apologists went to great lengths to describe God's existence and how it worked, arguing for its great meanings from all angles. In order to avoid criticism and reduce doubt, God was both everything and not everything, both logical and illogical, both personal and impersonal, and it has been shaped by various theological philosophers in different contexts that were similar or different. This kind of "assigned jobs" was, of course, not easy to succeed. Thus, the "Original Sin" and "Satan" appeared, representing the finitude of reason to remedy the flaws of the concept of

"God". In the Christian narratives, the basic pattern and order are exactly the opposite of those in philosophical discussions. Philosophical discussions usually start from the real world to explore and deduce the essence behind phenomena, while Christian narratives start from the God, the One, to the occurrences of history and reality, the many. Interestingly, God must first divide the formless and homogeneous world into different parts and create different individuals before he can unfold his story. This generative process vividly illustrates the rationale that differences must take priority. Therefore, philosophical discussions are convergent while Christian discussions are, quite "Algorithmically", divergent and explosive. It seems to be infinitely extending and evolving into the future. After realizing this "danger", it was forced to try to restrain itself. The concepts of "Father", "Son", and "Holy Spirit" could be literally applied well to the occasions in which they were produced, but the problem of their unity seems to have persisted to this day. Why did Jesus leave after his resurrection? Why will he return on the "Day of the Great Judgment" after he left? When will the "doomsday" be? Why will there be such a day? Questions like these are hard to withstand careful interrogations by doubters.

When a philosophy is exaggerated, it has the benefit of being examined more closely to find out what is wrong. The reason why nominalism developed so dramatically in the Middle Ages was that it hit the nail on the head of Christian philosophical realism.

As early as the time of Augustine (354-430), he had already laid the groundwork for nominalism. He said that one could doubt everything, but one could not doubt the actuality and definiteness of one's own *thinking*. Augustine even went so far as to prove the actuality and definiteness of thinking by saying that the human mind can produce errors. He said, "If he doubts, he lives... If he doubts, he thinks... Whoever then doubts about anything else ought never to doubt about all of these; for if they were not, he would be unable to doubt about anything at all."[8] Augustine's view implies the emergence of a thought as a kind of relatively independent object (and entity). This is the necessary foundation of nominalist philosophy. It is only on this basis that the following arguments of Boethius (c. 480-524) are to the point. He believed that "species" and "genus" were the "universals" formed by people collecting similar characteristics between many individual things, and these universals were a kind of thought that exists in people's minds, rather than something above people and concrete things.[9] This concise view is true even in relation to Aristotle. It corrects Aristotle's misconceptions about "species" and "genus". For Aristotle, the classification of "species", "genus", etc. did not seem to be the classification we think of today, but something outside of us, highly above the things, and governing the individual things. This is a Platonist way of understanding. Such an "entity" pretended to be higher than the individuals, but inappropriately became another "individual" and interacted "equally" with the individual concrete things, just as an ewe gave birth to a lamb. Obviously, this error came from the error in Platonic separation of Idea and things. Based on the hierarchical concept, Aristotle further expanded the definition of deductive method, proposing concepts such as "major premise" and "minor premise". These could all be misleading terms. Now, Boethius corrected these mistakes once and for all, namely, that the characteristic defined as a "universal" was itself part of the many characteristics of a concrete thing, and it should not be elevated just because other

---

8. Saint Augustine, "The Trinity", translated By Stephen Mckenna, Washington. D.C.: The Catholic University Of America Press, 2002, p. 308. The ellipses are added by me.

9. A. C. Grayling, "The History of Philosophy", New York: Penguin Press, 2019, p. 143.

concrete things also had such a characteristic. That is, *it is not that it is "greater than" a concrete thing, but that the concrete thing contains it.*

The reason why this concise and clear understanding is worthy of recognition is also relative to many latecomers. For example, even more than 500 years later, Roscelin (1050-1123) was still off track on this issue. Roscelin went to the other extreme, denying general truth, arguing that only individual things had objective truth. Universal was nothing more than a "breath of the voice" or noun, and was therefore empty. His view below may be taken as an illustration of his extreme nominalist position: the Holy Church of Rome was a false name, and only the churches in local places were real.[10] This seemingly extreme view has persisted to this day, and has long been hidden in the perceptions of academicians and the general public, that is, people only sometimes pay lip service to the importance of thought, but in fact they do not know what thought is, do not think that thought is "something", and do not intend to define what thought is. A thought seems to exist or not to exist, it seems to be important or not important, and people sometimes put it among their objects, and some other times they feel that it is not eligible to be among them. When Roscelin said that a universal was just a "noun", he was derogating both the universal and the noun: since nouns were not important, why did people introduce them? Weren't nouns introduced to make expressions concise and thus make ideas concise? Therefore, weren't the nouns some economic existences and therefore some substantial existences?

Roscelin's extreme views were quickly corrected by his pupil Peter Abelard (1079-1142). Abelard argued that a universal

---

10. Bertrand Russell, "A History of Western Philosophy", London: Unwin Paperbacks, 1984, pp. 428-429; Zhiwei Zhang (ed.), "A History of Western Philosophy" (in Chinese, 2nd), China Renmin University Press, 2010, p. 172.

was not just a noun, but a concept in people's minds, although he did not believe that ideas were objectively real. This is called "conceptualism" or a "moderate nominalism".

What is the relationship between the concepts of different individuals, since concepts are in the human minds? On this question, Averroes (1126-1198) and Siger of Brabant (c. 1240-c.1284) put forward an important argument that divided the soul into the soul common to all humankind and the individual soul. When a person died, the individual soul died, but the individual soul was formed by the union of the soul common to all humankind with the individual person, and the soul common to all humankind was immortal as a unified and unique soul, thus the spiritual entities of human beings are immortal.[11] This view already smacks of ATT. Human beings share a system of Instructions, and all the knowledge produced by the combination of Instructions and information can actually be regarded as "potential" and "predestined", except that each person has a different component of it. Given the obstacles created by limited computing power and big data, we as observers don't know exactly what this complete knowledge is. However, the asynchronous, ever-evolving existences of different people have led to human minds and knowledge bases appearing as if they could exist forever outside of the individual people. Such an Algorithmic view can be used to resolve the disagreements between Thomas and Siger about the individual soul. The individuality of a thought does not prevent it from being part of the human knowledge thesaurus.

Thomas made significant contributions to epistemology. He rejected the Greek tradition of opposing rational knowledge and perceptual knowledge and saw the two as complementing each other upstream or downstream. Sensory organs were only

---

11. Frederick Copleston, "A History of Philosophy", Vol. II, New York: Image Books (Doubleday), 1993, pp. 435-436.

used to form sensations and "images" when they came into contact with objects. *The concept of "information" was already coming into play here.* The human intellect processed sensory materials through means such as "abstraction" to *further* form something that were not present in sensations, namely, the universals. At the same time, Thomas had a relative attitude towards the relationship between universals and particulars. However, as a theologian, it was impossible for him to completely abandon the realist attitude of "universal first".[12]

The next prominent figure was William of Occam (c. 1300-1349). His more systematic nominalism was already calling on the later British empiricism. Special mention should be made here of his economics of thinking: Entities are not to be multiplied without necessity.[13] Universal was something that came out of human minds. This kind of thing could be produced, but not necessarily so far that it has become cumbersome, or even harmful. This was a rare and unambiguous statement of the economy of thought. From this perspective, there was a great deal of redundancy in theology and theological philosophy that needed to be eliminated. This was a call to the anti-metaphysical movement six hundred years later. In addition, William explicitly put forward the idea of establishing a language of thought[14], and hence he became a pioneer of Algorithmic Thinking Theory.

The pendulum would swing. The rebellion against God must not stop at individuality and particularity, but also extend to the social sphere. This was the revival of humanism in the Renaissance period. The philosophy of this period emphasized

---

12. Ibid, pp. 375-397.
13. Bertrand Russell, "A History of Western Philosophy", London: Unwin Paperbacks, 1984, pp. 462-463.
14. Pekka Kärkkäinen, "Mental Language", in Henrik Lagerlund (ed.), "Encyclopedia of Medieval Philosophy", 2nd edition, Springer, 2020, pp. 1160-1165.

human, human subjectivity, human dignity, human freedom, human desire, life value, and so on. Even the religious Martin Luther (1483-1546) said that "Who loves not woman, wine, and song remains a fool his whole life long"[15]. The figures of humanists were not only intellectual, but their thoughts or characters were subjective and "crooked". Even Machiavelli's depiction of the monarch's selfishness, insidiousness, and cunning[16] has revolutionary significance. This is all a reaction against the tall, righteous God. From an Algorithmic point of view, the logic here is particularly clear. This is like the political science discussed above: is order built around the monarch or around a large number of individual voters? These are two different distortive ways. While innovations are frequently happening that keep "straightening" the distortions to improve, social affairs need the ultimate adjudicator. The adjudicator is either the monarch or the electorate. In this sense, there is no such thing as perfect order.

## §152. Concluding Remarks

Let's wrap up the comments briefly. The mistake made by the realists to enshrine universals is related to a processing technique, that is, a universal cannot be regarded as the totality of a concrete thing, or, if the universal is to be regarded as the totality of a concrete thing, then the particular attributes of the concrete thing must be left blank in the universal model. It's like a fill-in-the-blank question, to be filled in by particulars. For example, when we speak of a "table" generally, this "table"

---

15. Zhiwei Zhang (ed.), "A History of Western Philosophy" (in Chinese, 2nd), China Renmin University Press, 2010, p. 231; And "The Musical World: A Weekly Record of Musical Science, Literature, and Intelligence", Vol VII, No. 83 (Oct 13, 1837), p. 65.
16. Niccolo Machiavelli, "The Prince", Ottawa, Ontario: East India Publishing Company, 2018.

does have certain characteristics, but its image is still relatively vague in general. This word "table" should not be considered meaningless, nor should it be considered to refer specifically to a table of a particular color and shape.

There are layers of information. One of the efficiencies of human thought and language lies in a certain ambiguity, that is, the use of short words or sentences to refer to a large number of concrete objects, to express something imprecise but by no means meaningless. Discussion along the path of "ambiguity -- precision" can make us realize that the so-called universals and particulars are not only relative, but also vary in degree. Some characteristics are common in a certain range but particular in a larger range. Universal and particular are themselves a simplified taxonomy that attempts to force the complexity of the objective world into line with the requirements of our human mental economy (in Augustine's words, "the unchangeable was to be preferred to the changeable"[17]). Excessive emphasis on universals will cause a great distortion in our understanding of the world, and will make us forget that the real reason for our worship of universals is nothing more than its economy that has pleased us. We worship it because we don't see our motives. In Freudian language, we need psychoanalysis and psychotherapy for ourselves.

In our writing, the word "reason" or "rationality" now clearly has a dual meaning, one referring to the conventional, narrow usage, namely, the objective and rational Algorithms as opposed to the subjective and arbitrary Algorithms, or the mainstream, deductive Algorithms as opposed to the alternative Algorithms. The second refers to the Algorithmical and broad meaning, that is, all Algorithms have their own

---

17. St. Augustine, "Confessions", translated by J.G. Pilkington, The Folio Society Ltd, 1993, p.122.

rationalities in their respective contexts. That is to say, it could be rational to use the deductive methods, and it could also be rational or reasonable to use other alternative Algorithms where it is irrational to use deduction. At this time, it can be argued that the use of the deductive methods has become "unreasonable". It is in this sense that the humanist movement was *rational* or *reasonable*, and the opposite, mechanical, and cold "rationality" was irrational and unreasonable. In other words, mental distortions are not necessarily bad, and operations of "straightening the distortions" are not necessarily good. Specific judgments need to be made in specific contexts. Given the limited choices of wording, we have to use these words temporarily.

Related to this topic is the word "knowledge". Although we have at the outset said that all the results of thinking are collectively referred to as "knowledge" because of the need for convenience, in fact, as the readers may have recognized, the necessity of the broad use of the word is now by no means limited to convenience. In the midst of the great diversity of knowledge that Algorithmic Theory presents to us, it is not easy for us to classify a specific piece of knowledge as a universal or a particular, truth or falsehood, and so on. This is not to say that there are no differences in quality or value between different pieces or types of knowledge. The certainty and constancy of the Instructional functions support the existence of these differences. The goal of computations and arguments between the actors in a specific scenario is just to identify these differences. That being the case, as constructors of general principles, we should transcend these differences and first adopt a neutral and descriptive attitude towards the activities of minds and their results. This attitude inevitably requires us further to adopt a uniform name for the computing results. Thus, my proposal is to expand the scope of the word "knowledge" to this maximum. Of course, there might be other alternative words.

There is also the word "soul", which needs to be analyzed again. In philosophical language to date, the word "soul" appears frequently. Obviously, sometimes it refers to the whole spiritual system or the system of thought, and sometimes it refers to that thing in the human mind that is particularly active, jumping around, and wandering freely. At this point, it is clearly referring to conscious activity. Algorithmically speaking, it refers to the "central processing unit", or to the "meta-computation". We think of the soul as actively "running around", which can be interpreted as different data moving in and out of the central processing unit. It is a relative motion. This relative movement does not prevent the soul from being able to engage in a large number of proactive "movements" in the intervals between passive movements (e.g., information-driven computations). I have also used this Algorithmic approach to discuss the topic of "immortal soul". Since the focus of this book is on principles and foundations, this topic will be left for now.

# CHAPTER 15
# MODERN PHILOSOPHY

## §153. Introduction

On one side were the things, and on the other side was the "Being" or God, and the role of human in it was ambiguous. In modern times, this situation had finally begun to collapse. For, at least some philosophers had come to realize that the latter was nothing more than ideas in the human mind, and that philosophy was only to discuss the nature, composition, origin, formation, and future of these ideas. According to this understanding, philosophy turned into epistemology, which was further manifested in the relationship between mind and matter.

However, the epistemological problems in modern philosophy were narrow, and the focus was still on continuing the spirit of Greek philosophy, which was the one-sided pursuit of high-quality knowledge (or "science") to the exclusion of other types of knowledge that were not so high-quality. In this way, the position and posture of philosophy changed literally, but its tone and style had not changed much; thus, epistemological philosophy was just a fine, upgraded version of Greek philosophy (and medieval philosophy).

Words such as Being, Substance, and God were now replaced by words such as ideas, truth, science, etc., but their statuses were still broadly similar. The "fact" that infallible knowledge existed, at least partially, was not doubted by most philosophers, and the problem was only how to interpret or illustrate it. Such a system would inevitably remain static. Even if the local, weak dynamics were accommodated, it still faced a final static ending. Once again, we can feel strongly how Algorithmic Thinking Theory is closely related to the theme of the history of philosophy, and how it involves every chapter and page of it. Since the mystery here is too simple, we can repeat it again: the innate mental apparatus must be thought of as discrete, diverse, and finite, and they work serially on a timeline to form both local or temporary equilibria and combinatorial explosions and infinite developments over the long term. If we take this Algorithmical theory as the concise answer to all these discussions, then we can see by comparison how each philosophy revolved around it but missed it, and that they advanced and attempted in different directions, and finally all failed to hit the bull's eye. The actual differences in the thinking of these philosophers were generally not as great as commonly assumed. Following the logic, we can even foresee how some inappropriate philosophies would emerge. In the vast history of philosophy, we cannot completely rule out (and even reasonably speculate) any possible proposition of ideas or theories similar to Algorithmic Theory. However, before the advent of the concrete and successful practical paradigm of computers, such a proposition, if it had been put forward, was unlikely to attract attention, let alone gain the upper hand or be universally accepted.

This is by no means to say that the spirit of science is not important. Computers themselves are a product of scientific progress. In fact, the scientific spirit originated from the West has become a key force leading the progress of human civilization. Although the obsession with high-quality knowledge is a kind of "mental distortion", it has objectively increased the impetus for scientific development. The Algorithmic philosophy can be embodied in today's famous saying, "Only the paranoid survive".

Kant initiated a crucial reversal in the direction of philosophy. Those ideas forgotten by scientists and their advocates would not be rediscovered until after Hegel. However, there was still a long way to go before these philosophical problems were to be solved.


## §154. Bacon, Descartes

In the history of philosophy, although Francis Bacon is only regarded as a forerunner of modern philosophy, I believe that his excellence even surpassed that of many later generations. His research on scientific methodology predates that of Descartes. His ideas and expositions on the inductive method are foundational in the history of science, and his relevant discourse became a sign of a major philosophical turn. The turn is that phenomena and sensations were no longer devalued, despised, or even antagonized, as in the Parmenidean tradition, but became the basis and starting point of knowledge. Based on this, people have developed thinking processes to try to find the truth, rather than assuming firstly the possession of the truth and then going back to the phenomena. This is the essence of epistemological philosophy, and it is also the essence of empiricism. Nonetheless, Bacon, like other later English empiricists, was not a one-sided, extreme empiricist. The label "empiricism" is merely a convenient term for him, and even a very large part of a mundane opinion. In fact, most of the British empiricists talked about experiences in the context of mind-matter dualism. Moreover, it seems that the mind-matter dualism in the context of empiricism has been expressed particularly clearly. An empiricist is by no means a person who has only "things" and no "mind" in his/her eyes. In the face of empirical materials, Bacon mentioned not only the importance of rational faculties, but also the need for a "marriage" between the two, which were the *instruments* and the methods (the famous metaphor of spiders, ants, and bees) for processing empirical materials. Bacon not only acknowledged that empirical materials were imperfect, but also believed that reason has a "remedial" effect on processing empirical materials. This perspective rightly places experience and reason in a position of *cooperation, complementarity, and competition* (this polygonal relationship actually relates to the relationship between different Algorithms or Instructions, or between computations for processing sensory materials and for deep thinking). It can be considered that this understanding is historically insightful. It rejects the opposition between sensibility and reason in Greek and medieval philosophy. How this position can be used to correct Berkeley's philosophy, as well as to illustrate Kant's philosophy, will be shown later. Moreover, there is also the meaning of "concrete rationality" permeated by this understanding. That is, not just to say that reason is nothing, or that it is not infinite, but to show how reason is *concretely finite*. Because only when reason (or rationality) is concrete can people understand and grasp its characteristics and thus can compare and match it with empirical materials and judge its merits and demerits. The following passage from Bacon can be used as a precursor to Kant's philosophy (and the Algorithmic philosophy), even better than Kant's own words:

"The human mind resembles those uneven mirrors which impart their own properties to different objects, from which rays are emitted and distort and disfigure them."[1]

---

1. Francis Bacon, "Novum Organum", New York: P. F. Collier & Son, 1902, pp.

In the history of philosophy, the first people to put forward creative ideas were not often the ones who became famous from the ideas. The contributions of the "masters" often lie in the development and argumentation of existing ideas, rather than the creation of new ideas from scratch. Descartes was like that. His argument of "I think, therefore I am" came from Augustine, but he expanded it and raised it to the level of "first metaphysical principle", and even God and external objects shall depend on "me" to exist. It overturned philosophy. Bacon emphasized empirical materials while Descartes emphasized the existence of the "mind", complementing the other party in the "mind-matter dualism". This forms the basic framework of modern philosophy.

Epistemology is always accompanied by methodology. If Bacon pointed out how to make empirical inductions relatively reliably, then Descartes' contribution lies in how to deduct relatively reliably and develop theoretical thinking. What were the methods recommended by Descartes? They were to find solid foundations, to simplify the complex, to go from easy to difficult, to compare all possible scenarios, and so on.[2] These principles, which might seem ordinary today, are in fact of great hidden significance that have not even been noticed. This is the *introduction of Algorithmic elements such as thinking time, space, discreteness, and plurality*. Thinking activity was seen as having a time *procedure*, and reasoning was the *activities* from premises to conclusions. Moreover, there were qualitative differences between different ideas, hence, choices needed to be made. Then, scientific work in pursuit of high-quality

---

20-21. The historic facts about Francis Bacon in this section come mainly from Zhiwei Zhang (ed.), "A History of Western Philosophy" (in Chinese, 2nd), China Renmin University Press, 2010, pp. 257-263, and Frederick Copleston, "A History of Philosophy", Vol. III, New York: Image Books (Doubleday), 1993, pp. 295-309.
2. Rene Descartes, "Discourse on Method", translated by Laurence J. Lafleur, New York: Macmillan; London: Collier Macmillan, p. 12.

thinking activities required researchers to make this choice: either choosing reliable premises, or giving *priority* to easy and certain jobs, and so on. This suggests that scientific work must *give up* something, and that it can only move forward conservatively. In particular, Descartes demanded that the topic of the study be reduced from big to small, and from complex to simple, so that it could be expanded in a time process, exchanging time for space, which refers to the serial and stepwise processing mode. It obviously has to be premised on the finitude of attention and meta-computation. The statement that "to make enumerations so complete, and reviews so general, that I would be certain that nothing was omitted"[3] is roughly in the mood of combinations and permutations. This is the inevitable situation that comes with a limited attention perspective. Although it is easy for combinations to explode, it is generally impossible to enumerate *all* kinds of cases; however, within the scope of a particular topic, those important cases are often worthy of detailed search and enumeration, and hence such efforts are generally necessary.

After philosophy has adopted such an epistemological stance, it has stood to reason that there should have been no more ontologies existing *in parallel* with epistemology. As mentioned earlier, I do not take the position that metaphysics should be abolished, but metaphysics should therefore logically become an epistemological appendage, and should not be independent of epistemology any longer. This is because metaphysics, as a generalized (and hypothetical) conclusion of the world, can only be a reflection of human's temporary and staged *cognition*, and if it is an ontology that exists in parallel with epistemology, it will not make logical sense—the readers may ask: where does this Being, Substance, or entity that has been detached from epistemology come from? It must be

---

3. Ibid.

understood that it is impossible for a person in the process of knowing to see the beginning and the end of the whole human cognition. However, most epistemological philosophers in modern times have added metaphysical ontology to epistemology. At this point, Descartes was not spared. His God and external objects were clearly derived from the "first principle", but they had to be redefined as "substance". He failed to give full play to epistemological philosophy in the same way that he did with Augustine's propositions. Moreover, although he also admitted the innateness of thinking ability, he insisted on the position of "innate ideas", which is redundant, leaving obvious room for criticism by other authors.

### §155. Descartes (continued)

However, among Descartes' critics, there is one whom we cannot agree with. He is Gilbert Ryle. Ryle said that Descartes' "I think" (cogito) was "the ghost in the machine" as a repeat of external objects, and was therefore a "category mistake"; then, it was necessary to keep external objects and dissolve the mind. On the basis of the previous (especially §44, Vol. I) refutation, this behaviorist view needs to be refuted again here.

As long as one acknowledges the real existence of thinking processes (which is the central Descartes' argument that has been widely endorsed), then the belief in the existence of external objects should in no way exceed the belief in the existence of the mind—at best, the beliefs in both can be equal. The latter situation means that the knowers have gained complete knowledge of external objects, so that the mind will not be needed anymore. It's like saying that my ears have heard enough of the outside world, so I don't need ears any longer. However, even then, it is not necessarily the mind (or the ear) that is to be dissolved, but also the external objects, as George Berkeley did. The reason for the dissolution of the mind can only be that the existence and reality of external things seen by the researcher are more than those of the speculated mental activities, thus, this dissolution must be based on the point that the mind is unreliable and insufficient to "reflect" external objects, and hence the mind and the things cannot be equal. Thus, the behaviorist's argument contradicts the above Descartes' argument, not to mention how absurd it is to think that a species that is characterized by the ability to think thinks that thinking does not exist!

Thinking is the human brain's own business. It can be said that in most cases, its contents are not "consistent" with external objects, but only in the process of "to be consistent". Even where there is a consistency, we must think that it is only consistent that the mind corresponds to or maps to the external objects, rather than simply equating them to the point where they can be substituted for each other. This approach is similar to the way people with color blindness perceive the world, assuming that both the minds and the objects exist and then carefully comparing them, *attempting to avoid both repetition and omission.* Since behaviorists pursue methodological rigor and prudence, then only from this mapping and colorblind perspective can we talk about rigor and prudence, otherwise, how can rigor and prudence be spoken?

*As long as we limit the activity of the real and live mind to meta-computation, the mind will not be a repeat of external objects, or of the stocked knowledge or other thoughts, or of itself* (because a meta-computation cannot work on itself), and it will be important for us to study the activity of the mind as an act or to study its contents. When we emphasize the physical, material, or substantial nature of thinking and the behavioral nature of mental activity, we seem to be expanding the concept of "behavior" from the narrow behavioristic concept of behavior to thinking activities, and thus seem to be expanding behaviorism. However, behaviorism itself is actually in an awkward position. The program of behaviorism is itself ignored by the mainstream academic community because of its emphasis on behavior as a flow, which potentially conflicts with the static characteristics of mainstream scholarship. The study of behavior is grossly incomplete since it does not include thinking behaviors. Conversely, it is only by studying both thinking behaviors and external physical behaviors that the concept of "behavior" can be correctly treated and probably resurrected. Moreover, through the rigorous and detailed description of mental processes, it can be considered that the Algorithmic method has greatly alleviated the defect that "mental processes are not convenient for an objective description". Considering that an external behavior is not actually as observable as it seems, the necessity and feasibility of directly studying mental activity are rapidly increasing. We'll continue on this in the next chapter when we discuss Ryle again.

We cannot ignore not only the study of thinking behaviors, but also the study of their thoughtful contents. The study of the contents of thought is not in conflict with the study of the forms of thought. It is impossible to ignore the language of software and use only the language of hardware *throughout* the research processes. The practice of behavioristic research has also shown that the original intention of behaviorism and its following consequences have not actually been to dissolve the mind, but to use the method of reductio ad absurdum to re-affirm the indispensability of psychological existence and mental processes, and *then enter into exploration of the psychological contents* (this is the reason why behaviorism is primarily a school of psychology, and it is also the most subtle, interesting, and paradoxical aspect of behaviorism). When an activity of the mind is studied as an act, an anonymous Instruction can be deemed generally implicitly used, but when the thoughtful contents are studied, the specific "identities" of the Instructions or information will have to be revealed. Obviously, Algorithmical discourses often take both approaches.

## §156. Hobbes, Spinoza

Thomas Hobbes, a materialist of the seventeenth century, resolutely raised the banner of atheism, and became well-known for it. Although the existence of God cannot be completely denied, as later Hume put it, this weakest reason is not sufficient to place God as a subject of great importance in everyday or academic discourse. In this sense, God itself is not worth talking about, and atheism can be admissible.

Hobbes creatively pointed out the fact that some of the characteristics of things were identified so much with sense organs that they could not exist independently of the sense organs, which is the precursor to Locke's concept of "secondary qualities". However, are the "primary qualities", such as the extension and movement of things, completely independent of the sense organs? Isn't it through their own feelings that people are able to understand and define these qualities? Hence, it is literally necessary to point out this specific dependence, but this dependence shall be not absolute but variable for different qualities of different objects. Then, what is the importance of this argument? In my opinion, it is moving towards the *emergence of the concept of information.* It is not the external object itself that enters the system of thought, but the "information"; "information" is the result of the interaction between the two kinds of physical objects, "sense organs" and "external objects", which is a kind of "being" that is different from both the external object and the sense organs, and this existence is matched with the thinking tools (Instructions) that naturally exist in the human brain, and is suitable for processing by such tools. *In the same vein,* we can understand the nature of thought: thought (and thus human's perception of external objects) is the result of the interaction of thinking tools with information, so that it is in principle different from both thinking tools and information—and therefore even more so from external objects.

The above was just the beginning of the computationalist atmosphere of Hobbes's philosophy. Hobbes clearly divided the thinking process into three steps: conception, judgment, and reasoning, which vividly demonstrated the serial processing of thinking activities based on the smallest units. This way of working is now finally being formalized precisely with the help of computer science. Hobbes astonishingly equates the notion of "computation" with reasoning: "by ratiocination (reasoning), I mean computation. Now to compute, is either to collect the sum of many things that are added together, or to know what remains when one thing is taken out of another. Ratiocination, therefore, is the same with addition and substraction"[4]. These words foreshadow that the UK's status as the birthplace of computer science and technology is no accident.

Hobbes's clear distinction between natural and artificial objects opened the way for him to become a social philosopher. Following Machiavelli's method and based on the human's "Algorithmical characteristics" such as short-sightedness, selfishness, malice, and violence, he proposed the "all against all" model of a jungle society, and then proposed the social contract theory, which still had a significant academic influence until the twenty-first century. Given that the original analysis of interests is attributed to Claude Adrien Helvetius in the history

---

4. Thomas Hobbes, "The Metaphysical System of Hobbes", 2nd edition, selected by Mary Whiton Calkins, Chicago: The Open Court Publishing Company, 1963, p. 7. The bracket and its content are added by me. The historic facts in this section on Hobbes are mainly based on Zhang Zhiwei, "History of Western Philosophy", pp. 277-286, and Frederick Copleston, "A History of Philosophy", Vol. V, New York: Image Books (Doubleday), 1994, pp. 3-32.

of philosophy (which will be discussed in the next chapter), Hobbes's ideas can be seen as a prelude to economic analysis, or rather a broad economic analysis. What is often referred to as the "trade-off" or "pros-cons analysis" shall not be limited narrowly to monetized items, but include other broader, non-monetary factors. Such considerations are undoubtedly as rational as economic computations, but they do not necessarily use quantitative data and methods. The means by which the actors pursue the relevant interests or avoid the relevant losses shall not be limited to voluntary, peaceful, and lawful means of buying and selling goods, but need to comprehensively include those such as fraud or anti-fraud, coercion or anti-coercion, violence or anti-violence, etc. Along these lines, contemporary economic research has expanded from commodity transactions to game theory. This is an extension of economics to the social sciences. Hobbes's analysis belongs to politics and social science. In the above sense, it can be integrated with economics. This topic pertains to the issue of the unity of the social sciences.

Hobbes's mechanistic materialism led him to reject not only God, but also the idealist concept of "free will". The latter rejection is in contradiction with his doctrines of artificial objects, social contracts, "Leviathans" (as a metaphor about the state), and so on. We can see how the concept of "freedom" has tormented modern philosophers and left them in a theoretical dilemma. Obviously, the scientific and rational elucidation of freedom can only be basically realized in the Algorithmic era.

After Hobbes rejected God, how could the world of mind and matter be left behind? To this, Spinoza gave his answer.

Spinoza could not tolerate Descartes' mind-matter dualism, and he wanted to eliminate it. This impulse clearly stemmed from the habit of traditional monist philosophy: it seemed that the world had been at peace, and all that was needed was just to eliminate this duality. As everyone knows, mind-matter dualism is the ladder to the philosophy of pluralism, as if a rat drags a shovel—the big head must be behind! Philosophy has been entangled in the dualism of mind and matter, lingering for too long time, so that it has not really entered into pluralism by far.

Spinoza's approach is creative. He said that there was only one substance in the world, and everything was a special manifestation of this substance, which was not only different from each other, but also interrelated and mutually restricted, forming a unified picture of all kinds of differences. As an example of this "special manifestation", he put forward the "mind-matter parallelism": everything in the world either belongs to the modes of mind, such as individual thoughts, ideas, emotions, sentiments, etc., or to the modes of matter with extension.[5] This is tantamount to acknowledging the differences and contradictions of things (including the processual conflicts). But this approach is different from the philosophical long-standing practice of treating phenomena discriminatively, and instead claims that phenomena, whether positive or negative, are "manifestations" of the same substance. In this way, the substance's generalization of phenomenon became comprehensive and unexceptionable, and a phenomena, whatever it might be, could no longer be used to falsify the substance. At this point, Fichte, Schelling, and Hegel could have no major creations. This was a unique invention of Spinoza.

Although this philosophy has been criticized from many angles in later times, it is still alive today and maintains its dominance within intellectual circles. Intellectuals simply wander and struggle between it and its critical voices, but this

---

5. Zhiwei Zhang (ed.), "A History of Western Philosophy" (in Chinese, 2nd), China Renmin University Press, 2010, p.290, and Frank Thilly, "A History of Philosophy", New Delhi: SBW Publishers, 1993, pp. 298-305.

dominance has not been subverted. The parallelism of mind and matter is still the main way for intellectuals to understand the world, that is, the mind and matter are at different levels of the same process, and can only be viewed *alternately*, not *simultaneously* and *mixedly*. The existence of a large amount of negative evidence against perfect rationality not only does not negate the paradigm of perfect rationality, but it is not even sufficient to arouse a sense of urgency in the search for new philosophical theories. This is also the case with the current economics profession.

Merely pointing out that such a theory is unfalsifiable is not enough to dislodge it entirely, because compared with this theory, its contrary theory, if any, would have made us feel more helpless and emptier than itself. Therefore, there must be a new theoretical construction to counter this theory, to give readers the opportunity to use it to fill the void that its departure will leave.

In contrast to Descartes' theory of innate ideas, Spinoza is very valuable in recognizing that high-quality knowledge is not innate, but is made by human with natural tools, and that this production takes place in the framework of mind-matter dualism: "The idea of any mode in which the human Body is affected by external bodies must involve the nature of the human Body and at the same time the nature of the external body."[6] "The intellect, by its inborn power, makes intellectual tools for itself, by which it acquires other powers for other intellectual works, and from these works still other tools, or the power of searching further, and so proceeds by stages, until it reaches the pinnacle of wisdom."[7] What these passages say is actually the roundabout method of production of ideas.

---

6. Spinoza, "The Collected Works of Spinoza", Vol. 1, edited and translated by Edwin Curley, Princeton, New Jersey: Princeton University Press, 1985, p. 463.
7. Ibid, p. 17.

However, since intellectual activities are presupposed with a "peak", there shall be nothing specially or essentially important about this method of production and these processes of production.

## §157. Locke, Leibniz

In the history of English empiricism, John Locke was a relay station between the past and the future, so we will be brief.

Locke's exposition of sensory experience, including the distinction between the two types of qualities of objects, is so brilliant and impressive that it seems that he deserves the label of "empiricist". Yes, if the title of "empiricist" has not been granted to such an author, who could it be granted to? However, Locke's refutation of the theory of innate ideas has been both paving the way for the elevation of experiences and removing obstacles to the theory of "innate tools": ability is innate, and knowledge is acquired. The famous saying "the mind is a blank tablet, a tabula rasa" is seriously misunderstood by people, because "tabula rasa" is also a "tabula" (or "slate"), and it is not nothing. It is precisely because this "tabula" resides in the human body and is innate that everyone does not have to worry about losing it, then Locke said: knowledge comes from experiences. The latter proposition is clearly a marginal and contextualized argument. Locke did not mean that "experience can unilaterally and completely determine knowledge". Think about it: even if sensory experiences were something Locke thought could not be determined by external objects alone, how could Locke think that knowledge could be determined by experiences alone? In particular, among the writers of the time, Locke typically and remarkably agreed with the importance of the deep processing of knowledge, namely, "introspection". Specifically, Locke spoke of the phenomenon of thoughtful distortion caused by further processing: the concept of "substance" lacked a direct source of experience and was created by the human mind. A substance, he said, was just an "abode" gathering the many concrete properties of things, which was then given a certain name. This argument clearly belongs to thinking economics, and it is brilliant and convincing. However, Locke's description of information processing was relatively simplified and failed to detail the distortion of the mind (the above distortive case he described seems to be an exception), which gave the impression that the front end of information processing was valued and the back end was ignored. This style is sort of consistent with the habit of contemporary information theorists to value information and miss Instructions. His dedication to arguing for the reality of knowledge, while acknowledging that "scientific will still be out of our reach"[8], reflects the overall style of British scholarship as a prominent mixture and a lack of internal chemistry.

Locke's opponent was Gottfried W. Leibniz. However, Leibniz's monadism is more worthy of discussion here than the issues they were arguing with.

After Democritus, Leibniz was one of the few authors who attempted to answer philosophical questions by introducing microscopic particles. Moreover, his "monad" especially includes spiritual elements, which is quite related to Algorithmic Theory. He once said that all the existing concepts in the world could be broken down into a limited number of simple concepts, and that they were like an alphabet, and that everything and its theoretical principles could be regained by correctly combining the "letters" in that "alphabet". He also

---

8. John Locke, "An Essay Concerning Human Understanding", Oxford University Press, 2011, p. 556. The historic facts in this section on Locke are mainly based on Zhiwei Zhang (ed.), "A History of Western Philosophy" (in Chinese, 2nd), China Renmin University Press, 2010, pp. 299-311, and Frank Thilly: "A History of Philosophy", New Delhi: SBW Publishers, 1993, pp. 308-325.

envisioned the existence of the "alphabet of human thought", thinking that various human thoughts were composed of combinations and permutations of these letters, so that through computation of these "letters", various simple or complex thinking activities could be completed.[9] This idea can obviously be seen as the prototype of today's AI large language models.

The fundamental philosophical question that Leibniz wanted to answer was unique. In today's parlance, it's a matter of discreteness. The world is seen as being made up of countless particles that move or combine in space, creating everyday phenomena. It can be said that this is a form of reductionist philosophy. It's easy to give a superficial impression of this kind of thinking, because people can naturally ask: Aren't there still the same problems in the small as those in the big? However, the Algorithmic theory tells us that even if we take this mere step, the effect is so big that it can solve most of the basic problems we face today. Since Algorithmic Theory, as well as any other doctrine, cannot solve all problems today or in the future, my goal is simply to bring about such a historic, phased progress.

Nor can we expect the theory of mind to be so fully constructed in the seventeenth and eighteenth centuries. However, starting from the monadism, many of Leibniz's subsequent ideas are quite Algorithmic. First of all, Leibniz emphasized the gradual and continuous nature of the changes of the world. Philosophers usually have the notion and habit of explaining the world as simply and purely as possible, and that small differences and differences in degree are always regarded as the "transitional" states between a number of "ideal states",

---

9. Xinmin Gao, Xuejun Shen, "Modern Western Philosophy of Mind", Central China Normal University Press, 2010, p. 433; And Donald Rutherford, "Philosophy and Language in Leibniz" in "The Cambridge Companion to Leibniz", Cambridge University Press, 1998, pp. 224-255.

and thus as theoretical triviality and impotency. However, if a phenomenon itself is so "trivial", isn't the proof of this "triviality" an explanation of reality? Isn't it a kind of theoretical success? A theory can be simple, but the results of operation of theoretical models can be complex, and the two can be compatible.

A Leibniz's basic idea was that microscopic particles should be regarded as having certain definite properties (e.g., the veins of marble), and that everyday phenomena and macroscopic phenomena could be formed by the repeated combinations of these properties in different ways. Since any phenomenon can be seen as the result of the combination of a number of definite elements, the phenomenon itself can then be regarded as "predetermined", and the historical process is a transition from potential to reality. Leibniz liked mechanistic theory, but after the introduction of microscopic particles, mechanistic theory became less mechanistic and began to change. Because the particles must exist in space and in the "gaps" between other particles. Such a mechanistic theory can accommodate both necessity and contingency. That's why Leibniz was keen to talk about "occasion".[10] Such a mechanistic theory also leaves room for freedom: monads can move and combine freely and autonomously while the consequences can still be predestined. As long as we add the Algorithmic theory, *such "determinism" can effectively break through itself*: although we can think that "there is a cause, there must be an effect", the combinations of the basic elements are so enormous that they are beyond our *observers'* ability to compute and predict, so *the observers, like the persons concerned, still cannot know for sure what the future will be*. In this way, the observers can in turn be "surveilled" and

---

10. Unless otherwise specified, the historic facts on Leibniz in this section are mainly based on Zhiwei Zhang (ed.), "A History of Western Philosophy" (in Chinese, 2nd), China Renmin University Press, 2010, pp. 312-321, and Frank Thilly, "A History of Philosophy", New Delhi: SBW Publishers, 1993, pp. 365-379.

"restricted", unlike in the current dominant determinism where the observers are hinted as having "heavenly eyes" and could see through everything in the world.

Secondly, under the Algorithmic conditions, although the consequences after decision-making (including the decision-making about computing jobs) are predestined, the flexibility of computing processes is huge, so *the space for subjective influence on the objective is huge, and the space for observers to influence actors is also huge.* The observers will not think that they cannot influence or intervene in the actors because of such determinism; instead, they may also see their influences and interventions as "predetermined". Both subjective and objective from this perspective have their own places to perform. The division of these places is very specific and clear. Moreover, *objectivity from this perspective has become a resource and tool for human*; without the existence of relevant objectivity, humans will have no channel to influence their objects.

## §158. Berkeley, Hume

In my opinion, George Berkeley is an interesting figure in the history of philosophy. The reason for this is that his proposition that "to be is to be perceived" sounds like a fallacy that lacks common sense, but it seems to be difficult to refute. In fact, I don't think philosophy so far has properly clarified and answered the set of questions that this proposition raises or involves. The bishop was like a mischievous child, laughing at the helplessness of his listeners being questioned. However, these questions can be answered Algorithmically.

Berkeley's line of thought actually unfolded along the lines we had above. What he asked was: if we recognize the principle of "I think, therefore I am", why should we set up again a separate substance? That is, if there is an epistemological philosophy, why should we have metaphysics again? Berkeley, in particular, defended his proposition on the following ground: "An idea can be like nothing but an idea."[11] It means that the mind cannot deal directly with external objects because they are of a different nature (which is similar to Gilbert Ryle's argument), and that what the mind perceives must be something that is consistent with the "format" of the mind. This kind of thing is a sense as an "idea". This strongly points to the concept of "information". The reverse is also true: foreign objects cannot enter the brain directly; only the senses come to the brain, and the senses come here for nothing other than to pair with the mind for the heart to "perceive". Although his aim was to dissolve the dualism of mind and matter, he had actually adopted the dualistic working of "mind + matter": to perceive and to be perceived. It's like people taking a binary approach of "tool + object" when doing their handwork. Therefore, while his proposition abolishes external objects, it highlights the mind. However, he emphasized that the perceiver and the perceived always appeared in pairs at the same time, and there would not be one without the other. This was his way of dissolving dualism. He explained the "perceived" and the "perceiver" in this way: "all the unthinking objects of the mind agree in that they are entirely passive, and their existence consists only in being perceived; whereas a soul or spirit is an active being, whose existence consists, not in being perceived, but in perceiving ideas and thinking."[12] "What I am myself, that which I denote by the term *I*, is the same with what is meant by *soul* or *spiritual substance*."[13] "Such is the nature of *spirit*, or that which acts that it cannot be of itself perceived, but only by the effects which it produceth."[14] It can

---

11. George Berkeley, "The Works Of George Berkeley", Vol. 1, London: George Bell And Sons, 1897, p. 182.
12. Ibid, pp. 243-244.
13. Ibid, p. 243.
14. Ibid, pp. 190-191.

be argued that these passages depict the working scene of active metacomputations in a "data-ridden" brain environment, and they emphasize the truth that a meta-computation cannot objectify itself.

There is no doubt that the mind and ideas in the brain cannot confirm the existence of external objects. However, this argument itself also answers the question of where an "external object" comes from: it is the product of the speculation and imagination of the human mind, an *idea* produced by the human mind that processes sensory materials, or a result of thinking, a *hypothesis*, and the *content* of a thought. As an assumption and speculation, it may be right or wrong, fit in a fact or not, which is precisely the characteristic of thought as the outcome of computations. Logically, it is not an entity that is equally juxtaposed with the "I" in "I think, therefore I am", and perhaps not as convincing as "I think, therefore I am". It is a result of the joint work of thinking tools and sensory tools. For example, I see the presence of a table. Through a lot of life experiences, I have accumulated a lot of information about the characteristics of tables and how they exist. Then I speculate that the table will still be there when I am not looking at it. *While what the eyes see is credible, what the mind speculates is not necessarily incredible*—as long as we look at and evaluate people's *senses and thoughts* equally or comparatively within a *relative* framework. There are a number of indirect ways to prove the reliability of this speculation. In this example, both I and the readers would know that this conclusion is very solid. Its reliability is not even inferior to the "fact" that I have seen, since sometimes the eyes make mistakes, and the sensory organs are not completely reliable, which is a common knowledge for everyone. If what is felt can be regarded as existent, why can't what is speculated by the mind be regarded as existent? This is where the flaw of Berkeley's logic lies. *Despite the fact that the sensory materials he valued were not entirely reliable, he required that the invisible be entirely reliable,* and then alleged the invisible as non-existent on the grounds that they were not reliable enough. Therefore, his criteria for determining an existence were actually internally inconsistent. The logic seemed to be rigorous, but in fact it was not sufficiently rigorous, and even quite arbitrary.

Obviously, from the perspective of epistemological philosophy, inferred substances can exist not only in the above senses, but also in a wide range and diversity. Material substances act as "the substratum that supports accidents", of which the identification and naming have significant computational economics. Other substances may or may not have extensions. They can be anything that can be named, or anything we think needs to be named. They can be everything, and not limited to those few substances identified by Descartes, stingily and on a case-by-case basis. *As long as we consider that such an identification is computationally necessary and advantageous, it is fine.* That's exactly where ATT stands. Epistemological philosophy should ultimately come to the Algorithmic standpoint.

Berkeley did not seem to be quite clear about the full significance of the philosophical arguments he held. One proof is that, while destroying the existence of external objects, he rashly assumed the existence of God, but this identification was still based on speculation. The God was not seen, but deduced with his own logic. This is another logical inconsistency in his argument. In this he is neither like Hume's claim that the existence of God can be neither proven nor falsified nor like Voltaire's claim that even if God does not exist, we must create it. Voltaire clearly recognized *the positive implications of distortions of thinking.* Since mental distortion can produce the most optimal and rational results, it is, of course, considered positive or beneficial in the places where it is applied, and even more worthy of adoption than other "non-distortive" methods.

This is a major principle that transcends the Berkeley era. The basic implication of this principle is that the philosophical dilemma did not come from elsewhere but that philosophers in the thinking process demanded too much, seeking infallible truths, and attempting to directly grasp the truth of the world beyond the course of history; to this end, they only focused on knowledge that they believed to be reliable, and ignored those general, imperfect, and "wrong" knowledge; knowledge was not treated in a comprehensive and undifferentiated manner, but only "correct knowledge", such as science, could find its way into the eyes of philosophers while others were neglected. Berkeley's God was only with science. The resulting tradition of scientists believing in God has continued to this day.

This "demanding" philosophy was finally visibly shaken by David Hume, the last author of English empiricism. Hume continued Hobbes's computationalist style, using words such as "compound", "transpose", "augment", or "diminish" to describe the processing of empirical materials. Coincidentally, his view of the self was similar to Berkeley's, and he emphasized the hybrid nature of the thoughtful world: the "mind" or "self" was a transcendent thing, we could only obtain a variety of special perceptions that were constantly changing, and we could not feel an abstract and general "self" at all, and the "mind" or "self" "are nothing but a bundle or collection of different perceptions, which succeed each other with an inconceivable rapidity, and are in a perpetual flux and movement."[15] Hume distinguished between "knowledge of ideas" and "knowledge of facts", with the former actually being knowledge about a priori tools. This distinction led to Kant's philosophy. Under this mind-matter dualism, Hume famously questioned the "knowledge of facts". This skepticism was so unquestionable

---

15. David Hume, "A Treatise of Human Nature", Vol. 1, London: J. M. Dent & Sons, Ltd., New York: E. P. Dutton & Co., 1911, p. 239.

that its effect was shocking. The world was finally beginning to understand the central meanings of epistemological philosophy, even though it seemed to have come a little later than it should have been.

To be precise, the term "skepticism" is not very suitable for Hume, who was actually referring to a theory of bounded rationality in its embryonic form. He clearly recognized that human reason was limited, and therefore advocated the moderate use of reason, especially not to transcend experiences, and *to avoid all lofty pursuits*. The pursuit of knowledge in an imperfect, relative framework shall not be a low goal. There is no need to be absolutely right, because the differences between higher-quality knowledge and lower-quality knowledge have already been important. Such differences are by no means optional or inconsequential in practice. "Life and practice are the cure for radical skepticism" was something that only an author who truly understood real life, not a nerdy type, could say. Philosophers use too much force, subjectively trying to supply the real society with as much perfect knowledge as possible, but the result is often the opposite, either misleading or hurting the world, or being rejected by the real society.

Hume's critique of religion is profound. And his praise of habits is unique and valuable.[16] This affirmative attitude towards habits is contrary to the traditional demeaning attitude towards habits. This is a precursor of Algorithmic knowledge theory.

---

16. The historic facts in this section on Hume are mainly based on Zhiwei Zhang (ed.), "A History of Western Philosophy" (in Chinese, 2nd), China Renmin University Press, 2010, pp. 333-341, and Frank Thilly, "A History of Philosophy", New Delhi: SBW Publishers, 1993, pp. 346-361.

## §159. Kant

The controversy between empiricism and rationalism, as well as the questions of metaphysics and freedom, finally had a major breakthrough with Immanuel Kant. It is no exaggeration to call this breakthrough a "Copernican revolution", because it did have the effect of reversing the direction of philosophy. Moreover, Kant's philosophy was precocious in relation to the philosophies of its contemporaries, and it can be said that its significance was not revealed until the Algorithmical age. Kant himself could not have entirely foreseen this. However, he deserved enormous respect for his groundbreaking achievements.

There is a certain ambiguity in this breakthrough. Historians of philosophy introduce Kant's philosophy in this way: on the one hand, it is true that our knowledge must be based on experiences, but on the other hand, the subject of epistemic activity himself has a whole set of *forms of cognition*; and, since these forms of cognition precede experiences and exist in our minds as conditions of experiences, knowledge is given a priori necessity and universality. In other words, experiences provide materials for knowledge, and the subject provides the forms in which knowledge is organized and produced; knowledge is empirical in terms of its contents, but a priori in its forms.[17]

The concept "innate thinking tool" has almost popped up here. In Kant's philosophy, it has been elevated to a very prominent position, to the point that it is incomparable with those relevant fragmented narratives in previous philosophy. As an exclusive invention, it forms the basis of the entire Kantian

---

17. The historic facts in this section on Kant are mainly based on Zhiwei Zhang (ed.), "A History of Western Philosophy" (in Chinese, 2nd), China Renmin University Press, 2010, pp. 389-423, and Frank Thilly, "A History of Philosophy", New Delhi: SBW Publishers, 1993, pp. 393-426.

philosophy. Knowledge, on the other hand, was explicitly seen as the product of *combining* such "forms of cognition" and empirical materials. *The binary structure of "Instruction + information" was beginning to take shape.* Such a philosophy was necessarily a bounded rationalism, so it was assumed that there was outside phenomena a "thing-in-itself", or many "things-in-themselves" that cannot be reached by the human mind, so that it or they could be contrasted with the phenomena and human's minds. Those who thought that the concept of thing-in-itself should not be proposed were, in fact, allies of George Berkeley. The key to recognizing the necessity of the concept is to recognize it as a hypothesis (a similar view was held by later "neo-Kantian" Cohen and Natorp[18]) rather than a traditional metaphysical entity. Since human reason is limited, a hypothetical method can be adopted. A hypothesis is not necessarily insignificant just because it is "hypothetical". Algorithmic Theory is devoted to arguing how significant and meaningful it would be to subjectively create a large number of "hypothetical" things!

Kant's philosophy was so shocking and so popular that it can be used as proof and a precursor of the effectiveness of Algorithmic Thinking Theory. However, the progress of philosophy was achieved so difficultly that Kant himself groped his way forward in obscurity. In the midst of the exuberant and recondite narratives, I think that, on the one hand, Kant was still very constrained by the old philosophy, and on the other hand, a large number of his discourses were either far-fetched and incorrect, or they only embodied a somehow appropriate direction, or they were only meaningful in specific sub-fields.

Making the demonstration of the necessity and universality of scientific knowledge a priority goal itself belongs to the old

---

18. Frederick Copleston, "A History of Philosophy", Vol. VII, New York: Image Books (Doubleday), 1994, pp. 363-364.

philosophy. Scientific knowledge should not enjoy a special status that is fundamentally different from other knowledge, since it is only of higher quality or other characteristics than other knowledge. Therefore, its "necessary and universal truth", if it meant its "infallibility", would be impossible to justify, and therefore any so-called "demonstration" must be far-fetched, even if it was detailed or of some value in other specific areas. The concreteness and definiteness of "innate thinking tools" have led people to be highly confident in certain logical and mathematical results, and even in some specific knowledge about the external world. However, this "a priori certainty" is different from "empirical certainty", and the two shall not be confused. Therefore, the relatively high quality of scientific knowledge cannot be recognized *conclusively* simply by analyzing the cognitive forms such as "synthetic judgment a priori". This mystical idea can, in fact, be naïve. It contains the flavor of the theory of "innate knowledge", which implicitly conflicts with his strong preference for the theory of "innate thinking tools". And, objectively, it caters to the idea that professional intellectuals can grasp the truth without leaving the university campus (Algorithmically, there is no need to deliberately find any particular reason for this, because the numerous "encounters" between innate thinking tools and information can stably guarantee this from a probability perspective). In the final analysis, it is also slightly similar to the basic idea of Parmenides' ontological philosophy.

In terms of the specific types of the "innate cognitive forms", although Kant proceeded from logic, he mistakenly regarded the elements of time, space, and categories as something like "a priori cognitive forms", even "a priori knowledge". Time, space, and categories are obviously all *acquired knowledge*, and they are the basic concepts that people arrive at using their own sensibility and reason to understand the world after birth. Because these concepts are basic, they are universally adopted among people (or, vice versa). However, they should not be mistaken for innate because of their universality. For example, when we realize that our bodies exist in a limited way, we naturally develop ideas of space and time. And, after we divide the external world into relatively independent objects, we must study the relationships between them. That's when "causality" as a "category" comes into being, even if it's not everywhere (or we cannot find it everywhere). If we can infer the processes by which these concepts came into being in the empirical world, there shall be no reason to believe that they are innate, and it shall be necessary to look for the more fundamental elements behind them.

One of the most regrettable parts of Kant's philosophical system is the discourse on morality. Kant failed to understand that morality, as a consequence of the bending of the mind, was only an imperfect knowledge. On the contrary, because he was obsessed with the positive meanings of morality too much, Kant inappropriately pinned the hopes of metaphysics and freedom on morality, which led to a series of lengthy and far-fetched statements. Kant should have recognized the engineering nature of morality, then he emphasized morality as a "law", namely, something that directed people to act. Kant perceived the existence of freedom from the disconnect between the field of knowledge and the field of engineering, and he also realized that the human mental system had the function of free will, but that freedom was deemed not manifested from other selective places, but from the self-discipline of the individual, then, wasn't such freedom too weak and far-fetched? Objectively, was there really an important difference between it and the laws of nature? Kant claimed "human as end in itself", but what is the meaning of "end" in such an environment of moral law? Nonetheless, Kant was not completely unaware of the bending of the mind. In addition to the (apparently unconsciously) use of the hypothetical method in the concept of "thing-in-itself", he also talked about the "transcendental illusion": because human reason had a tenacious tendency to grope, it was not satisfied to know mere experiences, and it must ask what was the basis behind experiences; therefore, it has assumed that as long as it exhausts the phenomena within the reach of experiences, it would know the basis behind the whole of phenomena, which makes it mistakenly equate the "ideal unity" of ideas with the "actual unity", thereby falling into the "transcendental illusion". However, this mental distortion was only used to critique existing metaphysics rather than on a broader scale.

Kant's system has a recognized static characteristic. He even recognized the diversity of innate forms of thinking—which is why he discussed them concretely and individually, and especially advocated "synthetic judgment a priori". Unfortunately, however, this fails to lead to the emergence of a dynamic schema composed of a series of concepts, such as meta-computing, serial processing method, knowledge stock, combinatorial explosion, and infinite development. This static system is inevitably another metaphysical system, and it will inevitably continue to carry the smell of metaphysics that he criticized. Without serial processing, an individual person cannot reflect on himself/herself, thus, Kant had to assert that "I think" itself could not be the object of judgment, and therefore "I think" could not become a substance. Not only did his argument for the "necessary and universal truth" of scientific knowledge give the impression of absoluteness, but he also absolutized the gap between knowledge and the objects themselves—these two absolutizations are apparently contradictory to each other. In this way, Kant initiated the kind of philosophy that seeks the *absolute limits* of rational thinking. This philosophy both opposes the old metaphysics and attempts to establish a new metaphysics in the old way, so it seems as if it is a *discount* to the old metaphysics. From an

Algorithmic point of view, although any meta-computation and current computation can be considered in principle to have not yet reached the objects themselves, the infinite development of knowledge will also lead to the infinite approximation to the objects—here we cannot but absorb the idea that "truth can be infinitely approximated" by Nicholas of Cusa, Giordano Bruno et al. Moreover, while the development of knowledge adopts the mode of infinite approximation to existing objects, it also adopts the divergent way of introducing new objects and new goals. Without this divergence, the persuasiveness of infinite development will be weakened. In particular, human engineering activities to transform the world, as a kind of divergent activity, are also the "transcendence" of objects, and the potential is obviously unlimited. It is a pity that Kant failed to integrate these various meanings of "transcendence", thus, his works can only be a foundation for a "transcendental" philosophy.

The lack of dynamics and development, in turn, left Kant unable to convincingly argue for freedom from the point of view that the natural world, which is even the kingdom of pure necessity, does not prevent human beings from having freedom. This is because the operating mechanism of the spirit itself gives the individual the freedom to deliberately ignore the objective laws, and also gives the individual the right to voluntarily bear the consequences caused by this ignorance. However, the lack of dynamics made it impossible for computations to close, then such a bend could not reasonably occur. Meanwhile, the mechanism of free will can also be regarded as a kind of "inevitability" that is "naturally" possessed by human, a "natural being", and it does not necessarily contradict the inevitability of other beings, and it can be said that these coexistent different "inevitabilities" can have their own characteristics, respectively. However, also due to the lack of dynamics, such free wills would have been futile to have their own characteristics, which would be used nowhere.

The lack of dynamics also led to a lack of flexible or *soft* elements in the whole system, and it seemed that the story had just begun (or rather, metacomputation had just begun), and the end was immediately seen. Words such as "legislation for nature" were also exaggerated. It was not the business of nature that human beings used their own thinking tools to produce knowledge for their own use. This excessive statement was not inconsequential, as its harm would soon manifest itself in later German philosophies.

## §160. Fichte, Schelling

Although Johann G. Fichte appeared as a follower and developer of Kant, in my opinion, he did not develop the revolutionary elements in Kant's philosophy, but instead devoted himself to suppressing and eliminating such elements in order to return to the old philosophy, or to establish a "new philosophy" that "changed the water in the soup but not its ingredients", and thus became a kind of preparation for Hegel's philosophy.

Fichte was committed to abolishing the mind-object dualism that had been the fruit of Kant's philosophy. To this end, he put forward the concept of "absolute ego" for the first time. At first glance, this "ego" is somewhat similar to the Instruction system that makes consciousness possible. Moreover, while this ego posits itself, it also posits the "non-ego" as an object—the Algorithmical objects are also "posited" by the ego in this similar way, to pursue computing convenience. Next, the ego and the non-ego oppose each other and penetrate each other, unfolding the historical process of "dialectical development", and finally, returning to the ego in the "satisfaction" brought by self-consciousness or practical activities, completing a circle that connects the beginning and the end.[19] This historical process seems to be dynamic, but since it has been set with an ending, it finally returns to statics. Thus, such an absolute ego is much the same as Parmenides's Being, Plato's Ideas, God, and Spinoza's substance.

In my opinion, such a philosophy is close to gibberish: differences, plurality, and contradictions were alleged as unity, and the ego was imagined as something with a high degree of unity that shuttled freely and discretionarily between division and unity. This created the seemingly unfathomable but actually irresponsible style of narrative of ego in modern times, that is, repeatedly playing with the "dialectic of the self" in places that were obviously unjustified, so that readers were like falling into clouds and mists, unable to understand, but afraid to question; thus, philosophical literature became a place for philosophers to do whatever they wanted. The principle of falsification (although it had not been explicitly put forward at the time) was completely set aside. The accommodation of dynamic processes was certainly an improvement. Perhaps for this reason, readers usually didn't pay much attention to the obvious question of "when will the historical process end" that could arise from his narratives. As specific issues in contradictions were resolved one by one, the readers might be speculating that a happy historical ending might soon be upon us—just as Christians have been waiting for the day when Jesus returns.

The dangerous factor inherent in this philosophy can be exhibited by Fichte's applied philosophy. Fichte, for example, believed that the government should govern society with force and a national spirit, and on the other hand, believed that all

---

19. The historic materials on Fichte in this section are mainly based on Zhiwei Zhang (ed.), "A History of Western Philosophy" (in Chinese, 2nd), China Renmin University Press, 2010, pp. 425-442, and Frank Thilly, "A History of Philosophy", New Delhi: SBW Publishers, 1993, pp. 446-448.

state organizations would one day become superfluous, and his doctrines would "free man from the shackles of things-in-himself and external influences", and that in the end, mankind would build an ideal society with free and rational actions. The shadow of Marxism has already flashed here.

After Fichte, Friedrich W. C. Schelling filled in a "weak link" in this "philosophy of identity", which was to see the natural world as an outward manifestation of the human mind. Since subjectivity and objectivity were considered to be unified or "identical", it was obviously not enough to only think that "human thought is a reflection of external objects", and there should also be people who advocated that "foreign objects are the reflection of human thoughts", then the "reciprocity" can logically be "completed". Thus, in the history of philosophy, Schelling's natural philosophy is a philosophy that can be predicted to emerge.

This philosophy did not adopt the "animist" approach of Greek philosophy, but adopted the scientific discourse of his time. Spinoza's substance was deduced in Fichte's knowledge on the one hand, and on the other hand, it evolved in nature. Driven by the contradiction between identity and difference, the material and the inorganic developed into the organism, the spirit, and even the natural sciences. Nature was considered to be "dumb, unconscious reason", and the evolutionary processes were deemed the processes by which the "soul of the world" moved from unconsciousness to consciousness, and the shell of matter gradually disappeared, and finally came to spiritual things such as laws and forms. Nature was the visible spirit, and the spirit was the invisible nature.[20]

We can now critique this philosophy of identity from

---

20. The historic materials on Schelling in this section are mainly based on Zhiwei Zhang (ed.), "A History of Western Philosophy" (in Chinese, 2nd), China Renmin University Press, 2010, pp. 443-446. and Frank Thilly, "A History of Philosophy", New Delhi: SBW Publishers, 1993, pp. 450-454.

another angle, that is, whether the statement that "contradiction drives the development of things" is reasonable.

This statement is puzzling when the subject is lifeless. What if "there is a contradiction in nature"? Is it true that the natural world, as Schelling and other philosophers said, is "dedicated" to dissolving this contradiction? Looking at it this way, it is clear that this is the result of the imposition of our own mental activity on external objects. "Contradictions" obviously only exist in our minds, and are the results of our human beings using our own thinking ability to understand external objects. In particular, they are the results of tailoring, regularizing, and idealizing the phenomena we observed as "human observers". A uniform "contradiction" is like reducing the shape of an object to a geometric figure, reflecting human preference for regularity in mental activity. This is because regularity is simple, economical, and easy to handle. Secondly, resolving contradictions and pursuing consistency are the psychological tendencies of human beings. A contradiction means that there is a problem. In other words, our many problems originated from contradictions. We human beings find opportunities in contradictions for thinking and action. In this sense, contradiction is indeed the driving force for the change and development of humans and society; this statement is not an exaggeration.

The above view of Algorithmic economics can be expanded again. Why do humans resolve contradictions and pursue consistency? As mentioned earlier, an important reason for this is obviously the pursuit of economy: because what is consistent is easier to deal with computationally than what is contradictory. Contradictory things must be remembered separately and dealt with separately according to different logics, while consistent things can be processed and remembered with a coherent logic in a unified system. The resulting orderliness makes economic sense. Therefore, we are not yet able to establish the proposition that thinking systems have the only one *natural* tendency to seek consistency. The thinking system just works in its natural way, and then finds some consistency and some contradictions. After comparing the two, it often decides to favor the former. This is just as if the ideas of right and wrong, good and bad, are not innate, but arise from acquired comparisons. These preferences are all just relative; in other cases, the latter may win out and be favored. We are not to detail them again.

The above method of distinguishing between an objective view and an imposed view can be illustrated by another example. A causal relationship between objects is usually recognized by people through various means such as experiments. A certain cause will produce a certain effect, which does not need to be understood in an *analogy with a mental process*. However, a "similarity relationship" is different from the above. We say that object A is similar to object B, and therefore they "have a similar relationship", which is directly dependent on the presence of our mental activity. When object A changes, there is no objective mechanism to cause object B to change accordingly; at most, we as observers guess whether object B will change, and then observe and test this guess. In my opinion, the contradictions in inanimate objects, both inside and outside them, belong to this nature. We observers cannot naturally speculate that a change will take place there because there is a contradiction there. This is a completely anthropomorphic way of thinking about inanimate objects— Unless the object is a human being, and he/she is aware of this contradiction, then we can speculate that he/she will deliberately try to resolve the contradiction.

Another problem that can be mentioned in passing is that among many philosophers from ancient times to the present day, there has been a widespread habit of talking about the human imagination at every turn. Modern theorists and empiricists are no exception to this habit. Since imagination is something that everyone possesses, it seems not surprising or questionable that the term appears frequently in philosophical literature. But how should imagination be positioned? Isn't it a type of thinking activity? Isn't it a universal and innate tool of human thinking? Philosophers talk about the reception, processing, reprocessing, and deep processing of sensory materials, as well as various forms of theoretical deduction, but have they ever thought of using some unified framework to *comprehensively* describe and analyze all relevant mental activities? At least, this tendency has not yet been seen in the narratives of the history of philosophy. "Imagination" was like an angel from heaven, and it came whenever it was said to come, without being asked what it was or why it was adopted. Then, on the basis of imagination, human beings were assumed to establish "ideals", which began to tear apart "rational" thinking activities, and then gave rise to some new problems. That's what Schelling's philosophy was.

## §161. Hegel

Hegel's goal of working on a philosophical synthesis is consistent with Algorithmic philosophy. This grand synthesis conceptually encompasses the entire range of mental activities, whether positive or negative, and whether scientific, social, or humanistic. This is also consistent with our Algorithmical goals. Hegel recognized and elaborated on the dynamic development of mental activity, which is particularly similar to Algorithmic philosophy. For these reasons, Algorithmic philosophy sees itself as an upgraded version of Hegel's philosophy, or as another solution to the synthetic philosophy.

However, Hegel's approach was disastrous. Considering the feedback and evaluation of later generations, this statement is not an exaggeration. Hegel's response to the challenge of Kant's philosophy was entirely old-fashioned. He developed old-fashioned metaphysics to the point of being rhetorical and embarrassing. In this "dialectical" way, he finally really "destroyed" the traditional metaphysics.

Although Hegel was knowledgeable and prolific in works, his philosophy was actually lacking in creativity. He borrowed the "absolute self" from Fichte and then divided it into "absolute" and "self" and used them separately. His idea that "there is spirit in nature" came from Schelling. Thus, his system has really been taking shape before him, and he simply filled it with knowledge, details, and arguments. However, even with his tongue-twister-alike dialectic to support it, his system still does not justify itself. From "absolute" to "absolute spirit" was the *developmental* process he deliberately described, but he insisted that it was to be a "circle". What, then, was to complete the circle? Evasively, he did not speak of it as a single entity such as "Being" or "God", but instead of words such as "unity" and "truth", saying that "the truth is the whole. The whole, however, is merely the essential nature reaching its completeness through the process of its own development".[21] How, then, did this "whole" return to itself? This did not make sense. Moreover, what was the point of its return to itself? Was it like a human suffering from homesickness? Or wasn't it the reason that philosophers had come up with in order to finalize their discourse? Here, dynamic was static, many was single, logic was history, opposition was unity, development was reduction, and are there anything more sophistical than these? Obviously, Hegel did not think that the recognition of contradictions was not evidence of a theoretical disability, but

---

21. The historical materials on Hegel in this section are mainly based on Zhiwei Zhang (ed.), "A History of Western Philosophy" (in Chinese, 2nd), China Renmin University Press, 2010, pp. 460-492, and Frederick Copleston, "A History of Philosophy", Vol. VII, New York: Image Books (Doubleday), 1994, pp. 170-244.

something that was worthy of showing off by theorists. Since the "absolute" army proceeded in two ways, where and when did they converge? For the Schelling-Hegelian philosophy, this obvious question had an obvious answer that Hegel seemed reluctant to say straightly, i.e., Hegel's own philosophy, the destination of the convergent process. This most arrogant answer must be a logical answer to be offered by Hegel's philosophy. From this, Hegel's philosophy becomes a philosophy about limited history and a philosophy that discriminatively treats different historical stages. I believe that *this violation of the principle of intertemporal equality can be recognized as a criterion of a bad philosophy.* Conversely, it is precisely in order to oppose and avoid such philosophies that we must establish this necessary condition for a desirable philosophy, the principle of "intertemporal equality": a desirable dynamic philosophy should equally treat each historical stage (development cannot be seen as a violation of this principle), and not isolate and discriminate against different historical periods on account of some (imaginary) "big event(s)"; history should not be a limited process with a beginning and an end, and philosophy must face the infinite development of history.

Another similarity between Hegel's philosophy and the Algorithmic philosophy is about the objectivity of thought. If we assume that there is a "human knowledge thesaurus", then the history of the development of human thought is the process of unfolding this "thesaurus" on the timeline. A range of Hegelian ideas related to this are valuable. However, it is only by comparing them with the Algorithmic philosophy that we can clearly see the gains and losses of Hegel's philosophy: The existence of thoughts as entities or "objective reality" is meaningful only when thoughts do not engulf their objects and thus return to the orbit of bounded rationality; Furthermore, although thoughts can be discussed *to a certain extent* apart from specific individual persons, they must ultimately belong to humankind; Apart from humankind, thoughts cannot be considered to exist, let alone thoughts "potentially" contained in the things objectified; The existence of the "human knowledge thesaurus" as a hypothesis does not tell us what its contents are, nor can it tell us the specific developmental route of knowledge, which is different from traditional determinism and does not exclude individuality, freedom, and subjective agency; Hegel's approach to humankind's minds as a whole has limitations, which can further be understood either as a discussion of the thinking activities of a typical individual, or as a discussion of some common parts of individual thoughts, and so on. For example, if there is a fixed periodic table of chemical elements, then the results of the evolution of matter in the universe can also be regarded as "predetermined", but this "predetermined" perspective does not give us much more than a holistic vision beyond the evolution of individual objects.

Why did history go back and forth between positive and negative phenomena? Struggling Hegel offered an answer to this question: it was called "the cunning of reason", that is, reason was mischievous and did not want to show itself directly, but acted in a roundabout way, forcing people to guess. This answer is actually central to the logical relations inside Hegel's entire system. However, it is highly anthropomorphic—although Hegel still insisted on the differences between an individual and the "absolute". Hegel seemed to believe that personifying his system would demonstrate its logical self-consistency. However, the problem of logical consistency is not the same thing as anthropomorphism. Even if the whole world behaves like a person's mental activity as a whole, it does not mean that the world is internally consistent, because the phenomena of individual internal contradictions, self-denial, etc., are not only obvious, but also explicitly recognized by Hegel himself. This argument was cunning in itself, and it established for later generations a once-popular but ultimately ineffective mode of sophistry. Moreover, this argument is narcissistic and anthropocentric. It reveals the idea that many of the phenomena presented by inanimate objects have "motives" that attempt to echo or influence our human beings —either to play with us humans, or to satisfy a certain psychology of our human beings, and so on. It's like someone in a group who always thinks that everything others say or do is related to him/her. In medicine, this is a sick psychology, and I cannot say much about it here. Then, is there any rationality in this? Obviously, what "the cunning of reason" was actually talking about is the phenomenon of mental distortions. Mental activities move forward in a tortuous way, and Algorithmically, it is "natural" for the cunning phenomena to occur. But these twists and turns are not necessarily to be deliberate, pre-arranged, or psychological, but primarily a consequence that has to be accepted.

Since the critique of Hegel's philosophy has already been developed implicitly in the preceding sections, there is not much that needs to be followed here. Let me now focus on the issue of the reformation of dialectics.

Dialectics emphasizes the importance and inclusion of opposites, but it needs to be recognized that the existence of contradiction is not so much an inherent property of the objective world as a reflection of bounded rationality. Because metacomputation has limited coverage, it is natural to overlook "that" when you see "this". Even, the neglect of the other point is precisely the result of the deliberate setting-up of "this object" based on the requirements of the thinking economy. For example, given the limited power of computations and actions, it is impossible for a political party to have a governing program that covers everything, which leaves room for the emergence of opposition parties. Furthermore, since the emergence of an opposite is related to the finitude of rationality, it is not only the opposite that is ignored by metacomputing, but also a large number of intermediate existences or states between the two poles. Then, this brings us to plurality. *Contradiction is only a special and extreme case in pluralism, so dialectics should be understood as a precursor to the philosophy of pluralism.* This has led to a series of issues such as mixedness and high-orderness. In short, dialectics can be absorbed by the Algorithmic framework.

Hegel's emphasis on self-reflection was at its peak. Hegel seemed to think that the unity or completeness of his theory was demonstrated by the constant emphasis on the self "returning to itself". However, Algorithmically, the mechanism of self-reflection is the same as the mechanism of objectifying external objects, and the two can be carried out frequently, freely, and interspersed with each other, and there is no longer any slight mystery here. Reflection occurs so frequently that there is no significant "cycle" or "circle" (and the contents of the "self" are generally always in flux) that can be used to justify the "end" of history. The self is not unified, at least not as unified as imagined or expected by the theorists. The mixed nature of an "individual" can be clearly shown in the Algorithmic framework, and it is only that it has a high degree of unity relative to a group of people.

Algorithmically, another example of Hegel's philosophical flaw is the characterization of the existence of social entities such as the state, political & legal systems, customs, and ethics as "objective knowledge". This is both an awareness of the solidification of the stock of knowledge and a misunderstanding of it. Moreover, they are just some types of knowledge, not any higher *levels* of knowledge. In the same way, art, religion, philosophy, etc., are only types of knowledge, not a higher *level* of knowledge (the "Absolute Spirit"). This error shares the same style as Kant's error.

## §162. Marx

In the foregoing discussion, we have not arranged a formal chapter for the philosophy of the French Enlightenment, in order to merge it with the discussion of Marxism.

If we don't need to be 100% reliable in our conclusions, then we can safely say that God does not exist. God exists as a doctrine, on the one hand, to satisfy people's curiosity for knowledge, and on the other hand, its function is to govern society. To a certain extent, society is governed by deception and self-deception. This is an application of Algorithmic principles. Sometimes a deception is benign and positive, and sometimes it is negative. And when society needs more individual freedom and creativity, and when the old system needs to be reformed, the image of God will be lowered, and the accusation that "religion is the opium of the people" will gain more social acceptance, and atheism will catch on.

When the spiritual weight decreases, the material weight will rise. In the framework of mind-matter dualism, this is a "seesaw" effect. Therefore, most of them, from the French Enlightenment thinkers to Karl Marx, favored or preferred materialism, which opened a major debate between idealism and materialism. Progressive or revolutionary thinkers tried to prove that the need for change was "objective" and must be accepted. For Marx, materialism largely meant economic determinism, namely, the decisive role of economic activity in social institutions and ideologies. With the emphasis on this, Marx added that the superstructure had a "reverse effect" on its economic base, and the relations of production also had it on the productive forces. This discourse, with its obvious logical flaws, actually reflects a general desire for a unified philosophy. We now know that we can satisfactorily settle this great controversy by concretely stating how mind and matter interact at the microscopic level.

Hegel's influence led Marx to be keen on the logic of dialectics, so his philosophy was called "dialectical materialism" or "materialist dialectics". However, in light of what we have said about dialectics, it is not difficult to see why dialectics has not played much of a positive role in the Marxist literature—other than to provide a comprehensive, holistic perspective and to transition between conflicting arguments at all times. Thus, what "dialectics" corresponds to is actually also an effort about theoretical synthesis. Another example is "alienation". Alienation is related to the self. With the illusion of self-unity, there has been the puzzle of alienation. Marx's rambling on the phenomenon of alienation is like Hegel's thoughts on the self, but in fact both are not enough to be profound in argumentation. On the contrary, now that we have comprehensively and Algorithmically answered the questions about the self and the self-objectification, the charm of the relevant passages in their writings will inevitably disappear.

Marxism is primarily a social philosophy.[22] Therefore, our discussion will be mainly in this area.

The first is the economy. The nineteenth century, in which Marx lived with a rapidly developing economy, a difficult life for the urban common people, and sharp class contradictions that left a deep impression on him of the failures of the capitalist system. These failures were mainly manifested in the gap between the high development of productive forces and the gross inequitable distribution of wealth. Thus, he proposed a radical economic theory that tried to prove that wealth was created by labor but was exploited by capitalists without compensation. What is puzzling about this doctrine is why a capitalist produces capital for production without being

---

22. For an overview of Marxism, see Leopold, David, "Analytical Marxism", The Stanford Encyclopedia of Philosophy (Fall 2022 Edition), Edward N. Zalta & Uri Nodelman (eds.), URL = <https://plato.stanford.edu/archives/fall2022/entries/marxism-analytical/>.

entitled to any compensation, and why should a person in possession of wealth give up his/her wealth for production? Marx (and his partner Friedrich Engels) proposed that the stocks of wealth should be "returned" to the public, and that the individuals should retain only the means of subsistence. In this way, there would no longer be the social problems with the means of production—it is clear that in this model capital still enjoys the right of income distribution, which is only covered up by the fact that the distribution is public. The Soviet Union, China, and other communist countries all established planned economic systems based on this assumption, but they have suffered a crushing defeat. At the same time, the Western countries, which continue to adhere to the capitalist system and the line of political reform, have made great progress. The collapse of the Soviet Union at the end of the twentieth century was seen as the finale of this experiment and competition.

These great historical events are extremely instructive for social philosophy, and for philosophy. As mentioned earlier, the idea of communism has existed since ancient times. According to Karl Popper, who was obviously quite right, its inventor was none other than Plato himself, the grandmaster of Western philosophy. The so-called "grand metaphysics", up to Marx's time, was expressed in the main sense that there was some kind of "absolute truth", which was simple in form, and which, if grasped, could dominate the whole world. The uneven minds of all human beings and their ordinary lives would eventually be attached to this truth. Being, Idea, God, Absolute, and so on have all been synonymous with this truth in different eras. Obviously, a logical development of this kind of thinking in the social sphere was the establishment of a planned economic system, or a communist system, in which a certain center controlled the whole society. In other words, *communism can be seen as the culmination of mainstream Western thought and philosophy since Socrates* (in fact, Parmenides). In particular, Marx emphasized that the conditions for the implementation of communism were becoming more and more ripe for the "socialized mass production" brought about by industrialization. Therefore, although communism did not appear until more than 2,000 years after Socrates, this emergence was the result of a series of subjective and objective conditions being met one after another. The mainstream academic community in the West has been speechless about this. Based on common sense and other branches of knowledge, such as political philosophy, most scholars immediately turned to criticism of communism, but privately they have remained both influenced and confused by it, until today. Obviously, most scholars believe that communism is wrong, but they don't know how to refute it. The existing criticisms have not been very convincing. This is a situation of "impotence".

This requires us to look at another thread, which is the development of the democratic and liberal system as a practical reality (and social engineering knowledge) in itself. The democracy of ancient Greece (as well as ancient Rome) was clearly established relatively independently of the influence of professional intellectuals, and its profound socio-historical influence greatly exceeded the influence of philosophers. Socrates and Plato's critique of democracy is a landmark event in the history of philosophy and the history of the Western world, and it is extremely thought-provoking. Throughout the Middle Ages, philosophy and absolutism were allied (albeit also at odds). From the Renaissance, the Enlightenment, to the Revolution, democracy has returned. Democracy has been transformed by thinkers such as Montesquieu, Locke, Edmund Burke, and John Stuart Mill to become more refined and effective. The decentralization system advocated by Montesquieu and Locke (very Algorithmically) aims to improve the efficiency of governmental services by simplifying the functions of the various branches of government and reducing the difficulty of computations. Burke, for his part, emphasized the importance of respecting traditions and gradual progressiveness.[23] Mill was committed to the construction of representative government.[24] The so-called "capitalist system" is based on nothing more than the natural economic system of all time, which has also been refined in the age of industrialization. There is a close kinship between this economic system and the superstructure of democracy & freedom, since they both rely primarily on, and believe in, the free and numerous individual actors. The natural, unstoppable, and long-term development of all fields of society constitutes the basic social laws that Algorithm Theory is to reveal.

In the nineteenth and twentieth centuries, these two forces clashed sharply. The reason for the latter's eventual victory, from an Algorithmic point of view, is obviously first and foremost due to the relatively conservative line it has taken, that is, the marginal improvement of the social system on the basis of continuing the existing traditional practices. This improvement must be within the limits of what real computing power can bear. The unequal distribution of wealth does not constitute a sufficient reason to overthrow and reconstruct the entire system. As long as we understand that human reason is inherently limited, we will not expect a perfect way of distributing wealth. The bourgeoisie, once it realized that the whole system was in danger of being subverted, was willing to make political concessions and reforms. Thus, Marx's prophecy that "the proletarian revolution will happen" was untenable— or rather, it implied a tendency to self-falsify. In the communist camp, on the other hand, Lenin rashly launched an armed

---

23. Leo Strauss et al. (ed.), "History of Political Philosophy", 3rd edition, Chicago & London: The University of Chicago Press, 1987, pp. 687-708.
24. J. S. Mill, "Considerations on Representative Government", Chicago: Henry Regnery Company, 1962.

revolution without a detailed and workable plan for the construction of the so-called "new society". The decision-making hierarchy, composed of a small number of people, did not have sufficient computing power to give correct and detailed guidance to everyone in society while pressing practical problems were haunting the decision-makers, which forced the new regime to inevitably adopt those simple and crude methods (which were inevitably still old-fashioned but only expanded). This single decision-making center would not be as competent as expected even if it was supported by scientists whose knowledge and capacity were also limited. The rulers of the new regime were not "philosopher-kings"—and there can be no "philosopher-kings". Even if they were a little smarter than ordinary people, they could not get rid of the various effects caused by limited computing power, such as emotions, desires, short-sightedness, selfishness, ignorance, and so on. On the other hand, after the public ownership of the means of production, the incentives for individuals were greatly weakened (as an Algorithmic effect), and the production efficiency fell sharply, resulting in the continuous occurrence of crises in the planned economy. Even if there was a period of prosperity due to the imitation of capitalism and the introduction of technology from capitalist countries, most communist countries eventually fell into a long-term decline. This imitation effect has been explained in §126-127.

## §163. Marx (continued)

This flippant idealism is worth reflecting on. As mentioned earlier, even a serious philosopher like Fichte would seriously predict the emergence of some kind of ideal society. It is true that since the speed of change in mental activity is independent of objective reality, it can *run faster than reality* and thus can predict or imagine the future. A history of continuous growth and development can also lead to optimism. This is the foundation that has produced idealism. However, another important reason obviously lies in the statics and ultimateness of traditional metaphysics. People who are influenced by this metaphysics will inevitably yearn for the moment when all their "secrets" will be revealed, and thus will inevitably despise the real world, the individuals, and the historical processes; and, they will regard all the laws and limitations in the subjective and objective worlds as temporary, and will believe that the future ideal life is a life without any restrictions. This is like the understanding of the speed of motion: the speed of transportation means used by human beings can gradually increase, but we cannot imagine that there will be vehicles with infinite speed, and that we will travel in a vacuum and weightlessness. The illusion of communism is similar: the illusion that human beings work without selfishness is like the illusion that physical objects on the earth will lose weight. *Knowledge will progress and artifacts will improve, but we must not envision that the physical laws and constraints of mental activity will disappear.* It is impossible to imagine that the computations of the human brain are carried out at zero time and infinite speed. In that case, the social problems we face will not be solved, but will be canceled, and there will be no social problems to explore and answer.

If there is any positive significance in the experiment of communism, it is that this experiment, at enormous cost, has deepened humankind's understanding of the workings of society. Until then, even leading intellectuals apparently did not know what the real constraints on the functioning of society were, and what its prospects were. Scholars tended to pursue static and ultimate knowledge, and had not yet recognized that knowledge was variable and continuously developmental in principle and in general, and that the *higher-order laws* of knowledge generation and change should be at the center of long-term predictions. It can be said that since then, the social sciences have been in a preparatory stage, until now. Marxism is also part of this preparatory work. On the positive side, its contributions in a number of areas are also quite unique and therefore need to be pointed out and discussed.

Marx emphasized and described in a unique way certain distortions of mental activity. Marx, for example, pointed out that there were certain systematic class biases with regard to religion, morality, ideology, and social institutions, i.e., they generally favored the rich to the detriment of the poor.[25] These biases were deliberately caused with money by the wealthy and by the political power of the dominant classes. In other words, social production was to a certain extent contrary to human ends and was therefore not democratic enough. In particular, Marx emphasized the cruelty of the conflict of interests between people, as well as people's subjective malice, deception, deprivation, and oppression towards others. Along this line, the school of conflict in sociology was later formed, as well as the branch of game theory in economics. People have a multi-faceted relationship with each other at the same time, such as cooperation and conflict. In order to reconcile these relationships, individuals often have many different options, and even an infinite variety of ways to conceive of them, and then they need to negotiate, contract, and execute the contracts with others. Marx apparently believed that the social system was malleable and could be innovated through consensus-building. There is a congruence between this idea and the social contract theory. The problem is that his blueprint is detached from reality, and hence he has tried to impose it on other classes. The approach of the violent revolution ignores

_____________

25. This view can be traced back at least to Baron d'Holbach (1723-1789). See A. C. Grayling, "The History of Philosophy", New York: Penguin Press, 2019, p. 271.

factors such as traditions, asset stocks, and processes, which shows the absence of relevant Algorithmic principles in traditional knowledge systems. In this regard, the later Austrian economists Ludwig Von Mises, Friedrich Hayek, and others have proposed relevant significant ideas.[26] The method of violent revolution did not provide the other classes with the right of speech and voting, and thus inevitably ignored the positive contribution of other classes to the economy and society, and its evil consequences were finally manifested in the practice of communism.

In contrast to the "Algorithmical Marx" mentioned above, there is also a highly mechanistic, deterministic, and "anti-Algorithmical" Marx. This is manifested not only in his economics, but also in his historical materialism. The latter doctrine was originally commendable as a form of dynamic and comprehensive social science. Because, then, and now, there were very few doctrines with such a broad and global vision. But it is overly simplistic, and has a prophetic determinist tone throughout, as if the authors themselves could (like other metaphysicians) look at the present from the standpoint of the future. In it, the relationships between the various parts of society are simple and mechanical. After going through a number of uniform social types, it finally came to the stage of "scientific communism", which echoed the beginning of primitive communism, thus completing the Hegelian circle. Historical materialism has the implication that the development of human society is ultimately governed by objective, material (rather than intellectual) laws, and therefore that human beings themselves have meaningless morals and values. This is complementary to Marxist atheism. When

---

26. Ludwig Von Mises, "Socialism: An Economical and Sociological Analysis", translated by J. Kahane, New Haven: Yale University Press, 1962, and F. A. Hayek, "The Fatal Conceit: The Errors of Socialism", The University of Chicago Press, 1989.

people no longer believe in God, the void God left shall be filled by appropriate philosophy, social science, and social engineering (a work that can now be done scientifically with the support of Algorithmic principles), or else it is dangerous. The lessons of history show that the Marxist-Leninist revolutionists were precisely such dangerous people, who were obsessed with what they consider to be the macroscopic logic of social history and regarded the individuals only as a tool for the realization of this logic. They flouted traditions and morality, and behaved ignorantly and fearlessly. Under Hegelian logic, they believed that when society concentrated power in the hands of one person, it would run in the most ideal way. As a result, most of them were greedy for power, considered themselves "the embodiment of truth", despised opinions of others, neglected the limitations of the regime's own capabilities, rushed to make big events, and were always inclined to use power to control everything (including the media, thought, and education) in order to carry out their own really limited, specific, and volatile agendas that concerned them momentarily. Logic such as "the cunning of reason" has become an excuse for their anti-moral atrocities and blatant criminal acts. Consequently, this unprecedented collective power has led to enormous destructiveness and oppression, causing unprecedented, even trans-century social catastrophes around the world—while the ideals and promises of the revolutionists were far from being realized.

Another idea that was different from Marxism-Leninism was the macroeconomic adjustment of the economy and society under capitalist conditions. Keynesian economics was an example of this kind of thinking, which narrowed the scope and intensity of social reform, and can therefore be regarded as a kind of rejection of Marxism. The enlightenment of Marxism lies in the fact that a society based mainly on private free competition has the *possibility* of macroscopic reforms.

Therefore, it is necessary for society to maintain an attitude of continuous examination and exploration in this regard. Macroeconomic management and the free market are mutually cooperative and competitive. The scope of traditional macromanagement was not broad enough, and the principle of Marxism is that no human system cannot enter the scope of such examination and exploration. For that matter, its challenging and enlightening shall be permanent.

In short, whether it is to criticize Marxism or to clarify its positive significance, Algorithmic Theory can play a crucial and unique role that has been difficult to play by any other theory. Moreover, precisely because the Algorithmic theory can be used to clarify the merits and demerits of organizational power, as well as the merits and demerits of markets, democracy, and freedom, and how the above two aspects compete and combine, its analysis and criticism of Marxism can be powerful, appropriate, and even conclusive. However, looking at the world today, a deconstruction of Marxism is still a practically important task. This is not just against Marxism, and the philosophy of history also needs a general reckoning. *The direction of philosophy needs to be fundamentally reversed, from the "Great Convergence" mode to the "Big Bang" mode.* Although the foundations for this reversal have been laid with Kant and the preparations have been made in many ways throughout the twentieth century, the final decisive step had yet to be taken. I believe that the Algorithmic logic can be overwhelming, and the Algorithmic scheme should be implemented.

# CHAPTER 16
# LATER MODERN PHILOSOPHY

## §164. Introduction

Hegel's extreme metaphysics gave birth to a large number of his opponents, because readers and commenters felt strongly the shortcomings of traditional philosophy re-interpreted by Hegel. This ushered in the era of what Chinese scholars called "modern philosophy", or the "post-Hegelian era".[1] This phase, here referred to as "later modern philosophy", continues to the present day.

I believed that the philosophy at this stage was firstly to raise questions and arguments to challenge the previous traditional and classical philosophy, and the next was to explore ways out and prepare tools for a new philosophy, and thirdly, to develop humanistic and social philosophy. The relevant challenging questions were either ignored by traditional philosophy or could not be answered. And in answering these questions, up to the point of the Algorithmic philosophy, efforts have generally not yet succeeded. This lack

---

1. Dunhua Zhao, "A New Edition of Modern Western Philosophy" (in Chinese, 2nd), Peking University Press, 2014, p. 1.

of success was either reflected in the fact that the authors themselves had not intended to propose a new system to replace the old one, or in the fact that the authors themselves mostly implicitly, or openly, acknowledged that their challenge was unsuccessful. The self-inconsistencies of several important philosophers became a prominent phenomenon in this period. However, progresses have been substantial in specific areas. As mentioned earlier, the line of *"logic – analytic philosophy – philosophy of language"* directly led to the emergence of computer science, while the line of *"irrational philosophy – economics of thought – pragmatism – hermeneutics – phenomenology – existentialism – structuralism"* provided the elements that need to be adopted for Algorithmic reasoning, as well as the conclusions that need to be drawn. The two lines gradually merge into a new panorama. Of course, due to the existence of inertia, there were many scholars who were obsessed with the unitary style of traditional philosophy. On the positive side, it led to efforts to pursue integration or unification. Then, the scheme of the new unified system is hereby given once and for all by Algorithmic Thinking Theory or the Algorithmic philosophy. Meanwhile, it needs to be emphasized that this new synthesis or unity is not traditional, but includes new elements such as plurality, infinite development, and so forth.

Let us now serially describe and interpret each advancement that has been made by its author at each locality.

### §165. Schopenhauer, Kierkegaard

Arthur Schopenhauer was a contemporary of Hegel, who died after suffering a crushing defeat in the university arena with Hegel. However, his philosophy gained more and more prestige after Hegel. The reason lies in the fact that he emphasized the power of emotions and desires as the "will", and that he borrowed Plato's theory of Ideas to elevate will to a metaphysical status as the essence of the world, and reason was deemed only an instrument of will. The shock that this re-positioning and narrative have brought to philosophers was not trivial. In this way, the "modernity" of *rebel instincts* was opened.[2]

Another characteristic of Schopenhauer's philosophy was his pessimistic attitude towards life. Will, born of desire, finally moved towards pessimism, abstinence, and nothingness in an endless impulse. This argument was a reaction against the optimism that had continued from the Enlightenment to the communist movement, so it was inevitable that this reaction would resonate with society. Optimism needs pessimism to neutralize itself, and then move towards the sobriety, sanity, and profundity of the modern age. It can be said that from modernity to postmodernity, it was an indispensable element of the times to bravely face failures with a healthy and strong mindset. This is certainly an element of bounded rationality and thus Algorithmic Theory.

From will to pessimism, the topics were in the fields of life and society. This was also a feature of later modern philosophy, in which the theme was predominantly social. Given that we believe that a proper unified social science would not emerge until Algorithmic Thinking Theory is proposed, modern philosophy as a whole can also be seen as a preparation for a unified social science.

However, Schopenhauer's position on will is not appropriate. Will, as part of the subject of "human", can have an ontological status, but this status is not as independent,

---

2. The historical materials about Schopenhauer in this section mainly come from Rulun Zhang, "Fifteen Lectures on Modern Western Philosophy" (in Chinese), Beijing: CITIC Publishing Group, 2020, pp. 33-41, and Frederick Copleston, "A History of Philosophy", Vol. VII, New York: Image Books (Doubleday), 1994, pp. 264-276.

absolute, mysterious, and extraordinary as he said. When a person stands in an empty square, he/she must choose and make decisions about the direction of his/her travel, that is, he/she must produce a certain will. This is an indispensable principle that wills are generated in human consciousness. In this sense, decision-making, and hence the generation of will, is a responsibility, a function of the human brain itself, or a way of working of the human brain. It has to be like this. *Whether in the cognitive stage or in the decision-making stage, an individual needs to generate wills at any time.* Knowing how to proceed next in an activity requires the support of will. This is because, at all stages of a computing task, more or less subjective decision-making is required. The word "will" clearly refers to subjective decision-making that requires subjective selection, highlighting the role of "will". In other words, the *emphasis on will was really primarily about the "subjective turn" of computations.* As for desire, it is true that it can continuously play a guiding role as a fundamental force of the entire thinking system, but as mentioned earlier, one of the ways to understand desire is not to turn to biology but to understand precisely the instrumental curvature of the thinking system itself. Organisms must have their own "biological" way of generating desires, but there is a similarity between this approach and the way the human brain computes. In particular, desire is the result of the organism's "conformity" to "formats" of the thinking system, and therefore, a "desire" itself is nothing but a *mental variable* that gives itself a certain place in the human body system by being able to interact with other thoughts, communicate the "demands" of the body, and guide decisions. It will be useless if it refuses to perform these functions. And in fulfilling these functions, it is similar to other "requests" received by the thinking system. For example, once an idea of interpersonal equity is established in the human mind, it will continuously "demand" that the relevant computations be adjusted to accommodate it. In this sense, this idea is a kind of "will", and many other types of knowledge also have the meaning of "will", or contribute to the production of wills.

After Schopenhauer, the panorama of modernity continued to stretch in Søren A. Kierkegaard. Kierkegaard's philosophy is relatively simple and clear, that is, it emphasizes the purposefulness, individuality, subjectivity, and infinite development of human beings. Emphasizing the purposes of humans is equivalent to emphasizing the practicality of knowledge, namely, emphasizing the branch of engineering. *Traditional epistemic knowledge is only a part of the knowledge system, and it is a kind of incomplete knowledge.* This knowledge needs to be extended to practicality in order to establish the whole chain of knowledge. The other extension is from universal social knowledge to the sphere of individual life, individuality, and the infinite future. Kierkegaard's discourse on the individual, life, and personality adopts a value-based or psychological approach. For example, he used the metaphor of the "*sleeping coachman*" to illustrate the pointlessness of a life that gave up one's subjective selection. He used the term "*continuous generative state*" to vividly illustrate the dynamics and infinite development of the social world, and used "anxiety" to describe the psychological feelings caused by infinite development. Contrary to the traditional understanding of faith, Kierkegaard particularly emphasized the personal and "private" nature of faith, which was consistent with his emphasis on subjectivity. His efforts to synthesize objectivity and subjectivity were reflected by referring to faith as the "*truth of faith*" alongside objective truth, and in his discussion of the development of the soul from the perceptual stage, the moral stage, to the stage of faith.[3]

---

3. The historical materials on Kierkegaard in this section are based on Rulun Zhang, "Fifteen Lectures on Modern Western Philosophy" (in Chinese),

However, the value-oriented and psychological methods are not as powerful and concise as a proper theory. With Algorithmic thinking, personality and interpersonal differences are so clear and appropriate that we avoid overemphasizing the sociality or individuality. As a partial and public knowledge extracted from the knowledge of many individuals, popular knowledge is not enough for personal life. The new popular knowledge must also be selected from the knowledge of individuals. In this sense, individuals take precedence. However, in the continuous development of social networks, individuals are always born to understand and learn social knowledge, and then to test and revise it; in this regard, society has priority. When combined, the question of "precedence" or "priority" itself is largely dissolved. The same is true of "subjectivity": we do not deliberately generate and maintain subjectivity to show off some values, but the mechanism of thinking forces us to have certain subjectivity. We both create subjectivity and try to eliminate it. When all of this is not properly treated within a coherent theoretical framework, they manifest themselves as a kind of academic dogma and the opposition between different dogmas—or as literary and psychological works that are out of touch with reason.

## §166. Nietzsche

Algorithmically, Friedrich Nietzsche is revolutionary in that his arguments about the Algorithmic elements and principles are probably the richest of his time, and his discussions of the nature and limitations of science are brilliant.

Nietzsche's "perspectivism"[4] embodies pluralism rather

---

Beijing: CITIC Publishing Group, 2020, pp. 48-58, and Frederick Copleston, "A History of Philosophy", Vol. VII, New York: Image Books (Doubleday), 1994, pp. 339-351.

4. Anderson, R. Lanier, "Friedrich Nietzsche", The Stanford Encyclopedia of

than dialectics. This pluralism is consistent with the Algorithmic inference that, in principle, the knowledge that can be obtained from any particular object is unlimited. His approach to pointing out the limitations of science on the basis of life, desire, and impulse is similar to Schopenhauer's. The reason why his "will to power" was misunderstood by the world is that he was actually explaining the Algorithmic principle of "factor completeness and the forced closure of computations": "The aim of knowledge is not to know, in the sense of grasping absolute truth for its own sake, but to master. We desire to schematize, to impose order and form on the multiplicity of impressions and sensations to the extent required by our practical needs. Reality is Becoming: it is we who turn it into Being, imposing stable patterns on the flux of Becoming."[5] This passage can be understood as emphasizing the simplicity and economy of what is commonly referred to as "knowledge". This passage also mentions something like the "cognitive format" that relates to an Instruction. Individuals have to direct their computations towards their own ends, and they have to be faced with an infinite number of variables, and they have to subjectively, even "capriciously", assign values to the variables. These characteristics are justified by the word "power". This extreme word emphasizes the subjectivity of computations in an impressive way. On this basis, Nietzsche's following brilliant arguments are now easy to understand: Truth is an error without which a creature cannot live; Literally, we know that concepts, names, or languages are not equal to things, but we can't help using them, otherwise, we can't live; The same is true of logical laws, and the reason why we believe them is not

---

Philosophy (Spring 2024 Edition), Edward N. Zalta & Uri Nodelman (eds.), URL = https://plato.stanford.edu/archives/spr2024/entries/nietzsche/, especially for perspectivism.

5.  Frederick Copleston, "A History of Philosophy", Vol. VII, New York: Image Books (Doubleday), 1994, p. 408.

because they have any transcendental and absolute truth, but because we cannot help believing in them; Truth and error are all our fictions, and they are not different in this respect, and their difference is just that errors are fictions that are not as useful as other fictions, and even harmful.[6] Here, in particular, Nietzsche pointed out the *relativity* of a difference in quality between different outcomes of thinking. Nietzsche should not have meant that usefulness was the only criterion for determining truth, but that on the basis of this relativity, we *technically* determine the line between right and wrong. Nietzsche did not point out such a line. Obviously, this line needs to be drawn by the Algorithmic theory, especially by the fixedness of the nature of Instructions. With this understanding of the nature of science, science will not only be inseparable from philosophy and metaphysics, but will also naturally become a subtype under the Algorithmic concept of "knowledge", and spiritual fields such as value and art can be saved.

Unlike Kant, Nietzsche also applied the perspective of relativity to moral issues. Nietzsche emphasized the relativity of morality that different people have different morals, and that morality was also developing; therefore, it was deemed necessary to revalue everything, to adopt an enterprising and creative attitude, so as to avoid mediocrity. Nietzsche's way of discussing morality showed that he had an understanding of the principle that morality was the result of a bent mind. Following this principle, we can understand concepts such as Nietzsche's "superman" and Schopenhauer's "genius". A world

---

6. The historical materials on Nietzsche in this section are based mainly on Rulun Zhang, "Fifteen Lectures on Modern Western Philosophy" (in Chinese), Beijing: CITIC Publishing Group, 2020, pp. 64-81, and Frederick Copleston, "A History of Philosophy", Vol. VII, New York: Image Books (Doubleday), 1994, pp. 407-420.

of subjectivity and difference is the right context to discuss these topics.

Nietzsche's failure lies in his concept of "eternal recurrence". This is a part that conflicts with other parts and reduces the quality of other parts.

## §167. Comment on Irrationalism

Now to a little comment on the so-called "philosophy of irrationalism".

Algorithmically, the "irrationalism" is nothing more than emphasizing the importance of other types of knowledge besides science as a sign of reason and that the methods other than the scientific method are also meaningful. Given that irrationalism, which emphasizes that desires, emotions, impulses, etc., can be viewed as hard software knowledge that is only comparatively subjective, the above unified perspective can be formed. Another way to achieve this unity is to argue for the relativity and finitude of science. For the sake of convenience, we have often referred to science as "high-quality knowledge", and it is necessary to add to this. The high quality of scientific knowledge is the general first impression that people have of scientific knowledge, but is it not possible to say that a work of art cannot be of high quality? Is there no mediocre scientific work? And in terms of method, does artistic creation not need deductive reasoning? Doesn't scientific research need imagination? Sometimes, the reason why a job is regarded as "scientific" may be neither qualitative nor methodological, but simply because it is closely related to existing scientific work, thus, it has been economically convenient to relate the job to science. In this regard, there is some truth to the statement that "science is a historical concept". In any case, however, we have to speak, and we have to use flawed but simple terms. The standards of science seem to be pluralistic and vague, and even both quantitative and qualitative elements must be included from the perspective of "softness". Fortunately, with the unified concept of "knowledge" and the concept of "type of knowledge", the importance of this issue has decreased significantly.[7]

It seems to be a difficult task to establish a unified framework that illustrates both "rational knowledge" and "irrational knowledge". Because, it has already been quite difficult to complete the former task alone, and this difficulty has already been shown by Plato, Kant, and others. But Nietzsche actually pointed out a path for philosophers: *it would be much easier to do both at the same time than to do one or the other alone.* This could be done by processing sensory materials with innate cognitive formats that produce a large number of differentiated outcomes (knowledge), and then, by comparing these results with each other, one could distinguish between higher-quality knowledge and lower-quality knowledge. The innate tools of thinking (although this is not Nietzsche's word) are fixed, and their functions are neither so good nor so bad, but concrete and limited (or just ordinary or modest). Then, the results of processing "raw materials" are various and mixed—it can be said that anything specific and finite, as long as it is used as a thinking tool, will lead to such an effect. Moreover, there are no ready-made methods and standards to distinguish the qualities of many thinking outcomes. As some types and some parts of the results of thinking, these standards and methods have also been naturally generated and gradually developed in

---

7. After many previous discussions, we have actually been able to try to give science a brief Algorithmical definition, that is, science is a relatively reliable type of knowledge developed using conservative strategies and aimed at explaining phenomena. However, I do not want to get involved too quickly in debates on specific branches of philosophy; instead, at present, I still focus on explaining the Algorithmical principles, as well as demonstrating its basic methods, so I would rather leave such work to scholars who are more professional in it.

specific comparative processes. Sometimes people judge by the effects of knowledge used to explain reality or guide actions, and sometimes they use logical methods (knowledge of logic was also discovered or built up in concrete comparisons although logical tools were used as innate thinking tools consciously or unconsciously) to do so with reference to other existing knowledge. This forms a distinction between empiricism and rationalism. At the same time, it can be speculated that a large number of thinking results (including methods) are neither entirely correct (regardless of the criteria used) nor entirely wrong or meaningless, and this is exactly what irrationalism finds or emphasizes today.

This requires us to take a holistic and all-encompassing view of all the results of thinking or knowledge and, simultaneously, to pull down all the lofty knowledge that has been offered on the altar and secularize it into the same identity as other knowledge. The differences between them can only be relative and technical, and cannot be considered absolute. These pieces of knowledge are used to selectively answer all kinds of questions, and the questions in each person's daily mental activities. Given the ubiquitous connections between things, any mental activity that involves decision-making, in principle, takes into account all the factors of everything in the world. However, limited by the limited speed of thinking, people have to make trade-offs and simplify. Such trade-offs or simplifications may have taken a structural or functional approach that particular areas or types of issues are not considered at all (e.g., natural factors are generally not taken into account when dealing with social issues). However, a more common scenario is that the types or structures of the issues considered remain unchanged while the accuracy of the consideration decreases. For example, in social issues, the impact of interpersonal interaction and strategy should have been considered in principle, but depending on the nature of the concerning specific issue, this consideration is often omitted or simplified to a greater or lesser extent. The trade-off or simplification can also take the form of merging, abstracting, fuzzing, and differentiating the relevant types *until the computing power can bear it.* It's like in a hunting activity in which multiple partners have to set up a formation and maintain a working surface so that they can take care of each other; and, an individual hunter should not go too far ahead, otherwise it will lead to some negative or dangerous consequences. Knowledge development, whether individual or collective, is also progressing gradually under the premise of maintaining a certain formation and working surface—and then historically forming different versions of knowledge systems (including metaphysics).

However, as we said in our commentary on Kant, Nietzsche failed to discover the discreteness of innate tools of the mind, otherwise, perhaps he would have discovered the principle of combinatorial explosions further without being forced into eternal recurrence.

## §168. Bergson, Freud

In this section, we continue to discuss how several modern philosophers have added Algorithmic elements to philosophy.

The first was Henri Bergson. Bergson emphasized in an impressive way the dynamic, generative, and unpredictable nature of the world (both physical and social), and was especially famous for what he called the "spatialization of time" in his critique of traditional philosophy: traditionally people have actually understood or spatialized time in terms of space.[8] Modern mainstream neoclassical economics is exactly

---

8. The historical materials on Bergson in this section mainly come from Rulun Zhang, "Fifteen Lectures on Modern Western Philosophy" (in Chinese),

what Bergson called this: a static model (space) is given first, and then a timeline is added to this model to extend it to the future, and the future situations are assumed to be predicted "rationally" in principle while the part that cannot be predicted is regarded as "random walk". It's as if a scroll drawing with a predetermined content gradually unfolds in front of the viewer's eyes: the future is only a relatively minor corner, an additional extra part of the drawing. It should be noted that this is the state of economics in the twenty-first century, whereas Bergson's above views were published in the nineteenth century. On the one hand, it shows that more and more philosophers in the nineteenth century recognized one of the great shortcomings of philosophy itself, that is, it tried to give a *predetermined* conclusion *in advance* to the unknown and infinite world that had not yet fully unfolded. On the other hand, it shows that by far philosophy has not yet made a decisive breakthrough, and that its central questions are still in a state of suspension.

Another unique aspect of Bergson is about intuition. This was an ancient topic with a long history. In today's cognitive science terminology, intuition is "automatic computation", i.e., the computation in the mind that happens automatically without the person concerned being aware of it. Here, we're going to expand on it a little bit and introduce how ATT embraces intuition. Specifically, we can assume that outside of the "central processing area", there are several "sub-areas" or "sub-centers" that are dedicated to handling certain types of computations under a specific overall arrangement. It's like a computer that, in addition to the main chip "CPU", is also equipped with other chips to carry out certain tasks. For example, a specific graphics chip, installed in the graphics card,

---

Beijing: CITIC Publishing Group, 2020, pp. 85-97, and Frank Thilly, "A History of Philosophy", New Delhi: SBW Publishers, 1993, pp. 577-580.

is used to perform computations related to the display of the computing results, and so on. The configuration of these subordinate chips does not fundamentally change the mode of serial computing in a computer, although it leads to the fact that there are actually multiple different thinking processes running concurrently in the computer. In the same way, we can also assume that after the above hypothesis is introduced, there are usually multiple thinking processes going on in the human brain, and they are not completely independent, and the central processing area is not aware of the internal structure and computational process of these sub-areas or sub-centers, but can only control their inputs and outputs. That is to say, the central processing area can decide what information is given to them for processing. It is common sense that if the brain does not pay attention to an object, it will not develop an intuition about that object. The results of the sub-areas or sub-centers as intuition are obviously automatically reported to the central processing area, just as a subordinate must report to a superior after completing a task. However, the central processing area can decide autonomously whether to adopt the results reported in its own computations, whether to modify or reject them. Thus, it brings up the discussion of our neglect or worship of intuition. Rationalists are usually wary of intuition, while irrationalists, like Bergson, value and even worship intuition. However, in the unified Algorithmic rationality, they are all biased.

The above mechanism of intuition is actually similar to the mechanism of hard software described in Chapter 5, and they are both an extension of Algorithmic knowledge theory. A considerable part of intuition must be produced by innate hard software (a chip is a kind of hard software). As for whether it is for all intuition, it is unnecessary to get into this for the time being, because I am not an expert in this specific field. However, it is important to emphasize that all knowledge stocks actually adopt the same operational manner to play their roles in computations; in this regard, intuition is completely indifferent from thought. Another related topic is the subconscious (or unconscious), which can be discussed similarly with intuition.

Sigmund Freud, a psychiatrist, has been widely regarded as a master of irrationalist philosophy. In a shocking way, he argued how sexuality quietly controls human life and behaviors. Sexual desire, as one of human desires, certainly can also apply to our theory of desire. Freud described how sexuality could *reasonably* have various consequences in a variety of situations. For example, a suppressed sexual desire may be sublimated to the creation of literature & art, or it may lead to psychosis. Sexual desire is usually not noticed when it comes into play in a person's behavior, so it is *latent*. It's kind of similar to intuition. The concept of "intuition" usually emphasizes that the person concerned knows or feels nothing of his/her thinking procedures but only the outcome. It's as if the person drops a task order into a black box and automatically gets the answer at the exit. The concept of "subconscious" emphasizes that while the whole process of computation is hidden, the answer may be hidden as well, and it may be secretly stuffed into the conscious activity. This is the concrete and subtle difference between these two concepts. However, Freud went on to say that what is latent can be unearthed and put in the spotlight, and become the content of consciousness, which can then be organized, managed, and reprocessed. This is very close to the self-objectification process in the Algorithmic theory of thinking. It's a pity that both authors have stopped here, not moving forward any more. They still adopt the discourse pattern of opposing the rational and the irrational (despite their attempts to combine the opposites), never realizing that the so-called "rational mental activity", that is, what they think of as "pure reason", actually works in the way they described as "irrational". Their theories can actually be regarded all as a prelude to the unified theory of thinking.

When Bergson talked about memory, about morality, and about the repression and rationality of religion, he was also kind of "Algorithmical".


## §169. Helvetius, Mach

The task of this section is to comment on Mach's idea of the "economy of thought". To this end, it is necessary to review and examine the history of economic analysis in philosophy.

Everything needs to be done economically in terms of the ratio of input to output. It's common sense. And we can be sure that this is common knowledge that has existed since ancient times. For example, since the trade in goods was already well developed in ancient Greek times, it is impossible to assume that people at that time did not know how to analyze the pros and cons, or the costs and benefits. The question is just how much influence this concept and method of economic analysis have on philosophy.

Philosophical research is also a job with real resource consumption, so it is also necessary to pay attention to its economy. I can be sure that this is also a kind of common sense or consensus that scholars have. For example, in any classical literature, the pursuit of simplicity and efficiency, and the avoidance of cumbersomeness and waste, have a self-evident legitimacy. The question is simply how much the pursuit of economics has an impact on the contents of philosophical literature.

A remarkable and influential arguer to date on the importance of thinking economy seems firstly to be Occam's William. As mentioned earlier, William advocated an economic methodological principle. His argument suggested that the contents of philosophy themselves should have been influenced by this principle, whereas most scholars at that time apparently had not discovered that the pursuit of economics was a dominant motivation in philosophy, and this motivation has profoundly influenced the contents and approaches of philosophy.

Before reaching Mach, we also need to mention the French philosopher Claude Adrien Helvetius (1715-1771). The publication of Helvetius's work coincided with (or even slightly prior to) Adam Smith. In particular, he emphasized the crucial role of selfishness, self-love, and self-interest in shaping *human society*. A textbook on the history of philosophy introduces him as follows: "Interest is the value standard for measuring all ideas and behaviors, interest governs all human judgments, and interest is a powerful wizard in the world. In the history of philosophy, Helvetius introduced 'interest' into philosophy as an important philosophical category for the first time, fully affirmed the role of interest in human society, and even regarded it as the decisive force for all human activities and social development, so as to explain the objective laws of human society."[9]

Now we need to think about what exactly is "interest"?

Interest refers first and foremost to a relationship. When object A (a thing or event) has an effect on individual B, the term "interest" may be used when the effect is *relatively clearly* related to B's purpose. That is to say, an appropriate condition for the concept of interest to arise is the existence of a finite object and its finite, identifiable impact. It is not possible to discern the influence of an infinite object, nor the infinite influence caused by an object. Even if some effects are inexhaustible, they do not cover all phenomena. As such, the

---

9. Zhiwei Zhang (ed.), "A History of Western Philosophy" (in Chinese, 2nd), China Renmin University Press, 2010, p. 368, translated by me. For English comments, see Irving Louis Horowitz, "Claude Helvetius: Philosopher Of Democracy And Enlightenment", New York: Paine-Whitman Publishers, 1954.

impacts can remain concrete and limited. Second, object A may be something or an act that belongs to someone else, or it may be something or an act of individual B's own. In the former case, B objectifies other people, while in the latter case, B objectifies himself, and these objectifications are all conditioned by the discrete nature of the things or actions, so that the world or one's behavioral flow can be segmented and inserted with the *thinking act* of "pros and cons analysis". The thing or action as an analytic object may have been constructed according to another logic, but is now analyzed for the pros and cons as a single and *integral* unit. This object probably also contains mental activities that have been conducted or are about to unfold; hence, these mental activities themselves are to be analyzed as part of the object. The results of the pros and cons analysis may lead to the evaluation, selection, or abandonment (when the object is a plan) of the whole object, or may lead to some adjustments to the internal structures of the object. However, this kind of adjustment usually does not reach the point of changing every element in the object, otherwise, the pros and cons analysis will displace the other thinking activities contained in the object, and thus the other thinking activities will lose their independence and there will be no room to exist. What we want to say is that the concept of interest, or the analysis of pros and cons, is a *derivative, higher-order*, and hence *local* existence or activity based on other *structural, serial, patterned* things or activities. Put simply, economic analysis is always computations upon *certain given* objects rather than all objects. *Without the discrete, serial, and high-order nature of thinking activities, there would be no the* "economic analysis" *as a type of computation.*

For example, before assessing the value of a commodity, the commodity as a product was manufactured by an engineer on a *technological* basis, including few economic considerations per se. The economic analysis begins with the regard of the product as a commodity. A would-be buyer as the economic analyst can choose to buy or not to buy the commodity, but is unable to direct the production process of the commodity. For another example, if I want to add a line to a drawing, I can evaluate the impact of the act as a whole, but how to draw this line is not something I can learn in economics class, but in geometry class. When this principle is applied to self-objectification, whether I evaluate my past work or future plans, I do so *intermittently*, i.e., I can only evaluate it *from time to time* in the chain of serial operations, but I can't evaluate it all the time and everywhere—otherwise I can't explain why I can *both think and evaluate the thinking activity*, and I will risk falling into the logical dilemma of *self-correlation* or *infinite regression*. Even if there are a lot of economic elements in the object, it is impossible for me to identify and *thoroughly* adjust them one by one, and to *fully* coordinate them with other activities that will be carried out after such an assessment. I am in the midst of a historical process, and I cannot wait for the historical process to be completed before making a prudent and most "sound" conclusion. I have to interrupt the historical process, insert it into it, look back and forth, and compute. This further means that the methods, bases, or criteria I use for the analysis are also modularized and known, and the results of the analysis can be some specific data that can be re-used clearly and directly—although they are not perfect. This discussion relates to the loudness, notability, accessibility, and limitations of the price system that we have explained.

This is what it might mean for Helvetius to introduce the analysis of interest. It seemed that Helvetius did not specifically discuss the pros and cons of mental activity itself, but it is safe to assume that this question must be included in the scope of his analysis (the pros and cons of mental activity itself have only come to the fore with the extreme development of neoclassical economics). That is to say, for the discourse of "interest" to have a place in philosophy, it needs to be conditioned by the revelation of a series of properties such as concreteness, finiteness, discreteness, seriality, reflexivity (or higher-order, as a special case of discreteness), patterning, etc. These conditions are the same conditions for economics and social sciences. In the discussion of Helvetius (and other writers on the same subject), we can clearly see how he juxtaposed and combined mental things (e.g., morality, state, etc.) with physical things.

Based on the concept of interest, we can make a generalization. Interest is resulted from Algorithmic persons' operations to shape their goals and values, and it is one of the many sorts of goals or values pursued by them. Besides interests, they can also pursue goals or values such as pleasure, leisure, virtue, reputation, etc. They are both interrelated and independent, and thus pluralistic. One is objectified or cited, which means this one is stopped and solidified, and another will start to work. The characteristics of "interest" can be further explored in comparison with other goals or values to identify the circumstances in which it is to be used appropriately (in most cases it is economic). This "defining" process is like what Fichte called the "positing" process. Actors not only posit goals, but also divide the world and define or posit different objects. This positing process is also like the making of knowledge. They are all the preparations made by Algorithmic persons for their current computations.


## §170. Helvetius, Mach (continued)

The protagonist, Ernst Mach, is now appearing, after a roundaboutness. In my opinion, Mach's proposal of the principle of "economy of thought" is a major event in the history of philosophy. Although this principle was famous at the time and has since been almost forgotten, its significance is in fact far beyond the scope of the scientific methodology in which it was founded. *It shall be a new premise on which philosophy historically reshapes itself.*

Mach explained his economy of thought in this way: "within the short span of a human life and with man's limited powers of memory, any stock of knowledge worthy of the name is unattainable except by the *greatest* mental economy. Science itself, therefore, may be regarded as a minimal problem, consisting of the completest possible presentment of facts with the *least possible expenditure of thought.*"[10] Therefore, science could be seen as a matter of minimalism, that is, to make the most perfect statement of the facts with as little thought as possible. Interestingly, starting from the principle of economy, Mach believed that there was a holistic relationship between theory and experience that was mutually substituting and transforming. Therefore, he sometimes regarded ideological activities as the "thought experiments", while the role of theory was to "*replace experience* and save experience".[11] From this point of view, it is clear that we can also think of experiments as a kind of "computational method", that is, when a researcher is unable to fully deduce and predict the reality in theory, the real object can be allowed to "come up" to operate and "compute" on its own, so as to showcase the real "computational results".

Obviously, this economic perspective can be extended to everyday thinking and all mental activities. Mach only explained the production of high-quality knowledge such as "science" from the logic of economy, whereas the economy not only caused a preference for high-quality knowledge, but also caused a bend in thinking, that is, the generation of low-quality knowledge. The latter also needs to be explained from the

______________

10. Ernst Mach, "The Science of Mechanics", translated by Thomas J. McCormack, Chicago: The Open Court Publishing Company, 1893, p. 490.
11. Ibid, pp. 481-494.

economic point of view. This was clearly something that Mach's time did not recognize. It can be said that the economy affects, tears, shapes, and forges all human thinking activities all the time.

Economics also had a significant influence on philosophy, which from the very beginning attempted to establish a perfect metaphysics once and for all. This effort led to a split in philosophy, making it difficult for its different branches to coordinate. The discovery of this subconscious economy in philosophy will lead to a revolution. However, the economic element is not enough to reconstruct philosophy alone, it needs to be combined with Algorithmic Thinking Theory to form a complete new framework.

In this new framework, it's not enough to talk about costs, savings, and simpleness. Like physical economic activity, mental activity will be an adventurous operation in an ocean of infinite possibilities, so it is necessary to discuss its *benefits* and trade-offs with costs. The trade-offs would probably result in a situation that is not contrary to the principle of economy, i.e., scholars rack their brains to lengthily write or argue on an inconspicuous issue. "Savings" does not simply mean a reduction in the amount of immediate direct expenditure. As long as the expected benefits outweigh the costs, both academic and practical computations will be feasible.

Behind this approach is a new, different, and subversive attitude towards mental activity, which is to see it as a group of discrete, concrete realities or entities, juxtaposed and interacting with other realities or entities. It will lead to an essential shift in the foundation, direction, and form of philosophy.

## §171. Dilthey, Gadamer

From an Algorithmic point of view, the significance of Wilhelm Dilthey's philosophy is to expand the scope of the concept of "knowledge" to the entire realm of thought and humanities while continuing to emphasize the meanings of life, spirit, and time (history), in conjunction with the philosophy of hermeneutics. This was an extension of the irrationalist horizon that has kept on moving in the direction of a holistic Algorithmic framework.

In Dilthey's view, the crisis of the times lay in the disconnection between knowledge and life, so much so that the system of values and meanings that make up Western civilization had lost its foundation[12], while the "human sciences" (Dilthey's term, including disciplines of both the social sciences and humanities), based on life, are actually in a permanent internal totality and interaction with life and the "lived experiences". Dilthey expounded the meanings of his "philosophy of life" and "human science" by contrasting them with the natural sciences. First of all, the philosophy of life is a combination of knowledge, emotion, and will, and not only perception, concepts, hypotheses, and reasoning, as in the natural sciences. Obviously, this puts "computing" in a framework that carries hardware, hard software, and intuition (automatic computing). Dilthey held a view close to that of Descartes' philosophy, that the human sciences can be superior to the natural sciences in the fact that the objects of human sciences are not the pure phenomena given in the external senses, the pure reflection of something real, but the present

---

12. The historic materials on Dilthey in this section come mainly from Rulun Zhang, "Fifteen Lectures on Modern Western Philosophy" (in Chinese), Beijing: CITIC Publishing Group, 2020, pp. 108-130, and C. L. Ten (ed.), "Routledge History of Philosophy Volume VII: The Nineteenth Century", ebook, Routledge, 2005, pp. 207-233.

reality itself, and the reality is given in a holistic nexus of internal experiences. Dilthey emphasized the precedence of lived experience over rational knowledge (a point that was later developed by Heidegger as "we are thrown into the world"), and that lived experiences commonly have not been analyzed, and thus are a raw wholeness. Therefore, he called this experience "reality" as if it were very different from rational cognition (which is not strictly correct, Algorithmically). At the same time, he emphasized that lived experiences are "historical" and that life and history are one and the same. It can be argued that this view raised the question of combining dynamics and statics. Lived experiences are humanistic and social, and they are the spiritual world's own business: "Nature is alien for us. It is a mere exterior for us without any inner life. Society is our world. We sympathetically experience the interplay of social conditions with the power of our total being. From within we are aware of the states and forces in all their restlessness that constitute the social system."[13] Such a perspective implies the idea that the main object of the humanities and social sciences is thought.

Therefore, epistemology must be expanded to include not only natural knowledge but also all kinds of human experience and knowledge. As an integral part of the latter, Dilthey emphasized and elaborated on his doctrine of belief and worldview: knowledge begins with belief, and all knowledge contains things that cannot be proved by pure reason or logic. The worldview is clearly an example of what Dilthey considered "faith": humans need a stable framework for understanding the world in order to grasp the diversity and changeability of life. These are the things that the Algorithmic concept of "factor completeness" emphasizes. In Dilthey's view,

---

13. Wilhelm Dilthey, "Selected Works, Volume I: Introduction to the Human Sciences", Princeton University Press, 1989, p. 88.

a worldview is not purely theoretical, scientific, or philosophical, but rather a combination of experience, reflection, and interpretation, but to a certain extent communal, and therefore classifiable. Moreover, such a spiritual science needs to be based on psychology, which in turn should be the "descriptive and analytic psychology". In doing so, Dilthey paved the way for his own "hermeneutic turn".

Hermeneutics, developed on the basis of analysis of ancient texts, became an ontological philosophy under Dilthey's pen. This is because lived experiences were reflected in language, which became the texts, and the texts then manifested them. It is not direct, but it is objective. Dilthey placed texts as language on an equal footing with religion, philosophy, literature, music, art, socio-political systems, scientific theories, expressions, tools, etc. as real social beings, and regarded them as the objects of study in hermeneutics. This attitude is very Algorithmical, and it is very different from the traditional philosophical attitude. For example, *to emphasize the difference between a text and the author's thoughts is to emphasize the solidity of the stock of knowledge.* In addition, in hermeneutics, there is a concept called "hermeneutic circle", which means that the researcher has to move back and forth between the whole and parts of a text. Dilthey understood this as a "production process" that was consistent with the above attitudes. This understanding is also quite Algorithmical. Nevertheless, Dilthey didn't know that the most fundamental way to explain this circle was the serial method based on the tiny computing power of metacomputation. From a metacomputation point of view, strictly speaking, this "circle" is not a real circle, because the objects for these different computations are generally not the same.

In order to emphasize the ontological status of text, Dilthey abruptly turned to a somewhat behaviorist style of discourse (behaviorism had not yet been formally put forward at the time), emphasizing that text was clearer and more objective than subjective experiences, and that if our understanding of a thing was different from the public understanding, then our understanding was basically invalid. Thereafter, these arguments were challenged by Gadamer.

As a twentieth-century hermeneutician, Hans-Georg Gadamer believed that the processes of reading and comprehension were the processes of dialogue between readers and authors and the processes of "fusion of horizons", rather than just the understanding processes that tried to conform to a certain standard. Furthermore, Gadamer believed that the stock of knowledge formed by education would dominate and distort a person's own reading and comprehension, but this "historicity" was insurmountable. Gadamer was very astute and quite Algorithmical in arguing that the Enlightenment actually had a very irrational preconception that people could come into direct contact with "reality" without authority and tradition, whereas tradition was something that preceded us whether we wanted it or not, and that we had to accept it, and it was a basic condition of our existence and understanding. Not only were we always in the midst of tradition, but tradition was always a part of us, and it was tradition that inextricably linked the perceived and the perceiver. It was impossible for us to go beyond the tradition and comprehend an object as a pure subject.[14] Gadamer believed that history was not a whole process of the unity of human existence and the world, but a one-way expansion starting from individual subjects. Therefore, knowledge was always temporary, and always

---

14. The historical materials on Gadamer in this section come mainly from Rulun Zhang, "Fifteen Lectures on Modern Western Philosophy" (in Chinese), Beijing: CITIC Publishing Group, 2020, pp. 368-386, and Richard Kearney (ed.), "Routledge History of Philosophy Volume VIII: Twentieth-Century Continental Philosophy", ebook, Routledge, 2005, pp. 296-322.

tended to be larger, but still limited, and never infinite or complete. These views are very Algorithmical. However, in the proposition that rhetoric was the only method of philosophy, Gadamer pushed humanism to an extreme.

Let me now make a few comments. It is an imperative step to extend the knowledge system to the field of humanities and look at humanistic works from the perspective of a unified ATT. We can clearly see how the history of philosophy moves stepwise and logically in this direction. As far as the synthesis of knowledge, emotions, and wills, or the synthesis of theory, history, and practice is concerned, how can we avoid the use of ATT? Since we should treat authors, texts, and readers as both interrelated and distinctive, why cannot we use the concise and effective framework of "Instructions + information"? Of course, it would take time for computer science to emerge, so those theoretical and logical relations in it had yet to be clarified. In desperation, philosophers frequently used vague terms such as "life", "relationship", "wholeness", and "history". When philosophy encountered obstacles on this issue, Dilthey suggested that philosophy could instead turn to the study of language and texts that were readily available to view or listen to. Thus, we can see that *the philosophy of language, hermeneutics, and behaviorist psychology emerged almost simultaneously after that.* This is a logical development of history.


## §172. Pragmatism

American pragmatism has a unique place in the panorama of the new system because it places special emphasis on the practical end of knowledge. Pragmatism, which may seem isolated, plays an indispensable and important role in the system. Three authors are involved here: Charles S. Peirce, William James, and John Dewey.

It is not enough for the traditional concept of "knowledge"

to be extended from the sciences to the fields of "hard software" and the humanities, but it must also be extended to engineering. In other words, the engineering contents of traditional knowledge need to be distinguished from the cognitive and scientific contents and then revisited. When we look at it in this way, the framework of time and space unfolds, and we will find that the epistemic or scientific contents and the engineering contents are located at different stages in the chain of thinking. Knowledge development can start in different locations and go in different directions. It can be developed sequentially from information to decision-making, or it can be reversed, from decision-making problems to seek its basis upstream. In this way, there will be extensive bifurcations and modularizations in knowledge development, and the connections between different modules will be loose or tight, dense or sparse. This discovery would be incompatible with the previous rationalist system in which the system of knowledge as a whole was assumed perfect. It was like a car running in a network of highways where it could freely go in any direction at a negligible cost, so it was not much important where the development of knowledge started, what the path was, how it forked, where it arrived, and what characteristics of its each phase had, and so forth. With the help of this comparison, we can recognize the differences between the old and new systems, and why the new philosophy is new and creative.

In traditional discourse, the field of action and engineering is called "practice". I prefer the word "engineering" in order to emphasize the division of disciplines, and simultaneously emphasize that the so-called "practice" field is not a field that cannot be systematized or documented. It is not only the epistemic or scientific fields that can be documented as formal disciplines within research and educational institutions. In the past, the word "practice" exactly had this inappropriate meaning. It created a psychological habit that as long as it is "practical", then those of you sitting here discussing at the moment will have nothing to say. The word "practice" also deliberately created a separation of mental activity from physical activity while ignoring the essential mental activity that occurs simultaneously in action. All mental activities (as well as physical activities) shall be included in our research, and the distinction between the particular and the general shall be deemed secondary and not always necessary.

Going back from a pragmatic point of view, one of the first important findings was that a large number of metaphysical issues were unnecessary or meaningless, neither verifiable nor falsifiable. In other words, this kind of study has been destined to be fruitless or inconducive to other mental activities. This was yet another blow to metaphysics. What it required was the refinement of philosophical and other academic studies. Second, it inevitably required adjustments in the goals, priorities, and directions of academic research. This requirement was consistent with that of positivism.

However, a difference between pragmatism and positivism is that positivism confines itself to the field of scientific research, working mainly upstream of the chain of thinking, while pragmatism focuses on the downstream, which causes it to (unconsciously) consider factor completeness and the forced closure of computations. As a result, pragmatism has made a series of important discoveries. The first is that it discovered that knowledge is essentially a "belief". Beliefs are entirely ideological, pure software. Therefore, this was a step forward from the hard software such as emotions and desires emphasized by irrationalism, and also a step forward from the "quasi-software" of Bergson's "intuition", closer to the Algorithmic theory. Second, the criterion for judging the usefulness of a particular knowledge is not only based on the effect of physical actions, but also on its effects on *other mental activities.* This attitude has essentially been a novel Algorithmical attitude, that is, both mental and physical activities are real, so that no matter which one is influenced by a particular knowledge, this influence can be used as a basis for evaluating that knowledge. Peirce specifically pointed out that different pieces of knowledge should not be indiscriminately treated just because they are beliefs[15]. Such a view can lead us to a unified vision that embraces all heterogeneity and irregularity.

William James emphasized the private, selective, and developmental natures of knowledge. He said that truth is not a discovery, but an invention, and that humans cannot arbitrarily produce truth, and that the production of truth needs to be subject to constraints, and that we still enjoy a certain freedom. Obviously, his relevant confusions could not be solved until it comes to the Algorithmic age. James's pragmatic view of truth unfortunately fell into the accusation of relativism[16], which could seemingly be remedied by the Algorithmic rationale that every specific decision can have a specific solution, and these solutions do not need to be consistent with each other. In other words, the solutions as knowledge can appear in the form of big data, not necessarily in a concise form. The pursuit of simplicity is sometimes an excessive demand unconsciously put forward by traditional philosophy based on computational economic considerations. The pursuit of both precision of a

---

15. Rulun Zhang, "Fifteen Lectures on Modern Western Philosophy" (in Chinese), Beijing: CITIC Publishing Group, 2020, p. 137, and Frederick Copleston, "A History of Philosophy", Vol. VIII, New York: Image Books (Doubleday), 1994, pp. 308-309. The historic materials on Peirce in this section come mainly from pp. 304-329 of the latter, and pp. 135-141 of the former.

16. Rulun Zhang, "Fifteen Lectures on Modern Western Philosophy" (in Chinese), Beijing: CITIC Publishing Group, 2020, p. 150, and Frederick Copleston, "A History of Philosophy", Vol. VIII, New York: Image Books (Doubleday), 1994, p. 337. The historic materials on James in this section come mainly from pp. 331-344 of the latter, and pp. 143-150 of the former.

solution in specific decision-making and universality (and thus brevity) in the solution can lead to a conflict—this was where James' misfortune lay. When he fell into the discourse of "truth", it showed that he was pursuing universality and excessive economy—especially in the context of morality. Since morality is rude itself, how could it be used as an absolute standard to measure everything? Thus, this sharp conflict highlighted the crisis of traditional morality, and the crisis of ethics itself.

Regarding Dewey, three additional comments can be made here: 1. He emphasized the anticipation, planning, and initiative of decision-making, which can be a footnote to the "factor completeness". 2. His "theory of inquiry" can be regarded as a preparation for Algorithmic logic. He particularly emphasized the need for reformation of logic. He believed that a thinking process is, in principle, a combination of multiple methods, and has spatiotemporal characteristics.[17] 3. In political philosophy, compared with the viewpoint of emphasizing the construction of institutions, Dewey emphasized education and the cultivation of civic quality[18], which formed a dispute between "system theory" and "quality theory". This question is very important for the development of democracy, and their integration can be carried out Algorithmically.

Finally, I would like to make a concluding remark. The starting point of pragmatism is particularly helpful in

---

17. John Dewey, "Logic: The Theory of Inquiry", New York: Henry Holt And Company, 1938.

18. The historic materials on Dewey in this section come mainly from Rulun Zhang, "Fifteen Lectures on Modern Western Philosophy" (in Chinese), Beijing: CITIC Publishing Group, 2020, p. 152-162, and Frederick Copleston, "A History of Philosophy", Vol. VIII, New York: Image Books (Doubleday), 1994, pp. 352-379.

establishing a unified vision that embraces different types of knowledge, in which each type of knowledge has a limited but unique role, competing and complementing each other. The whole body of knowledge is as limited in the face of specific decisions as it is in the face of specific phenomena. Regardless of whether it is a practical or a theoretical problem, an engineering problem or a scientific problem, the existing knowledge is generally insufficient in both quantity and quality, and is therefore barely used. On the other hand, the existing supply of knowledge would also be excessive and redundant, and a large part of it cannot directly contribute to solving the current problems—and the wrong knowledge in it would often be misleading and harmful. In this way, a complex, web-like correspondence is formed among the original information, the stock of knowledge, and the various problems. Understanding this network as a whole is important. Within the knowledge system, its structure is loose and developing, and order exists only partially. This is also closely related to Algorithmical convergence and divergence. In other words, pragmatism has a strong tendency to favor pluralism, discreteness, softness, and mixedness, and it did so in a simple and effective way, which is especially similar to the Algorithmic theory with the help of "decision-making – forced closure of computation – factor completeness" to the conclusion of the subjective turn. Therefore, I think that pragmatism is closer to the Algorithmic philosophy than European philosophy. We can find that American scholars and the general public with pragmatist ideas have gradually developed an open-minded, moderate, and inclusive character, as well as the rich and flexible means in dealing with practical problems. The American national character and the philosophy of pragmatism are mutually reinforcing, and they constitute an important feature of

American civilization.[19] In view of these practical effects, if we consider that the philosophy of pragmatism has been relatively successful, then we can regard this success as good news for the Algorithmic philosophy.

## §173. Frege

Gottlob Frege is an important philosopher who pioneered a generation. He is known to be one of the founders of mathematical logic, and philosophers have also elected him as the founder of analytic philosophy. Algorithmically, however, he outweighs these historical roles. Given that he is the founder of mathematical logic, I believe that he can actually be regarded as one of the pioneers of thinking theory, that is, a pioneer of the Algorithmic theory.

As mentioned earlier, Aristotle was the initiator of formal logic. However, Frege suggested that logic needs to be further symbolized. The reason for the symbolization is obviously that there are only *a few* typical logical reasoning activities, and by symbolizing them, a thinker *only needs* to remember the *finite*, abstract meanings and the operational rules that these symbols are given, and then they can perform reasoning activities as if they are mathematical operations, *without having to consider other factors*. A purpose of using symbols is to detach from natural language that has been not only imprecise but also often overly meaningful. Vague and rich meanings can be seen as an obstacle to standardized operations. A merit of mathematical operation is that this standardized symbolic operation will bring great convenience or efficiency (the computational economy). Frege apparently did not know at the

---

19. Daniel J. Boorstin, "The Americans: The Colonial Experience", Vintage, 1964; "The Americans: The National Experience", Vintage, 1967; "The Americans: The Democratic Experience", Vintage, 1974.

time that symbolic manipulation was beneficial to computer development because it reduced the kinds of operations that computers would have to simulate. Computers can use basic physical structures to simulate basic thinking activities, and then use a combination of these basic thinking activities to simulate higher-level, more complex thinking activities in a serial manner. This reflects the Algorithmical truth that simplicity and speediness should be highly valued, although they did not occupy an important place in traditional conscious thinking.

However, since this important work was carried out without a clear understanding of its significance, its limitations have been unavoidable. One of the limitations was manifested in the fact that symbolic logical reasoning was limited to the scope of logic rather than being treated as "behaviors", and thus did not include those administrative and service operations such as "data transfer", "search", "storage", etc. The latter types of operation were not added on until the advent of computer science.

A consequence of the fact that symbolic simulation was limited to logic was that Frege separated logic from psychology and emphasized the independence and "objectivity" of logic. Psychology has an implicit tradition and tenor of treating the mind as a substantive being, which was apparently not realized at the time. In view of those historical conditions of the time, this separation seemed necessary, because the synthesis of psychology and logic that we have reached today is first and foremost based on the formalization and clarity of logic. From mathematical logic to computer science, to artificial intelligence and Algorithm Theory, it was obviously a roundabout developmental process from complex to simple, and then from simple to complex. After the extension of logic to computer science, it had not yet formed a theory of thinking. Computer science plus the economics of thinking gives rise to the Algorithmic thinking theory. Correspondingly, in logic, the development of mathematical logic at Frege's time to the modern logic spawned by computer science, and the introduction of the thinking economy, bring us to the comprehensive "Algorithmic logic system" introduced in this book, which is equivalent to returning to the complex everyday thinking—at a higher level, of course. In this new integrated system, logical operations are a special case of mental activities, i.e., the consequence of ignoring the spatiotemporal and economic elements of computation. *Psychological factors, which Frege rejected back then, now logically return.*

Consistent with the rejection of psychological factors, all "wrong" or unreliable thinking methods, thinking processes, and thinking results were also excluded from Frege's mathematical logic that was only directly connected to "truth" and the real world. In other words, such analytic philosophy has been inevitably allied with *realism*. "Realism" was quite a new term. It can be considered, in modern philosophical literature, a variant of the traditional metaphysics marked by "Being" and "God". The term "realism" became popular obviously because traditional metaphysics had been intended to give up, which had been one of the goals of analytic philosophy, and the "rational elements" in traditional metaphysics had needed to be saved. Its core implication is that certain knowledge is perfectly correct and therefore should be given priority and special treatment. The existence of this type of knowledge is consistent with the belief in "perfect reasoning" and the belief in the authenticity of the external world. This notion was later summarized by Wittgenstein as the "principle of world-language-logic isomorphism".

As an example of this realism, Frege distinguished between the sense and reference of language.[20] He said that while a

---

20. The historic materials on Frege in this section come mainly from Rulun

noun might have a meaning in thought, the object to which it referred (e.g., a character in a mythological story) did not necessarily exist in the real world, and therefore, in logical reasoning, *it was necessary to distinguish between them.* In this way, the logician must always be concerned with the question of the truth or falsity of a proposition. Moreover, instead of determining the truth or falsity according to the actor who made the proposition, the logician oneself needed to determine it, and then modify the logical statement and logical operation accordingly. This meant that the *logician was directly involved in substantive problems of thinking.* Therefore, this approach pioneered by Frege was regarded as philosophical, not merely logical.

The philosophical significance of Frege's work has been stated earlier. In my opinion, it does not need to be a philosophy in this way. On the contrary, such an intervention is a serious malaise, because it violates the "content neutrality" that logic and languages are naturally and self-evidently supposed to observe. This neutrality means that logic and language, as tools, are only responsible for reasoning according to the given premises, or for expressing them according to the given contents, and have no rights and obligations to intervene in substantive argumentation of the relevant premises and contents. This principle of neutrality can be valid even in sentences that formally determine "true" or "false". For example, a proposition needs to be determined to be true or false, and the establishment of the proposition and the determination of its truth or falsehood shall be divided into two steps, which can in fact be a manifestation of the serial processing method—as Peirce said, a prejudice must first be

Zhang, "Fifteen Lectures on Modern Western Philosophy" (in Chinese), Beijing: CITIC Publishing Group, 2020, pp. 166-171 and A. C. Grayling, "The History of Philosophy", New York: Penguin Press, 2019, pp. 358-365.

accepted and then be tested.[21] However, this true-false determination can only be based on the premises given. Whether a premise itself is in fact true or not is a matter of the actor's own, and the author of the formal logic statement does not have to check it. Moreover, such a determination or examination must generally not be so easy as expected (later philosophers have tried, and it has been), and it is likely that the results are often inconclusive.

Unfortunately, this approach has been widely adopted by later scholars, not only in logic but also in language. A large number of authors seemed to want to discover the mysteries of the real world directly through the study of logic and language, just as Kant tried to discover a shortcut to truth directly through the study of those cognitive forms. This caused great confusion and led to a long-term, serious waste of energy—an ineffectiveness that even the analytic philosophers themselves finally acknowledged[22]. It can be said that it truly indicates that the "ghost" of traditional metaphysics has been haunting philosophy and never stopped.

Obviously, it has mistakenly skipped the link of "theory of mind". Between language and the world, what needs to be highlighted is thinking. People generate thoughts before they express them. Thought is not the same thing as language. This is common sense—although the Instruction system can be expressed as something called "machine language". Moreover, thinking is primary, and language is much less important than thinking—and this should also be taken as common sense. The study of language should be seen as a preparation (or "drill")

21. C. S. Peirce, "Collected Papers of Charles Sanders Peirce: Volume V Pragmatism And Pragmaticism", Cambridge, Massachusetts: The Belknap Press of Harvard University Press, 1974, p. 156.
22. Stuart G. Sbanker (ed.), "Routledge History of Philosophy Volume IX: Philosophy of Science, Logic and Mathematics in the Twentieth Century", ebook, Routledge, 2004, pp. 193-194.

before moving towards the study of the mind. All these can only be seen clearly when we come to the "Algorithmical state" now.

## §174. Russell

The discussion of Bertrand Russell begins with the problem of paradoxes. This discussion can serve as a corroboration for the validity of Algorithmic Theory, and of the above comments and opinions.

A common feature of set-theory paradoxes and semantic paradoxes[23] is that a paradox occurs if the corresponding proposition is considered to be self-referential. For example, in "X is mortal", the class of human cannot be a member of itself, otherwise, a paradox will occur. In "I am lying", the proposition cannot be directed at itself, otherwise, a paradox will occur. Russell's solution to these paradoxes was to propose the theory of descriptions. However, these paradoxes would not have occurred if we had understood mental activity in the Algorithmical way. This approach, as readers may have realized, is that any mental activity cannot contain itself in the first place under the Algorithmical processing mode. A thinker who is proposing a proposition does so through his certain mental activity, so that this mental activity he uses to formulate the proposition cannot be operationally and technically included in itself as an ongoing mental activity. Whether or not this ongoing mental activity and its result are applicable to the proposition it presents can only be based on a previous prediction or post-facto verification of the relevant contents in

---

23. Unless otherwise specified, the historic materials on Russell in this and next section come mainly from Rulun Zhang, "Fifteen Lectures on Modern Western Philosophy" (in Chinese), Beijing: CITIC Publishing Group, 2020, pp. 173-184, and Frederick Copleston, "A History of Philosophy", Vol. VIII, New York: Image Books (Doubleday), 1994, pp. 428-493.

the memory. However, this kind of prediction or verification itself is another new mental activity, in which the problem of self-inclusion could occur again, in the same way, and even infinitely. This determines that any proposition, no matter how "true" it is and how wide a scope it is assumed to cover, can in fact only be directed at *local* or *partial* objects. From the perspective of Algorithmic bounded rationality or concrete rationality, this effect must be inevitable.[24] Further, the problem of paradoxes only exposes the attempts of traditional extreme rationalists to establish an all-encompassing perfect theory. These attempts have been "greedy" to the point where they do not even give up an ongoing tiny and single mental activity.

Let's change into another way to solve the "golden-mountain paradox": "The gold mountain does not exist." "The golden mountain" is obviously something imagined by the human brain. To say that "the golden mountain does not exist" is not to say that "the golden mountain" as a fiction does not exist in the speaker's mind—if that were the case, it would be a real contradiction. Rather, it means that this fiction does not exist in the real world outside of the speaker. In fact, it's a common-sense understanding. Today, this is also an Algorithmical understanding, since "the golden mountain" as a conceptual entity can arise in the speaker's mind, which is now philosophically "legitimate". Although it is clearly originated by empirical materials from the real world (e.g., the "gold" and the "mountain", respectively) and re-processed by the brain to be generated, we can ignore the question of the appropriateness of this fiction. Because, the brain produces a lot of fictions and mistakes every hour of the day, and it is normal and unsurprising. In this case, clearly, the speaker has

---

24. Li, Bin (2022). "The Algorithmic Logic as a Synthetic or General Logic", Academia Letters, Article 4936. https://doi.org/10.20935/AL4936

already launched operations contrary to the above generative process to test whether what is imaginary in his mind corresponds to the reality of the physical world. Since thinking activity is a kind of relatively independent closed-door operation, this reverse operation is also necessary and normal, and in fact, it also occurs frequently in daily thinking activities. Sometimes it comes to a positive conclusion, sometimes to a negative conclusion, and in this case, the conclusion is unfortunately negative. All these are meaningful as long as we recognize the substantiality or materiality of thoughts, namely, the independent position of objects of thoughts in analysis. Its meaningfulness can be complete and undoubtable at all. The only thing that is problematic is the thinking of Russell and others, that is, the mistaken belief that they must first understand the "substantial truth" before they can logically reason or speak, otherwise, they will not even be able to speak, and even their minds will not be able to think.

This example highlights the importance of treating the human mind as a collection of separate entities (or reality) that are equal to, and distinct from, physical entities. Even the most correct idea must, in principle, be regarded as different from the object to which it refers. It is simply the result of the mind relating in its own way to the information from the objective world. If philosophers had positioned their thinking systems and ideas in this way from the very beginning, there would have been no such confusions.

Discussions of other aspects of Russell's philosophy can also be attributed to the above arguments.

As mentioned earlier (§55, Vol. I), Russell's logical atomism is quite close to Algorithmic Theory: everyday statements can be decomposed and transformed into atomic propositions (like Wittgenstein's "elementary proposition"), which state the smallest facts in instantaneous sensory experience. This theory implied the "Metacomputation = Instruction + information" structure. However, this doctrine was directed at language rather than thinking, so it had been unnecessarily complicated. For example, "Instruction + information" is a "verb + object" structure, while the basic form of language and logic is structured as "subject + predicate". For example, when a sensory material enters the mind, the mind processes it directly to form a mental activity, whereas in language it is a matter that needs to be expressed. The activity of thinking does not need to be expressed in the first place, and only in some cases does it need to be expressed. If the theory of thinking had been established, the question of language would have become the question of how to translate thoughts into physical symbols (words or sounds). Given that the formats of ideas are uniform and universal, it would then be appropriate to focus only on physical symbols. A rough judgment is that this kind of language research could have saved at least half of the efforts.

Second, Russell unnecessarily tied his logical atomism to his philosophy of realism. He went on to argue that atomic propositions corresponded to "atomic facts" in the objective world, just as atomic propositions constitute everyday language, and atomic facts constitute the world. Modern developments in physics suggest that the world is not only infinitely vast, but also infinitely divisible, and "atom" is not the smallest unit of physical materials. Arguments such as these are clearly a blow to all sorts of physical atomic theories. It can even be supposed that the infinite divisibility might also be applicable in mental activities, and the physical mechanisms and physical elements behind mental activity are likely to be infinitely separable. However, on the software side, the situation is different. We have reason to think that the smallest unit of mental activity that one can consciously manipulate does exist, which can be as convincing as the existence of the smallest limit to the size of an image that our eyes can see directly, even though the smallest image is still objectively divisible. On the other hand, with the help of a telescope or a microscope, there is no limit to the maximal and minimal sizes of objects we can see. In the same way, there is no maximum or minimum to the size of an object that can be involved in thinking, logic, and language. Human beings can dig a wealth of information and knowledge out of small objects, and can also summarize the objective world on a wide range in a few words.

## §175. Russell and the Vienna Circle

The difficulty in those pioneering works of philosophical forefathers can also be manifested in the logical constructivism proposed by Russell in relation to his logical atomism.

First of all, we need to review the so-called "elemental monism" that we have skipped. Mach divided what we now call "primitive information" into three categories: physical, physiological, and psychological, and argued that these elements can be used directly (in the form of functions) to draw conclusions beyond entities such as "mind" and "matter", so as to avoid the mind-object dualism of modern times. Coincidentally, his contemporary, William James, held a similar view, known as "neutral monism". James's writings persuaded Russell, who went one step further by proposing the concept of "sensibilia" in an attempt to unify these elements as empirical materials. But, dramatically, Russell, continuing his usual paradoxical style, has simultaneously made a breakthrough in the opposite direction. He said that subjects such as mind and matter were the "logical constructions" and had been used to govern the sensory materials. This is similar to my above view expressed in discussing Berkeley's "to be is to be perceived". Alfred J. Ayer argued that this was a "horizontal inference" (as distinct from "vertical inference"[25]), and the next question was, "How can the inference be justified?" Russell equivocated about this important issue.[26,27] We now know that the justification for the assumption of entities is the economics of computation, and the consequent bending of thinking. Moreover, the bending of the mind, as a major and important *phenomenon*, cannot be explained without introducing mindful entities, the Instructions, and Instructions can exactly be the variants of logic advocated by Frege, Russell, and others. Since all the elements and sensations can be recognized as "elements", why can't Instructions be?—Instructions can be spoken, and therefore must have been "felt" within the mind. Elemental monists, even if they did not recognize the minds of others, must recognize their own minds, because those sensory materials needed to be reasoned and calculated in order to reach a conclusion. Then, who and what had been making such computations? Was it the sensory materials that have computed themselves? In turn, after the Instructional entities have been identified, they can be ranked among the sensory data and then interact with data according to their respective properties. This is what we can do with elemental monism or neutral monism. After this tinkering, the logically constructed entities can coexist in comparison, competition, interaction, and complementarity with sensory materials on the tone of bounded rationality. This brings us to pluralism, of course, but also to the basic idea of monism. Personally, I even venture to believe that such a "tinkering" could not be rejected by monists, and perhaps even welcomed by them. The attempt to eliminate

---

25. A. J. Ayer, "Bertrand Russell", London: The Woburn Press, 1974, pp. 78-79.
26. Ibid, p. 74.
27. For a survey of this monism, from Mach to Russell, see Leopold Stubenberg and Donovan Wishon, "Neutral Monism", The Stanford Encyclopedia of Philosophy (Spring 2023 Edition), Edward N. Zalta & Uri Nodelman (eds.), URL = <https://plato.stanford.edu/archives/spr2023/entries/neutral-monism/>.

mind-matter dualism certainly stems from the time-honored habit of monism, but after this tinkering, monism, dualism, and pluralism should be able to achieve a great reconciliation.

The necessity of logically constructing entities needs to be illustrated by the approach of bounded rationality (or concrete rationality). In the same way, Russell's emphasis on the necessity of external relations also requires the help of bounded rationality. In the debate between Russell and Francis H. Bradley, Bradley proceeded from a neo-Hegelian standpoint and did not recognize that external relations should have an independent status. In my view, the rationale for this view lies in the fact that any "relationship" as a consequence or phenomenon should be regarded as the result of the interaction between the properties of the entities in question; however, the problem is that at any point in time, our knowledge of the properties of any particular entity should be considered incomplete, and therefore cannot be used to exactly predict what kind of relationship the entity will form with other entities. It is often only when this relationship is perceived that it is possible for us to come to realize the existence of some properties of the entity that we did not know before. Moreover, such a relationship is generally the product of the combination or interaction of related entities in *a particular way*; unless this way is identified and addressed, the properties of the entities alone might not be sufficient to be used to explain the formation of such a relationship. In these cases, the "relationship" must acquire a certain independent status, and cannot be completely reduced to a description of the properties of the entities.

The above explanation can be reduced to a single Algorithmic inference, that is, "phenomenon-entity-relation-change" constitutes a group of concepts, which are used in common, relatively, competitively, and complementarily to describe and explain the world. A single concept (e.g., an entity) cannot be expected to be fully effective, because the idea of "a single concept taking it all" is nothing more than a subjective desire created by us out of the motive of frugal mental activities.

In questions such as "the golden mountain does not exist" and "the king of France is bald", tracing back to the roots, it was obvious that the confusion caused by Plato's "three tables" in those years was flashing: the conceptual table, the real table, and the painter's table. This confusion has not yet been fully clarified. One of the key points is that we humans always think that the ideas in our heads are not just our own business, but also that of the objective world. This narcissism has always lurked in the discourse of philosophers in a variety of ways, to a greater or lesser extent. The following Algorithmic argument helps to complementarily cure this narcissism: The sensory materials about external objects enter the human brain, and although their formats have been transformed into "information" that matches the Instructions, their primitiveness and purity could be maintained to the maximum. This is because a metacomputation can be relatively independent of information, distinguishing itself from information, distinguishing different pieces of information, and also distinguishing itself from its result, i.e., knowledge. The distinction between people and objects now translates into the distinction between flow and stock within the human brain, and between different data. Information is not completely absorbed, assimilated, or completely "polluted" by the mind (as some writers fear) just because it contains subjective components. As a result, we are able to distinguish not only the original information from the knowledge, but also the pieces of information or knowledge at different depths of processing.

At the end of this section, we comment on logical positivism (or logical empiricism) in general terms in the context of the Vienna Circle. Logical positivism attempts to reduce all philosophical discussions either to logical problems or to concrete empirical materials. Indeed, this is the specialty and habit of scientists, and it is where the competitive advantages of scientists over ordinary people lie. Therefore, logical positivism actually has a spiritual essence, that is, the pursuit of certainty and the rejection of all ambiguity or summarization. This is in line with the spiritual temperament and preferences of the scholars in the "ivory tower". Their "professional", detailed, jargon-ridden, confident, yet sometimes confusing work used to shock people outside the circle. This quest for certainty further undermines traditional metaphysics and formally opens the historical process to the key answer to philosophical questions, a thinking theory. However, it all was explored in a semi-dark room. The explorers' mindsets were similar to that of pursuing Newtonian formulas of physics, always thinking that magical laws or truths can be discovered through the generalization of limited, individualized "reliable materials", to the exclusion of a global, historical perspective. Because their focus was on local "correct knowledge" and they did not see the meanings of other thinking activities and results, and thus other knowledge, they could not enter the social realm, whereas social issues are actually decisively linked to the "incorrectness" of thinking, that is, its substantiality or materiality. Since they did not understand this, it was impossible for them not to fall into confusion when they tried to interpret objects such as ethics while adhering to their extreme realist position. However, from Russell to Rudolf Carnap, they were frank and happy to talk about their explorations, reflections, and puzzles. The details[28] will not be reviewed here, as they are largely unsuccessful.

---

28. Zhiwei Zhang (ed.), "A History of Western Philosophy" (in Chinese, 2nd), China Renmin University Press, 2010, pp. 185-192, and Uebel, Thomas, "Vienna Circle", The Stanford Encyclopedia of Philosophy (Summer 2024 Edition), Edward N. Zalta & Uri Nodelman (eds.), URL = <https://plato.stanford.edu/archives/sum2024/entries/vienna-circle/>.

With regard to positivism, I believe that it is Mach, the spiritual godfather of the Vienna Circle, who is the most pertinent, as he often said: theory should be *as little as possible* beyond experience unless it is absolutely unavoidable, and theory should be verified, affirmed, or tested as *quickly* as possible.[29] Obviously, Mach did not confront the theoretical approach with the empirical method, but only expressed here a relative *strategy*, and the argument ended up on quantitativeness or softness, by no means as extreme as the Viennese scholars. In fact, many successful theories were not built outside empirical terms, but rather on vague and often abundant general experiences that were ignored by the average empiricists. These experiences are sometimes so pervasive that observers fail to detect them because of the effect of "darkness beneath a lamp". In my opinion, this is the case with the formulation of Algorithmic Theory. Moreover, I would like to emphasize that works on Algorithmic Theory are mainly and preferentially written for readers with a position of scientism or scientific realism. I'm focused on convincing those most stubborn minds, expecting that after accepting the basic Algorithmic elements, even if they continue to work with their habits, they will eventually come to the Algorithmic field.

## §176. Wittgenstein

With the above in mind, we need only make some additional, fragmentary comments on Wittgenstein.

Wittgenstein was a widely influential philosopher with a mysterious temperament. But, like many other prominent philosophers of the twentieth century, his thinking was self-contradictory, full of confusion, struggle, and even chaos. This

---

29. Zhiwei Zhang (ed.), "A History of Western Philosophy" (in Chinese, 2nd), China Renmin University Press, 2010, p. 543.

reflects the transitional features of philosophy in a historical development.[30]

First of all, let's talk about this richling's search for the meanings of life. Freedom is universally admired in the world, but when it comes, not everyone will know it. For Wittgenstein, who had attained "financial freedom", he did not have to run for a livelihood or dwell on mundane chores, but had essentially entered the realm of freedom. The number of people who can experience this state is only a very small percentage of the total population, and in this very small percentage, even fewer happen to be philosophers. Wittgenstein honestly wrote about his state of mind, which can be regarded as a philosophical voice for this part of the population. Indeed, this state of mind is typical. The idleness of the affluent population brings about emptiness, anguish, and the questioning of meanings of life. Theoretically, however, this kind of inquiry can be absurd, because what it has sought is nothing more than an attempt to put the free mind and body *back* under some necessities, objectivities, responsibilities, or ethical norms. One always says that he/she wants freedom, but as soon as he/she gets it, he/she might immediately turn to escape from it, and he/she might assume that it would still be the "happiest" days when he/she makes a little progress every day under the pressure of livelihood. This has been a common outpouring of this group of people. It seems that this mental anguish stems first of all from a psychological habit. In other words, it stems from a blind obedience to the hectic mass psychology. Philosophically, I think we should first

———————

30. Unless otherwise specified, the historic materials on Wittgenstein in this section come mainly from Rulun Zhang, "Fifteen Lectures on Modern Western Philosophy" (in Chinese), Beijing: CITIC Publishing Group, 2020, pp. 198-222, and Stuart G. Shanker (ed.), "Routledge History of Philosophy Volume IX", ebook, Routledge, 2004, pp. 162-193, and John V. Canfield (ed.), "Routledge History of Philosophy Volume X", ebook, Routledge, 2005, pp. 274-308.

(Algorithmically) clarify what a state of freedom is and what kind of psychology it will be. Once we step out of the above habitual mindset, objectively, calmly, and *at a higher order,* and realize that we have entered into freedom, then we will reshape our psychology into some new statuses, and our psychology will become stronger, and we will even be satisfied with this purposeless life, without falling into anxiety and panic. At this point, what Greek skeptics called "tranquil" could be referential to us. "Finding the meaning of life" is deemed a traditional task of ethicists, but it is actually not necessary. If there is an answer to this question, it may imply that freedom may have been lost. Research of ethics might need to be adapted in light of this understanding. It is a pity that, in contrast to traditional reflections, I do not think that Wittgenstein's reflection has made an important breakthrough.

In the philosophy of logic and language, it is not necessary to criticize the isomorphism again, but rather to reinvent it: logic (or thought) and language are *aimed at* specific objects in the world, and attempt to simulate and speculate on those objects, but different versions of logic (or thought) and language make simulations and speculations that may be highly different and irregular. Here, at best, the "isomorphic" relationship can be changed into the "corresponding" relationship. The fact that ideas and languages target specific objects does not mean that they are "isomorphic" to each other. Due to the "factor completeness", people in different eras often deal with similar objects and solve similar problems, but the methods, means, and effects of their actions are often quite different.

Wittgenstein recognized quite unequivocally the importance of thought over language: "It seems that there are certain definite mental processes bound up with the working of language ... The signs of our language seem dead without these mental processes; and it might seem that the only function of the signs is to induce such processes, and that these are the things we ought really to be interested in."[31] Wittgenstein believed that thought was made up of psychological constituents, but what were exactly the psychological constituents? He said he did not know.[32] Wittgenstein's following assertion is obviously incorrect: all ideas can be stated in propositions, and what cannot be stated (said) is what cannot be thought.

Wittgenstein's ideas of the early and late periods are not only contradictory, but also extreme. In his later years, he discovered the importance of common sense and the stock of knowledge. Just as he absolutized logic and language in the early stage, he has now absolutized common sense. He argued that common sense had a logical status different from that of language and mental activity: "Their status is so fundamental that they provide the grounds and framework for determining the certainty or uncertainty, the truth or falsity, for other propositions. They themselves, however, are without grounds and are incapable of being justified or supported by evidence. One might say these 'truisms' are prelogical even 'animal' in character. They determine the framework of a language system, but are not themselves hypotheses or suppositions, stated within the language-game they help to define."[33] Supposedly, since Wittgenstein recognized that such a "world-picture" was an "axis" or "scaffold" (a term I also like) and that it was pluralistic and changing, he shall not make these conflictive statements. Obviously, this is a consequence of the lack of the Algorithmic knowledge theory. Wittgenstein's statement on

---

31. Ludwig Wittgenstein, "The Blue and Brown Books", Basil Blackwell Oxford, p. 3. The ellipsis is added by me.
32. Ludwig Wittgenstein, "Notebooks 1914-1916", 2nd edition, translated by G. E. M. Anscombe, The University of Chicago Press, 1979, p. 131.
33. Milton K. Munitz, "Contemporary Analytic Philosophy", Macmillan & Collier Macmillan, 1981, p. 330.

factor completeness is quite wonderful: "A main cause of philosophical diseases—a one-sided diet: one nourishes one's thinking with only one kind of example"[34], so that philosophy needs an "overview", a "map" based on a survey, and a "geography" of our conceptual resources.[35] However, he thus pitted description against theoretical method: "we may not advance any kind of theory. There must not be anything hypothetical in our considerations. All explanation must disappear, and description alone must take its place."[36] This misunderstanding can be the result of the lack of Algorithmic logic, which can establish a rational logical relationship between seemingly fragmented elements and thus continue to apply them to theoretical deduction.

The lack of a proper theory of mind has also led philosophers to argue over private language. If we limit language to a tool for interpersonal communication, then Wittgenstein's insistence on excluding the possibility of private language is justified—and, it can be consistent with his own earlier arguments. However, mental activity, although different from language, can also be *expressed* as a special kind of language ("machine language"). Since data and meta-computations are independent of each other, they need to be recorded, and individuals need to record their own ideological activities and ideological conditions so that they can *communicate with themselves*. Then, it can be argued that many private languages must have been produced in this kind of recording and "self-communication" while a public language can be the result of the intersection, agreement, and

---

34. Ludwig Wittgenstein, "Philosophical Investigations", translated by Anscombe, Hacker, and Schulte, Wiley-Blackwell, 2009, §593, p. 164
35. Milton K. Munitz, "Contemporary Analytic Philosophy", Macmillan & Collier Macmillan, 1981, p. 317.
36. Ludwig Wittgenstein, "Philosophical Investigations", translated by Anscombe, Hacker, and Schulte, Wiley-Blackwell, 2009, §109, p. 52.

development of the private languages. From this point of view, Wittgenstein was wrong to equate his public language with thinking.

Algorithmically, Wittgenstein's "family likeliness" is popular because it proposes a much-needed element of "softness" that has been lacking in the social sciences, i.e., the redefinition or re-understanding of concepts in a mixture of vast similarities and differences. The concept of "language game" is also welcome because it (seemingly inadvertently) speaks to the crucial nature of human life and human society that it is a "human game" that has nothing to do with the natural world. Natural, physical elements, although they play a role in it, are indirect. The direct elements include the following propositions: they are all intentional and active conventions; although the conventions also need to take into account the limitations of objective factors, the limitations mainly and directly come from the field of thinking; factors of big data and combinatorial explosion lead to the fact that the processes of conventions are not completely deterministic, and the subjective factors and wills are very important. "Human games" include not only language games, but also "moral games", "political games", "economic games" and so on. Of course, the analytic philosophers have clearly not yet grasped the logic here. For example, all analytic philosophers, including Wittgenstein, have shown their confusion and incomprehension about ethics. And, Wittgenstein put it straightforwardly, "thinking really can't be compared to an activity at all."[37]

By the way, I would like to expand on a few other analytic philosophers. The mistakes made by the early analytic

---

37. Ludwig Wittgenstein, "Remarks on the Philosophy of Psychology", Vol. II, translated by C. G. Luckhardt and M. A. E. Aue, Basil Blackwell Oxford, 1980, §193, p. 39.

philosophers were often corrected by the later philosophers, which is a prominent feature of the school of analytic philosophy. In other words, the self-denial tendency of this school was quite prominent, although their rigorous and detailed analysis of language would certainly have certain referential significance in the Algorithmic analysis. For example, the theory of speech act advocated by John L. Austin of the Oxford School clearly distinguishes sentences into multiple types, which concretely shows how discourses can be viewed as *acts* with different purposes and functions. This perspective is Algorithmical. Leo Strauss and Willard V. O. Quine rejected analytic philosophy's total rejection of metaphysics, and instead extended analytic philosophy to the topic of metaphysics. Nonetheless, given the limitations of the basic framework of analytic philosophy, metaphysical research in this area has achieved little in itself except for the effect of self-denial.

## §177. Ryle

Gilbert Ryle is an important figure in Algorithmic arguments and hence deserves to be discussed again. Because, he is a pure and sharp opponent of debate. Like George Berkeley, he built an argument that was absurd, pure, and not easily refutable. For a long period before and after the publication of his The Concept of Mind, the behaviorism he supported was not successfully refuted, but instead became a guide for scientific research, dominating psychology and influencing many humanities and social sciences. He was a key voice for behaviorism in the field of philosophy. It was not until the second half of the twentieth century, with the rise of cognitive psychology, that behaviorism gradually declined. However, a decisive confrontation is still to take place. Part of the reason is that cognitive science itself is still faltering. In my opinion, it is necessary for cognitive sciences to absorb the Algorithmic principles and methods. In other words, today, we need to rally under the new Algorithmic program and launch a new counterattack against behaviorism.

As an analytic philosopher and philosopher of language, Ryle's defense of language adopts a singular behaviorist perspective, that is, language is a perceptible "act", one of many outwardly visible or perceptible "acts". In contrast, mental and intellectual activities can be regarded as non-existent, or in other words, there is a one-body-but-two-faced relationship between the two, and after studying one of the two faces, there is no need to study the other. And because mental activity was difficult to describe and grasp in his time, an inevitable conclusion could be that the study of external behavior shall *replace* the study of the mind. This was recommended as a methodological principle. On the other hand, if we study mind and matter side by side, or in opposition to each other as in modern philosophy, we will be repetitive, and will commit the so-called "category mistake". It's like committing a foul in a sports game.

The influences of this idea have been extensive. It caters to the traditional monist philosophy. We can see, for example, how much it fits into Spinoza's "mind-matter parallelism"! Even in the forthcoming phenomenological philosophy, there are similar elements lurking in it, which we will point out in a moment. Behaviorism implies the subtext that "we", as scholars, observers, and thinkers, are familiar with sensible, physical objects but not enough with our thoughts. Or rather, I see a guy on the road, and I go up to him and shake his hand and hug him and show friendship, and then the guy asks me who I am, and I reply, "I don't know who I am, please tell me!" That's where the absurdity lies.

However, such an absurd theory is very much in line with the minds of researchers. Ryle accused that Descartes was influenced by modern mechanistic physics, in fact, he himself might have been influenced by this more deeply; that is, since our knowledge and grasp of physical objects had been so satisfactory, it was better to study human and social objects by a simple extension of them; therefore, as long as the study of external behaviors could achieve the goal, then the psychological objects should be shaved off with Occam's razor.

"The Concept of Mind" lists multiple ways to try to "shave" the mind. It can be speculated that this method will never be useless, because there are always certain mental activities that have their external appearances. However, this method will never be completely successful, because there are also many thoughtful and psychological activities that do not have outward appearances. And, even if there are visual representations, they are generally unlikely to be "sufficient". Even if language is used to express ideas, it may not be sufficient.

Of course, the most critical rebuttals can only come from the cognitive or Algorithmical realm. This is: when we can now easily and clearly delineate, explain, and analyze the activity of thinking itself, is it time to tip the balance? Is it necessary for us to continue to prioritize the behaviorist approach? Obviously, the counterattack that can be launched at this time is systematic and overwhelming.

With regard to the question of categories, we need to answer: in what sense can mind and matter be juxtaposed as entities or objects of study? The answer is that, *in fact*, they have already been juxtaposed as our "phenomena" or "objects". A mind or thought is something that we can sense or feel clearly and intensely, not something outside of senses and feelings that we make up in order to explain certain phenomena (or for some other purposes). Humans have confronted these phenomena or objects since ancient times. Psychology and minds are not only materials for explaining other phenomena, but they are also phenomena, objects, and problems in their own right. At this point, all phenomena, objects, entities, or realities have the same status, and they are lined up in front of our senses or perceptual organs, presented to us separately, with or without weight or volume, with or without overlapping each other. This overlapping is simply an issue of the relationship between them. However, when they present themselves to us separately and independently, their respective independence is already evident, and even if some aspects of them overlap with each other, they generally cannot be regarded as completely overlapping. At this point, as we usually say, even if two objects are identical, they are the two objects because they are in different spatial positions.

## §178. Ryle (continued)

Even if psychology and thinking are indeed functions of the human brain, or of the nervous system, or of the whole human body (as the "embodied intelligence"), and the relationship between them is two-faced, this does not mean that the description and study of contents of the mind are superfluous. To think that this is superfluous is meant to *substitute* mental activity with the activity of nerves, or of the human body, or of the microscopic particles, but this substitutive description is actually extremely *difficult*. In this regard, as Descartes emphasized, it is the easiest, most immediate, and most economical way to record, reflect, recall, and state one's mental activities directly. In other words, in the case of software and hardware corresponding to each other, software language has a unique and irreplaceable role. Therefore, *discourses on software and hardware can be able not to repeat each other while showcasing their comparative advantages.*

The principle of linking and distinguishing software and hardware is a great contribution of computer science. The philosophical implications of this contribution are abundant. By showing how a content of thought is represented, generated, stored, changed, and lost in a physical entity, computer science *concretely* illustrates how spirit and matter juxtapose, interconnect, and interact with each other. Ideological content can be represented and transmitted on any material device that meets relevant technical requirements. Computer science illustrates how spirit depends on, and is independent of, matter. Computer science also accurately characterizes the spatial and temporal existence of ideas, indicating that they are only related to specific material bases (organs and tissues) and have no direct relationship with other things or objects. At this point, Ryle has been confusing the concepts. It cannot be said that because the mind is the "same" as its underlying physical materials, the mind is also the same thing as other unrelated entities or objects, and therefore it cannot be said that the opposition and interaction between the mind and the external objects are some false and meaningless scenes. This is one of the most basic meanings of "concrete rationality", or "concrete reason".

Moreover, computer principles in particular reveal in a metaphorical way how the mind and matter *interact* concretely: physical signals are converted into *information* in the formats compatible with those of thoughts (Instructions) through the sensory organs for use in the activity of the mind, and on the other hand, the decisions generated by the mind are *reversely* transformed into physical signals that then stimulate and control the relevant material organs of the human body to carry out physical operations, leading to the external visible behaviors. These processes of "modulation-demodulation" have now become a common part of information engineering. The relationships between the nervous system and other systems in the human body are clearly highly similar. Moreover, in the processes of external behaviors, the human brain must cooperate with the body to carry out executive and service computations. At this point, the mind and matter work closely together. Since computer science shows and implements all the details of this kind of computation, it would be eloquent to take these details to understand the relationships between mind and matter in the human body, and thus explain the substantiality or materiality of thought.

The theory of "category mistake" separates mind from matter and places them in two different levels of the world, which has a profound impact in the academic world. This position is "corroborated" and reinforced by the specious view that the activity of the mind is capricious, free-wheeling, coming and going unruly. Now, the thoughts have their "shapes", "places", and "volumes", and they have become real entities, and can coexist and interact with many physical entities. We need to realize what a tremendous change this is from the age of metaphysics and from the age of "materialism-idealism" confrontation! In this unified system, all kinds of philosophies have their rightful places. For example, let's not say that behaviorism has not been completely denied, the same is also true of realism: since none of our knowledge, including Algorithmic Theory, can be considered to be completely reliable, then, in statements, what does it matter to treat certain knowledge *directly* as truth which we consider in principle to be mere beliefs but is actually highly reliable? Will there be much negative consequence with this? Obviously not. Thus, in ordinary discourse, we can often omit the emphasis and statements on those higher-order philosophical principles of the fallibility of knowledge. In other words, the words and deeds of many of us can often appear to be realist alike, and the only exception is that we now have a different interpretation of these words and deeds, i.e. we do not think of ourselves as true realists, but the "Algorithmists" who like conciseness. These phenomena of hybridity also include the fact that it is only when individual actions are subjective (or so-called "irrational") that behaviorists care about them and recognize their "existence". Now, behind all of these, there needs to be a unified principle, and this unified principle needs to embrace the historical traditions and terminology of the academic community.

However, this inclusion can only happen after the ill effects of behaviorism have been cleaned up. Even in the philosophy of mind and cognitive sciences, there are still clear traces of behaviorism. For example, scholars often substitute the study of the spirit and the mind with the study of hardware. The work of establishing a software-only or software-based discourse system needs to be reinvented.

## §179. Brentano, Husserl

Algorithmically, phenomenology is a major achievement of twentieth-century philosophy. Its significance transcends all subsequent philosophies and is intimately linked to the Algorithmic thinking theory. Phenomenology is the philosophy closest to the Algorithmic philosophy. Therefore, I would rather value phenomenology, especially Husserl's phenomenology, higher than average historians of philosophy.

Let's start with the term "phenomenology". The Phenomenology of Spirit can be regarded as one of the shining points of Hegel's philosophy, because it presents human consciousness as a historical process that includes not only the "rational" and scientific parts that were usually given special attention, but the various types of conscious activities (i.e., mental activities) in general. Different kinds of ideas and intellectual activities are treated here equally as "phenomena", therefore, it is called "phenomenology". This attitude, although not entirely Algorithmical, is one step closer to the Algorithmical attitude.

Next is the word "intentionality". At first glance, this term from Franz Brentano (and medieval philosophical texts) has a certain superficial and ridiculous flavor, because when he said that a thought had the nature of "about an object", "reference to a content", or "direction toward an object"[38], it seemed that neither the speaker oneself nor the listeners were human, but physical objects, as if one object were explaining to another how the "new species" (i.e., "this thought") as seen this day differed from us "objects". Obviously, this was a behaviorist statement (although the behaviorist program was not yet explicitly put forward at the time). From a Cartesian standpoint, this tone and gesture must be comical. Of course, human researchers have expanded from the study of things to the study of humans themselves, so this historical sequence is understandable. It objectively indicates that people are more complex than things, and therefore the study of people has lagged behind things.

However, the term does say that "consciousness" actually has an instrumental nature, and that it is a way for humans as organisms to deal with external objects—or an integral part of this overall way including the sensory system. Specifically, it is used to process information (the intentional objects). My use of the word "instrument" here does not in any way contradict Kant's ethical proposition of "human as end in itself". The term "instrument" is relative to the raw material. It's like the word "stomach", when we see it, we will think of food, because the stomach is used to process food. In addition, it can even be said that I really don't know what other usage the stomach has, and what the other meanings or necessities of its existence are. In other words, the term "intentionality" actually establishes a

---

38. Franz Brentano, "Psychology from an Empirical Standpoint", translated by A. C. Rancurello, D. B. Terrell and L. L. McAlister, New York: Humanities Press, 1973, p.68.

conceptual pair that both distinguishes consciousness from information and strongly calls for it. A dualistic structure of conscious activity emerges. Some say that this is a revival of modern dualist philosophy. I would like to repeat that all efforts to eliminate dualist philosophy are a return to the old philosophy prior to the modern era.

Another valuable feature of the concept of "intentionality" is that it conceives of intentional activities as tiny and singular, thus tending to establish the smallest unit of mental activity. This paves the way for the distinction between the flow and stock of thought, and for the dynamics of computing activities.

Thus, on the basis of intentionality, Edmund Husserl proposed a preliminary theory of consciousness. In the absence of such innate thinking tools as Instructions, a reliance on this concept would be necessary. Conscious activity was interpreted as the two parts of "intentional activity" and "intentional object" (although Husserl specifically emphasized that this was a whole), which is similar to the binary structure of "Instruction + information". There was no discrimination among different types of intentional objects (assumptions, beliefs, imaginations, knowledge, etc.), and all of them were equally deemed the objects. The types of intentional activities include not only traditional cognitive activities, but also the high-order concept of "propositional attitude" (Russell's term), such as experience, command, hope, judgment, doubt, etc. This was a move toward a unified concept of "computation" (or thinking) in line with later computer science. Husserl recognized that the use of symbols was inevitable due to the limited capacity of a single intentional activity, and that the contents of symbols needed to be artificially given, so he proposed the concept of "meaning fulfillment". This obviously means something like "objects of the mind, or information, need to be reconstructed according to the cognitive formats". This construction is different from the subsequent deep processing of information. The latter distinction was also noticed by Husserl. At the same time, he further refined his theory of consciousness by emphasizing that consciousness could reflect on itself (what he called the "inner perception of intentional experiences") and that emotions were also intentional. [39]

On the basis of the above theory of consciousness, Husserl further proposed the two concepts of "suspension" and "reduction". What was suspended? What was reduced? According to Husserl's original intention, the answers are clear: to suspend knowledge so that we can reduce it to a priori consciousness and original information, or in other words, to the computational structure of Instructions plus information. Obviously, the suspension and reduction were intended to distinguish between the variable and invariable parts of the mind in order to critique and develop knowledge.

Many commenters view Husserl's early theory of intentionality separately from his later theory of the lifeworld, failing to recognize the intrinsic connection between them. Of course, Husserl himself did not clearly articulate this connection, except to say that the lifeworld was only an achievement of the transcendental self. However, Algorithmically, this connection is clear, direct, and intimate. Algorithmic Theory itself is also carried out in the order of first establishing a thinking theory and then deducing many Algorithmic consequences. To put it simply, in the course of time, such a dualistic theory of consciousness will inevitably deduce such a pluralistic, mixed, and developing ontological model of the "lifeworld".

---

39. Unless otherwise specified, the historic materials on Husserl in this section come mainly from Rulun Zhang, "Fifteen Lectures on Modern Western Philosophy" (in Chinese), Beijing: CITIC Publishing Group, 2020, pp. 260-284, and Richard Kearney (ed.), "Routledge History of Philosophy Volume VIII: Twentieth-Century Continental Philosophy", ebook, Routledge, 2005, pp. 8-25.

Husserl's originality is fitfully interspersed with many breakpoints. For example, in his early writings, he strongly opposed psychologism, not knowing that both logic and phenomenology could be treated as some special cases of psychology (or Algorithmic psychology). Without behavioral and psychological elements, the structure of consciousness will not unfold in the continuation of time, and thus the "lifeworld" will not be achieved. While discussing the types, natures, and contents of intentional activities, he said that the "pure Ego", "aside from its 'modes of relation' or 'modes of comportment,' is completely empty of essence-components, has no explicatable content, is indescribable in and for itself"[40]. It had been so close to the emergence of Instructions, but he stopped. Otherwise, with the concept of Instruction, with the certainty and clarity of the functions of instructions, his goal of "finding a reliable basis for all sciences" could be achieved, and he would not have to resort to vague concepts such as "Evidenz". The notion of "meaning fulfillment" seems to be associated with the development of knowledge, and Husserl's argument about it is also ambiguous. Moreover, he also set up the absolute knowledge, that is, "ultimate fulfillment". In his quest for objectivity, he simply appealed to intersubjectivity. However, if there is no criterion of objectivity within the subject, the objectivity generated between the subjects will be quite limited. Certain subjectivity is collective and cannot be eliminated through interpersonal hedging, because the subjectivity of interpersonal differences is different from the subjectivity of an individual facing the world alone. If there were Instructions and the discreteness of Instructions, none of these defects would have occurred. In particular, Brentano was vague on the important philosophical question of the

---

40. Edmund Husserl, "General Introduction to a Pure Phenomenology", translated by F. Kersten, Martinus Nijhoff Publishers, 1983, p. 202.

ontological position of intentional objects[41], which Husserl seemed not to have answered, either.

## §180. Heidegger, Sartre, Merleau-Ponty

Algorithmically, Heidegger compensated for the lack of dynamism in Husserl's philosophy. Husserl's philosophy is first a structure, then a picture (the lifeworld), lacking the time processes. Heidegger's philosophy, as the title of his famous book "Being and Time" suggests, is about time. Heidegger emphasized the importance of time processes in a strong way.[42]

This emphasis takes the form of a comparison between the opposites, "Being" and "beings", and their distinction theoretically means that dynamics cannot be reduced to statics, or that historical processes cannot be satisfactorily represented as the movement of certain given entities. Heidegger's philosophy repeatedly emphasizes this distinction from a variety of perspectives. The points similar to it are also repeatedly emphasized in our Algorithmical discourse.

We already know that Algorithmic Theory is particularly useful for elaborating on the relationship between dynamics and statics. An abstract and general person could be a static existence, while a concrete individual in a real spatio-temporal situation has to be dynamic. The latter type of individual is called "dasein" ("being-in-the-world"), who is clearly a finite

---

41. Franz Brentano, "Psychology from an Empirical Standpoint", translated by A. C. Rancurello, D. B. Terrell and L. L. McAlister, New York: Humanities Press, 1973, p.385.

42. The historic materials on Heidegger in this section come mainly from Rulun Zhang, "Fifteen Lectures on Modern Western Philosophy" (in Chinese), Beijing: CITIC Publishing Group, 2020, pp. 295-315, and Dunhua Zhao, "A New Edition of Modern Western Philosophy" (in Chinese, 2nd), Peking University Press, 2014, pp. 162-178, and Richard Kearney (ed.), "Routledge History of Philosophy Volume VIII: Twentieth-Century Continental Philosophy", ebook, Routledge, 2005, pp. 33-56.

being, shaped by circumstances and history, and has to deal with the world around him ("care" or "concern"), and therefore has to do current computations. Heidegger even used the words "readiness-to-hand" and "present-at-hand" to distinguish and refer to the difference between stocks and objects of current computations. Time is continuous, and dasein was first "thrown" into the world, and then there comes the roundabout production: the consequences of yesterday's actions become the conditions for today's actions, ideas are materialized into stocks, and then the stocks work in turn on actions, and so on. Dasein must plan for his/her own situations, looking back and forth, and must first accept the knowledge and social traditions that already exist. Then, dasein becomes an "ordinary person" (das Man, or "the one") with specific "understandings", attitudes, "emotions" (e.g., the "states of mind" such as "fear" and "anxiety"), and discourses. Then various sorts of "bends" take place, such as the "fallenness" of the "inauthentic self", and so on.

Algorithmically, Heidegger used a great deal of singular terms to show his determination to break with traditional philosophy. These terms deepened the reader's impression and brought out a strong humanist atmosphere, thus making his philosophy a fashion of the time. The notion of "dasein" emphasizes that an epistemic subject is, in fact, part of the objects (a scholar is also a social being), and then cognitive activities can only be done on the basis of decomposing the self and thus distinguishing the different selves at different moments from each other. However, there are connections between the different selves at different moments. For example, there are both distinctions and connections between the activities described by economic theoretical models and the activities of economists, i.e., between ontology and methodology (as Algorithmic Theory has recognized), but neoclassical economics cannot explain why people study economics per se and why public economic policies should be formulated. This is an essential conflict. This conflict determines that neoclassical economic theory is ultimately inappropriate. In this respect, Heidegger's critique of traditional rationalism is sharp and precise.

But, underneath this flamboyant exterior, it is clear that Heidegger's philosophy has some key problems. The first is the practice of pitting theory and practice, or rationality and "irrationality", which not only lacks theoretical breakthroughs, but also creates new misdirection. Heidegger's emphasis most of the time is actually the importance of common-sense knowledge. Although this kind of knowledge is different from the theoretical knowledge deliberately developed by intellectuals, there is no fundamental difference between the two. Therefore, the differences between them cannot be viewed absolutely; rather, it can be argued that every ordinary person has been actually inventing "theories" but most of the theories have not been documented into book knowledge. Here, Heidegger failed to recognize the role that computational economics had played. Throughout, his discourse failed to recognize the crucial role played by the economy of thought. Obviously, the reason why he used vague words such as "beings" to refer to this common-sense knowledge was because he was still living in the old-fashioned thinking that he himself opposed. Thinking and knowledge do not "exist" only when they are "wrong" or "non-theoretical", but also "exist" when they are correct, deductive, and theoretical. In the same way, there should be no "practical philosophy" that is fundamentally different from other philosophies. The new philosophy should be placed in an inclusive and unified framework.

In connection with these shortcomings, Heidegger absolutized the humanism he espoused. The division between the humanities and the sciences was deepened by Heidegger, so much so that to this day scholars still reject any effort of "grand synthesis". Science is science, the humanities are the humanities, practice is practice, and besides, there seems to be nothing more to say. Some of the contents of the humanities, which were originally compelled to exist because they could not be properly theorized and scientificized, have now become "justified" existences, and the possibility of their further re-classification and re-organization has disappeared. The humanities are completely detached from the judgment of their social practicality, and have become a form of privilege. This is similar to the principle of "professors governing the university": since society cannot simply leave the decision-making on academic development to practitioners who are particularly concerned with short-term interests, the principle of "professors governing the university" (which can be a mental bend) was established. However, this does not in any way mean that universities are free from social supervision, whereas society here has adopted an indirect and weakened form of supervision.

Another manifestation of the excessive humanism is Heidegger's critique of modernity. It is certainly the conscience and mission of intellectuals to criticize the evils of the times, but this kind of critique cannot be without a developmental perspective, which is exactly what Heidegger's philosophy lacks. In the early stages of its development, the modern way of life inevitably has defects of one kind or another, but it will continue to progress and improve. Science and technology can sustainably eliminate their own negative consequences, and the development of large organizations can coexist with freedom and diversity. However, Heidegger's excessive, absolutist critique not only failed to prevent large organizations from developing to the point of totalitarianism and war, but instead linked himself to them. This shows how important it is to achieve a real logical convergence between the different philosophical streams. What society needs is genuine persuasiveness, not stiff criticism. Philosophy urgently needs a process of synthesis or unification. Since a unified philosophy has not yet been formed, it is natural that Heidegger's later works (including his criticisms of so-called "humanism" or "anthropocentrism) caused confusions and criticisms.

Next, a brief comment on Jean-Paul Sartre. Sartre's philosophy has several impressive brilliances. First, he elaborated on the principle that "meta-computation cannot work on itself" (although there was no concept of meta-computation at that time), so that when an individual reflects on himself, that "self" is only a stock in memory, in an ordinary position alongside other stocked data. This can further lead to the establishment of the concept of metacomputing. The second is that he clearly saw emotions as the product of mental distortions, and described and rendered the distortions in a strange and interesting way: I figure that just blaming the grapes for being sour would solve my problem of not being able to reach them; this is an inert activity, a "degradation of consciousness".[43] The third is about freedom, and he emphasized in particular that people (in meta-computing) have to be free, and that freedom is an inescapable responsibility[44] —or, Algorithmically, freedom is an inherent property of consciousness. However, human, consciousness, or meta-computation is not "nothingness", and Instructions and their choices, and thus freedom, are in fact concrete and limited, although the range of choices is usually large.

---

43. Jean-Paul Sartre, "The Emotions: Outline of a Theory", translated by Bernard Frechtman, New York: The Wisdom Library, 1948, pp. 61-62; 75-77.

44. The historic materials on Sartre in this section come mainly from Rulun Zhang, "Fifteen Lectures on Modern Western Philosophy" (in Chinese), Beijing: CITIC Publishing Group, 2020, pp. 323-340, and Richard Kearney (ed.), "Routledge History of Philosophy Volume VIII: Twentieth-Century Continental Philosophy", ebook, Routledge, 2005, pp. 63-81.

Logically, the above meaning was discovered by Merleau-Ponty. Borrowing from the example of conditioned reflexes in psychology, Merleau-Ponty argued that there was an internal "*structure*" between the external stimulus and the behavioral response of an organism. This is an awareness that consciousness is not "nothingness". However, Merleau-Ponty was not able to directly see this structure as the structure of consciousness itself, but rather as an "intermediate realm" or "third dimension" between consciousness and natural objects, which could be used to bridge the mind-matter dualism. Merleau-Ponty tried to continue to use the expanded concepts of perception, body, language, history, etc., to make this bridge,[45] but he did not know that these were just trying to find a fish in a tree. On the road to a proper theory of mind, Merleau-Ponty completed a step and then deviated from that track.

## §181. Adorno, Habermas

In the history of philosophy in the twentieth century, we should mention Theodore W. Adorno in particular, because through his critique of the "philosophy of identity", Adorno became a philosopher who explicitly advocated pluralism. Pluralism, while particularly fashionable in today's socio-political discourses, has rarely been a clear and important philosophical proposition throughout the history of philosophy.

The so-called "philosophy of identity" refers to monistic philosophy like idealism or materialism. Identity is first and foremost a subjective construct, not the way the world

---

45. The historic materials on Merleau-Ponty in this section come mainly from Rulun Zhang, "Fifteen Lectures on Modern Western Philosophy" (in Chinese), Beijing: CITIC Publishing Group, 2020, pp. 343-362, and Richard Kearney (ed.), "Routledge History of Philosophy Volume VIII: Twentieth-Century Continental Philosophy", ebook, Routledge, 2005, pp. 88-99.

inherently is. According to Adorno, what people shall do is, first of all, to recognize the distinction between subject and object, and between all things, and even to recognize the rights of distinctions and differences. "Neither the undistinguished unity of subject and object nor their antithetical hostility would be conceivable in it; rather, the communication of what was distinguished. Not until then would the concept of communication, as an objective concept, come into its own. ... In its proper place, even epistemologically, the relationship of subject and object would lie in the realization of peace among men as well as between men and their Other. Peace is the state of distinctness without domination, with the distinct participating in each other."[46] However, Adorno argued that this was not to say that identity was useless, but that the activity of the human mind was just the activity of establishing identity (or consistency). On the premise of acknowledging differences and equality, the pursuit of identity resulted in the establishment of various relationships between different objects. Therefore, a holistic and appropriate attitude was to see both difference and identity. For example, in the exchange of goods, it was necessary to see equality and inequality at the same time. This example coincides with the one commonly used in our Algorithmic discourse. Adorno's critique of modernity based on pluralism is also to the point.

The importance of Jürgen Habermas comes from the novelty and importance of the topic of "social communication". As Adorno said, when there was difference, there was communication. As more and more scholars recognized the importance of subjectivity, interpersonal exchange, or

---

46. Adorno's words, in Martin Jay, "Adorno", Cambridge, Massachusetts: Harvard University Press, 1984, p. 65. The historic materials on Adorno in this section come mainly from this book, and from Rulun Zhang, "Fifteen Lectures on Modern Western Philosophy" (in Chinese), Beijing: CITIC Publishing Group, 2020, pp. 424-433.

communication, inevitably became an important philosophical issue. In the philosophy of monism, it was natural that the question of communication did not occupy a prominent place. Perhaps because of the uniqueness of this topic, Habermas noted that instrumental rationality was by no means the only rationality, and a more comprehensive and pertinent view of the question of rationality was necessary. Then, he argued that human beings had different types of behavior, different cognitive models, and thus different types of rationality, and that different types of rationality had their different requirements of justification. Even in the cultural and aesthetic spheres, it was possible to achieve a minimum degree of consistency. With the help of an expanded conception of rationality, Habermas also came to the conclusion that human life was becoming more and more rational. It could be said that this was an awareness of perpetual development—although these vague statements were not enough to achieve the goal of "a unified theory of society and rationality" that he pursued.[47]

We would like to take this opportunity to discuss a little more broadly the issues of technology and instrumental rationality that have been of concern to many philosophers. Algorithmical people are always trying to judge issues such as wrong and right, good and bad, rational and wrong with limited knowledge. As mentioned earlier, there is no natural absolute boundary in these distinctions. It can be assumed that the constancy of Instructional performance tends to lead to the conclusion that certain boundaries have been predetermined.

---

47. The historic materials on Habermas in this section come mainly from Rulun Zhang, "Fifteen Lectures on Modern Western Philosophy" (in Chinese), Beijing: CITIC Publishing Group, 2020, pp. 441-457, and Dunhua Zhao, "A New Edition of Modern Western Philosophy" (in Chinese, 2nd), Peking University Press, 2014, pp. 237-244, and Finlayson, James Gordon and Dafydd Huw Rees, "Jürgen Habermas", The Stanford Encyclopedia of Philosophy (Winter 2023 Edition), Edward N. Zalta & Uri Nodelman (eds.), URL = <https://plato.stanford.edu/archives/win2023/entries/habermas/>.

For example, in basic logical mathematical operations, such boundaries can be considered clear and absolute. But most of the conclusions that are used to deal with our everyday specific problems, such as the social problems debated by philosophers, cannot generally be considered to have absolute standards. This is because, Algorithmically, the solutions to these problems involve a huge number of operations, and the subjective elements in them are bound to be huge as well. Big data, or computational economic reasons, prevent people from coming up with clear, definite results. The certainty of the computing results fluctuates, sometimes decreasing, sometimes increasing, and given the heterogeneity in them, it is sometimes here and sometimes there, irregular. That is to say, the existence of so-called "rationality" must also be irregular; it must have different types, different rules of judgment, and it will also have different degrees. Different kinds of rationalities can only play their partial, relatively independent roles and cannot *fully* coordinate with each other. Moreover, "rationality" and "irrationality" are now the two sides of one coin, and every knowledge and every opinion will have a different degree of rationality and irrationality. A little more rational, a little less irrational, and vice versa.

In this pluralistic and flexible perspective, let's look at science and technology again. Science and technology are typical examples of instrumental rationality. In reality, however, it is by no means so pure, just as a deductive reasoning operation is not pure. Without passing the tests of higher-order Algorithmic logic and computational economy, deductive reasoning cannot be established, nor can it be carried out, let alone reach any result. In the same way, technology research and development are always carried out within a certain scope, and the "scope" here includes the conditions of purpose rationality, value rationality, etc. These conditions, although generally not rigid but elastic, have always been present. It is self-evident that developers need to comply with these conditions—although the scope for their freedom is also significantly large. As a result, technicians will not develop technologies that are contrary to human values and moralities from the beginning, nor will they develop technologies that are seriously unfeasible in their economies. The technical solutions that the developers provide to users and the market are generally significantly fewer than the technical options that could theoretically exist. The developers have screened relevant technical solutions in different phases in advance. In other words, the so-called "technology" seen by users or the public has implicitly contained the meanings of purposes, values, and the economy, and is by no means entirely "instrumental". The "instrumentality" here is only relative. The developers have not been able to judge these factors precisely enough, so they leave them to users and the public for further judgment. The division of labor and the social cooperation model as a whole are like this: in each person's own "process", it is as if all other external conditions are determined and hence solidified, and there is no need to think about them anymore, so that the person only needs to "technically" manipulate the individual variables left to him/her to complete his/her own task. Therefore, the changes of these variables within certain ranges, measured and decided here only according to some relatively simple criteria, are relatively independent and autonomous, and no longer constrained by other people or other factors—this is the meaning of the word "technical" or "instrumental". In this sense, everyone's work has both "technical" and "non-technical" components, or "instrumental" and "non-instrumental" components. In reality, it's just a way of unfolding the serial, discrete, economic, and imprecise *social computing*.

## §182. Structuralism

As a form of transcendental philosophy, structuralism takes transcendental philosophy one step further. What are the transcendental existences in the human mind? Previous transcendental philosophies were either vague (e.g., for Kant and Husserl) in it or alleged that they are the ready-made knowledge (e.g., for Plato). Structuralism, on the other hand, considers that the transcendence, or the a priori, is a kind of "structure" that is both relatively fixed but changeable, and that concrete phenomena in time and space are the results of these changes. This kind of thinking is quite close to the Algorithmic thinking theory. A problem with it is that the contents of the "structure" are still ambiguous and varied in different contexts. This casts a layer of mystery over the word "structure", as if it were some remarkable elements that are fundamentally different from ordinary objects. Now, when we look back, this is certainly not the case. The meaning of "structure" (and "system") is nothing more than that it contains a set of elements that are so closely interconnected that the "structure" as a combination of these elements can be seen as a whole and *a single object* beyond its constituent parts. Therefore, this problem pertains to the way in which objects are divided: there is a lack of consistency between objects divided by sensory materials and objects divided by computational convenience, and since the former objects have been too visually dispersed, the concept of "structure" is used to compensate for this defect. You can't think of a structure as something ideal or perfect. The sense-based division has not been completely abandoned, because changes of a structure under specific spatio-temporal conditions still need to be explained by the different permutations and combinations of its internal elements. Thus, the structuralist approach is really a mix of the holistic approach and the individualist approach. Further, it can be speculated that the description of a structure can also be replaced by a combination of "elements + inter-element relationships" (the effectiveness of this depends on the context). However, it is not just the structure or its constituent elements that operate in a specific space-time environment, there must be something else. Only in this way will the historical process not be completely reduced to a static structure itself. In this regard, the "Instruction + information" approach is really ideal, which can be used to mediate the oppositions between structuralism and existentialism, and between structure and subjectivity. Although the Instruction system as a structure is the same for everyone, it needs individual thinking activities to develop it, and the thinking activities of different individuals constitute *different processes* of operation of the structure, so that the "human knowledge thesaurus" and individual thinking have their own different meanings.

Now let's look at a few structuralist authors.

According to Fürternand de Saussure, it is important to pay attention to the interdependence and mutual constraints between the elements within a language system. He makes a clear distinction between language and discourse, where discourse is deemed something like specific permutations and combinations of words under specific spatio-temporal conditions, such as a specific text. This distinction clearly illustrates the difference and connection between statics and dynamics—a structure and the operations of the structure. On this basis, he distinguished between "synchronicity" and "diachronicity". The popularity of these concepts demonstrates the academic community's desire for a comprehensive theory of statics and dynamics. However, he said that language was a form, not a being. Such a statement obviously contains a remnant of the old philosophy.[48]

---

48. The historic materials on Saussure in this section come mainly from Xia

Noam Chomsky argued that while national languages have different grammatical rules, i.e., different surface structures, all national languages have universal syntactic rules, i.e., the common deep structures. Therefore, they can be translated and converted into each other. Why, then, are there generally the deep structures? According to Chomsky, this is because there is innately a mechanism or ability in the human mind to create or generate the deep structure of language.[49] Here the Instructional system is implicitly called upon again. Based on this idea, Chomsky is considered one of the initiators of the contemporary "cognitive revolution".

However, the idea of the universality of the deep structure of language shall not be overemphasized, because language is not thinking after all. The so-called "deep structure" is largely relative to the "surface structure". In particular, words reflect not only the tools and ways of thinking, but also information and knowledge. As a result, it is impossible to have strict one-to-one correspondence between words in different language systems. Therefore, the universal "deep structure" plus Quine's theorem of "indeterminacy of translation"[50] would be more comprehensive.

Next up is Leo Strauss. When anthropologists work in alternative societies that are very different from the mainstream, "difference" naturally comes first. Then, behind a large number of differences, it is natural to look for their commonalities and the common factors that produce different

---

Jisong, "A New Edition of Modern Western Philosophy" (in Chinese), Vol. 2, High Education Press, 1998, pp. 616-617, and Richard Kearney (ed.), "Routledge History of Philosophy Volume VIII: Twentieth-Century Continental Philosophy", ebook, Routledge, 2005, pp. 322-324.

49. Noam Chomsky, "Cartesian Linguistics", 3rd edition, Cambridge University Press, 2009.

50. John V. Canfield (ed.), "Routledge History of Philosophy Volume X: Philosophy of Meaning, Knowledge and Value in the Twentieth Century", ebook, Routledge, 2005, p. 23.

phenomena. This is the method that has been used in the history of academic, scientific work. In this sense, the use of "structure" is not really new, even if it is used to refer to something new that has not been emphasized in philosophy before. This new concept has different contents in different contexts, and its meaning is nothing more than to say that the structure cannot be reduced to a *single* ready-made object, nor can it be expressed as *a word* referring to this object, but rather a relationship between *multiple* elements, and so on. Among the many cases in which Leo Strauss said that different paradigms had the same structure, these cases were clearly related to the topic of "factor completeness and forced closure of computations": different groups of people solved the same or similar problems, which resulted in different versions of knowledge, and the same or similar elements lurked in them. However, the significance of the structuralist arguments emerged when he tried to prove that humans have a common mode of thinking across time and space. He argued that there was also logic in myth and totem systems, and that, although myth and science were markedly different, they had the same formal structure, a spiritual structure that was common to all.[51] Such an argument can be striking to modern people. He went a step further and argued that the mission of the anthropological science is to "dissolve man", which can be understood as an attempt to explain the individual in terms of entities smaller than the individual. This is consistent with Algorithmic Theory. But when he at the same time excluded the task of "constituting

---

51. Unless otherwise specified, the historic materials on Leo Strauss in this section come mainly from Rulun Zhang, "Fifteen Lectures on Modern Western Philosophy" (in Chinese), Beijing: CITIC Publishing Group, 2020, Beijing: CITIC Press, 2020, pp. 464-471, and Frederick Copleston, "A History of Philosophy", IX, New York: Image Books (Doubleday), 1994, pp. 412-417.

man"[52], he was incorrect and was clearly misled by the position he took in the polemics against existentialism, the opponent of structuralism.

The decay of diversity in modern society stemmed from the improvement of the means of communication and the growth of communicational activities in modern society. Once this is recognized, there will be no superficial lamentation that "diversity will disappear", because the increase in productivity brought about by communications will also stimulate new creativities everywhere at any time, thus arousing new diversity. However, Leo Strauss's emphasis on tolerance and cultural preservation as a "higher-order strategy" should also be adopted. Such adoption shall not necessarily contradict the modernization processes, but can also be part of an upgraded modernization or a healthier social policy.

## §183. Foucault, Derrida

The reason why Michel Foucault is regarded as a structuralist is obviously related to his uproarious proposition of "the death of man": human has dissolved into "existence" such as "unconscious structure", language, etc., so that the concept of "human" has become redundant.[53] Therefore, it is necessary to say a few more words about the inappropriateness of this proposition.

The fact that an individual human's consciousness, unconsciousness, and mind can be broken down into more

---

52. Leo Strauss, "The Savage Mind", London: Weidenfeld And Nicolson, 1966, p. 247.

53. The historic materials on Foucault in this section come from Rulun Zhang, "Fifteen Lectures on Modern Western Philosophy" (in Chinese), Beijing: CITIC Publishing Group, 2020, pp. 483-494, and Gary Gutting, Johanna Oksala, "Michel Foucault", The Stanford Encyclopedia of Philosophy (Fall 2022 Edition), Edward N. Zalta & Uri Nodelman (eds.), URL = <https://plato.stan-ford.edu/archives/fall2022/ entries/foucault/>.

fundamental elements and their relationships (structures) does not mean that the concept of "human" is superfluous. From the perspective of the computational economy, it will be very clear: each person uses his/her own computing tools to work in his or her own place, and the total amount of knowledge obtained by the whole society is limited at any point in time; without human, there is no "objective" "human knowledge thesaurus", we cannot know what knowledge is, there is no stock of knowledge, and it is impossible to develop the stock of knowledge. If there is one more person, the computing power of the society as a whole will increase, and the diversity of knowledge will also increase. It is especially important in view of the fact that the relatively independent knowledge system possessed by each individual is a condensed version of the knowledge system of the whole world. Of course, the meanings of the individual are by no means limited to this, but this economic way of understanding them is a fundamental way. Rejecting "human" for the reason that human can be broken down and analyzed is, first of all, a failure to understand the meanings of conscious and unconscious activity as an "activity" or "act"—of course, these meanings would only be clearest when it comes to the structure of "Instruction + information".

Another peculiarity of Foucault's work lies in its affirmative discussion of power. Foucault first revealed the tendency of the softening and refinement of power in modern society, i.e., the manners of use of power are no longer so drastic and destructive as before. According to Foucault, repression of people in modern society is often not through violent means, but through the proclamation of what is normal and the value standards associated with it; it is to constrain and manage people. Second, Foucault pointed out the wideness and inevitability of phenomena of power. It is impossible for humanity to get rid of power, just to transition from one governance to another. The power of modern society is mainly the "micro power" that permeates every corner of social life, and it constitutes the basic conditions of a certain way of life—the modern way of life. Power is the way of human existence, not just a means of repression; no one can monopolize power; and, everyone is being controlled by power and exercising power at the same time. Algorithmically, what did Foucault want to say? The answer is: a bend of mind. "Power", as a form of bending of thinking, and as a means of organization, has never left us. We cannot simply dogmatically condemn power, but need to rediscover its existence and its true face. This is a necessary beginning towards a truly appropriate social science.

On the basis of those modern authors, Jacques Derrida's philosophy[54] was further refined and thus more inclined to the Algorithmic theory. Derrida's "philosophy of deconstruction" first tends to dissolve a large number of issues, pointing out the inappropriateness of traditional philosophy in raising and discussing problems. In the tradition of Heidegger, Derrida continued to critique "logocentrism" and "metaphysics of presence". This critique can be traced back to Husserl, because Husserl's transcendental philosophy had an ideal component, namely, when reduced to transcendental consciousness, it seemed that computations became easier to grasp the essence. This tone is anti-developmental, as it implies that computational processes have been degenerating. In Algorithmic Theory, computations in the reduced state are called "pure simple computations", and they are impossible to grasp the essence of objects at once. In the same way, under the conditions of intellectual development, the self-identity of self-

---

54. The historic materials on Derrida in this section come mainly from Rulun Zhang, "Fifteen Lectures on Modern Western Philosophy" (in Chinese), Beijing: CITIC Publishing Group, 2020, pp. 495-503, and Lawlor, Leonard, "Jacques Derrida", The Stanford Encyclopedia of Philosophy (Summer 2023 Edition), Edward N. Zalta & Uri Nodelman (eds.), URL = <https://plato.stanford.edu/archives/sum2023/entries/ derrida/>.

consciousness is actually impossible. The identity and the present consciousness always require the Other and the non-present consciousness. That is, "a pure difference comes to divide self-presence."[55] Derrida invented the term "differenca" to illustrate that concepts could never be completely realized in reality, but be delayed infinitely. This is another way of illustrating infinite development, although it was still presented from the perspective of traditional philosophy, and he did not clearly and satisfactorily explain how infinite development could be justified.

Derrida's philosophy once again emphasized the need for philosophy to deal with all knowledge holistically and equally, that is, to see all human thoughts as within a unified system. Moreover, in this unified system, the inverted precedence in traditional philosophy should be inverted again: difference should precede identity, absence should precede presence, diversity should precede singularity, finiteness should precede infiniteness, flux should precede fixedness, particularity should precede universality, and so on.

Derrida referred to Husserl's argument that in Husserl's structural phenomenology, the meanings of objects and situations were not perceived by us at once as transparent and predetermined, but needed to be identified and distinguished; and, in order to be identified and distinguished, they must be relatively *persistent* in phenomena and not fleeting. But this persistence itself required a horizon structure in which they appeared, a horizon structure that contained our contextual beliefs about the objects. This means that the other knowledge that has been neglected by traditional metaphysics must in fact be regarded as a kind of normal knowledge, and Derrida demanded further that it must be regarded as a kind of priority

---

55. Jacques Derrida, "Speech and Phenomena", translated by David B. Allison, Northwestern University Press, 1973, p. 82.

knowledge. Then, how do we do this? Derrida said that the elements of time and events must become the basic elements here. This can be understood as pointing to the Algorithmic approach that starts from meta-computing: at first, people actually did quite helpless and random computations, and then a lot of "messy stuff" was generated. This is the "other priority knowledge". As long as these pieces of knowledge were not eliminated for particular reasons, they would of course exist and would work on a "first-come, first-served" basis in later computations. The problem, however, was that in the *midst* of all this mess, one occasionally found out *some* relatively high-value knowledge. People were amazed by what he/she found. Then, the passions of philosophers were ignited, and they expanded their imaginations about the possible "secret" that could exist behind all these discovered "truths", and racked their brains to grasp and understand it *solely*, so that they forgot the existence of other knowledge. In fact, it is much easier to look at and explain all the various thoughts of all humankind as a whole than to explain these "truths" alone. In my opinion, this is the major lesson that can be learned from the philosophical journey of the past 3,000 years.

## CHAPTER 17

## CONCLUSIONS & SUPPLEMENTS

### §184. On Economic Philosophy again

The task of this chapter was originally to examine contemporary or cutting-edge philosophies in order to further examine the effectiveness of the Algorithmic synthesis. However, in the process of the specific investigations, I feel that there are many difficulties. Obviously, the main reason is that because the dust has not settled, it is difficult to grasp the main points of the contemporary philosophies and make a comprehensive and general comment on them. Second, in terms of the scope of my coverage, I feel that there is not enough literature that is particularly meaningful to the subject matter of this book at the moment. Although there are many related achievements, they are all sporadic and scattered. As a result, the planned contents were reduced again and again, and in the end only a few sections remained, which were then presented only as the supplements along with the conclusion of the book. The first is the section on contemporary economics.

Algorithmic Theory originated from the exploration of economic theoretical problems. However, after completing a brief examination of philosophy and the history of philosophy, it is necessary to look back at the state of economics. At this time, I find out how faithfully economics has been following philosophy, barely crossing the red line by half a step. In this way, I understand why my early efforts to promote Algorithmic Theory in the field of economics have had little success. It is unlikely that economists will be able to solve the major problems of philosophical principles alone if the problems cannot be solved within philosophy. For most economists, philosophical questions have been marginal or even relatively unfamiliar. It is only after the philosophical problems are solved that economics can change radically. And, most likely, before that, there have been changes in the fields of psychology, sociology, political science, anthropology, law, etc. As is customary, changes in economics always lag the most behind. This is the case, for example, of the order in which the "cognitive revolution" movement spreads. In the same way, if the "Algorithmic revolution" can be carried out as expected, its impact on economic research will be far-reaching and long-lasting, but will also be subtle, especially on daily applied economic research, which would not be so easy to grasp. It is likely that this will be the case: scholars from all other disciplines of social sciences will jointly reconstruct the principles of the general social science, and finally economists will accept and implement them; creativity will probably only emerge in the process of concrete applications, or in the development of economics as a branch of Algorithmic unified social science.

However, it is interesting to analyze the pattern of economics and philosophy in contrast.

Among the existing active schools of economics, the style of neoclassical economics can undoubtedly correspond to traditional metaphysics. It extracts the most "reliable" parts out of common economic knowledge and forms a "complete" small model (general equilibrium) separately, which means that the world can be "condensed" into it, and the other "imperfect" parts can be technically ignored, the historical process can also be ignored, and the dynamics can be replaced by this static. Obviously, this model corresponds to Parmenides's "Being", Plato's Idea, God in the Middle Ages, the Absolute, and modern science. Then, by adding some real-world elements to this model and thus expanding it, the real world is given a certain "explanation". For example, after the introduction of strategies and conflicts, comes game theory. This corresponds to the expansion of the "Being" into dialectics. Both include conflicts, but both try to pretend to be unified and "uneventful". In this respect, Hegel's philosophy is the most representative and symbolic. After the Middle Ages, philosophy took a subjective turn, and epistemology came on the stage. Since Hegel, elements such as irrationality, time, and humanism have been highlighted. Correspondingly, in economics, after the introduction of time and bounded rationality, it came to evolutionary economics; after the introduction of money, statistics, and policy, it came to macroeconomics; after the introduction of "irrational behavior", it came to behavioral economics; after the introduction of institutions and transaction costs, it came to institutional and new institutional economics; after the introduction of those non-transactional, non-monetary social phenomena, it came to social economics, and so on. These derivative issues intersected with each other and further formed a variety of other schools. However, it was not clear how these "add-ons" were generated and came about. Philosophy was divided, and economics was divided as well. Up to now, not only has there been no trend towards unification, but even the efforts of the grand synthesis have been rejected by many scholars.

Philosophy has not completed the fusion between statics and dynamics, and economics has not, either. Philosophy separates the physical world from intellectual activity and human society, and the same is true of economics. Neither has yet been able to explain how those hypothetical mechanical behaviors can be extended to live, humanistic, and imaginative activities. As a result, they always treat issues absolutely. This absolutist attitude often creates antagonism, contention, and mutual negation. For example, to say that people are "irrational" has been meant to deny reason; to emphasize humanism has been meant to deny science, and so on. Ethics is seen as a relatively separate special topic, constituting a separate branch of philosophy and a type of economics. After the rest of the analysis is done, expand on it and discuss it. It's like doing some kind of routine work. It is the common sense shared by authors and readers that provides the adhesive needed for these separated parts to constitute a "wholeness". Unable to produce the adhesive along with the production of the parts, scholars have borrowed adhesives from the real world. After this borrowing has become so commonplace, even the "borrowing" itself is almost forgotten.

Since the Algorithmic integration of economics is so concise and clear, it is worth briefly repeating here: after the introduction of ATT, the neoclassical deductive method is reasonably and "optimally" extended to various subjective and objective Algorithms, and the various thinking activities of actors are regarded as "computations" and organized according to the Algorithmic logic. In principle, it can be said that the thinking activities that come out of this way are the real thinking activities that are exhibited by real actors. Such thinking activities are dynamic and perpetual, which leads to the dynamics and development of economic and social life. This kind of thinking activity is carried out in a roundabout way, generating and continuously calling on the stock of knowledge, which gives rise to the knowledge sectors, education sectors, institutions, organizations, states, ethics, and morality in the real world. Interpersonal differences, interactions, and games arise concurrently. Money is produced as a means of computation and a medium of information dissemination under the condition of bounded and concrete rationality. The primitive and endogenous pluralities lead to the confinement of commodity transactions to a certain scope, which equally exist and connect with other non-transactional, non-economic activities. The existence of bounded rationality has further led to the emergence of intellectuals and governmental agencies. Intellectuals can make suggestions to the governmental or ordinary actors, and the governmental agencies are engaged in macroeconomic adjustments. In this way, we actually come to a unified social science (and social engineering). In it, plurality and conflicts exist as primordial, processual, or technical elements, and frequently and mutually transform with consistency; they all share the "higher order consistency".

## §185. Some Philosophical Issues in Cognitive Sciences and Artificial Intelligence (1)

For the investigation of the frontiers of philosophy, a survey of philosophy of mind, cognitive science, artificial intelligence, and other relevant fields is indispensable. On a large scale, much of what is covered in this book can be considered a philosophy of mind. However, in the tradition of the discipline of philosophy, the philosophy of mind has been confined to a smaller field. In particular, contemporary philosophy of mind takes the mind-body relationship as its main area, namely, the question of the material source of consciousness. In computer language, this is the problem of "hardware-software interface". Philosophers of mind apparently fail to realize that the vast number of questions of consciousness that interest them can be answered in a purely software-based, Algorithmical way. Since we have already discussed this in some detail in Chapter 5, we leave it out here. The material, natural science approach shall not be the main answer to the questions of humanities and social sciences; even if it is inspiring somehow, it will ultimately be of little use. This argument has already been explained in §9.

The beginning of cognitive sciences was explicitly based on the binary framework of "nature + nurture" (e.g., Chomsky's "trans-formational-generative grammar"), as well as on computer science. Unfortunately, however, after a period of prosperity, its momentum has waned. Algorithmically, the obvious reason is that it doesn't realize that computer Instructions are the innate thinking tools that are of great significance. Early computer scientists generally drew an analogy between the human brain and a computer[1], but the focus of this analogy was information, and its counterpart, the thinking tool, the Instructions, were ignored, even though Instructions were made by their own hands. It's like when a person is faced with an object, he keeps thinking about how to deal with the object itself, but he doesn't realize that the way people deal with the object is actually limited, and there are only a few types of basic actions to be chosen, and the other actions are merely some combinations of the basic actions. The richness and infinity of the depth of information processing by computers also have tended to obscure the finitude of these "basic actions" (or rather, this finitude was only understood as the finitude of the computer itself, not the finitude of the human brain). As a result, the tradition of one-sided information theory has been long-standing and deep-rooted among professionals who specialize in technical work. Another foundation of information theory is symbolism. A "symbol" is a

---

1. See John von Neumann, "The Computer and the Brain" (3rd), Yale University Press, 2012.

physical object (although it is used to express an idea), so it guided the attention of researchers to the articulation with the philosophy of language. Another meaning of a symbol is the finite capacity of meta-computing, which requires that information and ideas must be simplified and condensed before the human brain can process them. The implications of this move in the direction of a computational economy were overlooked. Then, although cognitive sciences were once very vibrant, they finally failed to achieve results important enough. A large number of results, while meaningful[2], are fragmented and intertwined with hardware, natural science issues, and the progress obtained has been really trivial and slow. Research on the economics of computing, such as those on inconsistency, dis-equilibrium[3], laziness[4], and contextuality[5] is also fragmented.

The hallmark of the second generation of cognitive science was "embodiment", which emphasized that cognitive organs are not limited to the brain, but are found throughout the body. This argument, of course, is first and foremost in natural science approach and deviates further from the approach of software. Some literature takes a stance of opposing it to computationalism, which is also incorrect. In fact, it has a

---

2. See Bin Li, "Foundations of Algorithmic Economics: The Cognitive Revolution and the Grand Synthesis of Economics" (in Chinese), Beijing: Economic Daily Press, 2019, Section 2.3, pp. 87-93.
3. W. B. Arther, "Out-Of-Equilibrium Economics and Agent-Based Modeling", in Leigh Tesfatsion et al. (ed.), "Handbook of Computational Economics", Vol. 2, North Holland, 2006, pp. 1551-1562.
4. Leigh Tesfatsion et al. (ed.), "Handbook of Computational Economics", Vol. 2, North Holland, 2006, p. 1026; And, Marie Devaine, Jean Daunizeau (2017), "Learning about and from others' prudence, impatience or laziness: The computational bases of attitude alignment". PLOS Computational Biology 13(3): e1005422. https://doi.org/10.1371/journal.pcbi.1005422
5. See Shaun Gallagher, "Philosophical Antecedents of Situated Cognition", in Philip Robbins, Murat Aydede (ed.), "The Cambridge Handbook of Situated Cognition", Cambridge University Press, 2009, pp. 35-51.

positive Algorithmical significance, which is that it hints that activities such as bodily perception, response, emotion, and so on can be considered as some types of computation, which expands the concepts such as cognition, thinking, and computation within cognitive sciences. Meanwhile, this type of mental activity is further discussed in parallel and in combination with other (mainly physical) activities, which strengthens the substantiality or materiality of mental activity and the *totality of human physical and mental activities*. On the basis of computationalism, this perspective could wreak havoc again on behaviorism.

Cognitive science, after embodiment, is further integrated with neuroscience, artificial intelligence, and computer simulation research. Henceforth, let's discuss it in conjunction with the philosophical question of artificial intelligence.

Among the many explorations in the field of humanities and social sciences, I believe that the exploration of artificial intelligence is the most philosophical. A considerable part of these meanings has not yet been revealed, and they are closely related to Algorithmic Theory, so they deserve to be discussed here. At the same time, Algorithmic Theory can also be used to help solve philosophical problems in the field of artificial intelligence. This communication is a two-way street.

As mentioned earlier, early AI was computationalistic and symbolistic. Computer scientists used to be optimistic that with proper programming, computers could automatically do any work that humans did intellectually. As a result, a lot of bold work began to be tried. However, failures occurred in large numbers. The reason is that, just like our view that "syllogism requires a knowledge base", computers also need data and knowledge to reason, while the traditional deductive method requires a strict form of knowledge that is not easy to obtain. The application of one knowledge piece requires another knowledge piece, and the pursuit of such a thing is endless, and it is by no means something that computer professionals can satisfy in a short period of time. This reflects a truth of human knowledge: knowledge is by no means a complete and internally consistent system that can be simply deduced from a certain point, but an accumulation of a large number of scattered thinking results, in which the logical connections are partial or weak.

After accepting the above concept, "expert systems" were launched, which aim to establish electronic database systems by experts from all walks of life in cooperation with computer experts, which can then be processed by computers. Expert systems have achieved some individual successes, but their achievements are by no means universal,[6] because accumulating knowledge is easier said than done. How is it possible to collect a large amount of scattered knowledge about the real world and turn it into an electronic database all at once? Its difficulty was also reflected in the failure of the idea of "building a knowledge framework about artificial intelligence": AI philosophers once envisioned some "universal" knowledge framework that could be used in any AI system, like a general operating system in computers. This idea is a parody of common-sense knowledge. Obviously, this "universal knowledge framework", without recognizing that it is nothing more than ordinary knowledge, is either over- or under-conceived common-sense knowledge, a kind of knowledge that is similar to or equal to the knowledge that AI programs would target at with it. This idea seems to have discovered the roundabout production method for computing activities, but in fact, it misunderstood it. Simple computationalism seemed to have gone to a dead end.

---

6. For a short survey of expert systems, see M. Alroy Mascrenghe, "Expert Systems", in Philip L. Frana et al. (ed.), "Encyclopedia of Artificial Intelligence: The Past, Present, and Future of AI", Santa Barbara, California: ABC-CLIO, 2021, pp. 144-147.

By the way, it needs to be emphasized that AI engineering does not simply rely on its success to prove that a computer is a proper model of the human brain. The proof of this has also, implicitly, lain in its difficulties, failures, and setbacks. Because, the path of human thinking has never been smooth, and the struggles of AI engineering obviously resemble the torments of human minds.

## §186. Some Philosophical Issues in Cognitive Sciences and Artificial Intelligence (2)

That's when the connectionist approach came to the fore. The basic idea of connectionism is that the mental activities of the human brain are formed by the interaction of an extremely large number of relatively independent elements (neurons), in which there is no center and no strict serial operation as demonstrated by computationalism. At first glance, this idea is opposed to computationalism (and ATT). However, according to subjective feelings, the mental activities that each of us consciously carries out are actually mainly serial, and this seriality is different from the "seemingly centerless" connected networks that neuroscientists have directly observed in the microstructure of the brain. Correspondingly, the computational processes that computer experts can directly design and control are also serial. Therefore, the idea of connectionism, in its initial stage, is first embodied in the parallel operation of multiple serial operations and their controlled interactions.

Second, since it is a "first separate and then united" operational sequence, the independence and originality of each serial process are bound to be strengthened. Computations no longer need to be perfect, they just need to make some sense, and then improve gradually. This corresponds to the other side of the truth of the human mind, that is, the development of knowledge always starts in an attempt. We can literally accept the idea that "there is a lot of automatic computations concurrently in the brain", and these automatic computations generate numerous primary forms of knowledge, which are then consciously synthesized, refined, and re-processed. Moreover, even conscious computations are similar to such automatic computations. Conscious computations would be only rudimentary if they are not supported by various stocks of knowledge; and, automatic computation, obviously, also has a certain degree of continuity and accumulation. Computations in any part of the brain, as well as computations of any individual person, have always been in the same manner, and the so-called "global", "truth", "perfection", etc., are just the outcome of comparing the results of these computations plus an imagination (as a function of the brain, an Instruction, or an "Algorithm"). This is in terms of the levels of the computing results. In terms of the type of computation, there is also a need to draw analogies between deductive methods and other methods such as inductive methods, and look at them in relation to each other. Deductive methods are for reliable reasoning, and inductive methods are for unreliable reasoning, and they can be reconciled by adding a reliability factor between the two. In line with this idea, computer scientists have developed the method of "heuristics", or the "machine learning"[7]. Machine learning can be done in a controlled, continuous, and fast way—as stated earlier, classical serial computers could have also run continuously and

---

7. The word "machine learning" refers to the speculation or guessing made by a machine based on a clue. In humans, this type of thinking activity is the primary method of building propositions, and it has always been considered the most creative and challenging. Perhaps in an attempt to alleviate skepticism and criticism of AI engineering, AI scholars humbly refer to this type of activity as "learning", which is actually an inappropriate name. The human mind is not much more active than it, which is being strongly demonstrated today.

automatically, but since it would otherwise be easy to lose control from users and then become dangerous, they have been generally programmed to run only to a limited extent, manner, and time.[8] After a long period of time and extensive improvements, the machine learning method finally bore fruit at the end of 2022, that is, the large language model marked by ChatGPT has shown great practical value and has been enthusiastically sought after by the world.

On the basis of large language models, the above-mentioned "knowledge framework" idea is once again put on the agenda. Large-scale knowledge collection, accumulation, and development activities have taken place all over the world. As mentioned earlier, the idea that knowledge in computers has been growing so rapidly that it would exceed the amount of knowledge in living minds now becomes quite persuasive. The "artificial general intelligence" (AGI) developed through training in realistic environments may now logically catch up with or exceed the "common sense" in human brains—since the latter must be limited in quantity. It can be inferred from Algorithmic principles that the two kinds of knowledge will never be exactly the same, but the development of the former may also reach a certain critical point; after passing this point, people would generally believe that human common sense is "over" or the difference between the two is no longer of special importance. If this "general artificial intelligence" (the generality must be limited) can be successful, then it will be easier to establish special artificial intelligence models for specific problems and specific situations on this basis, and the continuous revision of general models and special models will be natural as well. "Superhuman intelligence" would be

---

8. For the history of artificial intelligence before ChatGPT, see F. Richard Yu and Angela W. Yu, "A Brief History of Intelligence: From the Big Bang to the Metaverse", Springer, 2023.

possible. However, this "transcendence" can only be understood as the transcendence of specific knowledge and intelligence over another specific knowledge, and cannot be considered to have any fundamental changes in the basic computing architecture of "Instruction + information" or the Instruction list itself.

With the advent of a new wave of artificial intelligence, the philosophical debate between connectionism and computationalism is also tending to come to an end. That's because today's successful connectionist AI uses only dedicated chips, along with a variety of other chips, to run on computers with traditional architectures. This clearly proves that the two are compatible without the need for other special arrangements. However, in my opinion, its philosophical explanation still needs to be carried out Algorithmically. It is firstly the correction of traditional concepts of reason, thinking, computation, etc. Computations can be rational, but this in no way means that they are purely deductive. Computations must *rationally* accept all kinds of less reliable but fast computations, and thus *rationally* accept, in principle, all kinds of imperfect computing results. Furthermore, since rational computations can be imperfect, why can't they tolerate the coexistence of multiple processes that have a *certain degree* of autonomy? As long as these *specific processes* have a certain competitive advantage in terms of computational efficiency and effectiveness, isn't it fine? Considering the widespread existence of heterogeneity, this logically proves the *possibility* and *legitimacy* of autonomous processes within a single computing architecture (or individual). The rest of the issues depend only on the competition and development of specific technologies. In fact, deep learning Algorithms had been around for many years without making breakthroughs. It is only when the machine model looks at human language in a purely formal way and uses real human big data for learning and training that its usefulness increases dramatically. A formal approach to human language (i.e., large language models) greatly reduces the requirement for computing power. The development of Internet has led to a large amount of real data about human life as the online data, so the training of models using these real data (rather than the data generated by the machine itself) has greatly improved the bases of computing. It's like the idea that to train a good scientist is first to bring him/her a good education. Only by adopting the approach of ATT can the reasons for this be clearly explained.

## §187. Some Philosophical Issues in Cognitive Sciences and Artificial Intelligence (3)

The success of large language models dealt a serious blow to J.R. Searle's "Chinese room" argument. This hypothetical experiment of the "Chinese room" argued that a person who does not know Chinese and writes in Chinese only by looking up dictionaries cannot be qualified as the one who "really" understands Chinese. However, since he can check the Chinese-English dictionary, it shows that this person has a certain understanding of Chinese. Even if this understanding has not reached the average level, it is better than knowing nothing. Obviously, Searle's understanding of the word "understanding" still came from the traditional misunderstanding that "understanding" must be standardized, and that the line between "not understanding" and "understanding" was absolute, not soft or developmental. It is the microscopic approach from computers that allows us to divide mental activity into extremely small steps or degrees, and thus establish the concept of "soft quantitative analysis" that has not been traditionally available. In what sense will ordinary people's understanding of real objects differ from the "understanding" of computers? Let's see the example in §32,

Vol. I again: For a stranger, we may simply remember his individual characteristics, such as "he is a relative of a friend" or "he is a tall man". Even for acquaintances of the stranger, his characteristics remembered by the acquaintances are not often too many. It is true that your knowledge of your families is much greater than that of a friend, but this great knowledge is only based on the premise of getting along with each other for a longer time, and thus is a composite of numerous pieces of data. Meanwhile, even so, the behaviors of intimate people can sometimes be unexpected. These characteristics are not only indifferent from those of a computer, but are also very similar. It can be inferred from this that the level of our understanding today must have been obtained through a long, circuitous, and fragmented process of historical accumulation and progress, and the complexity of this process can now be expounded analytically with the help of computer simulations.

Computers can help us to complete the reinversion of the philosophical system, that is, to pull down the "high-quality knowledge" that is high above and advances alone, and to put it together with other knowledge, and then establish a comprehensive and unified knowledge system. This kind of knowledge system will be more conducive to the improvement of the quality of knowledge. Computers are models of the human mind, so they can help us understand ourselves better. On the other hand, the updated philosophy can also help promote the use of computers. Obviously, artificial intelligence experts have also been groping purblindly without a clear understanding of the thinking mode of the human brain and its related philosophical issues. For example, like artificial intelligence engineering, computer simulations based on agents, the virtual entities, have brought many inspirations (such as computer experts recognizing that virtual humans must carry out certain political activities among themselves), but if the ideas of Algorithmic philosophy had been adopted in advance, those scholars would not have been in vain to build the "computable general equilibrium models"[9]. This deviation shows the importance of basic philosophical ideas.

The future development of artificial intelligence obviously has two lines. One is to pursue similarity with real people's thinking, then to replace some of real people's thinking. This may result in job losses. However, after people become free from the jobs that machines do, they can turn to create and engage in jobs that machines cannot undertake (the functions of any artificial intelligence products must also be limited), and thus to match and rebalance with machines, and to establish a new human-machine relationship. The second is to pursue differentiation from real people's thinking in order to assist, cooperate, and inspire people to enter higher-level and larger-scale thinking activities. This prospect of infinite expansion obviously requires the principle of combinatorial explosion to provide a theoretical basis.

The application of ATT in artificial intelligence can be multifaceted. Another dichotomy is the division between public and private AI systems. The current models are mostly public—although the use of them is mainly personal. A private system here refers to an AI assistant specifically for a single person, which can be developed from public systems and act as a subsystem or derivative of them, but under strict privacy protection rules, it is customized, cultivated, and used only by that individual, just like a personal sectary. Public systems can mainly be knowledge-based, while private systems are executive and service-oriented. The latter can run less quickly, as long as it is accurate, loyal, and reliable. The principles of Algorithmic economics ensure that this differentiation and

---

9. For a survey of this study, see Peter B. Dixon and B.R. Parmenter, "Computable General Equilibrium Modelling For Policy Analysis And Forecasting" in H.M. Amman et al. (ed.), "Handbook of Computational Economics", Vol. I, North Holland, 1996, pp. 4-85.

bifurcation, as well as other similar developments of individualization or specialization, are always meaningful.

Practical observations show that human thought and knowledge of the world have been on a continuous historic growth trajectory in terms of quantity. If we think of the world (or nature) as a given object, doesn't this growth show that the true "ultimate truth", if it exists, is probably not something simple or few? On the other hand, if we look backwards from such an "ultimate standpoint", the amount of knowledge will be shrinking, and the knowledge at the top, that is, the starting point of human history, is not only the simplest knowledge, but also the most "wrong" knowledge. This conclusion is contrary to the conventional wisdom that knowledge can eventually converge into a single, pure "Being". This further illustrates the inappropriateness of traditional philosophy. The collapse of traditional metaphysics raises a new question: what will be the future or "endgame" of knowledge development? The combinatorial explosion is just a basic, primary, and rudimentary perspective. This is not the end of philosophical thinking, but a new beginning.

## §188. Conclusions of the Book (1)

Finally, we go back to this formula again:

*Thinking = Computing = (Instruction + Information) × Speed × Time*

Just as a few mathematical formulas become the cornerstones of the edifice of physics, the formula above contains the fundamental secrets of philosophy, humanities, and social sciences. The acceptance and adoption of it will lead to the synthesis of various philosophies in the past more than two thousand years in fundamental and major respects, and the synthesis of all the philosophical branches—and it will also transcend existing philosophies by adding new contents. At the same time, the acceptance and adoption of it will allow a person with only a mind with logic, mathematics, and natural sciences to "naturally" enter into the agenda of the humanities and social sciences, as opposed to the current situation in which knowledge in the humanities and social sciences is fragmented as independent, scattered pieces, dogmas, or empirical rules. On the other hand, scholars in the humanities and social sciences do not need to emphasize how special their research is, because according to the Algorithmic logic, all research can now be indiscriminately interconnected. The Algorithmic logic here is not really a novelty, but a reproduction of correct common sense. It should belong to the kind of knowledge that "can be widely agreed upon as soon as it is spoken".

Instructions, which are the innate thinking tools, encounter and interact with information from the outside world, giving rise to something called "thoughts", "ideas", and so on. These are new things that the world did not have before. In principle, they are not only different from the information, but also from the thinking tools themselves. This is a basic "Algorithmic perspective"—Of course, in some *lesser*, extreme, or specific cases, thoughts can precisely match outside things. This is the Algorithmic neutrality and synthesis of mind and matter, or idealism and materialism. Correspondingly, we must think of thought as a fundamental entity or reality, or entities or realities in great quantity, which can be different from particles of matter, but can exist side by side with them, interacting directly or indirectly. In colloquial parlance, a thought must be a "thing" that arises, exists, moves, differentiates, combines, or dies in a certain way. Moreover, it shall not be conceived of as something invisible or untouchable like a gas, or as something that moves as rapidly as light, but as something that has been allowed to solidify or concretize, or something like a liquid or semi-liquid—or, as many scholars have repeatedly emphasized, a slow-growing organism. The mastery and application of Algorithmic Thinking Theory will inevitably produce such philosophical concepts; in turn, such philosophical concepts also require that a thinking theory at least be concretized into the mechanisms described above, otherwise, philosophical theories will remain vague or even stagnant.

Such a dualistic architecture necessarily takes the approach of bounded rationality, or "concrete rationality". The human knowledge system begins to grow and develop from a microscopic unit similar to an elementary particle—and then forms different versions of knowledge under the influences of a series of factors such as time, factor completeness, and the forced closure of computations, including versions of different periods, versions of different individuals, versions of different groups, and so on. Such a knowledge system already includes relatively high-quality knowledge such as mathematics and science. It is now possible to further understand why Instructions, which exist under the noses of so many scholars, have been ignored for so long time: because when traditional metaphysics was continuously dominating people's minds, the introduction of Instructions would be like inserting a wedge into the existing body of knowledge, and this would lead to the collapse of mainstream philosophy as a whole. In fact, in the history of philosophy, there were some scholars holding similar views. Kant was a figure who particularly aroused discomfort in intellectual circles, as can be seen from the successive attempts of later philosophers to dismantle subject-object dualism. One-sided information theory can be compatible with absolute truth, and Instructions are thus crowded out.

However, the emergence of a new system cannot be stopped. Algorithmic Theory proves that this is a marginal developmental process that can eliminate its opponents gradually. The one-way explosive development of knowledge is actually very satisfying, and can be in line with the wishes of intellectuals, which scholars need time to understand and recognize. The effects of this approach can be more satisfactory after we have carved out a relatively independent "manual Algorithmic approach" from the machine. Now that we equate Instructions with verbs in natural language, I think this approach's appeal is thus not weakened, but enhanced. It makes use of the work of computers, artificial intelligence, and linguistics, but simultaneously discards their drawbacks. Disadvantages of computers and artificial intelligence include that they are too technical, and the presumed equivalence of computers to the human brain is always in question. As mentioned earlier, a disadvantage of language is that it is too cumbersome. Moreover, only half of language is the mind, and the other half is the physical elements that have been neglected by linguists and philosophers of language. However, what we need is a theory of mind. Human beings must have a theory of mind. There has not been a proper theory of thinking or mind before. We realize this deeper only after we have obtained the Algorithmic theory. Therefore, *Algorithmic Theory does not need to be perfect in the first place, but we must have it first, and then we can consider the development on it.*

The more phenomena a theory explains, the more acceptable it becomes. Theories that explain the largest number of phenomena in the most concise form shall be the most acceptable. This methodological principle, which is based on the computational economy, has been widely accepted. When Algorithmic Theory is used to achieve synthesis between different theories, it is equivalent to explaining all the phenomena explained by all the related theories. Secondly, the existing theories that are synthesized are also a kind of "phenomenon" as the objects of ATT. This phenomenological principle can now be incorporated into the Algorithmic principles.

The argument for Algorithmic Theory lies both in its utility, that is, in the phenomena it explains, and in itself. The name "Instruction" may be a bit bizarre, but its contents have been so straightforward and simple. Do you have any Instructions in your head? Are they finite in number, and universal among people? Let's go through them one by one, and the answers will be there. Next, if you want to prove how every thought or idea comes from the process of combining Instructions and information, then you need to invite experts in the fields of computers, artificial intelligence, cognitive science, etc. to join in and start the technical work. However, it should not be forgotten that before the technical work, the basic analysis of the results and processes of the human mind had to be carried out manually. This part of the work still belongs mainly to scholars in the humanities and social sciences, and it has to be extended to the point where it is connected to the computerized simulative work, and then it can be transferred to the cooperation between theoretical experts and technical experts.

## §189. Conclusions of the Book (2)

It may seem unreasonable for a monograph with a lot of space to leave the examination of the existing literature mainly in the second half of the book, but I have to do so. One of the reasons is that the novelty and conciseness of the Algorithmic thinking theory are intuitive and self-explanatory, which I believe readers would be able to recognize even if I do not lengthily provide literary evidence at the beginning of the book—if any reader sees a similar theory, please write to me, which I would be very grateful to. Secondly, when we examine its intellectual origins, the connections are found to be too broad and interdisciplinary. Therefore, I adopt an arrangement, which is to examine its source and the development of relevant knowledge in different chapters, explicitly or implicitly, detailedly or concisely. For example, the development of computer principles and artificial intelligence is introduced in Chapter 3, Vol. I; and, the development of relevant philosophical thought permeates Chapters 15-16 of this volume. Thus, at the end of the book, we only need to add a few explanations and comments to accomplish this necessary job while avoiding a repetition.

The context of the development of each relevant discipline does not need to be elaborated here, and only those specific, direct forerunners are now to be addressed. According to my own limited (this limitation is, after all, inevitable) investigation, a forerunner directly relating to the origination of the Algorithmic thinking theory is William of Occam. He proposed not only the economy of thought, but also the concept of the language of thought distinct from natural language. This vein can be linked to the British tradition of computationalism, analytic philosophy, and philosophy of language. However, it has been slow to integrate with the continental philosophies on irrationality, the economy of thought, subjectivity, humanism, phenomenology, structuralism, and so on. This convergence can obviously only be achieved in the Algorithmic philosophy.

In 1883, Ernst Mach proposed his ideas on the economy of thought. Six years later, his Viennese native and economist Eugen von Bohm-Bawerk published the book "The Positivism of Capital", in which he proposed the concept of the "roundabout method of production", but discussed only the production of material goods, not the production of ideas. Decades later, in 1927, Heidegger published "Being and Time", in which he implicitly but vividly discussed the roundabout production of ideas, not knowing that it was a roundabout production. Around this time, the German philosopher Nicolai Hartmann also discussed the distinction between the flow and stock of thinking from the standpoint of "critical realism"[10]. Herbert Simon, an economist and computer scientist, made outstanding contributions to artificial intelligence engineering and explicitly proposed the concept of "bounded rationality", but he was also an important figure in behaviorism. It's incredible! This is as bizarre as Jerry Fodor as the author of the books of both "The Modularity of Mind"[11] and "The Language of Thought"[12]. The two books could have been integrated into one book. In Simon's time, the theoretical consideration of computational costs remained largely linear, that is, it had not yet been linked to changes in the contents of thought caused by the subjective turn. According to my incomplete search, the first person to discuss mental distortions under time pressure was Christopher Cherniak, an American philosopher and a neurologist. In his book "Minimal Rationality"[13], he frequently discusses the substitution relationship between computational speed and computational accuracy. Around this time, relevant literature began to appear in the field of economics. However, most scholars have been anxious to discuss the problem of specific decision-making under bounded rationality, or devote themselves to rejecting neoclassical rational models, without realizing that what has been touched upon here is the question of the overall transformation of the philosophical system. Those many deviations from the standard model have not been enough to lead to the creation of a new "standard model", even if it is realized that those patterns of behavior that are theoretically "heretical" but have practical significance are not

---

10. Nicolai Hartmann, "New Ways of Ontology", translated by Reinhard C. Kuhn, Chicago: Henry Regnery Co., 1953, pp. 80-86. In the works of critical realism, there are a large number of statements between traditional philosophy and Algorithmic philosophy, so it can be said that in principle it is also a transitional philosophy. For example, see pp. 23-29 of this book.
11. The MIT Press, 1983.
12. Harvard University Press, 1980.
13. The MIT Press, 1986.

"suboptimal" (Simon) choices, but optimal choices.[14] These can only cause a disruption, not a paradigm shift. The reason for this is not necessarily the "thick skins" of the scholars as Lakatos put it, but the lack of a constructive program. However, a vague Algorithmical program finally appeared in the field of sociology, which is Anthony Giddens's 1984 book "The Constitution of Society: Outline of the Theory of Structuration". However, the "structuration theory" in the book was too vague and crude, and did not draw on the computer principles that had already appeared at that time.

In the first two decades of this century, I have not found any important literature in this field. An examination of the latest literature has not only failed to find similarities in the Algorithmic thinking theory, but has also shown that the climate in academia has not changed significantly. A large number of online and offline exchanges with readers on Algorithm Theory have further confirmed its novelty and uniqueness.

It is not possible to have only thinking economics without Algorithmic Theory, and conversely, it is not possible to have only the framework of "Instruction + information" without thinking economics. Of course, the operational structure of "Instruction + information" itself naturally contains the element of economics of thinking, but this element needs to be clearly exposed to consciousness. Only in this combined way is it possible to answer the traditional metaphysical and epistemological questions (and informational questions), as well as a series of basic questions such as reason, dynamics, contradictions, pluralism, the future of the world, subjectivity-objectivity, absoluteness-relativity, humanism, methodology,

---

14. An early summary of this idea, see John Conlisk. "Why Bounded Rationality?" Journal of Economic Literature, Vol. XXXIV (June 1996), pp. 689-690.

and so on. All these questions can now be answered in one go. The question of pluralism can now enter into the core of philosophical theory, and be integrated with consistency through the dynamic, relative, and higher-order approaches. This is the key reason why I use the word "unity". The stock of knowledge is now receiving increasing attentions, such as the rise of the so-called "knowledge economics"[15] and "contextualization" (including emphasis on situations, backdrops, contexts, etc.) in the wake of "knowledge sociology"[16]. Again, a series of fundamental problems, or even a large number of fundamental problems within the relevant fields, can either not be solved, or can be solved in general at once. Only by understanding this overall framework can we understand Algorithm Theory. This is where the difficulties lie in understanding it, as well as in my explanation of it. It can be paraphrased with the saying: There are thousands of words, but I do not know how to say them; once I say it, all words become redundant.

## §190. Conclusions of the Book (3)

It now seems that for scholars accustomed to logic and mathematical thinking, there is something easy about the explanation of Algorithmic Theory: Initially, pure mathematical or logical computations were formalized and performed under completely abstract, hypothetical conditions; Then, such computations were put into actual environments by John von Neumann and others, for mathematical experts

---

15. Debra M. Amidon et al. (ed.), "Knowledge Economics: Emerging Principles, Practices And Policies", Tartu University Press, 2005.

16. The twentieth-century masterpiece "Ideology and Utopia" (Karl Mannheim, London: Routledge & Kegan Paul Ltd, 1960) once demonstrated in an impressive way the consequences of "knowledge" as an independent stock element carrying distinct subjectivity into social sciences.

looking for difficult practical problems to solve, so game theory was developed, which was initially positive and cooperative, but was later found by John F. Nash that people can be both antagonistic and negative and can still reach some equilibria; Now, when we add on space, time, speed, cost, and so forth, the computations are completely realized. Go computing! Go computing! Mathematical experts can play with calculations or computations as much as they would like, and even use the most advanced computers, but be careful not to forget the real constraints! I believe that now, they have no other choice but to cooperate with humanistic and social scholars. At this time, the computations will generate and exude the "human breath" that humanistic scholars are familiar with. This "human breath" can now be renamed "Algorithmic breath". Because, even in the public vocabulary, the word "Algorithm" is now increasingly inclined to refer to subjective methods of computation. This is its narrow usage. For humanists, the term may be wary, but for rationalists, it can be delightsome, even fascinating, because it combines rational principles with humanism that everyone likes, into a single logical chain. It's a compromise. Mathematical experts can now also find some opportunities to prove the actors wrong, or not smart enough. Then, this constitutes advice for the real world. However, given the reciprocity, adversariality, and mutual learning between people, there shall not be too many opportunities for researchers to guide the real world.

Thought of the natural sciences is prone to the defect of lack of plurality, while thought of the humanities is prone to the lack of logic. Both come with certain inefficiencies. Therefore, in terms of thought and method, we now need to adopt the "Algorithmical and comprehensive attitude". This attitude requires us to take a serial approach to a topic, that is, we can first look at its traditional and objective side, then look at its Algorithmical or subjective side, and then look at the wholeness formed by the combination of the two aspects, and examine its development (including interactions between the researchers and actors). This constitutes a basic and exemplary procedure for Algorithmical research. The Algorithmical theory and principles have been proposed, but exactly how to operate and apply them? The methods or rules in this regard are still under preliminary exploration.

Towards the end of this book, I regret that the book does not include a special chapter on the philosophy of sociology. I love sociology. All the discourses in this book have the goal of "reconstructing the foundations of sociology". However, the goal of "unifying the social sciences" is of the highest priority, and sociology is a part of it. I have only tried to incorporate the perspective of sociology into the relevant specific discourse. As for the synthesis between the existing sociological theories, since it is too obvious and hence I cannot provide many new meanings besides the existing narratives, I have to ignore it. As for the goal of "reconstructing macro sociological theory", I feel that there is no need to dwell too much on it at the moment, especially in this book. This kind of work should not be rushed. Do not be afraid of slowness, but be afraid of standing still. This conservative attitude is consistent with my own practice of not paying much attention to the specific contents and cutting-edge research of ethics and other social sciences.

I feel incapable of speaking head-on about the field of art. Moreover, historically, because art is not easy to reproduce, it has been monopolized by the wealthy and the upper classes of society. This leads to the consequence that the social status of art is likely to be unduly elevated. Now, in the informational age, the speed of reproduction and dissemination of works of art is accelerating, helping to bring art back to the people and to regain its vitality and relevance. Aesthetics and entertainment are the basic functions of art, and art should not be something to show off itself, nor should it be a tool for venting nostalgia. Therefore, I would venture to think that the philosophy of art, which has somehow divorced from the general humanistic and social doctrines, is itself suspicious in value, at least not so important as commonly believed.

Finally, the appendix to this book, "New Humankindism", should be mentioned. As it was written relatively independently a few years ago, it is presented here as an appendix. This is an example of how Algorithmic Theory can also play an important role in answering practical questions of our time. Although this article is mainly written for my Chinese compatriots, it can also be used as a reference for readers around the world because, in each country there are different degrees of questions about how to view the past, the future, and the aliens. In particular, in developing countries that are undergoing rapid changes in the tide of globalization, how should they view their own traditions and the different civilizations from other countries? The question has been acute. In other Algorithmical books, such practical discussions have always been interspersed from time to time. It's no different here. General philosophical discourse can respond to the ideological construction of the times. In this regard, the book says not too much, but too little.

# APPENDIX

# NEOHUMANKINDISM[1]

## 1. Where did Neohumankindism Come from?

Nowadays, people especially dislike grand concepts, and as soon as they hear a word with the suffix "ism", many of the listeners respond with disgust and then escape from it. This has been a manifestation of social progress. Because, since the founding of the People's Republic of China, people have been tossed and frightened by various "grand theories" of politicians and "experts", and generally they just want to live an ordinary life quietly and plainly. The fact that the word "expert" is laughingly equated with its Chinese homophone "brick master" is proof of this attitude. This equation implies that the so-called "experts" are actually only worthy of being slapped with a brick on the back of the head. There is a strong sense of democracy in this humor.

Not so much in the 1980s. At that time, many kinds of "isms" were floating in the campus and in society, and people were arguing about these grand concepts, as if once they chose

---

1. This essay was originally written in July 2015 as the last section of the first draft of my book, "Foundations of Algorithmic Economics", then was removed from the book before its publication.

the right path of development, the "ship of China" would be navigating well all along afterwards. However, with the ruthless loss of years, the "patriotic youth" finally understood that before "saving the country", the most important thing was to save themselves first. In social circumstances, the tradition of caring for national affairs has gradually faded and been replaced by individuality, money, consumption, and enjoyment. The "Peking ruffian literature" of Shuo Wang became popular, interspersed with bizarre, somewhat vulgar and decadent films, television, music, and literature imported from Hong Kong and Taiwan, where words such as "big money", "bigwig", "tycoon", "big brother" and the like were pervasive. The intense contrasts and impacts made the audience uncomfortable. There were a lot of people who were not keen on this style; and, there were other people who liked the other "lofty" cultures, either the retro style in the words of "palace" and "emperor", or the Western aristocratic and gentlemanly taste. This indicated the spirit seeking new sustenance, reflecting the anxiety and gropes of the times. We used to have problems of how to achieve specific purposes, but then the purposes themselves became a problem, and we didn't know what to pursue. This has been not only the anguish of any individual or group, but a universal (certainly not all) and social psychological trait.

However, the big question of "what path the country shall take" still exists. The collapse of the Soviet Union and the upheavals in Eastern Europe were once astonishing, but the subsequent catastrophic consequences were disappointing. For Chinese people who advocate the Western-style system and Western-style life, their feelings of anxiety and confusion have intensified. The great reforms of the 1990's have actually been carried out in this mood. The prosperity at the turn of the century gave birth to the unilateralism of the United States in the international community, and then the economies of the United States and Europe experienced a serious crisis, and the state of "crisis management" has not yet been completely lifted by far. Have Western democracy, freedom, and markets reached the end of their road? Can the Chinese therefore be complacent about their own developmental model? If not, then what is the truth?

The resurgence of the leftist movement in China has been around for at least a decade, and it has prompted people to re-examine Western civilization and the history of left-wing movements. Another trend is the resurgence of the study of ancient China in recent years, and even some people come to wear the ancient costumes. The rise of sinology indicates some dissatisfaction with the imported left-wing and right-wing ideas. For some Chinese, if the "truth" is not here, it must be there. In short, their priority job is always to resort to the extant books where they are convinced that the ready-made answers must be lying.

This large-scale interweaving and pluralistic competitions further stimulate the desires to pursue "truth", including the "social truth", the essence of which is to seek a unified framework of social theory in order to get rid of anxiety and confusion. Up to now, it can be said that this work has been preliminarily completed in theory. However, sorting out the existing materials is a bit tedious after all. When a person reaches his middle age, he may be reluctant to look backward, but be quite interested in looking forward. The Algorithmic perspective reminds us that there are many disappointments in both the old and the real. As the saying goes, "If you want to eat something delicious, cook it yourself." The key is the future, both for individuals and for a country. In view of the fact that "innovation" has become an unavoidable means of survival, how should we innovate, and what principles and basic methods do we need to adopt in innovation?

In the process of thinking about these issues, in an earlier period, I had come to mind a term called "New

Continentalism", which meant that the Chinese of the present era should have the courage to create a continental culture (or more broadly called "civilization") that shall be different from the "port culture" of Hong Kong or "island culture" of Taiwan, to meet our own needs—and then use it to influence the world. Later, however, I came to realize that there was something of vainglory in the concept that "I innovate for the sake of differentiation from others, or my own 'superiority' over others." I didn't like the word anymore, but I felt there was still something in it that needed to be said.

Around the turn of the century, a beautiful new word, "New and New Humankind" became popular[2], and the penetrating power of the word immediately attracted me, not only because it contains the meanings I wanted to express, but also because its popularity showed that there must be numerous "soulmates" of mine in the society. A large number of contemporary people think of the same thing at the same time, which often indicates that the matter has a higher value. Since I haven't seen any social science interpretation of the word, I think I can do something to fill it and interpret it. And since what I'm expressing is, of course, mainly my own meaning, this can also be counted as a borrowing. Then, I decided to revamp the word a little and rename what I wanted to convey as the "Neohumankindism".

"Neohumankindism" is an attitude that Chinese can adopt towards the future in this era of radical change. This attitude can find a strong philosophical basis in the Algorithmic Thinking Theory (ATT). With ATT, we can make a quite concise and precise exposition of "neohumankindism", which would be thorough and convincing, and thus easy to grasp and

---

2. According to public information on the Internet, the term seems to have first become popular in Taiwan around 1990.

apply. It shall be most appropriate to place "neohumankindism" under the Algorithmic framework.

The process of democratization of society is a process of marginalization of intellectuals and academics, and a process of academics becoming an ordinary profession. But an era that doesn't like grand theories doesn't necessarily mean that thought is not needed, and that thought is not to be produced effectively. At this time, intellectuals can (and can only) do the following: pre-produce some ideas, publish them, and wait for them to be used by society when they are needed or interested.

## 2. Everything Is Equal before Thinking

The word "thinking" has many meanings, but here it refers to the "thinking me", the "thinking activity", the "active computation", or the "meta- or current computation". Algorithmic Theory helps us clarify the relationship between the flow and the stock of the mind, and thus, firstly, it helps us reflect on the question of "who I am". At this time, we find that "I" is actually a rather vague concept. The "active computation" is certainly "me", but isn't the stock of "sleeping" thoughts in my brain not "me" or part of "me"? In this sense, "I" is just a useful concept that can bring some convenience, but it is really crude.

Algorithmic Theory can help us to undertake the philosophical task of "dissolving the self" well and appropriately. However, the word "I" still needs to be used. In front of "me" or in front of my thoughts, there are not only physical things in the world, but also mental beings such as memory, knowledge, concepts, systems, organizations, cultures, and interpersonal relationships, which exist partly in my mind and partly in others and society. The meaning of "equality before thinking" is, first of all, that "I" can identify their formats, understand and evaluate them, and process and transform them, and secondly that the relationships are all *equal* among information or data, current computations, computing results, and thoughtful stocks. Since we can clearly describe the transformative processes among them, the mysteries surrounding some of them can be removed, and since we have understood the mechanism of "mental distortion", despite the extant knowledge and relationships, we can *deliberately* build some different new relationships between the "me" and the "distorted objects", and these new relationships would be expected to be more harmonious and more successful. Based on these new relationships as new knowledge, the degree of rationalization of our behaviors would increase, and each of us would enter a more *intelligent, free*, and *creative* state, and thus create a new "self" and a new "human being" that is different from the past.

In the current Chinese society, this seemingly abstract and plain idea is actually of great practical significance.

First, it deals with how we come to understand who we are. The interpersonal universality of the Instructional system means that, in fact, each of us is similar to anyone else, and hence there is a fundamental similarity between Chinese and foreigners. This is the foundation of interpersonal, interracial, and cross-border exchanges. On the other hand, there are differences between people. Despite the differences in appearance, interpersonal differences can mainly be differences in the stock of thoughts, which can be divided into the innate and the acquired. Innate differences are clearly present, but they can hardly be systematic, and their distribution among the population seems to be so even that it is difficult to say that one group is significantly superior to another. In particular, it is difficult to say that the innate intelligence of one nation or race is significantly superior to that of another. More importantly, no matter how different one's innate intelligence is from another's, acquired efforts can add on or make up for it to varying degrees. There is a commensurability between the innate stock and the acquired stock, and there is also a commensurability between current computations and the knowledge stock. This unified principle technologizes and secularizes all interpersonal differences in the stock of thought, and places them in a secondary position. This is an encouragement to our underdeveloped Chinese nation, and it is also a wake-up call for advanced Western countries. Equality, democracy, fraternity, and "universal harmony" shall be the general trends of the world.

The principle that "the identity is to identify differences" means that an identity is only a means of survival, and generally it should not be pursued as an end. The concept of "Chinese" means that a person has certain physical and physiological characteristics, and he/she may also have certain characteristics in personality, temperament, thoughts, knowledge, habits, hobbies, etc. These people who are called "Chinese" are, first of all, ordinary "people"; second, they happen to have the above characteristics, so they are called "Chinese". However, at least some of these characteristics can be changeable. If these characteristics change for a person, he/she may no longer be a "Chinese"—but he/she will continue to exist as a "person", or a person with another identity.

On the other hand, the concept of "Chinese" can also be changed. *If some characteristics of the majority of Chinese people change, the connotation of the concept of "Chinese" will also change, and Chinese will have a new image in the world. Therefore, we cannot associate and fixate our own identity absolutely with certain characteristics.* It doesn't always have to associate us with certain symbols (such as Tang costumes, red, lion dance, or Chinese cuisine), nor does it always have to associate us with the history we already have. *History is only a memory, while symbols are a tool, and they are all for our use, not to limit us.* They are created by us or our ancestors, not for us to worship. *"I" or "we" means not only something that is attached to us as a result of past actions, but also something that we are conceiving or will create in the future.*

After more than 150 years of ups and downs, the Chinese nation has re-emerged. As one of the world's four ancient civilizations, China is regaining its important position in the world. However, what is different from the past is that this rise of China's national power is not a simple repetition and continuation of its existing civilization, but a re-opening of the process of Westernization and globalization that has begun in modern times. It is a bit strange that the rise of a country's power has been accompanied by the decline of its traditional civilization. However, it is easy to understand that China is undergoing a great civilizational shift—from traditional civilization to (primarily) Western civilization. And, the rapid development is brought about exactly by this shift. The breadth, depth, and speed of this shift, while perhaps rare in the course of world history, may not be clearly perceived by most insiders. In fact, it involves all aspects of the economy, politics, law, culture, thought, customs, life, interpersonal relationships, and so on. Let's look at our everyday life; for example, the style and furnishings of our homes are rapidly becoming Westernized, as are the clothing and utensils. In traditional societies, people had great difficulty in traveling and hence knew little about each other, whereas currently we are rapidly understanding the customs, habits, personalities, and cultures of different regions and provinces. Underneath the superficial similarity, different groups of people or individuals can have striking differences in the way they think and behave. Since their own dialects are prevalent in their own places respectively, it can be said that we do not have a unified national language, and Mandarin is actually only in the process of being promoted. Similarly, we don't have a national menu, and our restaurants and kitchens are far from modernizing (including standardizing).[3] We are actually in the process of being *"nationalized"*. This process is both intertwined with internationalization and simultaneously a basis for internationalization. Most of this process is taking place under the banner of "modernization", because it already contains a lot of our own creations. However, "Westernization" is still the main ingredient of it; it's just that we don't usually like to emphasize it.

The process of modernization and Westernization is also the process of civilizational rupture. We break away from our traditional system and join a new "tradition" and a new system. We usually say that this is a process of "integration" between China and the West, which is a more positive statement, and of course a "correct" statement. However, the Algorithmic perspective tells us that there must be a lot of stiff and regrettable ruptures, abandonments, mixedness, and forced acceptances. The process will never be so harmonious and wonderful, nor will it be so quick and certain, nor will it be perfect. Reinvention after acceptance and rediscovery after abandonment will also occur from time to time, but the likelihood, timing, and pattern of their occurrence will not be very regular. Traditional Chinese medicine is an example. The medical profession always says "the combination of Chinese and Western medicine", but because Chinese medicine and Western medicine were developed according to different basic

---

3. I hope that this statement will not cause misunderstanding. In traditional societies where different regions have not been so closely interconnected, it is inevitable that each region's food would have more distinct characteristics. The strengthening of regional ties will lead to an active process of exchange, reference, transformation, uniformization, and innovation. Then, the activity will decline, and the variety, quality, and production process of diets will gradually converge to a relatively stable state. This is not to say that all the menus shall be entirely monolithic, nor that they are no longer evolving, but that Algorithmically, such a convergent process must be a common phenomenon during the course of industrialization and modernization.

ideas and logical systems, the combination between them cannot be easy, and in fact, the relevant specific results are far from reaching the level expected commonly. Traditional Chinese medicine may have potential, but that's for another story, and its potential may not be revealed until the distant future—or not even at that point.

This rupture of civilization threw us Chinese into an extremely anxious mood, and as a result, a sentiment similar to that of the "Boxer Rebellion" broke out in contemporary China. The main characteristic of this sentiment is xenophobia, hostile to everything that comes from abroad. Just as the governmental policy of "Reform and Opening-up" is a continuation of the process of Westernization in Chinese modern times, this sentiment is also a continuation of the earlier xenophobic tide. The social forces that support it come mainly from those who have little connection with international affairs or who have not benefited much from the opening-up policy. The ultra-leftists who advocate "orthodox Marxism-Leninism" are part of this; this is because Marxism-Leninism has been indigenized and hence is already seen as part of the "tradition". What distinguishes this extreme sentiment is the nostalgia shown by the majority of the population. People travel passionately to monuments, ancient towns, and villages in search of tradition, and invest heavily in the preservation of artifacts and antiques. To a large extent, the craze for the study of ancient China is also a reflection of nostalgia.

However, history cannot be retained, it will eventually pass. The preservation of the historical heritage should be left to relevant experts. Monuments, ancient towns, and villages can be developed as tourism projects, but most people can't expect to continue living in them. *Tradition is just a resource, which is placed in front of us on an equal footing with other imported resources, for us to choose and use.* If we recognize that the good past and our sense of belonging to it are largely just memories at work, our nostalgic sentiments will no longer be so strong, and our minds will become stronger. We need to understand that psychological warmth is just the result of people "telling stories" and comforting each other. We must learn to survive in a state of lack of psychological sustenance, less warmth, and moderate anxiety. We must calm our sentiments, wipe away tears, restrain our longing for our hometown and the past, and bravely welcome the future. The philosophy of Confucius and Mencius has excessively softened the spirit of us Chinese, and it is time to correct this weakness. As for those who stubbornly stick to the old ways and do not take the initiative to change their ways, history will also mercilessly grant them failures, forcing them to reflect again in the regret of failures.

## 3. Let Reason Lead Us

Algorithmic Theory can enlighten us that there must be many inappropriate aspects in our attitude towards life. Often, we always remember the past much more than we plan for the future, that is, *we are heavily biased towards the past, and the past and the future are in a state of severe asymmetry in our brains.* We always look back at history over and over again. We look back too much on history. The written history of mankind is only a few thousand years long, and the history of mankind itself may be, at least, millions of years long. Considering the history of the universe and the infinite future that humanity will face, it can be seen that we have given too much preference to this short period of several thousand years. Of course, one of the reasons for this "preferential treatment" is that history, as a fact that has already happened, represents "existence", while the future is uncertain, and the discussion of the future can only be carried out under the premise of assumptions, which is highly subjective and pluralistic, so it is not easy to form a platform that can be used unanimously for interpersonal communication. However, on the other hand, history has been precipitated and cannot be changed, whereas we have a great opportunity and freedom to determine the future, which leads to the fact that history can and can only be used as materials for us to plan for the future. This shall be the real significance of history.

One indirect piece of evidence of the preferential treatment of history is regret. Regret has some benefits, but we often regret excessively. For example, we have been so bitter about the loss of knowledge and traditions during the Cultural Revolution and the Mao era that we often regret it too much. The losses were indeed severe, but these special experiences must be compensated—and have been in compensations. Without the painful lessons of that era, the "Reform and Opening-up" might not have come so quickly. These lessons will be continuously learned by the people of China and all humankind. It is true that this period of history has damaged the continuation of Chinese civilization and tradition to a certain extent, but it has not destroyed all the things that are beneficial. Given that the main historical mission of the present era is to modernize and go global, many aspects of Chinese tradition need to be abandoned in the first place. If we can recognize this abandonment, it will be possible to turn losses into gains, thereby successfully accelerating our development.

We need to change our traditional attitudes of being too attached and adoring to the state, and we need to change our overly strong national consciousness. Between the domestic and external worlds, we place too much emphasis on the domestic and too little on the outside. This is not conducive to our development. The only reason why we attach importance to domestic affairs should be the geographical proximity of domestic people and things to us; other reasons either should not exist or can only be derived from it. We neglect international affairs for the opposite reason. It's the same thing that there is a difference between the energies we spend in the past and the future. This is also one of the meanings of "everything is equal before thinking".

China was once ahead of the world in terms of development for a long time, and later regarded as the leader of a certain region, while the ancient Chinese long regarded China as the center of the world. This arrogance has been ruthlessly destroyed by recent history, and we have turned to seclusion. Internationally, we have been either trying to reshape our "hegemon" status or adopting a posture of indifference, passivity, or inferiority to "tailgating" international affairs. Just as we need to establish the right attitude towards the state and the nation, we also need to establish a right attitude towards other countries, international affairs, and the people of the world. This attitude is, first of all, to correct the previous passivity and to shift to a two-way interaction with other countries. Secondly, of course, it is mutual respect, equality with each other, peaceful coexistence, and so on. These norms should not only be used as diplomatic rhetoric, but should be delivered from the heart and implemented in all aspects of foreign exchanges, both governmental and non-governmental. In this sense, hostility to the West should no longer exist. Finally, we need to look back at the current foreign affairs from the prospect of "globalization" and "world government" to re-examine our current attitude. In my opinion, one of the gists of this attitude should be that we do not just passively and half-heartedly accept the market, freedom, and democracy, but also be the vanguard and active advocator of outstanding universal value and globalization; we should proactively and far-sightedly promote globalization, even at the expense of participating in some affairs that are ostensibly not closely related to us. This is not only sensible and in our interests, but also, in the long run, in the international interest (also in line with the notions of openness and globalization in our ancient civilization). And, in order to effectively shoulder this responsibility, as a result and a step in reforming our domestic ideology, we must also show our ideological tendencies (even progressivism) internationally. This is unavoidable. Otherwise, we will not be able to fulfill our role as a promoter of globalization.

As part of the push for globalization, we Chinese must also rethink our identity and our future destiny. In recent decades, many Chinese have immigrated to other countries, just as many foreigners have immigrated to live in China. This is a continuation of the long-term migration process that has begun since ancient times. This tide is unprecedentedly turbulent and is bound to become even more turbulent in the future, which forces us to ponder the following questions: Is the flow of immigrants beneficial to the country or not? Do people who have emigrated to other countries still need to bear any more responsibility for China? Does China still need to bear any more responsibilities to overseas Chinese? Should we strive to integrate ourselves into the international community along with the globalization process, or should we deliberately maintain our differences from other nationalities and races? Even if the reflection on these issues does not produce concrete policy consequences, it is bound to once again impact our national concepts. It shall not be enough to live in the memories and yearn for the past; however, the consciousness of some people in our society is indeed still stuck in the ancient feudal era. In parallel with the progress of our physical apparatus and conditions, a great emancipation of minds and a prospective thinking are necessary, and the social exchange of ideas must be carried out in some way.

Prospective thinking means that innovation is inescapable. A meaning of the term "development" in the narrow sense is indeed imitation, but pure imitation is, in fact, extremely rare, and different situations must lead to more or less different decisions and behaviors. To a large extent, *"innovation" is just an objective consequence of people's conscious computations based directly on the interests, the pros and cons of the matter itself, rather than a deliberate purpose.* Innovating is neither for the sake of innovating itself nor for catering to some other big concepts or big narratives. The "natural" actions of hundreds of millions of people "naturally" bring about creative consequences. Therefore, it is uneasy to deliberately obtain innovation, or to deliberately avoid it.

On the other hand—and we always adopt this "two-sided" approach, which is actually hard to avoid in a comprehensive framework—this doesn't mean that we can't work at all on managing and designing innovation. In this regard, what advice can we give to our compatriots in the motherland?

The advice is: to vigilantly and skeptically weigh all ideas, theories, impulses, feelings, emotions, authorities, idols, norms, and values, and to place them *equally* on the scale of *"reason"*. The core of Algorithmic Theory is *not to praise or belittle "irrationality", but to disenchant "irrationality" and incorporate it into the rational system.* The result is inevitably to make us stand higher and see farther than before, and thus our reason is developed and expanded. Such theoretical tools encourage and support us *to dare to apply our various abilities to understand, analyze, judge, imagine, and design any objects,* whether physical or ideological, practical or cultural, political or non-political. Especially in such an era of great change, we cannot expect that everything that suits us has already been made by our ancestors or foreigners, so that we just need to find out and introduce it. We cannot expect too much from something traditional or be intimidated by it; neither can we expect too much from something foreign or be intimidated by it. We must not be stuck in the old ways, nor be so busy looking for authoritative guidance that we forget or look down on ourselves. *Any idea, assumption, or plan, as long as it has passed the test of our reason, including the test of risk management, we must dare to come up with it and try it.*

Since Plato, Westerners have developed a cautious attitude towards emotions, whereas the tradition in our country is the opposite. We love sensationalism, and we love to live in the midst of emotions. Confucius and Mencius put us in emotional struggles, anesthetizing each other with a sense of belonging to each other while believing that we have found some true meanings of life. This can be called "emotional worship", a relatively negative and corrupt state of mind that is not conducive to development. It frees us too cheaply from the confusion, anxiety, and loneliness that innovators have to face. We must return to the truth of the world. Thousands of years ago, when our ancestors created national totems, designed various apparatus, and arranged our way of life, had they foreseen that these things would be worshiped by future generations? What were the actual situations at that time? Was the concept of the "Chinese nation" designed by someone in advance and deliberately implemented in history? There is a lot of evidence that the real way of ancient life and the mental state of the ancient Chinese were quite different from what we have imagined today. In view of the fact that the whole world is in the midst of rapid development and change, how will human beings be in the future? How will we be in the future? How will our descendants be in hundreds, thousands, or tens of thousands of years? And, how will we or they live and think in the future?

*The flourishing of futurology will be a sign of sanity.* The benefits of speculating and planning the future shall be enormous—even when most of them have been lost. Speculating about the future will first of all enable us to develop a broad and long-term vision, and avoid falling into the triviality and futility of short-term activities. Nowadays, people tend to pay too much attention to the things in the present. Because there is a lot of uncertainty and fear of wasting energy (it is believed that, on average, the return on this "waste" shall be very high), they often do not focus on medium- and long-term issues. Furthermore, because medium- and long-term issues receive less attention, the opportunities in them are often left unattended. However, the principle of heterogeneity can tell us that short-term predictions may not be easy, and medium- or long-term predictions may not be more difficult than the short-term ones.

Here is an example of the importance of developing a medium- or long-term perspective.

All kinds of indications show that under the impetus of science and technology, the basic way of life of humankind is likely to undergo tremendous changes in the near future, and humankind is likely to make tremendous progress in a short historical period. These changes will inevitably be reflected in ethical and moral fields. In China, some people have been so bitter about the moral deterioration caused by business activities that they spend their days scolding it on the Internet. However, these people do not seem to realize that since society is changing so rapidly, how can it be hoped that the level of morality remain unchanged? If morality should not be enshrined generally as a fixed code of conduct, it can be expected that some old moralities will decline and be replaced by new moralities that are to be established gradually, then, how can the two processes be perfectly coordinated? In fact, even with only a little reasoning, you can conclude that *the moral system can never be perfected in times of great economic and social change; only when economic and social changes slow down or even stagnate will it be possible to speed up the construction of morality.* In this sense, we can even say that the high level of morality and rule of law that exist in Western societies today may be a consequence and evidence of their relative lack of social vitality. It's hard to make the best of both worlds. With this medium- to long-term perspective, one can reduce those excessive complaints about the status quo.[4]

Nor does the preferential use of reason imply that practice is devalued. The primary goal of the use of reason is to achieve some practical effects. Ideas and culture can be endogenous and controlled by people themselves, so a far-sighted strategy is to give priority to objectivity over subjectivity, thereby prioritizing various practicalities. This is one of the things in which Western civilization is more sophisticated than our Eastern civilization. We have focused too much on the spiritual world, and as a result, we fell behind. For this reason, we understand "practicality" (or pragmatism) as a subordinate criterion of reason or rationality—even though the principle of "practicality" and the principle of "rationality" appear side by side in many discourses.

Summing up all the above arguments, it is called "reason first, all others behind", or "let reason lead us". I recommend it as a basic attitude and a method of exploration that we can adopt when facing the world and the future.

Although the slogan of "national rejuvenation" has received a certain amount of popularity, it contains more or less the meaning of "restoring the oldness", so I believe that it is somewhat misleading. This "rejuvenation" of a nation, a state, and a society must be accompanied by the destruction of its traditions and the rise of a great deal of new things, which are mainly the results of the efforts of *individual* persons and

---

4. Many people express regret and shame when they see reports of negative behaviors of Chinese tourists abroad, and I'd like to persuade these people to ease their feelings temporarily. Is there no resemblance between these Chinese's impact on the Western order and the nineteenth-century Westerners' impact on the tranquil and orderly life of the Qing Empire of China? This is certainly not to imply some kind of intentional revenge, but to say that this "Algorithmic effect" is largely inevitable when a rapidly developing society encounters a slow-growing society.

entities (e.g. corporate and governmental entities) in solving their *specific* problems, and are therefore local, scattered, irregular, mixed, and even bizarre, to a large extent. *We should not directly analyze the big concept of "nation" from a macro perspective, but can only base ourselves on each part and its rationality and practicality, and let the big concept develop mainly as a result. We must also distance ourselves from tradition and allow it to compete for its survival in the test of reason and practicality. If tradition is gold, let it shine on its own in the open competitions!*—I hope that those who are passionate about upholding tradition will also recognize this as a desirable strategy even in terms of their own goals.[5]

I believe that readers will not misunderstand me as trying to deny the interdependent relationships among the rights, responsibilities, and interests that must occur when an individual faces any collective organizations, including the nation and the state. However, *in the present era, we must never be conservative,* and in any field such as technology, economy, politics, society, culture, thought, academics, lifestyle, etc., it is better to take the initiative to plan and participate, rather than passively waiting for the impacts of changes. This is one of the main appeals I would like to make. This appeal, and all the discussions in this essay, can be summed up in the following word:

Neohumankindism.

---

5. For example, considering the lack of openness, free competition, reasonable rules, and the rule of law in the research of traditional Chinese medicine and the use of the research results, it is doubtful that China will be able to maintain its historical leadership in this field. Even in the study of Chinese history, leadership seems to be quietly shifting abroad.

# ABOUT THE AUTHOR

Bin Li, a visiting scholar of Center for Urban & Regional Studies, University of North Carolina at Chapel Hill, used to be an independent scholar and a columnist in Shanghai, China. Email: libinw2025@hotmail.com

Personal Webpages:

    https://pcc.web.unc.edu/faculty/bin-li/

    https://unc.academia.edu/BinLi

    https://www.researchgate.net/profile/Bin_Li197

    https://scholar.google.com/citations?hl=en&user=qkCLlowAAAAJ

    https://algorithmicalbinli.wordpress.com

    Chinese site: http://blog.sina.com.cn/libinw

    Chinese Weibo: https://weibo.com/u/1400692850

    Chinese Podcast:

    https://www.ximalaya.com/zhubo/185996474

Books:

    Li, Bin (2005). "Reformation of State-Owned Enterprises: A New Scheme" (in Chinese, original title: "The Constitution of State Capital: A Mechanism-Design for Management of China's State Capital"). Beijing: Economic Daily Press, 2005.

    Li, Bin (2009). "Algorithm Framework Theory: A Basis for Unification of Social Sciences" (in Chinese). Beijing: China Renmin University Press.

Li, Bin (2012). "A Preliminary Inquiry into Principles of General Social Science: The Algorithmic Approach" (in Chinese). Beijing: China Renmin University Press.

Li, Bin (2019). "Foundations of Algorithmic Economics: The Cognitive Revolution and the Grand Synthesis of Economics" (in Chinese). Beijing: Economic Daily Press.

Articles:

Li, Bin (2006). "The Algorithmic Economics: A General Theory on Bounded Rationality" (in Chinese). Economic Research Information, No.6. 3–14.

Li, Bin (2011). "The Synthesis of Various Economics: An All-in-One Solution". Annual Conference of Association for Heterodox Economics (AHE), Nottingham, UK. https://www.hetecon.net/wp-content/uploads/2019/12/Li_AHE201106IR.pdf

Li, Bin (2014). "The Grand Synthesis of Economics" (in Chinese). The Chinese Symposium On Interdisciplinary Theoretical Innovation, Unirule Institute.

Li, Bin (2015). "The Endogeneity of Institutions & Organizations: The Algorithmic Approach" (in Chinese). The annual conference of China's Institutional Economics.

Li, Bin (2019). "How could the Cognitive Revolution Happen to Economics? An Introduction to the Algorithm Framework Theory". World Economics Association (WEA) online conference: Going Digital. https://goingdigital2019.weaconferences.net/papers/how-could-the-cognitive-revolution-happen-to-economics-an-introduction-to-the-algorithm-framework-theory/

Li, Bin (2019). "Ten Lectures on Algorithmic Economics" (in Chinese). free e-book online, downloadable at the personal English webpages.

Li, Bin (2020). "The Birth of a Unified Economics". MPRA (The Munich Personal RePEc Archive) paper, downloadable at https://mpra.ub.uni-muenchen.de/110155/

Li, Bin (2020). "Why is Algorithmic Theory a Necessary Basis of Economics?" MPRA (The Munich Personal RePEc Archive) paper, downloadable at https://mpra.ub.uni-muenchen.de/110581/

Li, Bin (2022). "How Various 'Irrationalities' Proven to be Rational". Academia Letters, Article 4579. https://doi.org/10.20935/AL4579 [peer reviewed]

Li, Bin (2022). "Algorithmic Economics as an Economics of Thought". The International Journal of Pluralism and Economics Education, Vol. 13, No. 2, pp. 176-191. [peer reviewed]

Li, Bin (2022). "The 'Algorithmic Logic' as a Synthetic or General Logic". Academia Letters, Article 4936. https://doi.org/10.20935/AL4936 [peer reviewed]

Li, Bin (2022). "How can a Human be Modeled 'Alive'? The Scientific Endogeny and Manifestation of Subjectivities", in "Human Rights, Religious Freedom and Spirituality", edited by Yashwant Pathak, A. Adityanjee. Pune: Bshima Prakashan, downloadable at the personal English webpages.

Li, Bin (2022). "Algorithmic Economics". MPRA (The Munich Personal RePEc Archive) paper, downloadable at https://mpra.ub.uni-muenchen.de/113563/

Li, Bin (2023). "A Unified Psychology as Part of a General Social Science". Qeios. doi:10.32388/GGSOLK.3. [peer reviewed]

Li, Bin (2023). "From General Equilibrium to Algorithmic Equilibrium". Qeios. doi:10.32388/3WoJ51.2. [peer reviewed]

Li, Bin (2023). "The Unrevealed Causes of Prosperity". Qeios. doi:10.32388/KLR222.4. [peer reviewed]

Li, Bin (2023). "Como Várias 'Irracionalidades' Dão Provas De Serem Racionais". Revista Paranaense de Filosofia, v. 3, n. 1, p. 220 – 232, Jan./Jun., 2023.

Li, Bin (2024). "The Algorithmic Philosophy: A Synthetic and Social Philosophy". Qeios. doi:10.32388/SoAQEE.2. [peer reviewed]

Li, Bin (2024). "The Thinking Theory Unifying Grandly". Under review.

Over one hundred column articles (in Chinese) in Securities Times Newspaper, mostly on China's public economic policies.